SHAKESPEARE AND PHILOSOPHY

VIBS

Volume 256

Robert Ginsberg
Founding Editor

Leonidas Donskis
Executive Editor

Associate Editors

G. John M. Abbarno
George Allan
Gerhold K. Becker
Raymond Angelo Belliotti
Kenneth A. Bryson
C. Stephen Byrum
Robert A. Delfino
Rem B. Edwards
Malcolm D. Evans
Roland Faber
Andrew Fitz-Gibbon
Francesc Forn i Argimon
Daniel B. Gallagher
William C. Gay
Dane R. Gordon
J. Everet Green
Heta Aleksandra Gylling
Matti Häyry
Brian G. Henning

Steven V. Hicks
Richard T. Hull
Michael Krausz
Olli Loukola
Mark Letteri
Vincent L. Luizzi
Hugh P. McDonald
Adrianne McEvoy
J.D. Mininger
Peter A. Redpath
Arleen L. F. Salles
John R. Shook
Eddy Souffrant
Tuija Takala
Emil Višňovský
Anne Waters
James R. Watson
John R. Welch
Thomas Woods

a volume in
Philosophy, Literature, and Politics
PLP
Edited by Leonidas Donskis and J.D. Mininger

SHAKESPEARE AND PHILOSOPHY
Lust, Love, and Law

Raymond Angelo Belliotti

Amsterdam - New York, NY 2012

Cover Illustration: Canaletto: Rialto Bridge. Oil on canvas. (private collection)

Cover Design: Studio Pollmann

The paper on which this book is printed meets the requirements of "ISO 9706:1994, Information and documentation - Paper for documents - Requirements for permanence".

ISBN: 978-90-420-3598-0
E-Book ISBN: 978-94-012-0872-7
© Editions Rodopi B.V., Amsterdam - New York, NY 2012
Printed in the Netherlands

For

Marcia, Angelo, and Vittoria

*Il successo non è mai definitivo;
l'insuccesso non è mai fatale.*

CONTENTS

EDITORIAL FOREWORD BY LEONIDAS DONSKIS   xi

ACKNOWLEDGMENTS   xv

INTRODUCTION   1

ONE   *The Merchant of Venice*: Tests of Our Humanity   5

     1. Venice and Belmont   5
     2. Why is Antonio Sad?   6
     3. Philosophical Interlude: Individualism and Community   7
     4. The Contract: Bonds of Commerce   8
     5. Philosophical Interlude: The Notion of Desert   10
     6. Who is Shylock?   17
     7. Philosophical Interlude: Existential Authenticity   22
     8. The Casket Test: Bonds of Intimacy   24
     9. Philosophical Interlude: The Contours of Love   28

TWO   *The Merchant of Venice:* The Trial and Judicial Decision Making   35

     1. The Breach   35
     2. Philosophical Interlude: Basic Contract Law   36
     3. The Trial of Venice: *Stage One:*
         The Duke Reasons with Shylock   40
     4. Philosophical Interlude: The Rule of Law   42
     5. The Trial of Venice: *Stage Two:*
         The Presiding Jurist Enters and Renders Judgment   48
     6. Philosophical Interlude: Mercy, Equity, and Forgiveness   52
     7. The Trial of Venice: *Stage Three: The Sting*   56
     8. The Trial of Venice: *Stage Four: The Annihilation*   59
     9. Philosophical Interlude: Judicial Decision making   64

THREE   *The Merchant of Venice*: Bonds Repaired   71

     1. Broken Vows   71
     2. Philosophical Interlude: The Symposium   74
     3. Love, and the Condition of Souls   81
     4. Human-All-Too-Human   85
     5. Summary of Philosophical Lessons   91
         A. Beware of Claims Lodged in the Name of Desire and Desert   92

	B. Beware of Rigidity and Inflexibility	93
	C. To Know the Good is Easier Than to Do the Good	94
	D. Both Communities and Individuals Reap What They Sow	95
	E. We Find Solace, but Not Salvation, in Love	95
	F. Love Requires Sacrifice, Risk, and Heightened Mutual Vulnerability	96
	G. Money Cannot Buy Happiness	97
	H. The Power of Feminism	99

FOUR *Measure For Measure*: Law and Order   101

    1. The Delegation of Authority   101
    2. Philosophical Interlude: The Art of Delegation   102
    3. The Crime   106
    4. Philosophical Interlude: The Doctrine of Desuetude   108
    5. Comic Relief   112
    6. Philosophical Interlude: The Threat of Nihilism   114
    7. The First Plea   120
    8. Who is Angelo?   123

FIVE *Measure For Measure*: Lust and Death   129

    1. The Second Plea: The Proposition   129
    2. Who is Isabella?   130
    3. Philosophical Interlude: Is Premarital Sex Morally Wrong?   132
    4. Downbeat Consolation   137
    5. Philosophical Interlude: The Specter of Pessimism   137
    6. The Family Feud   139
    7. Philosophical Interlude: Life & Death   141
    8. The Bed Trick   148
    9. Philosophical Interlude: If Premarital Sex is Morally Wrong Should it be Legally Prohibited?   150
    10. The Betrayal   154
    11. Philosophical Interlude: What Punishment Fits the Crime of Fornication?   155

SIX *Measure For Measure*: Law and Marriage   159

    1. The Head Trick   159
    2. The Trial, Stage One: Isabella's Accusation   160
    3. The Trial, Stage Two: Mariana's Confession   161
    4. The Trial, Stage Three: Wedding Bell Blues   161
    5. Philosophical Interlude: The Paradox of Agapic Love   162

6. The Trial, Stage Four: The Grand Resolution	166
7. What Type of Betrothal Agreements did Claudio-Juliet and Angelo-Mariana Contract?	171
8. Theological Interlude: Religion and Jurisprudence	180
9. The Aftermath	182
10. Philosophical Interlude: Refashioning Viennese Jurisprudence	184
11. Summary of Philosophical Lessons	188
A. Judging Others Requires Self-Understanding and General Knowledge of Human Nature: Pretension and Arrogance Undermine Success	188
B. The Interrelations of Opposites	189
C. The Human Condition Merits Sympathy	190
D. Patriarchy Dehumanizes Women	192
E. Beware of Existential Inauthenticity	192
F. Sex Can be Dangerous	193
G. Fear of Death Can be Overcome	195
NOTES	201
BIBLIOGRAPHY	213
ABOUT THE AUTHOR	219
INDEX	221

EDITORIAL FOREWORD

William Shakespeare is likely to have become a modern sensibility. Like Niccolò Machiavelli or Shakespeare's own contemporary and Significant Other, Christopher Marlowe, Shakespeare's world seems to have been developed into a modern moral and political sensibility, a criterion to assess the modern project, and even a symbolic design within which we perceive and interpret ourselves and the world around us.

We cannot bypass Shakespeare when we encounter a problem of evil, both in its classical forms and in its modern incarnations. The psychogenesis and sociogenesis of modern feelings and sentiments, namely, love and friendship, as opposed to traditional forms of our grasp of the world and of human powers of association, are also inseparable from Shakespeare's sonnets and plays. It is with sound reason that such modern sensitivities as loyalty, intimacy, and privacy are closely observed and examined as early as in the world of Elizabethan dramatists.

Shakespeare appears not only as a miracle of his time; he comes to us as a mystery and as a pivotal test of our sensitivities. Whether he existed and whether he wrote his plays and sonnets is a secondary issue in the face of the miracle of his profoundly modern perception of human reality whose embodiment and symbol he has become. The quarrel over the definitive and final stroke of a loose brushwork as to whether it was executed by Rubens or his entourage, Rembrandt or Ferdinand Bol or Aert de Gelder, is as senseless and meaningless as the ink spilled in the countless debates on whether William Shakespeare from Stratford-upon-Avon wrote his immortal plays. The miracle of Shakespeare has little if any to do with who exactly Shakespeare was.

The way Shakespeare was perceived by Goethe and Schiller tells us something of critical importance about the clash of modern sensibilities in the epoch of Friedrich the Great and of the Sturm und Drang movement when the principles of Bildung and Kultur prevail over that of Zivilisation – in an epoch where moral and political sensibilities are shaped by the conflict of the then semi-feudal and the emerging modern approaches to the world.

The way in which Shakespeare was grasped and interpreted by Leo Tolstoy tells us something of critical importance about the encounter of opposing modes of discourse and also of Eastern and Western European hermeneutics, especially in interpreting modernity. At the same time, the way in which Shakespeare is assessed by Sigmund Freud tells us something disturbing about a problem that Shakespeare poses for a modern world which, no matter how egalitarian, is tinged with some elitist interpretations and distrust for the natural-born genius of a person who cannot pass for a mystery of blood, class, creed, or tradition. Thus, Shakespeare posthumously lends his life and biography to the scrutiny of modernity with its promises of equality, pursuit of happiness, and human spontaneity and unpredictability.

Far exceeding and transcending the boundaries of Renaissance perceptions of the human world, Shakespeare offers, in Hamlet, not only the idea of *la mente audace* as a clue to the concept of the brave mind of a modern hero who thinks while he acts and who acts while he thinks – and who, in doing so, bridges thought and action; Shakespeare also comes up with a strikingly modern idea that the will to understand the world around us lives side by side with the will to misunderstand it; that the religious and erotic feelings can easily roll into one (as if we can doubt this after Jean Fouquet's painting *La Vierge à l'Enfant*); that there is something deeply erotic about exercise of power and frighteningly powerful about intimacy; that we tend to speak the unspeakable and to think the unthinkable quite often; that we choose to be deceived or to deceive ourselves – as the truth is unbearable for us. In this, Shakespeare obviously precedes and even anticipates Freud.

Like in Hamlet, the emergence of the individual can signify the marriage of thought and action. The aforementioned ideal of the brave mind put forward by Renaissance humanists is obvious in Hamlet's ability to outsmart and get rid of his treacherous friends Rosencrantz and Guildenstern. Yet the arrival of the modern individual may also signify the reverse tendency, the divorce of thought and action, which is the case with Hamlet and which becomes the reason of his defeat – albeit political rather than moral – and death.

Raymond Angelo Belliotti's book, *Shakespeare and Philosophy: Lust, Love, and Law*, strikes a readership as a perceptive and profound study of Shakespeare as a philosopher. It is a timely study of the timeless Shakespeare. The subtle points that Belliotti makes about two of Shakespeare's plays, The *Merchant of Venice* and *Measure for Measure*, allow him the point of departure in combining, as Belliotti put it, literary interpretation, legal theory, and philosophical doctrine. Belliotti's mastery shows itself in his elegant assumption that

> Unlike academic philosophers, religious reformers and custodians of societal traditions do not craft sophisticated deductive arguments to prove their moral conclusions. They do not seek to persuade through logical wizardry; instead, these influential paragons tell stories. Thus, the Bible is rich with imaginative parables that press themselves upon our minds, stir our deepest emotions, and teach us moral lessons in unforgettable contexts. Likewise, Aesop's fables cascade through generations with greater social impact than any syllogism or categorical moral imperative. The power of parables and folklore arises from their accessibility, colorful cast of characters, and magical allure. Events occur in stories that transcend the natural laws of reality: animals are active moral agents, supra-human beings intervene, and miracles spring up at propitious occasions. Moreover, comedic and tragic artistic considerations often demand the inclusion of episodes that require the audience to execute astounding leaps of faith. As a result, parables and folklore are exquisitely more entertaining than a painstaking, pedantic

philosophical demonstration. But parables and folklore are also less rigorous than philosophical arguments: conflict, tension, and outright contradiction pervade Biblical parables and Aesop's fables when each set of moral tales is considered as a whole. Perhaps that is their greatest lesson: the human condition resists neat, fully coherent explanations and principles that might capture the complexity of our moral life.

Belliotti is at his best when he defines, in the following passage, what he terms the existential tension, the latter clearly being the nexus of his study:

> Throughout history, many writers have argued that existential tension is at the heart of human experience: our yearning for intimate connection with others and the recognition that others are necessary for our identity and freedom coalesces uneasily with the fear and anxiety we experience as others approach. We simultaneously long for emotional attachment yet are horrified that our individuality may evaporate once we achieve it. If we experience too much individuality we risk alienation, estrangement, and psychological isolation. If we experience insufficient individuality we court emotional suffocation, loss of self-esteem, and unhealthy immersion in the collectivity. This disharmony may never be fully reconciled once and forever, and so we find ourselves making uneasy compromises and adjustments during our life's journey as we oscillate along the continuum whose endpoints are 'radical individuality' and 'thorough immersion in community', respectively. This existential tension replicates itself at numerous levels: the individual confronts family, the family confronts wider community, communities confront society, and society confronts the state.

It is with good reason that Shakespeare appears as nearly a perfect guide into the troubled, albeit fragile and vulnerable, world of modern tensions and identity dramas. In more than one way, Shakespeare's plays anticipated the tensions between the individual and family, family and community, community and society, society and the state. Shakespeare may have had anticipated and drawn, long before Ferdinand Tönnies, the dividing line between Gemeinschaft and Gesellschaft. Shakespeare paves the way for a study of such existential tensions as those between tradition and rationality, intimacy and expertise, the ought and the is dimensions, value and fact, determinism and unpredictability, destiny and free choice. In Shakespeare, history and tradition are merely the masks on the face of modernity.

We owe much to Raymond Angelo Belliotti's book for reminding us of all this, and for a daring and deeply meaningful move to bridge philosophy, literature, and politics.

Leonidas Donskis

ACKNOWLEDGMENTS

Numerous people contributed to this work directly or indirectly. As always, my family comes first. My wife, Marcia, combines the mental acuteness of Portia with the generosity of Isabella, all without the occasional emotional manipulations and meltdowns of Shakespeare's literary characters. My son, Angelo, bears no resemblance to his namesake in *Measure for Measure*. I admire his work ethic, sense of humor, refusal to make excuses, and glistening intellectual talent, which far exceeds that possessed by his father. My daughter, Vittoria, is too complex for even Shakespeare to capture in literary form. Her unwavering sense of justice, boundless capability to love, and intense family pride are prized by all who know her. As always, that this book will long outlive its author and my words will be available to torment my children when I am no longer here warms my spirit.

Thanks also to Eric van Broekhuizen, who steadfastly supported this project and was an ongoing source of sound advice and good cheer. I deeply appreciate the efforts of Leonidas Donskis in providing an exquisite Foreword to this work. Finally, this book would not have been possible without the expertise and energy of Joanne Foeller in proofreading and preparing the manuscript for publication.

Finally, I thank the following publishers for their permission to reprint and adapt material from my books and articles:

> Rowman & Littlefield for *Happiness is Overrated* (2004);
> Lexington Books for *Roman Philosophy and the Good Life* (2009)
> Lexington Books for *Niccolò Machiavelli* (2009);
> Temple University Press for *Justifying Law* (1992);
> University Press of Kansas for *Good Sex* (1993);
> Rodopi Editions for *What is the Meaning of Human Life?* (2001);
> Wiley-Blackwell for *Dante's Deadly Sins: Moral Philosophy in Hell* (2011);
> *The International Journal of Applied Philosophy* for "Gloom and Doom: Executing the Eighth Amendment," 3 (1986): 43-57;
> *The University of Western Ontario Law Review* for "The Rule of Law and the Critical Legal Studies Movement," 24 (1) (1986): 67-78;
> *Albany Government Law Review* for "Billy Martin and Jurisprudence: Revisiting the Pine Tar Case," 5 (2012): 210-239.

INTRODUCTION

This book is an interdisciplinary work that weaves literary interpretation, legal theory, and philosophical doctrine into a coherent mosaic in the context of two of Shakespeare's plays: *The Merchant of Venice* and *Measure for Measure*. Although Shakespeare did not "invent the human,"[1] Bloom's intimations to the contrary notwithstanding, he did grapple with questions of enduring human concern. This work aspires to reveal, explain, and analyze paramount philosophical and legal questions raised by these two Shakespearean plays. In the process, I will advance literary interpretations of the plays that will include character studies of some of the main protagonists. My aim is partly theoretical but mostly practical: to demonstrate what we can learn about living a robustly meaningful and significant human life by taking Shakespeare's work seriously from contemporary philosophical and legal vantage points.

In Chapter One, we begin *The Merchant of Venice* and enter the intriguing cities of Venice and Belmont. The environments of commerce and romance form the background in which the resident alien moneylender, Shylock, invokes the law to assert his equality only to have his jurisprudential theory turned against him by a fraudulent jurist possessing an acute legal mind and superior knowledge of extant statutes. In this chapter, I describe the different social atmospheres in Venice and Belmont, and provide character studies of Antonio and Shylock. Moreover, I introduce four crucial philosophical doctrines: the paradox of individualism and community; the notion of personal moral desert; Heidegger's understanding of existential authenticity; and an analysis of the phenomenon of erotic love. Finally, I discuss the bonds of commerce, as exemplified in the contract executed by Shylock, Bassanio, and Antonio; and the bonds of intimacy, as illustrated by the casket test used to discover a suitable husband for Portia.

In Chapter Two, we find that Antonio cannot fulfill his obligations under the bond with Shylock. The Jewish moneylender sues Antonio and demands the penalty provision for breach of contract that was included in the bond: he claims a legal entitlement to cut one pound of flesh from the area nearest Antonio's heart. Despite the entreaties of the Duke of Venice, numerous prominent Venetian citizens, Antonio's friends, and the fraudulent jurist, Balthasar-Portia, Shylock remains firm. However, his refusal to extend mercy to Antonio will seal his doom as Balthasar-Portia first leads him to believe that his legal argument will prevail only to later use Shylock's jurisprudential theory to eviscerate his dignity and shatter his sense of identity. During the course of the literary interpretation, I introduce three pivotal legal theories: the foundations of contract law; an analysis of the virtues of the rule of law, a necessary but not sufficient condition of justice; and the principles of judicial decision making. Furthermore, I include a philosophical examination of the nature of mercy, equity, and forgiveness.

In Chapter Three, Belmont provides the setting in which Portia struggles to repair her marital bonds with Bassanio. The literary scene provides the backdrop for an extensive discussion of the relationship between whom we love and the condition of our souls. I sketch the theories of love contained in Plato's *Symposium* and *Phaedrus* to inform that discussion. This leads to an understanding of what it means to be human-all-too-human. Finally, I explain a host of philosophical lessons that can be derived from *The Merchant of Venice*: Beware of claims lodged in the name of desire and desert; Beware of rigidity and inflexibility; Understand that to know the good is easier than to do the good; Be aware that both communities and individuals reap what they sow; Know that we can find solace, but not salvation, in love; Recognize that love requires sacrifice, risk, and heightened mutual vulnerability; Accept that money cannot buy happiness; and Acknowledge the power of feminism.

In Chapter Four, we leave Italy and travel to Vienna. In *Measure for Measure*, we find a seemingly intractable problem: the laws of the city are uncommonly strict and also immutable; the Duke of Vienna has enforced them negligently for at least fourteen years; and Vienna has become a nihilistic society where sexual license, disease, and fractured community are pervasive.

The Duke decides to delegate temporary political authority to Angelo, a deputy widely known for his high rectitude and uncompromising approach to law. Angelo promptly applies the law literally and unconditionally. A young nobleman, Claudio, is arrested and condemned to death for violating the fornication statute. His friend, Lucio, implores Claudio's sister, Isabella, a novice nun, to plead Claudio's case to Angelo. Overcoming her initial reluctance, Isabella does so. In this chapter, I provide a character sketch of Angelo. Furthermore, I introduce two philosophical doctrines: an analysis of Machiavelli's advice on the art of political delegation; and an examination of Nietzsche's depiction of the nihilistic moment. Finally, I sketch the legal theory of statutory desuetude.

In Chapter Five, Angelo propositions Isabella: he will spare Claudio's life if and only if she will have sex with him. Isabella is distraught. After Claudio is given a downbeat description of the value of human life by the Duke of Vienna, who masquerades as a Friar, he still tries to convince Isabella to comply with Angelo's distressing offer. Isabella snaps harshly at Claudio and departs his cell. The Friar-Duke convinces Isabella and Angelo's jilted ex-fiancée, Mariana, to participate in a bed trick: Isabella will pretend to agree to Angelo's offer, but Mariana, not Isabella, will be his sexual partner. The arrangement is consummated, but Angelo reneges on his original proposition and orders the execution of Claudio. In this chapter, I provide a character sketch of Isabella. Additionally, I state, explain and answer three philosophical and legal questions: Is premarital sex morally wrong? If premarital sex is morally wrong should it be legally prohibited? What punishment, if any, fits the crime of fornication? Finally, I discuss philosophically the relationship between life and death, and how human beings might strive for robust meaning and significance in confrontation with their finitude.

In Chapter Six, stymied in some of his well-intentioned but fraudulent manipulations, the Friar-Duke decides to facilitate the execution of a condemned criminal, Barnardine, and substitute his head for that of Claudio. Unfortunately, Barnardine refuses to comply. However, luck favors the Friar-Duke and yet another substitute is found. A grand trial occurs in which the Duke, stripped of his false Friar's frock, presides over Isabella's accusations against Angelo. After numerous meanderings, Isabella extends mercy to Angelo. The Duke eventually resolves all lingering problems by ordering a series of marriages, and by proposing marriage to Isabella. In this chapter, I examine the type of betrothal agreements entered into by Claudio-Isabella and Angelo-Mariana. Moreover, I address the philosophically perplexing notion of agapic love in the context of analyzing Mariana's affection for Angelo. I also examine the relationship between religion and jurisprudence while demonstrating some of the biblical principles about judging other people that underwrite the play. I also argue that refashioning the jurisprudence of Vienna is required if the city is to go beyond the nihilistic moment. In that vein, I provide a concrete proposal for salutary change. Finally, I explain a host of philosophical lessons that can be derived from *Measure for Measure*: Understand that judging others requires self-understanding and general knowledge of human nature. Pretension and arrogance undermine success; Recognize the interrelation of opposites; Be generous and accept that the human condition merits sympathy; Acknowledge that patriarchy dehumanizes women; Beware of existential inauthenticity; Understand the circumstances under which sex can be dangerous; and Learn how fear of death can be overcome.

We can interpret Shakespeare from the lens of the Elizabethan age, or from our contemporary vantage point, and/or from historical loci in between. Each type of interpretation can vivify our understanding of the human condition. I am not concerned with discerning Shakespeare's actual motivations and intentions, or extracting from those mental states what his plays "really mean." The numerous ways Shakespeare's plays have been staged over the centuries suggest that his work permits different plausible interpretations of the main characters. For example, Shylock has been portrayed, among other ways, as a comic villain, a misunderstood victim, a vicious blight on society, a "hallucinatory bogeyman," and a sympathetic existential hero.[2] Angelo has been depicted, among other ways, as a sexual predator, a political patsy, a personification of "everyman" caught in moral conflict, a frigid hypocrite, and a victim of his nihilistic society.[3] Accordingly, to argue that we should struggle mightily to discover Shakespeare's original authorial intent and remain true to those interpretations of his plays is literary imperialism. Instead, in this work, I am using Shakespeare's plays as a springboard for deriving enduring philosophical lessons related to living life fully.

My project does not assume that Shakespeare has a tightly defined moral system that he is urging upon his audience. He is not a moralist in that sense. Instead, Shakespeare challenges his audience to struggle with moral complexity as they confront conflicting elements surrounding legal and normative issues presented in his work and within the souls of his characters. His issues and their conflicts are also ours. Accordingly, we can extract from Shakespeare a broad philosophical and legal framework that requires specific prescriptions for practical enactment. In this work, I am concerned mostly with highlighting that philosophical and legal framework, and with enhancing its acuity with contemporary understandings. This is not to say that Shakespeare was profoundly philosophical or deeply theoretical. Much of his work consists of raising weighty questions inextricably connected to the human condition and inviting his audience to ponder possible answers. In my judgment, the philosophical lessons about living our lives meaningfully and significantly that we can derive from Shakespeare are simple yet powerful. In effect, I am reading Shakespeare, but seeing philosophical and legal theory.

One

THE MERCHANT OF VENICE: TESTS OF OUR HUMANITY

Unlike academic philosophers, religious reformers and custodians of societal traditions do not craft sophisticated deductive arguments to prove their moral conclusions. They do not seek to persuade through logical wizardry; instead, these influential paragons tell stories. Thus, the Bible is rich with imaginative parables that press themselves upon our minds, stir our deepest emotions, and teach us moral lessons in unforgettable contexts. Likewise, Aesop's fables cascade through generations with greater social impact than any syllogism or categorical moral imperative. The power of parables and folklore arises from their accessibility, colorful cast of characters, and magical allure. Events occur in stories that transcend the natural laws of reality: animals are active moral agents, supra-human beings intervene, and miracles spring up at propitious occasions. Moreover, comedic and tragic artistic considerations often demand the inclusion of episodes that require the audience to execute astounding leaps of faith. As a result, parables and folklore are exquisitely more entertaining than a painstaking, pedantic philosophical demonstration. But parables and folklore are also less rigorous than philosophical arguments: conflict, tension, and outright contradiction pervade Biblical parables and Aesop's fables when each set of moral tales is considered as a whole. Perhaps that is their greatest lesson: the human condition resists neat, fully coherent explanations and principles that might capture the complexity of our moral life.

In any event, *The Merchant of Venice* is a magical, moral fable. But after over 400 years of critical commentary on the play, the precise nature of the moral lessons of the play remains contestable. Each generation must confront and interpret the work anew. The play addresses enduring human questions that resist univocal, timeless solutions. This, along with its glistening artistic value, accounts for why *The Merchant of Venice* remains vibrant and didactic.

1. Venice and Belmont

The play is set in Venice and Belmont. Venice is a bustling, sophisticated, prosperous city centered on trade, commerce, and international business. Colorful and vibrant, Venice exudes competitive market places and courtrooms. At its best, Venice is a metaphor for the world of contracts: fair, arm's length bargaining allows people to exercise their agency and flex their freedom to craft their own lives and make their own way—at least if one is a full citizen of the state. Belmont is located on a mountain across from the sea. It is more a fairyland of lighthearted love and magical transformation. Venice stands for the pursuit of self-interest under law, and mercantile values; appearances, self-pride, and rhetorical flourishes preside. Belmont stands for love, compassion, and beauty; spirituality, heightened mutual vulnerability, and lofty ideals prevail. Or so it first seems. However, as the play is set around 1600, patriarchal prerogatives are firmly in place in both Venice and Belmont.

2. Why is Antonio Sad?

The Merchant of Venice opens with Antonio, a wealthy, well-respected businessman, declaring his melancholy: "In sooth, I know not why I am so sad" (1.1.1). His friend Salerio suggests that perhaps the state of his business is troubling Antonio. No, that is not it. Another friend, Solanio, wonders if Antonio is in love. Antonio denies that he is in love. He concludes that the world is "a stage where every man must play a part, /And mine a sad one" (1.1.78-79). The reason for his melancholy, which persists through most of the play, is never explicitly revealed. But two possibilities, which are not mutually exclusive, recommend themselves. In general, Antonio finds his business success and the easy camaraderie of Venetian traders insufficient spiritual solace. Even if he is not in love, he yearns for deeper human connection. More specifically, Antonio probably is a homosexual who is in love, but the object of his affections, the heterosexual Bassanio, has indicated his strong interest in a woman of Belmont, Portia. Much of the play focuses on Antonio's deep affection for Bassanio and includes times when Antonio vies with Portia for Bassanio's favor.

Careless in both romance and economics, Bassanio has squandered his money and is in debt. He asks Antonio for a loan in order to square his accounts and finance a trip to Belmont to wine and dine Portia. A romantic adventurer who likens his quest to that of Jason, Bassanio understands that a union with Portia will remedy his material destitution once and forever. But Bassanio is not merely an unabashed golddigger. He recognizes that Portia embodies resplendent beauty, virtue and intelligence. He considered her well-named: the wife of Brutus, a Portia of the late republican era of Rome, was celebrated for her courage and faithfulness.

> In Belmont is a lady richly left;
> And she is fair and, fairer than that word,
> Of wondrous virtues; sometimes from her eyes
> I did receive fair speechless messages;
> Her name is Portia, nothing undervalu'd
> To Cato's daughter, Brutus' Portia. (1.1.161-166).

However, Antonio lacks the cash on hand to satisfy Bassanio's request. He has invested heavily in putting his ships to sea. But he instructs Bassanio to seek a loan elsewhere using Antonio's credit as surety.

3. Philosophical Interlude: Individualism and Community

Throughout history, many writers have argued that existential tension is at the heart of human experience: our yearning for intimate connection with others and the recognition that others are necessary for our identity and freedom coalesces uneasily with the fear and anxiety we experience as others approach.[1] We simultaneously long for emotional attachment yet are horrified that our individuality may evaporate once we achieve it. If we experience too much individuality we risk alienation, estrangement, and psychological isolation. If we experience insufficient individuality we court emotional suffocation, loss of self-esteem, and unhealthy immersion in the collectivity. This disharmony may never be fully reconciled once and forever, and so we find ourselves making uneasy compromises and adjustments during our life's journey as we oscillate along the continuum whose endpoints are "radical individuality" and "thorough immersion in community," respectively. This existential tension replicates itself at numerous levels: the individual confronts family, the family confronts wider community, communities confront society, and society confronts the state.

Despite his resignation, Antonio is not merely a player on the stage of life. He is not merely reading a script that others have written or that nature decrees. His melancholy flows from spiritual impoverishment: he desires a more profound sense of community than he enjoys. He yearns for a deeper bond with Bassanio in particular; he wants more intimacy in general than the level provided by the competitive, contractual amiability exuded in Venice. Antonio is a lover beset by a vague understanding that his deepest aspirations will forever go unrequited. Antonio needs a different stage. More precisely, Antonio resides in a community where his personal fulfillment will never rise to the level of his commercial success.

The individual confronts others, of varying numbers and powers, at many different levels. As we meet others at institutional and not merely personal levels, the stakes rise in some respects. Our need to retain individual freedom and resist coercion intensifies when our relations are impersonal, where we experience less direct control over our destiny, and when entrenched bureaucracies seem ready and able to usurp our autonomy. Our existential dilemmas deepen as we choose and mold the appropriate forums in which to live out the human drama of individualism versus community. The aggravated dangers accompanying societal and state levels recommend strategies to moderate the perceived threats and amplify the potential benefits. As ever, our sense of possibility will be a major player in our solutions. Circumscribed by socioeconomic reality, the relentless socializing of the established order, and the inherent inertia of the masses, our sense of possibility resists extinction and thereby honors the human craving for context-transcendence. Antonio, however, has lost his sense of possibility. He feels doomed by past and present circumstance. As such, he wallows in existential inauthenticity: he underestimates his freedom and opportunities for transcending his current conception of the self, while exaggerating the power of his past and present contexts.

4. The Contract: Bonds of Commerce

Bassanio approaches the notorious financier, Shylock, and requests a loan of 3,000 ducats for three months with Antonio standing as surety. Shylock is a Jew whose living is based on usury. Venetians, following Christian tradition, did not permit the institution of lending money for interest, but Jews, considered alien heathens, were allowed the practice which was as necessary as it was disparaged in such a commercial city. In the late sixteenth century, almost thirty years prior to the composition of *The Merchant of Venice*, the lending of money at interest at or below 10 percent was legalized for Christians in England. Still, usury was considered to be an unsavory, unworthy practice.

Shylock labels Antonio a "good man" (1.3.12). When Bassanio incorrectly assumes that Shylock is referring to Antonio's virtue, the moneylender corrects him: he speaks only of Antonio's ability to repay the loan. Shylock is aware of the ships that Antonio has at sea and the financial danger he bears, but concludes that Antonio is still a sound risk. In fact, Shylock understands all too well the possibility that should the ships be wrecked or pirated at sea that Antonio would be at his mercy.

Bassanio invites Shylock to dinner with Antonio and him. Shylock ungraciously but honestly refuses: "I will buy with you, sell with you, talk with you, walk with you, and so following, but I will not eat with you, drink with you, nor pray with you" (1.3.37-39). In fact, Shylock loathes Antonio:

> I hate him for he is a Christian,
> But more for that in low simplicity
> He lends out money gratis and brings down
> The rate of usance here with us in Venice.
> If I can catch him once upon the hip [gain an advantage over him],
> I will feed fat the ancient grudge I bear him (1.3.43-48).

Shylock will not resort to lawlessness to gain his ends. Instead, he places his faith in guile and gamesmanship woven within the bounds of law. He relates approvingly the Biblical story of how Jacob craftily deprived Laban of his sheep (1.3.73-91).

Of course, Antonio neither borrows nor lends money on interest. But, for Bassanio, he is willing to make an exception; Antonio assumes that Shylock will charge him interest on their contemplated loan. Shylock recounts the numerous times that Antonio has berated Shylock on the Rialto—spewing ugly epithets such as "misbeliever" and "cut-throat dog;" spitting on his "Jewish gabardine" and kicking him (1.3.112-119). Antonio, ungraciously but honestly, informs Shylock that he will continue to abuse him. Antonio does not seek friendship with those he perceives as alien beasts. He suggests that Shylock lend him the money "rather to thine enemy, / Who if he break, thou mayst with better face/ Exact the penalty" (1.3.135-137).

After exchanging unpleasantries, Antonio and Shylock agree to a "merry bond": Shylock will lend Bassanio 3,000 ducats over three months at no interest with Antonio standing as surety. However, should the borrower renege on the bond, Shylock will be entitled to carve a pound of flesh from Antonio in whatever part of Antonio's body Shylock chooses (1.3.147-152). Bassanio prudently resists the overture, but Antonio is confident that he will easily repay the bond once his ships return. Shylock disingenuously points out that a pound of a man's flesh, unlike the flesh of animals, brings no profit and falsely presents the terms as amicable. Bassanio is not convinced: "I like not fair terms and a villain's mind" (1.3.181). However, Antonio is convinced he risks nothing and is undoubtedly pleased to avoid interest charges. To conclude that Antonio was lured into accepting the terms by Shylock's feigned good will is spectacularly unreasonable.

How much is 3,000 ducats? Estimates vary wildly. One way of calculating the sum is to multiple the amount of gold in 3,000 ducats by the current price of that metal per ounce. The total amount of gold in 3,000 gold ducats was about 332 ounces. In 1990, gold sold for about $400 per ounce which would total around $132,800. In 2010, gold sold for about $1540 per ounce which would total around $511,280. Obviously, the price of gold is so volatile that putting a current value on 3,000 ducats held in 1600 by this method is problematic. Intuitively, how deeply in debt could Bassanio have been? How much would he need to woo Portia? Within the text of the play, Portia describes 3,000 ducats as a "petty debt" and offers to repay it "twenty times over" to prevent Shylock from exacting his terms (3.2.309-310). Calculations by Shakespearian editors place the value of 3,000 ducats between $2,000 and $2,500.[2]

In any event, why would Bassanio go to Shylock for a loan? Why not tap into Antonio's wide network of Venetian business associates or the circle of those whom Antonio had helped in like situations? Why approach a loan shark whose hatred of Antonio was profound and understandable? And why accept the terms of a bond that is anything but "merry"? Surely, Antonio could have insisted on paying interest or, failing that, could have sought another financier. Remember, though, that moral parables and folklore require the suspension of belief on matters of detail.

Antonio taunts Shylock by assuring him that in the future he will continue to abuse him. Friends do not charge interest when lending to friends. Instead, Shylock should consider this a loan to an enemy; if Antonio breaches the contract Shylock may then exact the penalty without qualms. Despite Antonio's surliness, Shylock responds generously: "I would be friends with you and have your love,/Forget the shames that you have stain'd me with,/Supply your present wants and take no doit/ Of usance for my moneys, and you'll not hear me:/This is kind I offer" (1.3.139-143). Shylock thus offers Antonio an interest-free loan. On cue, Bassanio perceives the offer as kind. Immediately, Shylock calls into question the sincerity of his response to Antonio by inserting the penalty provision for breach: a pound of Antonio's flesh. Sure of his ability to repay the loan because he anticipates the lucrative return of his ships, Antonio eagerly accepts the terms despite Bassanio's misgivings. Shylock describes the arrangement as "merry sport" (1.3.147) and "this merry bond" (1.3.174) even though throughout the play he is about as merry as a heart attack.

For Antonio, friendship is a higher good than commercial success and he will not suddenly pledge his friendship to Shylock on the basis of one interest-free loan. Such an offer might be necessary for establishing a relationship of friendship, but it is far from sufficient. In fact, perhaps Antonio accepts the penalty provision so readily partly because it underscores the personal distance between him and Shylock. From Shylock's perspective, he blocks Antonio's possible complaint that Shylock has done what all despised aliens do: practice usury. Moreover, should Antonio default Shylock will surely have him "upon the hip." Finally, Shylock might harbor the small possibility that Antonio will voluntarily come to a more favorable view of Shylock because of this transaction. (I find this to be a long shot, however, given Antonio's surly speech and the fact that Shylock will continue to practice usury in the future.) At bottom, a bond with a harsh penalty provision for breach may be the only way that Shylock can avoid being despised yet again as a usurer, yet place Antonio under obligation to him; Antonio can save face by not accepting a gift, an interest-free loan, from his enemy; and the basic inequality and enmity between the two can be preserved.

Shylock and Antonio share striking personal similarities. They are bonded by their mutual enmity; by their isolation from intimate community—neither is married nor in a requited loving relationship, both are alienated to different degrees from Venice's commercial ethic; neither finds personal fulfillment in the accumulation of wealth; and both are predominantly melancholy. At one level, Shylock and Antonio richly deserve each other.

5. Philosophical Interlude: The Notion of Desert

One of the recurrent themes of *The Merchant of Venice* is the inadequacy of the notion of personal desert as a moral measure. Although mercilessly abused during the climactic trial, Shylock can be seen as deserving his end. In crucial respects, Antonio and Shylock deserve one another. During the casket trial, one of Portia's suitors erroneously believes that because he deserves love he will win Portia's hand. In these and other instances, Shakespeare underscores the notion that personal desert cannot capture the entire truth about appropriate outcomes.

Although the principle of desert seems intuitively obvious, it exudes ambiguities which merit examination. I will focus only on the concept of *personal* desert. Accordingly, I will not discuss other locutions and questions of desert such as "Do beautiful artistic pieces deserve attention?" or "Do useful, valuable material objects deserve care?"

A few general principles:[3]

> If people deserve something they do so on the basis of some prior performance or by virtue of some possessed characteristic.
>
> If someone deserves something then that is a good reason for giving that something to him or her but not always a sufficient or conclusive reason.
>
> The nature of the something to be distributed—whether it is a prize, reward, blame, punishment, praise, or the like—will determine, at least partially, the nature of the basis that warrants the person's claim of deserving that something.

Typically, for someone to claim to deserve something he or she must point to some prior performance that might warrant the claim: The person must have done something in the past. We deserve something in virtue of prior acts for which we are responsible. In some cases, though, we may justifiably claim to deserve something based on our possession of a relevant characteristic and not on a prior performance.[4] For example, I deserve equal consideration of certain of my interests, along with those of other human beings, based only on my possession of humanness. However, a person who lacks both a relevant past performance and a relevant characteristic has no legitimate claim based on desert. For example, we cannot justifiably claim that we deserve to win the New York State Lottery or that we deserve our natural talents. In the case of the lottery, merely purchasing a ticket and wishing on our lucky stars that we might win are past performances that are not enough to support a justified claim of desert. In the case of natural talents, we possess them due only to the genetic lottery; we did nothing, we were nothing, prior to our birth.

Claims of desert are typically, although not always, connected to the results of voluntary actions over which we have major control. The notion of desert is often invoked to treat human beings appropriately given that they are responsible for their actions. Having no control over the amount and type of natural talents we possess or over who wins the New York State Lottery, we can assert no credible claim of desert in either case. If a person deserves something then he can advance a reason why he ought to receive that something, but the reason is not always a conclusive consideration establishing that he ought to receive it.

Claims of desert must be distinguished from claims of entitlement, another principle of justice. Consider the following example: The Buffalo Bills play the Miami Dolphins for the right to enter the Super Bowl. The Bills prove conclusively that they are the better team and also that they exerted the most effort on this particular Sunday. However, because of a stunning series of lucky breaks, fortuitous decisions by the game officials, and cooperation of the weather, the Dolphins win the contest, 21–20. To claim that the Bills *deserved* to win—Should not the better team that tries harder be declared the more deserving?—is reasonable. But even if the Bills are unanimously deemed the more deserving team, they are neither *entitled* to play in the Super Bowl nor do they have a *right* to play in the Super Bowl. The Dolphins, the less deserving squad, is entitled and has a right to compete in the Super Bowl. By the same token, the winner of the New York State Lottery did not deserve to win, but is entitled to the prize.

> Someone is *entitled* to a prize if and only if he or she has fulfilled the qualifying conditions specified by the rules determining who receives that prize.
>
> Someone *deserves* to win a prize if and only if he or she demonstrated to a higher degree than all other competitors the skill and effort set forth as the basis of the competition.

Accordingly, one may be entitled to something but not deserve it, and one may deserve something but not be entitled to it. For example, children may work steadfastly to support their elderly, disabled parents and observers may well conclude that the children deserve a reward for their effort, commitment, and contribution, but there may simply not be a reward for which they qualify and thus none to which they are entitled. Having been legally designated in a will, Jones may be entitled to a huge inheritance that observers might accurately conclude Jones does not deserve based on their examination of Jones's life. Desert and entitlement, then, are two distinct claims of justice that sometimes conflict when others determine what one ought to receive as his or her just due. Although they deserved to win the crucial game, the disappointed Bills cannot legitimately claim they are entitled or have a right to compete in the Super Bowl. The right to compete in the Super Bowl is conferred on that team that fulfills the relevant qualifying condition—winning the preceding playoff game—and not necessarily on the team that deserved to win that game.

> If someone deserves something it does not follow that he or she has a right to that something.
>
> If someone is entitled to something then he or she has a right to that something.

Again, a person may deserve something although not be able to lodge a justified claim to it either because there is no prize or award to be claimed or, even if there is such a prize or award, because he or she has not fulfilled the qualifying conditions to receive it.

Consider the following:

>Mary deserves praise
>Mary deserves blame
>Mary is entitled to praise
>Mary is entitled to blame

Under the appropriate conditions, the first three attributions make sense. But the fourth is problematic. While a person may deserve either praise or blame (or reward or punishment), the claim that a person is entitled to blame (or punishment) rings hollow. Entitlement is a consideration of justice that applies only to things that people desire or ought to desire. In contrast, desert is a consideration of justice that sometimes applies—in the cases of punishment and blame—to things that people typically do not desire. In that vein, to claim that someone has a right to praise or reward is compelling under the appropriate circumstances, but to claim that someone has a right to blame or punishment is odd. Accordingly, the notion of rights is tightly connected to the concept of entitlement, but not to the concept of desert. In that vein, the notion of personal desert is mainly or entirely pre-institutional; it is a natural moral notion that is not conceptually tied to political institutions, social structures, and legal rules. The notion of entitlement is mainly or entirely institutional; it is an institutional notion that is logically linked to political institutions, social structures, and legal rules.

This distinction, though, is far from iron-clad. Several desert claims do presuppose a sociopolitical context because of the nature of the treatment or object at stake. For example, to say that Mary deserves a Pulitzer Prize, Vito deserves the Medal of Honor, and John deserves a long stretch in prison are all legitimate assertions under the appropriate circumstances, and they all presuppose the existence of different social, military, and legal institutions. Still, claims of desert, unlike those of entitlement, do not arise merely by fulfilling the conditions specified in an institutional system of political or legal rules. Mary, Vito, and John may have satisfied the conditions laid down for their respective treatments, but doing so is not the basis of their desert claims. That there are such things as the Pulitzer Prize, the Medal of Honor, and imprisonment is a function of institutional arrangements. But desert claims, unlike entitlement claims, related to these awards and treatments must be grounded on bases other than satisfying the qualifying conditions specified for them. The basis of desert, then, remains certain qualities that Mary, Vito, and John embodied and how those qualities animated their respective actions.

Numerous bases have been offered in support of claims of desert. For example, a person may lodge a claim of desert based on moral worth; on success in contributing to society; on general productivity; on effort expended in seeking to contribute to society or to general productivity; or on the possession of relevant characteristics. Of course, these considerations do not always coalesce easily. Who deserves the prize—the person who made the most effort or the person who demonstrated the most skill and produced more? The nature of the object at stake and a series of value judgments will typically determine the appropriate basis of the desert claim. For example, if a scarce medical resource can be administered to only one of two equally needy patients, one of the possible recipients might be more deserving of the resource based on her superior contributions to society. Of course, that she ought, all things considered, to receive the resource based only on the fact that she is more deserving is another matter. In other contexts, claims of desert based on greater societal productivity are irrelevant. For example, a renowned, stunningly productive citizen is not allowed to vote more times in a national election than an ordinary person.

Controversy swirls around the question whether need is a legitimate basis for desert claims. We might see need as the type of personal characteristic that grounds desert claims to, say, medical treatment or allocation of food. But need is less a personal characteristic and more a (hopefully) temporary condition or situation. A person is needy not because of his or her inherent personal attributes but because of a series of describable choices, causes, and events. In fact, we are all antecedently needy until our biological, psychological, and material desires are satisfied to one degree or another. But what of a person whose needs flow from an extraordinary run of misfortune, none of which is due to her misdeeds or shortcomings? To conclude that she deserves a break or some good fortune is not misplaced. We would be assuming that nonculpable people should not be subject to a disproportionate amount of bad luck. We hope that luck would finally even out or at least occasionally smile on those it had unduly assaulted. Such a desert claim would underscore the disparity between a person's blameless performance and massive misfortune. Having not deserved relentless battering from lady luck, the person now deserves a squaring of accounts. Of course, such a claim appears platitudinous. Having no control over the whims of fortune, we are casting only a hope into the wind.

Suppose you had one delicious slice of pepperoni pizza to bestow and two possible recipients. Both were strangers who were equal in all respects—contributions, effort, productivity, and the like. However, one had been the constant victim of bad luck, while the other was unremarkable in that regard. Would you conclude that the nonculpable victim deserved the food more than the other person and you now had a chance to reverse the cycle of misfortune, at least to a small extent? Although the two possible recipients are equally needy in terms of food, they are unequally needy in terms of reversing past outrageous fortune. Neither is entitled nor do they have a right to the slice, but a review of past circumstances might well impel you to decide in favor of the unfortunate pilgrim. Still, the case is not clear-cut. If the two famished people are equal in respect to contributions, effort, and productivity, then more credit might be given to the person who battled through more adverse circumstances; perhaps effort is not equal after all. Or perhaps the more unfortunate of the two was blessed with greater (undeserved) innate talents that permitted her to equal the production of her more fortunate but less naturally gifted colleague. If so, attributions of desert are more ambiguous. In any event, appeals to need are better severed from appeals to desert. The two types of appeals often constitute conflicting claims to just distribution of social goods. However, innocent suffering and bad luck can affect a person's desert claims in indirect ways.

The Merchant of Venice is most concerned with the notion of moral desert. Moral desert arises from voluntary choices, deep intentions, sincere efforts, and cultivated character. But from a human perspective the idea of rewarding or punishing the internal origins of moral desert is highly problematic. Lacking unambiguous access to motivations, intentions, and past socialization, human evaluators cannot easily separate what someone genuinely deserves from what someone acquired by luck. For example, calculating what Shylock deserves involves weighing a host of competing vectors. He is harsh, inflexible, and often ill-motivated, which inclines us to conclude that he brings upon himself and thus deserves much of his fate. However, how much of his approach to life is an understandable response to being treated cruelly and unjustifiably by the Venetian commercial establishment? Having been spat upon, vilified, and shunned for no other reason than his ethnicity and religion, Shylock's deficiencies in graciousness and benevolence are unsurprising. Still, is he not responsible for allowing the transgressions of others to harden his soul? Unraveling what Shylock deserves given his social context is no small task.

John Rawls argues that none of us deserves our innate talents and initial social position.[5] After all, none of us can point to any prior performance or antecedent characteristic by virtue of which a legitimate claim of desert for those things could bloom. Rawls concludes that we do not deserve those rewards and prizes that flow from such undeserved qualities. He suggests that the major bases for desert claims—effort, productivity, contribution, and even moral worth—greatly depend on undeserved innate talents and initial social position. Even our willingness to make an effort and fulfill one of the major bases of desert depends largely on our initial starting position, social circumstances, and innate talents. Rawls tacitly accepts the principle that we deserve something if and only if we deserve the characteristics by which we obtain that something. (The principle would hold for all desert claims other than those based on possessing relevant characteristics, some of which would not be deserved.)

However, even if *willingness* to work is a character trait that a person embodies because of the luck of the genetic lottery, *actual* work and effort may still underwrite a genuine claim of desert. The mere possession of desirable character traits flowing from the genetic lottery such as high intelligence, willingness to work, physical strength, natural wit, and the like do not produce genuine desert claims. Lacking the animation provided by effort, such desirable characteristics produce little or nothing. Possessing desirable characteristics as innate gifts is one thing, but exercising those characteristics is quite another. Manifesting and exercising desirable character traits requires concentrated effort that vivifies legitimate desert claims. To treat people as they deserve is to respond to them as autonomous, free beings responsible for their actions. Doing so also heightens our understanding that by crafting our actions in certain ways, we can strongly influence how others will respond to us. When others treat us as we deserve they are responding to us according to our deeds, commensurately to what we have earned.

Of course, even if a person does not deserve something it does not follow that he ought not to receive it or even that he is not entitled to it; it follows only that the notion of desert cannot provide him with any claim to it. Rawls highlights the problem that while a person may well deserve certain things, it is typically impossible to calculate what she genuinely deserves and this epistemological problem renders the notion of desert a feckless practical guide to the distribution of social goods. To calculate what accomplishments, exertions of effort, notable deeds, and the like flow from characteristics that a person deserves or has earned and what arises from undeserved initial social position and innate talents is virtually impossible.

Are human beings genuinely free? Can we deserve certain treatment even though we do not deserve our initial starting position, social circumstances, and innate talents? How can we separate the effects of innocent suffering, bad luck, and the like from the results of our actions for which we are fully responsible? How do the different bases of desert interrelate when calculating a person's overall moral desert?

As existentialists are fond of reminding us, experience is the greatest "proof" that human beings have freedom. We cannot deny our freedom once we experience the anguish of choice, profoundly sense we could have done otherwise than we did, and, at times, break entrenched habits and patterns by apparent acts of will. Although neuroscience may insist that my decisions and choices are conjured in my brain prior to my consciousness of them, my felt experiences persist. Even if science repeats that my mind is subject to the typical material pattern of causes and effects, even if all events are determined by prior chains of causes and effects, we cling to a thin reed: causation need not be compulsion. My choices are neither random nor coerced. If freedom requires making choices and acting on the basis of reasons that are not causes then rationally establishing freedom is gravely problematic. But our experiences scream out and win the day: How could we live and act under the self-conscious view that we are unfree? How would we experience the world? If we are antecedently constructed to experience and thus believe that we are free, what rational evidence could change our manner of living other than in a purely academic way? Even if we are convinced by the evidence against human free will, we must heed Jean-Paul Sartre's slogan, "We are condemned to be free," and paraphrase it: "We are condemned to live *as if* we were free." Sartre insists that we are radically free and fully responsible. His rallying cry of "No Excuses" amplifies that theme. As a matter of theory, Sartre may well be incorrect, but as a function of practice—how we must live our lives—his program resonates deeply. We are biologically constructed to live as if we are free. No other practical alternative is available.

Accordingly, we must *assume* that human beings are autonomous, responsible, free moral agents responsible for their actions. The conundrums of the principle of desert may well be unsolvable by human beings. Still, the notion of personal desert bears significant moral currency if employed artfully.

In sum, the notion of desert attaches to justice, while the experience of love embodies sacrifice, forgiveness, compassion, and mutuality. One of the lessons of *The Merchant of Venice* is that as flawed, fallible human beings we all require mercy, the extension of compassion that we do not strictly speaking deserve. Such compassion nourishes our relationships, allows us to navigate the individual-community continuum with aplomb, and promotes the bonds most essential for our flourishing.

6. Who is Shylock?

Greedy, uncompromising, ungracious, conniving, vengeful, opportunistic . . . Shylock is all of these things and more. Venice branded him as an alien, restricted his opportunities to forge a livelihood, then hypocritically demeaned him for his usury—an institution that facilitated the commerce and trade that underwrote the city's glory. Prominent citizens such as Antonio freely hurled epithets at Shylock, physically assaulted and spat upon him with impunity, without any fear of legal redress. Venice regarded him as a lowly cur and treated him worse than they would treat a beast.

Christian citizens sung paeans of praise to the theological virtues of faith, hope, and charity, and facilely invoked the glory of understanding, intelligence, and mercy. But their practice rarely mirrored their rhetoric. Portia recites critical lines on that score: "If to do were as easy as to know what were good to do, chapels had been churches and poor men's cottages princes' palaces. It is a good divine that follows his own instructions: I can easier teach twenty what were good to be done, than to be one of the twenty to follow mine own teaching" (1.2.13-18).

Shylock seethes at Christian hypocrisy, yearns to avenge his systematic mistreatment, and often strikes out inappropriately. His servant, Launcelot Gobbo, leaves Shylock's house and considers him "the very devil incarnation"

(2.2.28-29). His daughter, Jessica, elopes with a Christian to escape Shylock's tyranny: "Our house is hell" (2.3.2). What is Shylock's response? He unsentimentally dismisses Launcelot as a lazy, ravenous drain on household resources: "The patch is kind enough, but a huge feeder; / Snail-slow in profit, and he sleeps by day / More than a wild-cat: drones hive not with me; / Therefore I part with him, and part with him/ To one [Bassanio] that I would have him help waste/ His borrowed purse" (2.5.46-51). When Shylock learns that Jessica has run off with the Christian, Lorenzo, he is outraged. When he learns that Jessica has absconded with much of his wealth, Shylock is apoplectic: "My daughter! O my ducats! O my daughter! / Fled with a Christian! O my Christian ducats! / Justice! The law! my ducats, and my daughter!" (2.8.15-17). When he begins to assess the extent of his losses—a diamond that he had purchased for 2,000 ducats, other precious jewels—he senses a curse upon his people: "I would my daughter were dead at my foot, and the jewels in her ear! Would she were hearsed at my foot, and the ducats in her coffin!' (3.1.91-93). When his friend, Tubal, tells Shylock that other men suffer misfortune—such as Antonio whose ships were lost at sea—Shylock is momentarily heartened. But Tubal adds that Jessica squandered 80 ducats in Genoa, Shylock is dismayed and has only one avenue of retaliation: "I'll plague him [Antonio]; I'll torture him: I am glad of it" (3.1.121-122). Tubal adds that Jessica traded for a monkey the turquoise ring that Shylock had given his wife prior to their marriage. Shylock is distraught.

Shylock's identity is defined by his wealth and his remaining family, his daughter. Losing his daughter—to a Christian, no less—and part of his fortune jeopardized his sense of self and undermined his already-fragile sense of security. His two major channels of exercising control, of ordering his world, and exerting his power are collapsing. Shylock was the master of his household, but he has been deserted by his daughter and his main servant. Shylock was the architect of his wealth, but much of that has been pilfered by his wayward daughter and her Christian paramour. He has only one apparent avenue of redress, one way of reasserting a sense of control and order to his life: Shylock will demand the penalty clause of his "merry" bond with Antonio, who cannot repay the loan. He will carve Antonio's flesh just as Shylock's own flesh has been carved by years of Christian hypocrisy and abuse, and by his own daughter's betrayal. Shylock will exact his revenge upon Venice and partially reinstate his self-worth in one fell swoop.

Judged by strict existential criteria, Shylock acts inauthentically. He takes little or no responsibility for the person he has become. He notes accurately the unfair professional slights and unjustified spiritual assaults that Venetian life has inflicted upon him. But he claims to reflect only what the hypocritical Christians have taught him. He postures as a once empty vessel now filled only with venom poured by Christian adversaries. While we sympathize deeply with his social predicament and understand well his zeal for revenge, we cannot ignore his flight from responsibility. Is he not the agent of the condition of his household? While his freedom to affect Venetian public life is severely circumscribed, is Shylock not the sole designer of his "hellish" home? Certainly, Shylock cannot persuasively blame the inhospitable Christian public sphere for his own tyrannical private domain. While he apparently remains true to his departed wife and the life they shared, we find little else to recommend in Shylock's character and actions.

When Antonio's friend, Salerio, questions the value of taking Antonio's flesh as penalty for his failure to repay the loan, Shylock does not miss a beat: "To bait fish withal: if it will feed nothing else, it will feed my revenge. He hath disgraced me, and hindered me half a million; laughed at my losses, mocked at my gains, scorned my nation, thwarted my bargains, cooled my friends, heated mine enemies; and what's his reason? I am a Jew" (3.1.55-60). The time has come for Shylock to strike back, not only at Antonio but at the entire set of past and present circumstances that have brought him to his moment.

The rest of this speech is the famous "Hath not a Jew" soliloquy. But even here, at his literary zenith in the play, Shylock strikes an existentially false note. He points out unassailably that Jews, like Christians, have eyes, hands, organs, dimensions, senses, affections and passions. Both sets of religious followers are fed with food, hurt with weapons, subject to diseases and changes in the seasons. Undeniably, Christians and Jews are biologically indistinguishable: "If you prick us, do we not bleed? If you tickle us, do we not laugh? If you poison us, do we not die? and if you wrong us, shall we not revenge? If we are like you on the rest, we will resemble you in that . . . The villainy you teach me, I will execute, and it shall go hard but I will better the instruction" (3.1. 68-76). After sketching a host of strictly biological reactions, Shylock jumps to a normative response: how people answer wrongs. If Jews are like Christians biologically, Shylock concludes that Jews should respond to transgressions in the same pitiless fashion that Christians do.

Of course, evaluative and moral conclusions do not follow from purely descriptive (biological) premises. That Christians and Jews are biological similar cannot establish the foundation for how they should respond to wrongs. Shylock might be assuming that avenging wrongs is itself a purely biological response. Here, though, we might still argue about proportionate retaliation— Should Antonio be killed in order to square the books on his own past mistreatment of Shylock? Is such a response proportionate and thereby justified? Is Antonio, instead, the appropriate, involuntary redeemer of *all* atrocities levied against Shylock by Venetian citizens? Even if so, does the punishment fit the collective misdeeds of the city?

That Shylock is making such arguments is doubtful because he admits that what he seeks is "villainy" because that it is what Christians have taught him by their example. Thus, Shylock does not believe revenge—at least of this type and scope—is a purely biological or natural response. Instead, Shylock takes his revenge to be justified because of what he believes Christians would do if the tables were turned and because of their own past hypocritical mismatching of their ideals and actions toward him. Let one of them feel the lash of disproportionate, merciless hatred. Shylock will mete out to Christians precisely what they *deserve*. Again, Shakespeare places a red flag on actions and judgments grounded in someone's perception of what another person deserves.

Shylock flees from responsibility. He refuses to view himself as an active agent in forging the person he is becoming. Rather, he is only a once-empty vessel into which Christian teaching by example has poured moral poison. Shylock is only a victim who now feels justified in retaliating against his tormentors. In existential terms, he views himself as pure facticity, while denying his freedom to transcend his current self-conception and denying his collaboration in forming the person he is becoming.

Primarily, Shylock is imprisoned by avarice.[6] Greed signals an obsession with material accumulation such as wealth, status, and power. Focused too acutely on the wrong objects of desire, greed distracts us from loftier pursuits. Avaricious people yearn counter-productively to calm their restless spirits with tangible goods. Money and property—which often spawn social power and privilege—are their means of keeping score and measuring self-worth. They conjure the most chilling images of Plato's insatiable tyrant flailing futilely on a treadmill of desire: the more he strives and strides, the more deeply he is imprisoned by desire. Successful accumulation breeds only more desire. Nothing can fully satisfy the avaricious as they impale themselves on a pendulum of frustration: If their desires are unfulfilled they are frustrated and disappointed; if their desires are satisfied they enjoy a temporary joy that is soon overwhelmed by more rapacious desires. Worse, the single-minded quest for material accumulation typically spawns a host of evil deeds that trample on the interests of other people, destroy salutary human community, and obstruct spiritual endeavors. Greed often breeds disloyalty, betrayal, hoarding, theft, robbery, and fraud.

The literary image of Ebenezer Scrooge, before he turned soft, resonates. He, like Shylock, warped his own soul by attributing false, inflated value to material accumulation. He sacrificed the bounty and adventure of life on the altar of possessing for its own sake. Scrooge's possessions ruled him by directing his energies and molding his daily tasks. He found himself on Plato's endless treadmill where the more he exerted the less he developed as a person. His face betrayed his character and chronicled his spiritual deprivation. Avarice deflates the heart, misdirects our energies, fetishizes commodities, and alienates us from others. Possessions become our measuring stick and our instruments for wrongdoing. The avaricious are self-defined by the desires they gratify and material objects they amass. The worst case scenario: a virtually infinite, insatiable yearning for more. The result: a selfish quest for material accumulation that transgresses upon the needs and entitlements of others. In sum, the avaricious have a distorted sense of boundaries and wrongful priorities; they are emotionally aloof and profoundly insensitive. Thus, emerges Shylock, but without the intercession of the benevolent ghosts who influenced Scrooge.

However, we must understand that avarice is not always centered on material accumulation. At points during the trial when he thinks he has a genuine choice, Shylock will refuse double and triple repayment of his loan to Bassanio and Antonio. Instead, he will demand his forfeiture under the bond: a pound of Antonio's flesh. A person who was greedy only for money would choose otherwise. Still, Shylock is plagued with avarice. But his greed focuses on an outlet for his vengeance and frustration. Having been relegated to third-class resident alien status in Venice, having been gratuitously mistreated by Antonio—a beloved symbol of the Venetian commercial spirit, and having been betrayed by his daughter, Shylock's avarice takes a nonmaterial turn. He is greedy for revenge; he is greedy for a way to legitimize his personhood; he is greedy for equality under the law; and he is greedy for cathartic relief from his pent-up frustration at being labeled "the other" and the concomitant indignities thereby thrust upon him.

Shylock is also encased in wrath. Prominent citizens of Venice, such as Antonio, have abused him terribly; worse, his daughter has eloped with a Christian, converted to Christianity, and stolen some of Shylock's wealth. He has been objectified as less than human and he has been played for a fool. His familial bond has been broken in a far more threatening way than Antonio's default on their contractual bond.

We should distinguish between righteous anger and wrath. At times, as recognized by thinkers from Aristotle to present, anger is a salutary passion that motivates virtuous action. Outrage at injustice, the conditions of poverty, forced ignorance, and the like stirs us to forge remedies. Indeed, anger is an antidote for sloth. The Bible reports that on Palm Sunday, righteously indignant at sacrilege, Jesus scattered the moneylenders and drove them from the Temple in Jerusalem. After all, suppressing justified anger, turning it inward, leads easily to resentment and depression. Aimed at appropriate targets and intelligently discharged, anger animates our sense of purpose, underscores our highest values, and externalizes our commitment to a better world. Anger, then, motivates actions, whether wisely or not. At times, the call to simmer down is nothing more than a ploy to demean and suppress an appropriate response to injustice. Yes, anger is accusatory, judgmental, and unpleasant. But numerous events in the world merit such a response. To care deeply about anything is to risk outbursts of anger. Reason without passion is vacuous, while passion without reason is directionless.

In contrast to righteous anger, wrath is excessive, misdirected, and erroneous. Lacking a justification and connection to the good, wrath differs from anger. Wrath is even more accusatory, judgmental, and unpleasant than anger, but wrath lacks a righteous basis and is severed from intelligent expression. Anger is divisive in that it distances us from a pernicious segment of society, but anger can unite us with a righteous part of the community. Wrath is the love of justice wrongly inflated to revenge and spite. Wrath either divides us from almost all of society or severs us from the righteous sector while joining us with noxious elements of the community. Wrath is a fixation, an inordinate desire for retaliation, a hardened heart, an overly resolute spirit, and a knowing and willing expression of malice. Wrath inflames envy, arrogance, resentment, and greed. Righteous anger expresses our considered judgments, while wrath suffocates our ability to make rational evaluations. Wrath too often consumes those who choose to use it as a weapon against others. Shylock is a case study in the counterproductive effects of unconstrained wrath.

Fueled by avarice and wrath, Shylock will place his faith in the strict application of law. He will take solace in the rule of law virtues of generality, impersonality, and objectivity. For once, he and the Christians will at last enjoy the same status. Better still, Shylock has finally caught Antonio "upon the hip." Shylock has fulfilled his duties under their "merry bond," but Antonio, having lost his ships at sea, cannot repay the 3,000 ducats. Happily, Shylock will be able to use Christian legal ideals against Antonio. Shylock's anticipated triumph will not be grounded in personal vengeance but, instead, will be crowned with the luster of law.

7. Philosophical Interlude: Existential Authenticity

Martin Heidegger gave to existentialism the terminology of authenticity. He described inauthentic human living as distinguished by wrongly denying freedom and succumbing to false ideas of inevitability. He suggests at least five, partially overlapping, ways in which I might be living inauthentically, denying my individuality.[7]

I am *sunk in everydayness* if I live in the "they" and consider myself as *das* Man—which translates roughly to generic humankind; thinking and acting in accord with "what one does" or "what people do"; subjugating myself to the mass of others; regarding myself as a member of a kind or type. If I accept the seductions of conformity, then a banal life of habit and routine, punctuated by diversions follows. A particular example of this is distancing myself from reflection on my mortality. If I recognize abstractly that all human beings are mortal, but insist that my death has nothing to do with me now, then I prevent myself from consciously and continually creating who I will be. Heidegger calls this a mark of *falling*.

I am *denying my freedom and transcendence* if I think of myself as *necessarily* being who and what I am. Regarding the roles I play and the categories to which I belong as necessarily part of who I am reneges on my capability of transforming who I am.

I am *kneeling before false necessity* if I take my decisions, choices, and actions as being the appropriate, natural, inevitable result of the kind of person that I am. Doing so relegates my future to my unalterable nature.

I am *clinging to fixity* if I accept that I have a fixed, unalterable essence. Doing so denies my transcendence—my freedom and capability of transforming who I am—and overly empowers my facticity—my givenness, aspects of me that cannot be changed, such as my birthdate, biological inheritance, birth parents, and the like.

I am *settling for chatter* if the overwhelming bulk of my conversation with others centers on small talk, babble, gossip, and shop. I am merely squandering time in non-threatening ways. I avoid profound issues such as politics, religion, philosophy, and race because discussing such topics jeopardizes my acceptance by *das* Man. In sum, *das* Man, necessity, fixity, fallenness, and chatter are the standard bearers for inauthentic living.

For Heidegger, authentic human living focuses on transcendent self-creation in the context of one's facticity. *I must recognize my uniqueness* and not identify as a member of a kind or type. I must embrace *consciousness of my particular death* by heightening my awareness of my mortality instead of regarding mortality abstractly as universally pertinent. I must *embrace my freedom* by concentrating on the decisions, choices, and actions that constitute my life and that help form my self. I must *shape my future in context* by denying that I am a fixed essence, by accepting the limits of my facticity, and by understanding my transcendent possibilities. I must *appreciate the contingency of kinds and types* by viewing them as accidental memberships subject to re-imagination and revision. Although none of us is entirely authentic or inauthentic, we differ in degree and those differences distinguish the quality of our being.

The primary existential values are authenticity and intensity. Embracing a tragic sense of life, reaffirming the beauty of life while honestly facing its horrors, recognizing that suffering and anguish are required for fully human life, accepting our freedom and taking complete responsibility for our choices and actions, distancing ourselves from the petty fears and hopes of the faceless masses, heightening our consciousness of the human condition and of our own mortality, and bestowing our energies and enthusiasms upon the world are all paramount ways of manifesting and sustaining those values.[8]

Judged by Heidegger's criteria, Shylock's life seems significantly more inauthentic than authentic. Critical to this judgment is the undeniable observation that Shylock neither displays a conscious desire to change in salutary ways nor does he participate in new projects or relationships that might have that effect. Instead, he accepts his current self-understanding as definitive of who he is; he views himself as a finished product, an essence from which the remainder of his life will flow. Shylock perceives his judgments, choices and actions as naturally arising from the sort of person he is and he thereby unwittingly worships the flimsy idol of false necessity.

8. The Casket Test: Bonds of Intimacy

Belmont is bustling with the business of marriage. Portia's father decreed in his will that she would wed only the man who passed a trial of the understanding. Suitors must choose among three caskets, each structured of a different metal and adorned by a different description: the gold casket advertises, "Who chooseth me shall gain what many men desire"; the silver casket beckons, "Who chooseth me shall get as much as he deserves"; and the lead casket cautions, "Who chooseth me must give and hazard all he hath" (2.8.21-39). But those who step up to select must take an oath: They may not reveal to third parties the choice they made; if they fail to win Portia they cannot marry anyone else; and if they fail to win Portia they must depart immediately and not trouble her again (2.8.10-16).

A host of lotharios have contemplated taking the test. Portia judges harshly a Neapolitan prince, who talked expansively about his horse, and a County Palatine, who exuded deep melancholy: "I had rather be married to a death's head with a bone in his mouth than to either of these" (1.2.53-55). A French lord, young baron from Falconbridge, a Scottish lord, and a German nephew of the Duke of Saxony meet a similar fate and judgment. Although Portia feels the sting of patriarchal privilege in her father's impulse to control her future from the grave—"the will of a living daughter curbed by the will of a dead father" (1.2.26-27)—she reconciles with her destiny: "If I live to be as old as Sibylla, I will die as chaste as Diana, unless I be obtained by the manner of my father's will" (1.2.116-118).

Why would Portia's father decree such a matrimonial test? Surely, no strict correlation between being a successful game show contestant and a worthy husband exists. Moreover, any reprobate off the street has a 33% chance of lodging a lucky, Portia-winning guess. Also, the oath each suitor takes is hardly enforceable other than by a personal code of honor. Finally, even if a suitor has the "correct" *understanding* of love and marriage—which is, after all, the best that the casket trial can hope to discern—it does not follow that the correct *practice* of love and marriage will dog the steps of such understanding. Portia has already instructed us that "If to do were as easy as to know what were good to do, chapels had been churches and poor men's cottages princes' palaces."

Given these obvious points and that her entire future is at stake, why would Portia comply with the casket trial? As an intelligent, resourceful, uncommonly perceptive woman, Portia is unlikely to swallow the premise of the test. Even if she feels a deep allegiance to her father why should that translate to submission to a fatally flawed exercise upon which so much turns? Portia's waiting-maid, Nerissa, gives a plausible explanation: "Your father was ever virtuous; and holy men at their death have good inspirations: therefore the lottery, that he hath devised in these three chests of gold, silver, and lead, whereof who chooses his meaning chooses you, will, no doubt, never be chosen by any rightly but one who you shall rightly love" (1.2.30-35).

Again, moral parables and fables require that we suspend belief about and take numerous leaps of faith with details. No sane person would genuinely propose the casket trial as a reasonable way to secure a spouse. Online dating services such as E-Harmony.com, word of mouth referrals from experienced yentas, and even arranged marriages are more likely than the casket trial to maximize the possibilities of a successful union. Accordingly, we must cast our literary judgment with that of Portia's father: the successful suitor will possess both a keen understanding of the nature of love and marriage, and he will prove himself a wonderful husband in practice. Although it appears that her dead father has commodified Portia as the prize in a fatuous game show, appearances, as the play will demonstrate throughout, are often deceiving.

The trial, itself, is not exactly subtle. Three criteria of love and marriage are embodied in the descriptions dressing the caskets: love based on desire; love grounded in personal desert; and love flowing from mutual vulnerability. Moreover, these three themes vivify the greater scheme of the play. They suggest standards by which a society might distribute social goods and they underscore the importance of the individual-community continuum.

Shakespeare shares the reasoning of the final three suitors. The Prince of Morocco, noting his tawny complexion, boosts of his past romantic and military successes. Assured by Portia that she will abide by the results of the casket trial, Morocco dismisses the lead casket as unworthy of pursuit: lead is not a metal that merits hazarding all he has. Morocco has obtusely confused the composition of the casket with the prize at stake. After all, the correct choice secures Portia not the value of a casket. Morocco demonstrates that he is a simpleton lured only by surface appearances. He selects the gold casket because so many suitors from so many places desire Portia. Because she is widely desired and because gold, too, is widely desired and highly valued, Morocco chooses the gold casket. Morocco unlocks the casket and is shocked to discover a skull, within whose empty eye contains a scroll: "All that glistens is not gold" (2.7.66). Morocco strikes out because desire and attractive appearance are radically insufficient for love.

At best, they constitute an initial allure to another person, but they fall far short of grounding the emotion of love. By stressing only the anticipated gains of love, Morocco misunderstands its nature. Morocco has no clue of to what love amounts and chooses only on the basis of what he and others want. Portia sniffs, "Let all of his complexion choose me so" (2.7.79). Apologists for Portia may suggest that "complexion" should not be taken literally, but only as a metaphor for those likely to be non-Christians and thus undesirable spouses. But is religious bias less virulent than racial bias?

The next candidate is the Prince of Arragon. He is both sharper and ruder than Morocco. He quickly dismisses the lead casket: "You shall look fairer, ere I give or hazard" (2.8.22). Unwilling to make himself vulnerable, he demonstrates immediately that he misunderstands love (or seeks Portia only as a prize or meal ticket). Headed for matrimonial Palookaville, Arragon spurns the gold casket because the desires of the masses are unworthy. If the multitudes desire something then Arragon is suspicious of the value of that something. The masses are fools and he who follows their judgments is doomed to mediocrity. Arragon selects the silver casket because it distributes social goods on the basis of personal desert. Arragon is convinced that his merit glistens. He unlocks the silver casket and gets precisely what he deserves: "the portrait of a blinking idiot" (2.8.54). But stressing only his perceived merits and how they should be rewarded, Arragon misunderstands the nature of love. The claim of personal desert is inadequate to ground love and marriage. Love is bestowed, not claimed on the basis of one's own assessment of his personal worth.

The final candidate is the Venetian scholar and soldier, Bassanio. He had previously caught Portia's eye and she fervently hopes that he will select wisely. She entertains the idea of teaching Bassanio the correct answer to the test, but realizes that cheating would undermine the purpose of the trial. Still, she offers a hint: "One half of me is yours, the other half yours, / Mine own, I would say; but if mine, then yours, / And so all yours" (3.2.16-18). Portia senses that Bassanio, in part, desires her for her money. But she just as keenly intuits that there is more to Bassanio than meets the eye. She instructs that music will play as he makes his choice. The song selected may well have aided Bassanio in his romantic quest: the end words of the lines of the first stanza all rhyme with "lead," and the song's message warns against choosing on first appearances. Moreover, Portia garnishes her conversation with Bassanio with additional clues: she employs the words "hazard" (3.2.2), "venture" (3.2.10), and "sacrifice" (3.2.57), all of which link up with the inscription on the lead casket. Granted, few literary interpreters have portrayed Bassanio as intellectually brilliant, but we may well suspect that Portia's aid has the desired effect. Has Portia obeyed her father's will literally, but nevertheless violated the spirit of the test? Do her actions anticipate Shylock's position at trial—when he rejects the spirit of contract law and demands a literal decoding of the bond? Will Portia's marriage end as disastrously for her as Shylock's trial does for him? Or is a more nuanced reading recommended?

Bassanio is a master of appearance—charming, physically attractive, uncommonly glib. He is a master rhetorician who has an intuitive knack for eloquently articulating the precise message his audience needs to hear at a particular moment. Unlike Morocco, he understands deeply the false allure of the very appearances he embodies: "The world is still deceiv'd with ornament" (3.2.74). Bassanio will not be suckered by the glitter of gold: he remembers the story of Midas. Instead, he is drawn to the meagerness and paleness of lead. He will approach love and marriage with humility and tenderness. He unlocks the casket and finds his prize: a portrait of Portia confirms that Bassanio is our medalist in the love and marriage game: "You that choose not by the view, / Chance as fair and choose as true/ . . . Turn you where your lady is/ and claim her with a loving kiss" (3.2.132-139).

That Bassanio would love Portia is clear. She has money, intelligence, virtue, grace, wit—she is the entire packet of excellences a young man might seek. But why would Portia love Bassanio? Is he not the embodiment of the very appearances he otherwise disparages? He has played upon Antonio's generosity and love for him; he has squandered his money on good times and idle pursuits; he may have an understanding of what the good is but he has significant difficulty in practicing what he grasps intellectually; and he consistently promises much but delivers little. Bassanio is long on excuses and vows of reformation, but short on firm commitment, discipline, and personal responsibility. Worse, as a master rhetorician he almost always knows the effective thing to say and has an acute sense of his audience. At first blush, he seems to be the ultimate, unwitting con man, the Sultan of Scam. Bassanio appears such not because he consciously and deliberately hatches plots or conjures manipulative schemes, but rather because he has an uncommon zeal to be appreciated. Moreover, he loves the thought of being in love, and he is drawn to the drama and passion of the romantic play. He believes what he says when he says it. He is neither disingenuous nor mendacious. Bassanio seems not a charlatan, but an attractive, immature, romantic adventurer: perhaps all sizzle, but no steak.

Portia, however, intuits deeper truths about Bassanio. Or at least what she takes to be deeper truths. She is impressed by his comportment after his correct selection of the lead casket. Instead of jumping about in smug exultation and unabashed self-congratulations—as we might suspect Morocco and Arragon would have exuded in like circumstances—Bassanio does not claim Portia at all. Instead, he asks for her acceptance of him: "So, thrice-fair lady, stand I, even so; / As doubtful whether what I see be true, / Until confirm'd, sign'd, ratified by you" (3.2.147-149). Moved by his humility and graciousness, Portia offers her spirit to "her lord, her governor, her king" (3.2.167). She bestows a ring upon Bassanio and cautions that should he lose it, give it away, or part with it in any way "Let it presage the ruin of our love" (3.2.175). Right on cue, Bassanio accepts it with rhetorical flourish: "But when this ring/ Parts from this finger, then parts life from hence; / O, then be bold to say Bassanio's dead!" (3.2.185-187). Do we genuinely believe that Portia will consign herself to dutiful obedience to Bassanio's will? Has Bassanio, once again, played to his audience? Does Portia have insight into Bassanio's idealized possibilities? Or, ironically, has she fallen prey to "ornament" and forgotten her own teaching that, contra Socrates, to know the good is easier than to do the good?

The scholarly debate over whether Portia provides Bassanio the correct answer to the casket test centers on a false dilemma. The actual choice is not between whether Portia wrongly advantages Bassanio by offering him a host of clues or whether Portia completely complies with her father's casket test rules. Instead, Portia acts as a midwife to what already resides within Bassanio—namely, the correct answer which signifies his potential to practice love as sacrifice and risk. In true Socratic fashion, Portia does not confer knowledge or learning upon her student. If she had offered the same verbal clues and background song to Morocco and Arragon, we must assume they would have still flunked the quiz: they lacked the ideal possibilities embodied by Bassanio. We must be clear that Bassanio at this point has not actualized his best potentials; he is not yet prepared to practice love as sacrifice and risk. Although he always talks a beautiful game about love and friendship, he remains too immature to practice what he orates. He will need the ongoing midwifery skills of Portia to realize his highest potentials. When Bassanio informs Portia that "I freely told you, all the wealth I had/ Ran in my veins" (3.2.257-258) he relates not only that his finances are low and his breeding high, but on my reading, he hints at his unrealized potentials; he suggests the potential nobility of his soul. The likes of Morocco and Arragon, however, are incapable of understanding and practicing the nature of love as conceptualized by Portia's father. Not even Socrates could elicit that which does not reside within them.

In any event, the lessons of the casket trial are numerous and bright. First, appearances are deceiving: Do not accept first impressions without deeper investigations. Second, distribution of love or social goods on the basis of desire is wildly off the mark: Desires flow effusively, but love and other social goods are appropriately gleaned in other ways. Third, distribution of love or social goods according to personal desert is deeply problematic. That one can claim to personally deserve love because of his or her past deeds or inherent characteristics is not enough to attain it. Love involves mutuality and reciprocity; in love, sacrifice is crucial to receiving. Fourth, love also requires heightened mutual vulnerability: risk, sacrifice, commitment, widening one's subjectivity, and forging enduring bonds are critical. Fifth, loving someone is more than merely appreciating their current embodiment of excellences. Sixth, to know the right thing to do is easier than to perform the right action. Even the wisest among us are sometimes victims of appearance, indolence, and weakness of will.

9. Philosophical Interlude: The Contours of Love

To understand the general phenomenon of love, I will briefly discuss the particular form most familiar to us. Righteous, erotic love is an inherently discriminatory notion. I cannot be a lover, in the deepest sense, to everyone even if I was so inclined and even if everyone was morally good. I would still not have enough time and I could not expend enough effort to pursue the common commitments and joint activities that genuine love requires. This underscores why trading-up is misplaced in genuine erotic love. While I may perceive, accurately, that a stranger possesses a higher degree of excellence—more desirable qualities and properties—than my love, our past connection and mutually satisfying relationship exude currency. My lover and I are not at *lontananza* (a distance), but forge a shared identity. Our relationship, if profound enough, entails that my interests are not experienced as fully apart from my lover's interests and vice versa. Relationships, of course, vary in intensity and depth, but all genuine loves share this element.[9]

Accordingly, I would not trade-up easily because my current lover and I share a relationship that has valuable ramifications for who I am. I would recognize the transition costs—time, energy, uncertainty, and changes to my self-image—of substituting the stranger for my current lover. I would also understand that even if the stranger bears more excellent properties than my lover, the stranger cannot exemplify those properties in the same way as my lover. The excellences of my lover and that of the stranger will differ qualitatively in the particular ways they are manifested. Just as the stranger may be more physically beautiful than my lover, the stranger does not have more of *my lover's* beauty. The unique way my lover embodies and expresses beauty may be more appealing to me than the way the stranger expresses his or her admittedly greater physical beauty. Finally, the historical relationship lovers have shared has special significance that should not be dismissed. Lovers form a union or federation that is not defined merely by adding the interests of the parties together. In genuinely loving relationships and in well-functioning marriages, the whole is greater than the sum of the parts. The bond or union or federation that lovers nurture transforms the parties. The historical relationship that chronicles that development bears independent value in a way similar to the value produced by positive family relationships. Shared memories, gratitude, reciprocal self-making, and a sense of belonging make trading-up in loving relationships problematic. Where trading-up does seem to happen easily we can legitimately call into question whether a fulfilling, deep love was present. In friendships the situation is somewhat different. Often, instead of facing a choice of trading-up—dumping our current friend for another person—we can simply add to our list in a way that is precluded in romantic love. Still, practicalities limit even the number of close friends with whom we can share deep relationships.

The task for Portia and Bassanio will be to transform the infatuation that is mutual longing and passionate anticipation into the emotion of love that includes shared purpose and joint identity. The joint identity principle I am urging will trouble some philosophers. They will screech that my standard of love is too high as it requires a loss of individual autonomy. Once we talk of extended or shared identity, we seem to infringe on an individual's freedom of choice and independence. My choices, projects, and actions are no longer *mine*, they are *ours*. Does this not demand concessions of the individual's will?

The short answer is "yes, but why the surprise?" Every intimate relationship has that consequence. Can we coherently conjure, say, romantic love where each spouse retains full, individual autonomy? Living together, sharing a life, pooling material resources, planning for the future require joint decision making, reciprocity, and mutuality. To believe that full independence can be retained is fatuous. The deepest versions of intimacy transform our characters. Why should we shrink back in horror when we find that our independence is no longer sacrosanct? A world of strangers may be a world of complete independence for individuals, a community of lovers and friends is not.

We care about our lovers and friends, at least in part, because we perceive that they bear excellences or admirable qualities. We could be mistaken in that assessment, of course. Our evaluations are not infallible, our perceptions are not flawless. Once we realize our error, the incipient friendship may end. But the ground of our initial attraction is the value we think the other possesses.

A critic might rejoin, however, that making the perceived value of the other the ground of love is troubling. First, our real focus seems to be on that value, wherever it may reside, and not on a particular person. Human beings are not merely repositories of value, nor does value alone define who we are. We have other qualities—beyond our glorious value—that are neutral in terms of value or that are imperfections or disvalues. To focus only on the other's value is to love her only for a part of her personhood. Second, to ground love in only the other's current perceived value is to freeze the other in time. We all change, grow, and regress. To rivet a loving relationship in the current image of the other is to deny inevitable change. Again, such a love is not directed at a whole person but at certain value which we now think we have found in the other.

These criticisms are difficult, but not impossible, to answer. To establish a love of whole persons, our critic is correct: we must appreciate more than the current perceived value of each other. Each of us is a compendium of qualities, not all admirable, wrapped together by our unique way of embodying and expressing those qualities, seasoned by hosts of possibilities (potential qualities that we can develop into actualities). By considering the other person's qualities beyond their perceived value, we parry the charge that we are drawn only to value not whole people. By attending to the other idealized possibilities, we block the charge that love wrongly freezes the other in the present. Friends affect each other's choices, actions, and personal development. They do not simply take the other as a fixed, permanent character.

One of the functions of love is to control access to ourselves and to regulate our privacy. Intimacy is mutually nurtured in several ways: through privileged self-disclosure, participation in shared projects, discerning and advancing each other's best interests, and having a roughly similar system of values. Bonds of trust, far beyond the level we enjoy with strangers, flow from the heightened mutual vulnerability distinguishing deep intimacy.

With apologies to the new age of promiscuous public disclosures of virtually everything on the internet, we typically reveal information about ourselves to our lovers and friends that we keep shrouded from the general public. In so doing, we regulate our privacy—permitting more access to those whom we choose—and both acknowledge and reinforce the bonds of trust between our lovers and ourselves. By participating in shared projects, lovers and friends reveal and sustain the projects of their most profound concern. Lovers and friends share activities at least partly for the sake of sharing them. They often strive to advance each other's interests. I can advance my lover's interests only after appraising what her best interests are. Throughout all these processes, the values of the parties are paramount. Sometimes lovers come to their relationship with roughly similar values. Sometimes they develop roughly similar values as a consequence of their relationship and shared activities. In any case, lovers mutually influence each other's values in proportion to the closeness of the relationship.

I may be drawn to or try out a new value or project simply because my lover already embodies the value or pursues the project. But my initial attraction need not translate into final acceptance of the value or project into my life scheme. We should recognize a distinction between what motivates my desire to try out a new project or examine a new value—I pursue them just because they rivet my lover's concern—and the grounds upon which I will decide whether to adopt the value or project as my own. My lover's values and projects never fully define mine. I must make a relatively independent assessment of the new value or project at some point.

Portia and Bassanio must negotiate not only a relationship but also their shared purposes. Each needs to connect to projects beyond themselves and beyond each other. Their pursuit of meaningful, valuable lives may well falter if their mutual affection is overly insular.

Love is also an exercise in self-making in proportion to the closeness of the relationship. Aristotle insisted that human beings are social animals. A person alone in a desert island might be a beast or a god, but not a human being. We need others to help understand and define ourselves. Those closest to us play a disproportionately strong role. The annoying parental warning—"Be careful who your friends are, don't associate with the wrong crowd"—hits the mark squarely. Lovers and friends influence the people we are becoming.

Love is, accordingly, a process, not a fixed condition. It begins in lack and is grounded in power. But the grandeur of love is that it is not a commodity: it cannot be bought or sold, yet it is not costless. Love struggles to overcome its internal paradoxes of consolation and growth, dependency and freedom. The uniqueness and specialness of the lovers—not in terms of their facility in guiding the mutual quest for individual perfection—form the core of the relationship. Love is a mysterious mixture of choice and discovery that changes our perception of the world without actually changing the world. Love is transformative but not redemptive. But, mostly, it is an acknowledgment of bonds not fully chosen.

Love cannot be an arm's-length, mutual aid exercise in individualism. Lovers cannot be creators at *lontananza*. No, love widens our subjectivity and creates a new identity that immediately embodies its own unrealized ideals. And the unrealized ideal possibilities of lovers-bound are never merely the sum of the unrealized ideal possibilities embodied by the two individuals. The love is not two minds thinking or valuing as one. Even the most committed lovers must retain a healthy measure of independence.

Love is also dangerous. No one can betray us more hurtfully or thoroughly than a lover. Any time we heighten our vulnerability through revealing special information about ourselves, sharing intimate activities, forging bonds of trust, and relying upon the good will of others, we not only enjoy the fruits of positive self-making but also risk treachery. My lover knows more about me, has shared and helped to shape my values, and benefits from my trust. She is in a better position than the general public to advance my best interests but also to frustrate my deepest aspirations.

Who is better able to betray and destroy Bassanio than Portia? Intuitive and psychologically acute, Portia could easily eviscerate the self-worth of the romantic, vulnerable Bassanio. Or she could, through the arts of a Socratic mid-wife, elicit Bassanio's highest unrealized possibilities.

Are the risks worth the value of love? Love increases our flow experiences by energizing our efforts in the projects at hand. Shared activities and commitments are also necessary for moral and intellectual growth. Lovers help us accurately evaluate the quality and meaningfulness of our lives. The sense of belonging and intimate validation love produces soften our fears that we are alone and powerless. Because we are social animals, love is valuable for its own sake, not just for benefits directly derived from the relationship.

Desire and love, properly directed and in an appropriate measure, are the best antidotes to the seven capital vices: arrogance, envy, avarice, wrath, lust, gluttony, and sloth. The account of righteous, erotic love and deep friendship can be extended to include healthy desire of other worthy objects, projects, and values. Unfortunately, we are inherently fallible and flawed: the human condition and our required but threatening connection to wider communities suggest we will always struggle mightily with the seven capital vices, particularly envy, arrogance, and lust. We are born of dust and to dust shall we return.

Portia and Bassanio have forged a bond of intimacy grounded in their mutual understanding of the nature of love; Portia's current and Bassanio's potential capabilities of practicing the genuine nature of love as mutual vulnerability, sacrifice, and risk; and their respective needs. For example, Bassanio seeks financial solvency provided by a virtuous, intelligent, beautiful woman; while Portia seeks to transcend the material comfort she appreciates but finds inadequately fulfilling. To attain robustly meaningful, valuable lives, Portia and Bassanio must go beyond their current self-understandings.[10]

Meanwhile, Antonio and Shylock have voluntarily agreed to a material bond, an interest-free loan benefiting Bassanio but for which Antonio stands as surety. Now that his ships have apparently been lost at sea, Antonio has breached the terms of the contract. As Antonio had freely described the contract as between enemies, Shylock, with deranged avidity, now sues to exercise lawfully the penalty provision for breach of the contract: he demands to cut a pound of flesh from Antonio's body. The "merry bond" has turned gruesome.

Two

THE MERCHANT OF VENICE: THE TRIAL AND JUDICIAL DECISION MAKING

Salerio informs Bassanio that all of Antonio's ships have been destroyed. Bassanio is stunned: "Hath all his ventures fail'd? What, not one hit? / From Tripolis, from Mexico and England, /From Lisbon, Barbary and India? / And not one vessel 'scape the dreadful touch / Of merchant-marring rocks?" (3.2.267-272). Salerio adds that Shylock is adamant that his bond must be enforced. Although twenty merchants, the Duke of Venice, and a host of prominent Venetian citizens have tried to persuade him otherwise, Shylock demands what he takes to be his due. Jessica affirms Salerio's information. She has overheard Shylock talking to two of his Jewish friends: "[Shylock said that he] would rather have Antonio's flesh / Than twenty times the value of the sum / That [Antonio] did owe him" (3.2.289-291).

1. The Breach

Feeling responsible for his friend's precarious situation, Bassanio tells Portia that the sum owed is 3,000 ducats. Portia responds: "What, no more? / Pay him six thousand, and deface the bond; / Double six thousand, and then treble that, / Before a friend of this description / Shall lose a hair through Bassanio's fault" (3.2.302-306). She then offers Bassanio enough gold to repay the "petty debt" twenty times over. Portia and Bassanio will marry, but he will leave immediately for Venice. They will sexually consummate their union only after Antonio's predicament is favorably resolved.

Meanwhile Shylock resists all overtures of mercy. He will have his bond. His Christian tormentors have called him a dog and they must now beware of his fangs:

> I'll have my bond; and therefore speak no more.
> I'll not be made a soft and dull-ey'd fool,
> To shake the head, relent, and sigh, and yield
> To Christian intercessors. Follow not;
> I'll have no speaking: I will have my bond (3.3.13-17).

Shylock, the despised outsider, seeks equality before the law. Even if Venetian citizens deny him human status, the indispensable institution of law must recognize Shylock's personhood. The rule of law virtues of generality, impersonal application, and universality must be honored. Venice may not care even one iota for Shylock and his ilk, but Venice must uphold rule of law virtues to ensure its own self-interest as a center of international commerce. The sanctity of contracts lies at the core of Venice's economic success and reflects Venice's self-image as a community. Shylock shrewdly intuits that in Venice only the law is antecedently committed to recognizing his claims to equality. Although enforcing the terms of his bond with Antonio is undoubtedly inhumane, Shylock will now use the law to assert his own humanity.

No one understands this more clearly than Antonio. When Solanio desperately offers him the consolation that the Duke of Venice will never uphold the terms of the bond, Antonio knows better. The consummate businessman is just as keenly aware as is Shylock that much more turns on this case than the fate of a 3,000 ducat loan. The commercial and communal nature of Venice is in play.

> The duke cannot deny the course of law:
> For the commodity that strangers have
> With us in Venice, if it be denied,
> Will much impeach the justice of his state;
> Since that the trade and profit of the city
> Consisteth of all nations. Therefore, go (3.3.26-31).

In Belmont, Portia takes measures to ensure Antonio's success at trial. First, she entrusts her household to Lorenzo under the cover that she and Nerissa will be staying at a nearby monastery until Bassanio and Gratiano, Nerissa's husband, return. Then Portia dispatches a servant, Balthasar, to Padua with a letter for her cousin, Doctor Bellario. The good Doctor will provide Balthasar with "notes and garments" which the servant will bring to the Belmont ferry headed for Venice. Finally, Portia unravels her scheme to the trusted Nerissa.

Portia also knows that should Antonio be legally slain or gravely injured by Shylock because he stood surety for Bassanio, his status would rise extravagantly. Bassanio would be both racked with guilt and utterly awed by Antonio's sacrifice on his behalf. Portia is well aware that competing with a martyr, hero, or saint for Bassanio's affections is unwise.

2. Philosophical Interlude: Basic Contract Law

In the Middle Ages in England, courts of equity and courts of law were distinct. Each type of court followed its own procedures, arrived at its own substantive judgments, and forged its own remedies. Courts of law interpreted and applied the common law, from which developed rules that were often rigidly formalistic. Courts of equity, under the administration of the Chancellor and deputies, crafted a host of equitable principles that softened the often draconian judgments of courts of law. The distinction between the two types of courts was part of the jurisprudence that the United States inherited from England. But the division between courts of equity and courts of law disappeared gradually at both federal and state levels in the United States. In this way, equitable principles became part of the law as such and not circumscribed to a particular type of court.[1]

Accordingly, contemporary jurisprudence cannot be accurately understood as fundamentally a conflict between law and mercy. The merging of courts of law and courts of equity ensured that much of what was described as "mercy" in the sixteenth century is now part of the law itself. As noted, the sanctity of freedom of contract is adjusted by explicit considerations of public policy, conscionability, and procedural and substantive fairness that in earlier centuries would be consigned to courts of equity or to discretionary invocations of mercy by decision makers. In that vein, to conclude that mercy must rule law or that law necessarily excludes mercy is mistaken. The fusion of courts of equity with courts of law expanded the definition of "law" and permitted judicial decision making to more closely approximate "justice."

The basic remedy for breach of contract is expectancy damages, which aim at compensating the injured parties by placing them in the position they would have enjoyed had the breaching parties fulfilled their contractual duties. That is, the aggrieved party receives the monetary equivalent of what he or she expected under the terms of the contract. In general, the aggrieved party should not receive more than expectancy damages because the intent of contract is only to compensate the injured party; contract law does not aspire to punish the breaching party. Awarding damages higher than the expectancy standard would also undermine the motivation to contract because parties would be reluctant to assume high liability for breach. Also, the aggrieved party should not receive less than expectancy damages because contract law does not typically aim at encouraging parties to renege on their obligations. Awarding damages lower than the expectancy standard would deflate people's confidence in the terms of their contract. Thus, in general, awarding expectancy damages for breach of contract is the preferred way to promote voluntary agreements. Parties can rest assured that in accordance with the terms of their contracts they will receive either performance or equivalent compensation if the other party breaches.[2] Bear in mind, however, that contract law recognizes a host of qualifying principles that sometimes limit the recovery of injured parties to below their lost expectancy.[3] Moreover, in a few situations in breach of contract courts will award injured parties reliance damages instead of expectancy damages.[4]

At times, parties stipulate in their contract the amount of damages owing to one in the event of a breach by the other. This is called a liquidated damages provision. In case of a contractual breakdown, parties can thereby avoid the time and expense of calculating and proving damages. Liquated damages also provide both parties with notice as to the consequences of a breach and an incentive to avoid a breach. Courts will honor liquidated damage provisions only if the agreed-upon amount is "a reasonable forecast of just compensation for the harm that is caused by the breach" and "the harm that is caused by the breach is one that is incapable or very difficult of accurate estimation."[5] Of course, those two conditions coalesce uneasily: they require "a reasonable forecast" of a harm "that is incapable or very difficult" to estimate accurately. A good faith estimate, apparently proportionate to the damage of the breach, is required. Courts often refuse to enforce liquidated damages provisions if they appear to be penalties or would result in a windfall for the aggrieved party.

In contrast to money damages, specific performance—which requires that the breaching party undertake to perform or to complete performance of his obligations under the contract—is a less frequently invoked contract law remedy. This remedy is awarded only when money damages are inadequate to make the aggrieved party whole. Typically, this occurs when the subject-matter of the contract is unique such as in land sales or one-of-a-kind goods such as sports or entertainment memorabilia. Courts often refuse to grant specific performance when the aggrieved party's conduct was unsavory: for example, if the plaintiff engineered an unconscionable bargain or under circumstances where awarding specific performance would produce injustice or be, overall, inequitable.[6]

Freedom of contract presumably honors and encourages the exercise of individual liberty and autonomy; facilitates efficient allocation of resources; and thereby promotes economic growth. But the principle of freedom of contract is not absolute. Numerous voluntary agreements will not be enforced by courts.[7]

For example, contracts to perform illegal acts, such as embezzlement or prostitution, under state or federal criminal law are not enforceable. More important, the doctrine of unconscionability allows courts to refuse to enforce contracts on grounds of unfair surprise, disparity of bargaining power, and procedural or substantive unfairness. Procedural unconscionability includes the presence of duress, fraud, undue influence, failure to comply with the duty to disclose, obscure terms, vastly unequal bargaining power in adhesion contracts, and the like.[8] Substantive unconscionability includes the presence of contractual terms that are strikingly immoral (for example, the sale of a baby) that contravene public policy (for example, contracts that include penalties of physical punishment for breach or delay), or that unjustifiably subvert a party's purposes for contracting (for example, radically one-sided contracts).

Furthermore, a defaulting borrower has a right called "equity of redemption," whereby the delinquent borrower may retain his property that he is about to forfeit because of his default by curing the default—making payments due within a reasonable time plus all accumulated costs as well as interest.

Given this sketch of basic contract law, we can understand why contemporary courts would refuse to enforce the bond between Shylock, Bassanio, and Antonio. To undermine the legal force of the contract between Shylock and Antonio, we might invoke procedural unconscionability or fraud. But this is unlikely to succeed. While Shylock called the bond "merry" and stressed the worthlessness of a pound of human flesh—perhaps undercutting the seriousness of the penalty provision of the bond and his intent to ever enforce it—that does not rise to the level of procedural irregularity or fraud in the inducement. Bassanio, especially, understood the gravity of the penalty provision as did Antonio. Antonio agreed to the provision not because he was lured by Shylock's representations;

instead, he was certain that he could easily repay the bond once his ships returned from their voyages, and by accepting the forfeiture penalty he could symbolically highlight his love for Bassanio. Furthermore, that Antonio was gulled into thinking that one pound of his flesh had no value to Shylock, a person whom Antonio had abused and loathes, is unreasonable. Although Antonio's flesh has no value in the public market, Shylock values it as a souvenir of revenge. Finally, Antonio appreciated the no-interest feature of the loan, which was tied to the penalty provision.

The bond might also be invalidated as an unenforceable gambling contract: an agreement whose essential purpose was to gamble on Antonio's life. Such a strategy is a long shot because the counterargument that the essential purpose of the bond was the conveyance of an interest-free loan is strong. However, as we shall see, the strategy gains traction by Shylock's early conduct at trial. He refuses two and three times the amount of his principle because he is determined to exact the penalty provision of the bond. From Shylock's vantage point it seems that the essential purpose of the loan was the gamble on Antonio's life, not the repayment of the 3,000 ducats. But the appeal to unenforceable gambling contract will prove to be superfluous once we pinpoint the more precise reasons why the penalty provision of the contract is invalid.

First, one might argue that the contract is illegal as such because, as we shall see, under Venetian state law should an alien, such as Shylock, directly or indirectly attempt to take the life of a Venetian citizen, the intended victim is entitled to one-half of the perpetrator's material goods, the state will confiscate the other half of his goods, and the perpetrator's life can be spared only by a pardon from the Duke of Venice. Thus, this bond promotes the performance of an illegal act. But a counterargument is available: the bond is not precisely a contract to perform an illegal act because only Antonio's breach triggers the attempt to extract his flesh. That is, instead of an illegal act being the subject of the bond, it is merely an ancillary provision invoked only by breach.

Second, a compelling case can be advanced that the substantive terms of the bond are unconscionable: they include a penalty for breach that involves physical abuse and, more likely, death. As such, the contract wrongfully commodifies human flesh, treating it as a mere object. Even if the contract is not illegal as such, surely its penalty clause for breach is unconscionable, in violation of public policy, and thus unenforceable. The substantive unconscionability arises not from one party using his bargaining advantage or economic leverage to overwhelm his weaker negotiating partner, but from the immoral commodification of human flesh.

Third, we might construe the extracting of flesh not as a penalty for breach but as a request for specific performance on the part of the breaching party. Such an interpretation is a stretch. But even if we are persuaded, the bond should not be enforced because demanding specific performance would be, overall, inequitable. This is especially the case where an award of money damages can easily make Shylock, the aggrieved party, whole.

Fourth, one might argue that the pound of flesh forfeiture is a type of liquidated damage clause. This is beyond a stretch because liquidated damages are invariably monetary. Putting that aside, the desperation move fails because a pound of flesh is not a good faith calculation of just compensation for the harm that is caused to Shylock by the breach; nor is the harm that is caused by the breach one that is incapable of accurate estimation. Shylock's contractual injury is readily calculable in monetary terms.

Shylock might have also argued that the forfeiture provision of the contract had a legal purpose: to promote Antonio's repayment of the loan. After all, Shylock had not charged Antonio any interest and to safeguard Shylock's principal a special incentive for repayment was appropriate. Still, under contemporary contract law and even under sixteenth-century contract law no court would enforce a penalty provision triggering mutilation and probably death.

In sum, a reasonable court should award Shylock his principal of 3,000 ducats, with appropriate interest. Money damages based on Shylock's expectancy are sufficient to make him whole under the contract. Also, Antonio could have cured his default and retained his flesh (and blood) by invoking equity of redemption. In fact, as we shall see, Bassanio's offer at trial to repay the debt twice over and Balthasar-Portia's refashioning of that offer to thrice over provide much more than is required under equity of redemption.

The trial of Shylock v. Antonio should consume only a few minutes once both parties stipulate to the terms of the bond. In real life, the trial would either never have taken place or been dully brief. But moral parables and didactic fables do not submit readily to the categories of reality. The drama must continue if practical lessons are to emerge.

3. The Trial of Venice: *Stage One: The Duke Reasons With Shylock*

The climactic act of the play is the trial. The trial is in fact a series of overtures, offers, refusals, manipulations, and coercions. We must address each stage of the trial in turn if we are to understand fully its implications.

In a version of a pre-trial conference, The Duke of Venice implores Shylock to soften his position. The Duke advances several reasons: exacting a pound of flesh is wanton cruelty that lacks a justifying cause; exacting a pound of flesh will result in Shylock losing his 3,000 ducats, but also will sever Shylock from gentleness and love; a show of mercy is appropriate given the unforeseen and significant losses that Antonio has incurred at sea (4.1.20-30). In effect, the Duke suggests that Shylock should simply cancel the contract.

Shylock is unmoved. He need give no reason when he is interrogated about why he chooses to enforce the bond: "I'll not answer that: / But, say, it is my humour / . . . Mistress of passion, sways it to the mood / Of what it likes or loathes /. . . So can I give no reason, nor I will not, / More than a lodg'd hate and a certain loathing / I bear Antonio" (4.1.42-61). Shylock underscores that the Duke's duty is to uphold the law: "To have the due and forfeit of my bond: / If

The Merchant of Venice: *The Trial and Judicial Decision Making* 41

you deny it, let the danger light / Upon your charter and your city's freedom" (4.1.37-39).

Bassanio points out that malice falls short of a justifying cause, but Shylock, taking comfort in his perceived legal rights, reiterates that he is under no obligation to give answers as to his motives nor does he require a justifying cause: "I am not bound to please thee with my answers" (4.1.65). Shylock's position is clear and telling: Look here, if I have a legal right to enforce this bond—freely and knowingly entered into by Antonio, Bassanio, and me—and if you, the Duke of Venice, desire to uphold the law and Venice's position as a commercial center then render to me that to which I am entitled. The principle of sanctity of contract does not require that I furnish a reason to enforce the bond that satisfies you. I demand my legal rights as the aggrieved party: Antonio has breached our contract.

Antonio, the consummate businessman, understands and ratifies the force of Shylock's argument. Basically, he implores Bassanio (and the Duke) to stop wasting time trying to appeal to the better angels of Shylock's nature: they do not exist: "Let me have judgement and the Jew his will" (4.1.83). Antonio is prepared to die and why not? Suffering from (what I take to be) an unrequited homosexual love of Bassanio, finding his past commercial success spiritually unfulfilling, and recently destroyed financially by the loss of his ships at sea, Antonio is no longer merely habitually melancholy—he has good reason to be profoundly depressed. Also, he appreciates Shylock's claims about sanctity of contract and what is at stake in Venice. Finally, what better way to die than in service to his beloved Bassanio? When all is seemingly lost, to die at the right time in a glorious cause can add luster to a person's biographical life.[9]

Still, Bassanio, enriched by Portia, offers Shylock 6,000 ducats as payment. Bassanio offers Shylock the traditional measure of breach of contract: money damages, in this case, generously doubled. Shylock scoffs that he would refuse six times that amount. Shylock is greedy, but not for money. The Duke reenters the conversation: "How shalt thou hope for mercy, rend'ring none? (4.1.87).

At the early stages of the trial, Antonio, Bassanio, Gratiano, and the Duke all demand mercy from Shylock, while simultaneously disparaging his harsh heart and wolfish nature. But mercy by definition is not a benefit to which a guilty person can claim entitlement. All of the participants are locked into a pridefulness and certitude that precludes their genuinely offering or receiving mercy. They do not approach the dispute with humility, generosity, and a sense of sacrifice. The adversaries stand as arm's length bargainers, rather than collaborators seeking a just resolution. They are all Venetians, saturated with the false glitter of materialism and the flimsy substance of tribalism.

Shylock points out that as the aggrieved party he is in no need of mercy. He fulfilled the terms of the contract, Antonio did not. While the Duke may be referring to mercy in the afterlife, Shylock is unswayed by Christian appeals. In fact, Shylock takes the opportunity to jab at Christian hypocrisy one more time.

He brings up the slave trade in Venice. Just as upright Venetian citizens purchase and use their slaves as property and prosper from their labors—all of which is accepted and enforced by the law—so too does Shylock seek to enforce his legal rights:

> The pound of flesh, which I demand of him,
> Is dearly bought; 'tis mine and I will have it.
> If you deny me, fie upon your law!
> There is no force in the decrees of Venice.
> I stand for judgment: answer; shall I have it? (4.1.99-103)

The Duke has no other response to Shylock. He has asked a learned doctor, Bellario from Padua, to preside over the actual trial.

4. Philosophical Interlude: The Rule of Law

Proponents of the rule of law strive to ensure neutrality, uniformity, and predictability in the formulation and application of law. In crafting law and establishing the conditions needed for realizing the truth of the slogan "a government of laws, not of people," legal systems try to ensure that all citizens have notice of the law's requirements, which implies that those requirements must be accessible and capable of being readily understood; that legal requirements are written in a general and impersonal fashion; that law is sovereign in the exercise of state power; that in the absence of relevant and established law there is neither crime nor punishment; and, in most legal systems, that a separation of powers among the various branches of the state facilitates all of the above.[10]

In applying law and establishing the conditions needed for realizing the truth of the slogan "treat like cases alike," legal systems try to ensure that every person has the right to a meaningful day in court; that officials preserve the state's neutrality among class and interest groups; that decisions of state officials are free from bias; that *ad hoc* decision making and the enforcement of retroactive or *ex post facto* law are prohibited; and that judicial decisions are reasoned and rationally justified publicly.

Substantial state compliance with the elements of the rule of law allegedly establishes the formal equality of all people before the laws, as well as imposes important limitations on the exercise of the state's power of coercion. In sum, substantial compliance with the elements of the rule of law presumably nurtures individual freedom and autonomy, and constitutes a necessary (although not sufficient) condition of justice.

Shylock places great faith in the rule of law. Indeed, as the play vividly depicts, Shylock's faith in the rule of law lays the groundwork for his own humiliation and domestication. His major error is in thinking that rule of law virtues are sufficient (and not merely necessary) for arriving at substantive justice. Shylock is convinced that if only the rule of law, accompanied by simple decoding of contractual language, is applied then he will receive the equality and justice for which he yearns. Rarely has a mistake in jurisprudence produced such disastrous consequences for a litigant.

Criticisms of rule of law ideology: Leftist critics first argue that the rule of law rests on a view of judicial decision making that is absurd. The rule of law maintains that judges must remain close to the consensus of received opinion because they are presumably constrained by authoritative materials. Judges also have the freedom to adjust and interpret, acts manifest when judges reject certain received interpretations as mistakes. But critics rejoin that there is no pure method of analysis that yields determinate answers to all or most legal questions. That is, there is no self-evident place where justification of received opinion ends and revision begins; there is no available meta-logic capable of determining the "correct" relationship between justification and revision. Instead, judicial decision making reflects the conclusions of numerous, conflicting wills working at cross-purposes in different historical periods. In the absence of an immanent moral rationality, this body of decisions cannot be articulated by a single coherent theory.

As a result, critics contend that judicial decision making is radically indeterminate. There is no distinct mode of legal reasoning that can be validly contrasted with political rhetoric. Hence, law—the product of legal reasoning—is merely politics clothed in more seductive dress and surrounded by a more pompous and elaborate mystique. In fact, law is nothing more than the product of the contingent outcomes of ideological struggles and historical accidents. Legal doctrine cannot generate determinant results in concrete cases because it can be manipulated to "justify" an almost infinite number of possible rationalizations for various legal outcomes. In addition, a plausible argument can be advanced that any of these rationalizations and their corresponding outcomes have been deduced from preexisting legal doctrine.

Critics are correct in debunking the pretenses of an extreme formalism that holds that the law is a coherent, consistent doctrinal body with only marginal aberrations which can be correctly stigmatized as "errors." Indeed, there is considerable flux and conflict in various areas of law—for example, constitutional law—which reflect intramural disputes among political philosophies. Judicial decision making is inescapably political in the sense that interpretation and judgment are required. However, such an admission does not imply cataclysmic conclusions about the possibility of attaining rule of law virtues. Only if the rule of law is grounded in a mechanical, formalistic mode of judicial decision making would devastating consequences emerge from this admission. But attaining rule of law virtues does not depend on mechanical, formalistic judicial decision making. The presence of some indeterminacy, conflict, and flux in law is compatible with a rule of law jurisprudence that concedes that judges must interpret statutes, precedents, and administrative decisions from the background of what judges take to be the most coherent explanation of the political and legal system. For who believes that statutes, precedents, constitutions, and administrative decisions are self-executing? Believers in mechanical or strictly formal decision making, like hobgoblins, trolls, and extra-terrestrials, are more easily imagined than discovered.

Of course, Shylock is one such imagined believer in mechanical jurisprudence. But we will discover that his legal theory sows the seeds of his destruction. Shylock naively concluded that the marriage between the rule of law and formalistic judicial decision making was happy and inexorable. As such, he made himself vulnerable to leftist criticism of the rule of law. More important, he exposed himself to the legal machinations of the fraudulent jurist Balthasar-Portia who cleverly turns Shylock's legal theory against him.

In sum, the application of the rule of law is not dependent on a mechanical or strictly formal mode of judicial decision making. Recall, substantial compliance is all that is required if legal systems are to realize rule of law virtues. Given the impossibility of a purely mechanical mode of judicial decision making and the omnipresence of human fallibility, that is all for which we can hope.

Critics also point out that paeans of praise are sung by advocates of the rule of law about the formal equality that results when official decision makers view litigants as faceless, impersonal, abstract legal entities. Under the rule of law, the requirements of law are applied to all equally and without regard to the sexual, racial, religious, or social circumstances of the respective litigants. This is thought to be necessary in order to prevent judicial bias and ad hoc decision making, both of which undermine rule of law virtues.

Systematically disenfranchised by the Venetian establishment, Shylock stakes his fate on formal legal equality. He is convinced that only within the impersonal application of law can he attain equality and elude bias and discrimination. Sadly, he will discover that he is not formally equal in the eyes of the law in all respects and where he is formally equal he will suffer.

Critics regard formal equality suspiciously. Because formal equality fails to consider the vast disparities of economic, political, and social power among litigants, critics allege that formal equality begets substantive inequality. That is, the elements of the rule of law prevent the benevolent exercise of power that might be used to redress obvious social inequalities that often antecedently exist between litigants. Leftist critics regard formal equality before the law as obviously undesirable where inequalities of power already exist between litigants. For, under such circumstances, formal equality can only exacerbate, rather than ameliorate, inequalities among the people in the state.

In response to the leftist critics: First, it is unclear whether the judicial decisions of liberal capitalist regimes invoking the rule of law result in as much substantive injustice as critics imagine. Second, even if we concede the truth of the critics' claim—that substantive inequality results from the application of the rule of law in our and other predominantly liberal capitalist systems—the question arises whether that is due to the nature of the rule of law or to the dominant liberal ideology that the rule of law invokes and sustains. Clearly, liberal ideology includes a firm conviction in formal equality of opportunity, but it is not automatically repelled by substantive inequality in result. For example, the (modified) classical liberal ideology of the United States allows for and even encourages inequalities in economic, political, and social power among people. In part, the "American Dream" is to accumulate more such personal power than the amount possessed by one's parents and grandparents. Thus, if the critics' claim—that actual legal decision making heightens antecedent inequality among citizens—is sound that is due to the nature of the dominant background ideology of the United States and its embrace of a certain form of competition that engenders inequality of results; it is not because the nature of the rule of law is to perpetrate substantive injustice. At worst, the rule of law is an unconscious collaborator, compelled to participate in widening substantive inequality by the set of background moral and political assumptions with which it is saddled by the dominant ideology of the liberal-capitalist state. Critics are correct only in that the rule of law is a tool of the background moral and political ideology of the state that invokes it, and the rule of law cannot be an independent force for guaranteeing substantive equality. But no serious thinker believes that the rule of law is a sufficient, rather than merely a necessary, condition of justice. The critics' attack in this case is thus focused on a "straw person."

Imagine a state committed to a radically egalitarian ideology. Such a state would extol substantive equality of results. In this system, judges would strive diligently to ensure that litigants ended up with or retained equal political, economic, and social power. Such a legal system could and should still invoke the rule of law. For example, litigants would be on notice that regardless of race, creed, or ethnic affiliation the aim of law—substantive equality of economic, social, and political power—would be applied impersonally and without bias. Like cases would be decided alike and all decisions would be reasoned and rationally justified publicly. Of course, the criteria for determining "like cases" and the arguments viewed as persuasive would be animated overwhelmingly by the dominant background ideology of radical egalitarianism. Given this different set of background moral and political assumptions, the application of the rule of law would not work substantive inequality (from the perspective of leftist critics), but would be necessary to attain substantive equality. My point is only that the rule of law, of and by itself, is not the reason why either substantive justice or injustice results from the judicial decisions of various legal systems.

The message to Shylock is clear: pay greater attention to the substantive law; place less faith in alleged procedural safeguards that are abstract; and never forget the social context within which judicial decision making operates.

This is not to say that the elements of the rule of law are, in any profound sense, neutral. Stripped of all background sets of moral and political assumptions, the elements of the rule of law are abstractions that in themselves are inapplicable. The rule of law is "neutral" only in this trivial sense. But once the elements of the rule of law are made applicable by being commandeered in the service of a dominant state ideology, basic neutrality evaporates. For any dominant state ideology already embodies a host of moral and political values, which serve to fuel the substantive results arising from the application of the rule of law. In the service of the (modified) classical liberalism of the United States, the application of the rule of law produces a certain set of substantive legal results that seem noxious from the vantage point of leftist critics. But it is an error to stigmatize the rule of law as the perpetrator of the offense. For in service of the radical egalitarianism preferred by many leftists, the application of the rule of law will produce substantive results amicable to leftist aspirations.

In sum, most elements of the rule of law are not indigenous to and inseparable from only liberal-capitalist regimes; the application of the rule of law is not neutral, but reflects the background ideology informing a particular legal system; the rule of law itself can neither ameliorate nor remedy perceived defects of the background ideology that invokes it; and the rule of law itself does not prevent the benevolent exercise of state power, although it may have that implication when yoked in service to certain background ideologies.

I will address one other leftist criticism of the rule of law. Leftists claim that the rule of law spawns pernicious hegemonic and legitimating effects. While judges intend to treat like cases alike, the definitions of similarity and difference are determined by invoking moral and political criteria supplied by the dominant ideology of the state. Legal decision making is thus a kind of intramural exercise with the dominant background ideology, limited only by logical constraints of coherence and consistency. But the appearance of formal equality undermines any claim that the legal system is an instrument of substantive injustice and social oppression. Instead, the pretenses of the rule of law have the effect of legitimizing and further entrenching the mystical power of the established dominant ideology, thereby frustrating the development of a consciousness of egalitarianism that might replace the false consciousness of the classical liberal state. To leftist critics, the more citizens believe and accept rule of law ideology, the less they understand the terms of their enslavement.

Of course, this is precisely Shylock's fate. By placing too much faith in rule of law ideology he comes to believe that the rulings of Balthasar-Portia reflect merely the demands of law. Perplexed and befuddled, Shylock becomes an unwitting collaborator in his own ruin.

Leftists claim that liberal ideology obscures and often denies the value choices inherent in the application of legal rules. Liberal ideology thereby legitimates the view that the existing social hierarchy is not merely the result of contingent, historical political struggles. Political mystification, in part, proclaims that the current political and legal order is objectively correct—as corresponding to a transcendentally appropriate standard resulting from an inherently fair process of choice. Regardless of whether such mystification occurs through use of concepts such as natural rights, unchanging human nature, the dictates of a Supreme Being, ideal observers, reflections of human reason, or appeals to a neutral method of value selection, the practical result of this (often subconscious) process is to freeze the fundamental terms of social debate, diffuse social conflict, and elevate the political status quo to the objectively necessary and rationally uncontestable. In this manner, by reification and sanctification and through the connivance of its hegemonic political ideology, liberal jurisprudence isolates itself from instability that is any more disruptive than marginal adjustments and incremental changes.

While it is undoubtedly true that in liberal-capitalist regimes the rule of law serves hegemonic and legitimating functions, this could hardly be otherwise. One of the purposes of any type of legal system is to reinforce the normative suppositions of the existing state ideology in the consciousness of citizens. Law must be widely viewed as emanating not merely from brute power, but also from normative mandate. Thus, in the radically egalitarian paradise imagined by leftists, the invocation of the rule of law would legitimize and normatively sustain radically egalitarian ideology. The rule of law is conservative in that sense: it is status quo preserving. The leftist dispute is directed most accurately at the rule of law's pretense of neutrality among class and interest groups and, most particularly, with the dominant ideology of liberal-capitalist states.

Leftists here echo a recurrent Marxist theme: the rule of law ratifies the necessity of an adversarial, competitive, atomistic conception of human relations—conceptions that leftists find historically inaccurate, sociologically distorted, and morally bankrupt. While leftists are correct in denying the historical or objective necessity of liberal-capitalist systems, they are incorrect in blaming the rule of law for perpetrating those myths. The servile marriage of the rule of law to the mastery of classical liberalism is what reinforces what leftists take to be pernicious descriptive and prescriptive world visions. If the rule of law is invoked by radically egalitarian regimes it would legitimize and reinforce a very different world vision amicable to leftist aspirations. In sum, the background normative assumptions of the dominant ideology that happens to employ the rule of law will be mainly responsible for substantive injustice or justice in that state. Harping on the alleged inherent inadequacy of the rule of law itself is interrogating the wrong suspect.

Thus, Shylock's cruel end is not the result of deficiencies in the rule of law. Instead, the architects of his destruction are his own misunderstanding of the rule of law and misguided faith in mechanical jurisprudence, the intrigues of a false jurist, and the substantive deficiencies of some Venetian laws.

The mystifying effects of law are overrated by leftists. If the application of the rule of law was truly, irremediably, and thoroughly unjust it could not mask oppression or legitimate class structures. A necessary condition for hegemonic effects of law is that the law correlates substantially with conventional social morality and displays an independence from unjust manipulation. Belief in rule of law ideology extends to state officials as well and this belief constrains their behavior. The powerful and ruling classes accept willingly a degree of self-limitation in order to govern effectively. Through a process of internalization—the acceptance of rule of law ideology as a moral and not merely a prudential imperative—law becomes more than the self-serving creation of the ruling class. Because both rulers and those ruled act on their beliefs that the legal system possesses at least some of the virtues embodied by rule of law ideology, that ideology cannot merely be sham and pretense. To think otherwise is to suggest that social relations can be understood independently of the meaning and values that people who participate in those relations attribute to them.

Although a prominent and pervasive feature of jurisprudential discourse, discussion of the rule of law is often a surrogate that partially masks the genuine source of legal disputes, which are waged from fundamentally different descriptive and prescriptive visions of social life. Accordingly, the rule of law and the ideology it embodies are necessary but not sufficient conditions of achieving substantive justice in a state. Thus, the rule of law is more important for attaining justice than is supposed by leftist critics; while it is less important for attaining justice than is supposed by Shylock.

5. The Trial of Venice: *Stage Two: The Presiding Jurist Enters and Renders Judgment*

Bassanio, ever the sweet talker, tells Antonio that "The Jew shall have my flesh, blood, bones and all, / Ere thou shalt lose for me one drop of blood" (4.1.112-113). Antonio brushes the offer aside and asks Bassanio to write his epitaph. Meanwhile, Gratiano berates Shylock with the harshest condemnations in the play.

Dressed like a lawyer's male clerk, Nerissa bears a note from Doctor Bellario commending a young doctor from Rome, Balthasar, to the Duke of Venice. Bellario is too ill to preside over the Shylock v. Antonio trial, but he assures the Duke that he has brought Balthasar up to speed on the facts of the case. Balthasar is none other than Portia, dressed as a male jurist.

Noting that the case is one of first impression, Balthasar-Portia leads Antonio to confess the bond. Apparently signaling that in the light of the stipulated facts Shylock's position is legally sound, Balthasar-Portia asks Shylock to render mercy. When Shylock wonders how he might be compelled to do so, Balthasar-Portia advances a beautiful paean to the quality of mercy. Mercy is not coerced; instead, it drops as a "gentle rain from heaven." As a divine attribute it elevates both giver and recipient; most important, mercy is required for salvation because justice is inadequate for the task. Even though Shylock's cause is just, he must render mercy to mitigate the harshness of the legal remedy in play (4.1.185-205). As did the Duke, Balthasar-Portia suggests that Shylock should simply cancel the contract and forego his 3,000 ducats. Unwittingly following the paths of Morocco and Arragon in the casket test, Shylock insists on getting what he desires and thinks he deserves; sacrifice is out of the question.

In response to Balthasar-Portia's stirring notes in praise of mercy, Shylock, giving credence to the negative evaluations of his spirit, is unmoved: "My deeds upon my head! I crave the law/ The penalty and forfeit of my bond" (4.1.206-207). Shylock reiterates yet again that he will assume responsibility for his deeds. He desires only the correct application of law and the penalty stipulated by the contract that was breached by Antonio.

Upon questioning from Balthasar-Portia, Bassanio informs the court that Shylock has refused payment of 6,000 ducats to discharge the contractual debt. Predictably, Bassanio emboldened by Portia's wealth, ratchets up the rhetoric: "if that will not suffice, / I will be bound to pay it ten times o'er, / On forfeit of my hands, my head, my heart" (4.1.210-212). He beseeches Balthasar-Portia to ignore strict application of law in the instant case and, instead, "To do a great right, do a little wrong" (4.1.216). Balthasar-Portia rejects Bassanio's invitation and repeats the analysis advanced earlier by both Shylock and Antonio:

> It must not be; there is no power in Venice
> Can alter a decree established:
> 'Twill be recorded for a precedent,
> And many an error by the same example
> Will rush into the state; it cannot be (4.1.218-222).

Balthasar-Portia's initial sympathy with Shylock's legal position lures him into accepting her as an authoritative voice of law. She becomes the personification of what he seeks: an objective, impersonal adjudicator who will bring him equality: "A Daniel come to judgement! Yea, a Daniel! /O wise young judge, how I do honour thee!" (4.1.223-224). Shylock does not thereafter question Balthasar-Portia's rulings other than to inquire, "Is that the law?" (4.1.314) when the judge informs him that should he spill even one drop of Antonio's blood in extracting the pound of flesh Venice will confiscate all his material holdings. Also, Balthasar-Portia's initial rulings reinforce Shylock's resolve to settle for nothing less than the forfeiture provision of the contract: a pound of Antonio's flesh.

Shylock, then, is moved by the jurist's reasonableness. After examining the bond, Balthasar-Portia seemingly renders the final judgment:

> Why, this bond is forfeit;
> And lawfully by this the Jew may claim
> A pound of flesh, to be by him cut off
>
> Nearest the merchant's heart. Be merciful:
> Take thrice thy money; bid me tear the bond (4.1.230-234).

In case the crowd had not been listening, Shylock repeats that his legal position is nonnegotiable: he demands the terms of his bond. Growing more impatient, Antonio begs the court to render its judgment forthwith. Balthasar-Portia makes it official: "You must prepare your bosom for his knife" (4.1.245). (Notice that Balthasar-Portia has seemingly enhanced Bassanio's offer of 6,000 ducats by another 3,000 ducats.)

At first blush, it may appear that by refusing twice and thrice the repayment of his principal, Shylock has abrogated his greed: no amount of money will substitute adequately for what he desires and thinks he deserves. Bear in mind, however, that Shylock may not have entirely abrogated his materialistic mindset. It may seem that refusing twice or thrice the amount of his principal for releasing Antonio from the forfeiture provision of the bond demonstrates that Shylock's avarice has disappeared or at least changed its form. But with Antonio out of the way and the number of interest-free commercial loans thereby decreased, Shylock anticipates that his usury business will expand: "will have the heart of him, if he forfeit; for, were he out of Venice, I can make what merchandise I will" (3.1.131-133). Perhaps, for Shylock, refusing 6,000 or 9,000 ducats as repayment of Antonio's debt is sound long-term financial strategy. (But how great a financial threat could Antonio pose to Shylock's business now that Antonio's ships have presumably sunk?) In the end, I would think that Shylock's motives are complex: a Christian, Lorenzo, has insinuated himself into Shylock's family, stolen his daughter, who has converted to the despised religion that has oppressed Shylock and his people; Shylock's long term financial security is his sole refuge from continued Christian assaults; Shylock has his main tormentor, Antonio, the symbol of Christian commercialism, "upon the hip" and can gratify both his financial interests and his thirst for lawful revenge by demanding the forfeiture provision of his bond.

Upon questioning from Balthasar-Portia, Shylock avers that he has a scale at hand to weigh the flesh extracted from Antonio's body. The jurist asks whether Shylock has a surgeon at hand to stop the bleeding, lest Antonio die from the procedure. Shylock points out that no such accommodation is required by the terms of the bond. Unless Shylock is legally compelled—bound by the terms of his voluntary agreement with Antonio—he will provide no such solace.

Balthasar-Portia asks Antonio if he has any final words prior to the execution of judgment. Antonio bides a loving farewell to Bassanio and asks him to inform his wife: "And when the tale is told, bid her be judge / Whether Bassanio had not once a love" (4.1.276-277). Right on cue, Bassanio turns up the heat:

> Antonio, I am married to a wife
> Which is as dear to me as life itself;
> But life itself, my wife, and all the world,
> Are not with me esteem'd above thy life:
> I would lose all, ay, sacrifice them all
> Here to this devil, to deliver you (4.1.282-287).

Taken literally, Bassanio values his wife as highly as his own life. But he would sacrifice his life, his wife's life, and the entire world to save Antonio from his plight. Always pleasing his immediate audience and always prepared to risk everything by words if not in practice, Bassanio leaves Antonio with evocative images. Balthasar-Portia sniffs that Bassanio's wife would not have been pleased to hear his poem had she been present.

Not to be left behind, Gratiano, a pale copy of Bassanio as an orator, adds that although he loves his wife he wished she was dead and in heaven so she could convince a power to change Shylock's obdurate heart. The disguised Nerissa informs Gratiano that he is fortunate that his wife was not present to hear his desire. Shylock, as always shocked by the cavalier attitude of Christian husbands toward their wives, bemoans his daughter's marital union to Lorenzo.

We should be clear that Shylock has no intention of murdering Antonio as such. He yearns for lawful imprimatur; he seeks law because he is firmly convinced that it bestows what he has hitherto been denied: equality. Shylock aspires to use Venetian ideals against Antonio, the symbol of commerce and mercantile collegiality. His error is in thinking that rule of law virtues are sufficient—in contrast to merely being necessary—to ensure substantive equality. An unpopular alien, such as Shylock, will be wary of appeals to judicial discretion, which are unlikely to favor his cause. Instead, he will place his faith in the mechanical application of the results of simple decoding of statutory and contractual language. But formal equality, as encased in rule of law virtues, is simply inadequate to achieve Shylock's aspirations. Yoked to the explicitly discriminatory Venetian ideology that insists that Christian citizens enjoy a higher social status and more legal protection, at least criminally, than do non-Christian resident aliens, invoking the rule of law cannot ensure substantive equality for the likes of Shylock. On the contrary, under such circumstances invoking the rule of law can only deepen Shylock's dire predicament.

Balthasar-Portia brings the proceeding back on point: "A pound of that same merchant's flesh is thine: / The court awards it, and the law doth give it" (4.1.299-300). By enforcing the penalty provision of the bond, Balthasar-Portia awards Shylock a type of specific performance measure of damages. Shylock is prepared to exact the penalty specified for breach of his contract with Antonio. Shylock has apparently achieved his goals: equality before the law, full recognition of his personhood, vengeance upon Antonio as an individual and upon the state generally, all of which is sanctified by the ideals of the most powerful instrument of social control in Venice. The merchant of Venice has apparently reneged on his final commercial transaction. But, remember, appearances are often deceiving. Formal equality, as encased in rule of law virtues, is simply inadequate to achieve Shylock's aspirations.

Shylock seeks the law, not justice. More precisely, he craves the formal and substantive equality conferred on citizens of Venice by law. Who has ever conferred mercy upon Shylock? He will not budge even an inch partly because he has never been granted any gratuities when Venetian citizens have maneuvered him "upon the hip." Furthermore, appeals to mercy are unreliable because they are discretionary. As bestowing mercy upon the guilty is not mandatory—not part of the law— mercy may or may not be granted. Under such circumstances, who is most likely to benefit from appeals to mercy? Despised resident aliens such as Shylock? Not likely. Only antecedently advantaged Venetian citizens—the Antonios of the state—will evoke the sympathy from powerful decision makers that will issue in mercy. Shylock understands the appeal to mercy as yet another ingredient of his inequality. Instead, he demands the impersonal, general application of the rule of law. Shylock mistakenly believes that simple decoding of statutory and contractual language and mechanical application of the results will ensure substantive equality before the law. This philosophical error will deepen his alienation and seal his fate. In the end, the law will prove to be yet another instrument underscoring Shylock's inferior status in Venice.

6. Philosophical Interlude: Mercy, Equity, and Forgiveness

Establishing the proper relationship between law and mercy, or between courts of law and courts of equity, is critical in *The Merchant of Venice*. Mercy can be bestowed only where a normative standard, either moral or legal, has been applied to render a verdict or judgment; or when a person is otherwise legally vulnerable to a stronger party. Perhaps kindness or generosity can be bestowed without such a judgment, but not mercy. Put another way: the invocation of mercy in legal contexts typically presupposes guilt. Antonio has breached the contract with Shylock; he has wronged Shylock to that extent; he is civilly guilty. Balthasar-Portia beseeches Shylock to render mercy despite acknowledging these facts. The judge's request is eminently reasonable. We recognize the forfeiture clause of the bond as grossly inappropriate, even if Antonio voluntarily and recklessly agreed to it. Surely, Bassanio's offer to pay two or three times the principal more than compensates Shylock for Antonio's breach. At the very least, the presence of a medical doctor would ameliorate the health risk to Antonio should Shylock extract a pound of flesh. Certainly, justice demands that law be tempered with mercy.

Equity demands flexible, situational judgment; we must attend to the particulars of the instant case.[11] The generality and impersonality of law opens gaps that must be remedied by judgments focusing on the specifics of a case. Also, bright-line rules cannot capture fully the complexities of normative judgment. Mechanical application of bright-line rules will work injustice in certain instances. A striking tension exists between the clarity of general maxims and the complex variables attending human action. To compose bright-line rules that could consider adequately all such variations is impossible. Even if somehow possible, the resulting concoction would be no more transparent than a kaleidoscope (witness portions of the tax code). The outcome would be application of law that was over-inclusive in some cases (punishing the innocent or excessively punishing the guilty) and under-inclusive (failing to punish the guilty or punishing them insufficiently) in other cases.

Equitable judgment often requires that we judge not only from the perspective of an ideal observer, but also from the vantage point of the perpetrator of an alleged wrong. Of course, strictly speaking, close attention to the specifics of a case does not automatically mitigate judgment or soften punishment. On the contrary, aggravating circumstances may be evident that suggest a sterner response than is typical. In criminal law, at least, mitigating the severity of a sentence is less problematic than increasing the severity of a sentence. Rule of law virtues are less forgiving of the state's excessive use of power than the state's imposition of less than it is entitled to exact.

In sum, equity requires decision makers to respond to a person's individual circumstances and the specific features of the instant case when the relevant law is unable to consider them. Equity, then, refuses to apply mechanically legal rules in deference to consideration of the individuating dimensions of a case. Equity, however, remains within the domain of justice. That is, equity emerges from our commitment to attain justice. As such, equity adjusts the generality of law in order to honor the principle of justice.

To act mercifully is to refrain voluntarily from using one's power or to use that power to a lesser extent against another who is vulnerable to that power. Merciful agents act against existing reasons to act in ways that would cause or refrain from alleviating the vulnerable person's suffering. Merciful acts, however, need not arise from praiseworthy motives. For example, Shylock might have been merciful to Antonio because he thought so acting would be sound long-term business strategy. Perhaps, Shylock's reputation would thereby be enhanced and his usury transactions would increase or that Antonio would thereafter forego rendering interest-free loans that interfered with Shylock's business. If so, calling Shylock's waiving of the penalty provision of his bond with Antonio an act of mercy would be appropriate even though his motivation would be purely self-interest. But I do not think that every reason of self-interest would do. In the narrative of the play, we will discover that Shylock does not enforce the penalty provision of the bond, but he does so only because his own life is in jeopardy. To call Shylock's actions merciful under such circumstances sounds a sour note, especially because Balthasar-Portia had already instructed us that mercy cannot be coerced but must flow "as the gentle rain from heaven" (4.1.185). While her suggestion that mercy springs only from praiseworthy motives is incorrect, her intuition that "coerced mercy" is problematic, perhaps even an oxymoron, is persuasive.[12] I would argue that a necessary condition of merciful action is that it be voluntary. Shylock's coerced relinquishment of the penalty provision is not voluntary, whereas mercy dispensed for some nonpraiseworthy reasons, such as Shylock's waiving of the penalty provision for reasons of self-interest in the hypothetical above, is voluntary.

In legal contexts, merciful acts occur when one party is vulnerable to the legal power of another party; the vulnerable party is susceptible to suffering or other detriment as a result of the legal power of the party in the superior position; the party with the power advantage recognizes the vulnerable party's situation and refuses voluntarily to exercise his or her legal power or does not wield it to the typical extent; and as a result, the suffering or other detriment of the vulnerable party is softened. Mercy is an appropriate response to remorse, repentance, and atonement.

Mercy, then, is voluntarily exacting less than we are authorized or in a position to impose, or extending ourselves more than is typical given the situation. Compassion and empathy are crucial to a merciful mindset. In judicial contexts, mercy implores us to accept less than what justice requires. In judicial contexts, mercy alleviates suffering that is legally deserved or which authorities are otherwise entitled to exact.

One reason underlying merciful legal action is empirical: psychological and institutional vectors typically facilitate harsher punishments than deserved. For example, we tend to overestimate the role of individual character and underplay the role of natural and social conditions as causes of human actions (call this our "existential bias"); public relations campaigns against crime almost always ratchet up the rhetoric about getting "tough on crime"; legislators have enacted fixed penalties and mandatory sentences for a host of crimes; law-biding citizens too often are drawn to such campaigns and enactments, and reward politicians identified as being tough on crime with their votes; and we tend to ignore any collective responsibility for the social conditions that nurture crime. In such an atmosphere, opportunities for dispensing mercy allow us to thwart injustice done in the name of justice.[13]

What factors might incline us toward mercy? A perpetrator's sincere remorse or well-intended attempts at restitution; an offender's especially gruesome socialization that fueled his or her depraved character; particular circumstances that led a perpetrator to act lawlessly in this case, but contrary to his or her general character; and cases where offenders have already suffered greatly for their misconduct and full additional punishment would seem disproportionate to the deed. In all such cases, what the miscreant deserves is unchanged. However, the inclination to be merciful centers on special hardships and circumstances that incline us toward meting out less punishment than deserved.

Of course, the notion of desert, as previously sketched, is a slippery concept. At the legal level, an offender deserves punishment in accord with the gravity of the offense committed and in the absence of justification or excuse. None of the factors inclining us toward dispensing mercy rise to the level of justifications ("I did what is typically wrong and was responsible for doing it, but in this case the act was permissible because of a special set of circumstances") or excuses ("I did what was wrong, but in this case I was not completely responsible for the act because of a special set of circumstances"). Of course, at a moral or psychological level, we can explore the notion of desert further: Does an extraordinarily severe socialization soften a person's responsibility for the ensuing deplorable character he displays? What follows normatively from the fact that none of us deserves our initial starting position in society or our genetic inheritance?

We are all the product of biological and social conditions that at least partly undermine justice and salutary intimacy. Although existentialists remind us fondly that we have no excuses and we are condemned to our freedom, they tend to overlook or downplay the effects of our socialization and genetic inheritance, and are too often overly scrupulous in holding us fully accountable for our characters. They spill much ink over the respective roles of facticity (our unalterable givenness) and transcendence (our freedom and capability of going beyond our current self-conceptions), but almost always end up glorifying our freedom, scolding us about taking more responsibility, and effacing the effects of our background natural and social conditions. The call for mercy flows from an appreciation that human beings are flawed, fallible creatures prone to sin and vice. Extending mercy underscores our solidarity and refuses to see ourselves as immune from common transgressions. Moreover, mercy, unlike equity, is not limited to the domain of justice. That is, mercy emerges from our commitment to humanity and as an adjustment to our tendency toward harsh judgments. At times, dispensing mercy transcends considerations of justice and equity.

If mercy is a value independent from justice then conflicts between the two may arise. However, it does not follow that mercy is therefore unjust. Dispensing mercy need not ignore or wrongly trample upon the imperatives of justice. Instead, mercy is considered only after an offender's just deserts have been calculated. At its best, mercy can temper justice to arrive at the best overall normative result. Remember Aristotle's words: where justice is in place, friendship is still necessary; but where friendship is firm, justice is unnecessary. Justice is a crucial to, but not the exclusive component of, the best overall resolution. Clearly, even if Aristotle overstates the case, human relationships are grounded in normative considerations beyond those of justice.

Forgiveness, in contrast to equity and mercy, abrogates negative attitudes and hard feelings toward the offender as a person, while continuing to acknowledge the wrongness of the action and the perpetrator's responsibility for that action.[14] Neither equity nor mercy presupposes forgiveness. Forgiveness, then, divorces the offender from his or her transgression in terms of how we perceive and feel about the offender. Thus, by renouncing negative perceptions of and feelings about the perpetrator, while retaining our conviction that the action was wrong and the perpetrator was responsible for it, we view the perpetrator more favorably than her act. We no longer evaluate the offense as definitive of the perpetrator's character. In so doing, we underscore our own fallibility in connecting what a person deserves, morally and psychologically, with what that person has done in this case. While determining legal desert is often straightforward, determining moral and psychological desert is inherently paradoxical. In addition, forgiveness highlights the difficulty of evaluating fully the character of others and resists the human-all-too-human inclination to define others by the worst actions they perform.

Forgiveness, unlike equity and mercy, does not always involve actions toward the other. I can forgive another person without any accompanying acts and without the other person ever being aware of my change of heart. At its core, forgiveness concerns how I perceive and feel about the other person, while equity and mercy concern how I act toward them. Also, where forgiveness is accompanied by action it need not be merciful or compassionate. I can forgive someone who has transgressed against me, in the sense adumbrated here, yet require that the offender compensate me fully. Just as clearly, I could act mercifully toward the offender and waive my right to compensation because I was influenced by the hardship the offender would experience, or the sincere remorse the offender expressed, or the like, but I might still not forgive the offender for his or her deed. I could still regard the offender as defined primarily by her wrongful act. Forgiveness, then, often involves reconciliation or repair or the beginning of a relationship, whereas equity and mercy have no such implications. In order for this to occur, either the perpetrator must distance herself from her wrong—perhaps by remorse, repentance, or reformation—or the victim of the wrong must unilaterally create the distance between the perpetrator and her wrong. Even in the absence of the perpetrator's efforts, the victim can decline to define the perpetrator by her misdeed. This can result from, among other reasons, consideration of a past nurturing relationship between the parties, viewing the instant wrong as decidedly out of the perpetrator's general character, or from the judgment that the perpetrator had suffered sufficiently from her wrongdoing.

7. The Trial of Venice: *Stage Three: The Sting*

Then Balthasar-Portia wipes the smugness from Shylock's countenance. As the bond specifies that Shylock is permitted only a pond of Antonio's flesh, should Shylock shed even one drop of Antonio's blood he will have exceeded his entitlement. If that happens, all of Shylock's land and material goods would be confiscated legally by Venice (4.1.306-312). Having placed his faith in simple decoding of legal materials and mechanical application of the results, Shylock will now experience the lash of what he desires and what he thinks he deserves.

To this point, Shylock had been nobody's fool. Shrewd, malicious, and greedy, his intelligence is surpassed only by that of Portia. Yet, confronted with this legal twist from nowhere he can mumble only, "Is that the law?" (4.1.314). In reality, the answer is clearly "no."

Contracts rarely if ever spell out every means necessary to secure the main goals of the terms. If flesh cannot be extracted without shedding blood and if the extraction of flesh is permissible under contract law then the shedding of blood while extracting the flesh is an implied condition of the agreement. It need not be expressly stated in the bond. Also, Shylock might question the proportionality of the penalty: If he sheds even one drop of Antonio's blood he forfeits his entire trove of material possessions. Why? Is that because he is a Jew and he would have exceeded his legal entitlements against a Christian? Is that because anyone who goes beyond his legally decreed contractual remedies is subject to forfeiture of all his material goods? If so, Venice is an extraordinarily dangerous place to conduct business. But we must not dwell on such details. After all, *The Mer-*

chant of Venice is a moral parable and we must submit to its understandings in order to derive its lessons.

In any event, Shylock's bravado begins to melt more quickly than a snowman in June. With Gratiano cheering Balthasar-Portia in the background, Shylock caves: he will accept the 9,000 ducats offered earlier as full discharge of his legal remedies against Antonio.[15] Bassanio presents the money, but Balthasar-Portia rules the settlement out of order. The recurrent themes of desire and desert are paramount. Shylock desires application of law by bright-line rules and understanding contract provisions by de-coding the express terms contained therein. Shylock will get precisely what he desires. Shylock has refused Bassanio's generous settlement offer earlier in the proceeding and he has spurned all invitations to bestow mercy upon Antonio. Having offered no mercy, Shylock does not deserve mercy now. Shylock will get precisely what he deserves. Balthasar-Portia refuses to allow Shylock to revisit past settlement possibilities.

Balthasar-Portia taunts Shylock and deepens his predicament: He is legally entitled to one pound of flesh, but he must not shed any of Antonio's blood and he must extract exactly one pound of flesh. Any violation of these terms—the shedding of even one drop of blood, the extracting of even one iota more or less than one pound of flesh—and Shylock will lose all his material holdings and he will be executed (4.1.332). Gratiano, absolutely giddy at this turn of fortune, sneers, "Now, infidel, I have you on the hip" (4.1.334).

By stressing that Shylock must not shed a drop of "Christian" blood, Balthasar-Portia rubs his nose in his otherness. In Venice, Shylock is an alien and if he thinks that formal equality before the law is sufficient to efface his otherness he is wildly mistaken. Furthermore, if he extracts any more or any less than precisely one pound of flesh that would demonstrate his noncompliance with the terms of the bond—after all, Shylock demanded a simple decoding of contractual provisions— and not only will all his land and goods be confiscated but Shylock will be executed: "Thou diest and all thy goods are confiscate" (4.1.332).

From whence did the death penalty emerge? Perhaps Balthasar-Portia could conjure a justification, based on attempted murder or wrongful assault, if Shylock extracted more than one pound of flesh from Antonio. Although the penalty applied in some such cases seems disproportionate—Should it be triggered if Shylock takes a barely discernible amount of flesh more than one pound?—at least a rationale can be advanced. But what is the justification for executing Shylock should he extract less than that to which he is legally permitted? True, he would not thereby comply precisely with the penalty provision for breach, but he would not have disadvantaged Antonio; quite the opposite. Balthasar-Portia has turned Shylock's jurisprudential theory against him with relish. Philosophical error has rarely garnered such retribution.

Shylock does not inquire as to the justification of the potential penalty. Under these terms, Shylock will lose all his holdings and be subject to execution if he extracts even a fraction of an ounce less than one pound of flesh even if he somehow manages not to shed a drop of Antonio's blood! That is, Shylock will have all his material goods confiscated by the state and be subject to execution for taking less than that to which he was legally entitled. The regime of bright-line rules and decoding express terms has morphed into tyranny.

Thoroughly disheartened, Shylock accepts Balthasar-Portia's interpretation as unassailable. Having lost all rational acuity, Shylock can offer only another compromise: he will accept the principal of his loan to Antonio, 3,000 ducats, as full discharge of his legal remedies. Again, Bassanio offers the purse. Again, Balthasar-Portia drops the hammer. Having earlier refused such monetary settlements, Shylock is barred from accepting them now. Shylock desired what he took to be justice—defined by bright-line rules and decoding express terms—and that is precisely what he shall receive. Shylock must now enforce his legal remedies under the perilous conditions that the judge has outlined. Thus, when Shylock offers to take his principal, end the trial, and go home, the judge rejects his initiative (4.1.336-339).

Shylock does not point out that he had rejected earlier settlement offers only because Balthasar-Portia had led him to believe that he would prevail on the legal merits. The judge had not given Shylock notice of these other dangers he would face if he enforced his legal remedies. As such, Shylock's rejection of settlement was not rendered in the full light of the alternatives. The judge lured Shylock into believing that he would win a judgment, which provided no incentive for Shylock to settle the case, and then the judge refused to allow Shylock to settle once he understood fully what was at stake.

Yes, Balthasar-Portia gave Shylock some hints: what Shylock takes to be justice is inadequate for salvation; a person must offer mercy to others to deserve mercy from others; legal remedies can be harsh if not mitigated by kindness; and we should often provide more than the law requires (for example, an attending surgeon when we extract flesh from another person).

Still, who is this judge? First, Portia is an imposter. In contemporary terms, she perpetrates a fraud by posing as a judge. Second, Portia has a vested interest in the case. Even if she was a bona fide judge she should recuse herself from presiding over this trial. She is the wife of an interested party—Bassanio is the direct recipient of the 3,000 ducats that constitute the bond—and she has a strong bias to favor Antonio, her husband's close friend. Moreover, she has a financial interest in the case. The money that Bassanio has offered as settlement is hers. Portia has good reason to reject Shylock's belated requests for settlement. Shylock has a compelling procedural claim: he has been denied an impartial, fair hearing of his legal case.

What can justify Portia's fraudulent, biased actions as judge? Shylock's obdurate, vengeful posture seems excessive. Especially in the light of his having been offered two and three times the principal of his loan as settlement of the debt, Shylock's insistence on enforcing the forfeiture clause of the bond earns him no sympathy. Additionally, Shylock's actions threaten the three marriages centered in Belmont: Portia and Bassanio, Nerissa and Gratiano, and Jessica and Lorenzo. Portia's rulings as judge, along with Antonio's sentence provisions,

The Merchant of Venice: *The Trial and Judicial Decision Making*   59

ultimately promote the happy resolution of those three couplings. Finally, Portia's judicial rulings demonstrate the inadequacy of viewing the law as defined merely as decoding statutory and contractual language and mechanically applying the results. Courts of equity must soften the results of courts of law.

Whether these lessons could have been learned absent Portia's legalistic chicanery is a critical question. One may well wonder whether Portia's participation as a fraudulent jurist with a major stake in the outcome of the trial—not to mention her conjuring of obscure statutes and peculiar interpretations out of thin air as she entraps Shylock after leading him on—sullies the ends she secures. (Even after the trial, Balthasar-Portia accepts the gift of a ring from Bassanio, an interested party in the litigation.)

But Balthasar-Portia has not completed her destruction of Shylock. Meting out a brand of justice that she is convinced Shylock has courted himself—through his desires and deserts—the fraudulent judge has a final trump card to play.

8. The Trial of Venice: *Stage Four: The Annihilation*

Balthasar-Portia next informs Shylock that independently of the penalties he will incur should he shed even a drop of Antonio's blood or extract even an iota more or less than one pound of flesh from him, Shylock has already violated Venetian law. Should an alien, such as Shylock, directly or indirectly attempt to take the life of a Venetian citizen, the intended victim is entitled to one-half of the perpetrator's material goods, the state will confiscate the other half of his goods, and the perpetrator's life can be spared only by a pardon from the Duke of Venice. Accordingly, prior to even trying to enforce the penalty provision of his bond with Antonio, Shylock was already in violation of the criminal law. Balthasar-Portia turns the civil case of Shylock v. Antonio into the criminal trial of Venice v. Shylock.

The only person seemingly aware of this law is Balthasar-Portia. Should not all aliens have been put on sharp notice of this decree? Given their precarious status in Venice, would not all aliens have made it their business to learn of the legal inequities to which they were subject? If not all aliens, certainly highly intelligent commercial agents such as Shylock should have known about this law. Yet, Antonio, Bassanio, the commercial traders of the state, and the prominent bystanders do not seem aware of it. Even the Duke of Venice is taken by surprise. The existence of an alien attempted murder law ("the Alien Statute") implies that Shylock arrived at the trial already condemned; at least once the facts of the bond were stipulated and Shylock refused pre-trial settlement offers. Much of the civil trial was pure theatrics.

The substance of the Alien Statute is stunningly unjust: it wrongfully discriminates against noncitizens; it is overly broad in that it can be applied to mere intentions ("contriving") to act and not only to direct acts against the lives of citizens; it contains no exculpatory justifications or excuses, not even self-defense, for acting against the life of a citizen; and its extreme penalties will often be grossly disproportionate to the offense. Where, as here, the resident alien has caused no bodily harm and seeks to jeopardize the life of a citizen only if lawful, the penalties of forfeiture of all property (half to Venice, half to the intended victim) and execution are draconian. The procedural unfairness of the Alien Statute—its utter obscurity and the lack of notice provided to resident aliens—only adds to its villainy.

Of course, Gratiano cheers unabashedly from the sidelines as the Duke of Venice, brimming with self-congratulations, contrasts the merciless Shylock with what he takes to be his own merciful spirit. The Duke will pardon Shylock and spare his life; half of Shylock's wealth will flow to Antonio; and the other half will be confiscated by the state; but should Shylock display remorse, the Duke will reduce the confiscated sum to a mere fine and permit Shylock to retain almost half his present wealth.

For a few, brief shining moments, Shylock's defiance returns. He sputters that he seeks no pardon; he tells the Duke to take his life; after all, by seizing his livelihood and the means by which Shylock supports his household, the state would have already taken his life in every critical respect except biologically. Shylock is clearly underwhelmed by the Duke's "mercy."

Balthasar-Portia then asks Antonio what mercy he would render Shylock. Having earlier instructed the parties that only the Duke of Venice could render mercy under the Alien Statute, the judge now seeks counsel from the defendant in the civil case. Delicious irony, that. The apparent losing party in the civil trial becomes the sentencing agent in what is in effect Shylock's criminal trial. The justification of this intrusion is Antonio's right to one half of Shylock's current material holdings under the Alien Statute.

Antonio's "mercy" may well seem even harsher than the clemency offered by the Duke.

The merchant sketches four conditions: (1) waive even the fine that was suggested in lieu of the confiscation by the state of one-half of Shylock's goods; (2) Shylock will place the remaining half of his material wealth in trust under the administration of Antonio. At Shylock's death, the trust will be rendered to Lorenzo, Shylock's Christian son-in-law; (3) Shylock must convert to Christianity; and (4) Shylock must execute a will such that upon his death he bequeaths all of his possessions to Lorenzo and Jessica.

Let's compare the two extensions of "mercy." The Duke's sentence: once Shylock shows sufficient remorse, he can retain his life and almost one-half his material holdings, while the other half of his wealth goes to Antonio. Shylock rejected that offer, preferring death to material and personal dishonor. Antonio's sentence: Shylock retains his life and one-half of his material holdings, the other half of his wealth endows a trust to be administered by Antonio with Lorenzo named as beneficiary upon Shylock's death. Upon his death, Shylock bequeaths all his holdings to his daughter and son-in-law; and Shylock converts to Christianity.

When asked by Balthasar-Portia to render Shylock mercy, Antonio begins by "generously" suggesting that even the Duke's fine (in lieu of the state confiscating one-half of Shylock's goods) should be forgiven. Of course, Antonio had no antecedent claim based on the Alien Statute to that half of Shylock's property. According to the statute, only the state was entitled to seize those goods. Although Antonio is entitled to the other half of Shylock's property, he offers to administer a trust that designates Lorenzo as the beneficiary (or "remainderman") upon Shylock's death. Antonio does not name the income beneficiary during Shylock's lifetime. The most likely candidates for income beneficiary are Antonio, Shylock, or Jessica and Lorenzo. By far the most probable result is that Antonio will be the income beneficiary. But Antonio also asserts control over all of Shylock's property at his death, That is, not only does Antonio control one half of Shylock's present holdings, he will also direct the wealth Shylock acquires after the trial at Shylock's death, all of which will revert to the heirs named by Antonio: Jessica and Lorenzo. Antonio's assertion of power over Shylock's right to dispose of his assets at death is not grounded in the Alien Statute. We should consider it a condition precedent to Antonio waiving his right to seize one half of Shylock's wealth straightaway.

But Antonio's terms are harsh: he arrogates to himself Shylock's right to control his assets and help shape his posthumous legacy, while naming the daughter who betrayed Shylock and the Christian son-in-law Shylock despises as his heirs. The sentence forces Shylock to benefit Antonio, Jessica, and Lorenzo, none of whom appear on a list of Shylock's dearest associates. Finally, Antonio conditions his "mercy" on Shylock's conversion to Christianity, which implies the loss of Shylock's profession as well as the even greater loss of his sense of self.

In fairness, an audience in late-sixteenth or early-seventeenth century England might interpret Shylock's conversion differently. For example, they might view it as an opportunity for Shylock to finally redeem his heathen soul. Nevertheless, conversions under duress lack the requisite faith and bear no recommendation. Futhermore, Antonio assumes the role of surrogate father to Jessica and Lorenzo in usurping Shylock's prerogative to dispose of his wealth upon death and to name the beneficiary of the court-imposed trust. As such, Antonio short circuits Shylock's interests in channeling his assets and forging his legacy posthumously. Accordingly, to praise Antonio for his bestowal of "mercy" upon Shylock is misplaced.

At the end of the trial, do we genuinely believe that Antonio has been transformed, that his heart has elevated, that he has discovered kinship with resident aliens such as Shylock? Not likely. Instead, his solution is to convert Shylock under duress, warmly embrace the Alien Statute, and seize Shylock's interests in controlling the disposition of his assets and legacy posthumously. Also, during the negotiations for the 3,000 ducat loan, Antonio dismissed all thoughts of reconciliation with Shylock. On the contrary, he assures Shylock that his abuse will continue. When Shylock had earlier demanded the enforcement of the forfeiture provision of the bond, Antonio ignored his own gratuitous abuse of Shylock and inauthentically blamed Shylock entirely for the enmity between them: "I oft deliver'd from his forfeitures/Many that have times made moan to me, /Therefore he hates me" (3.3.21-24). Antonio is the Christ-like figure of the play in only one dimension—his willingness to give his life to "redeem" Bassanio. Otherwise, any resemblance Antonio bears to the philosophy and practice of Jesus is purely accidental. Venetian "mercy" is more revenge against a resident alien whom the state perceives jeopardizes its stability.

Why would Shylock acquiesce to Antonio's sentence after just rejecting the Duke's proposal? What is more akin to spiritual death for Shylock than converting to Christianity? He has defined himself and has been defined by the citizens of Venice as a despised outsider. To convert to Christianity, even if only in form but not in worshipping substance, annihilates Shylock's self-image and eviscerates his self-worth. If he considered the loss of just over one-half his wealth tantamount to destroying his life in all critical spiritual respects, what should conversion to Christianity under duress add to his assessment?

Yet, upon questioning from Balthasar-Portia, Shylock claims that he is "content" with Antonio's sentence (4.1.394). How is this possible? To believe that Shylock's conversion is sincere—perhaps a sacred recognition of Christian mercy and generosity in the face of his own maliciousness—is spectacularly unreasonable. Nothing Shylock has been subjected to at the trial would lead him to revise his antecedent evaluation of Christians: hypocrites who fail to live up to their moral ideals. To believe that Antonio's requirement is even intended as merciful—perhaps because as a Christian he is convinced that only the faithful will attain heaven and Antonio now wishes to save Shylock—is equally unreasonable. Under Christian doctrine, profession of Christian faith (under duress?) and the sacrament of baptism (under protest?) are insufficient to earn eternal salvation. The conversion of Shylock is most reasonably interpreted as his most profound humiliation. Yes, the Duke of Venice pressures Shylock to acquiesce to Antonio's sentence: "He shall do this, or else I do recant / The pardon that I late pronounced here" (4.1.391-392). But so what? Shylock had already apparently accepted death when he rejected the Duke's own sentence proposal.

Perhaps I am missing something about the terms of the trust. Who is the intended beneficiary of the trust income during Shylock's lifetime? We know that at death, Shylock must bequeath the trust to Lorenzo. But Antonio did not specify the beneficiary of the trust during Shylock's lifetime. If might be Antonio himself. After all, under the Duke's initial sentence proposal Antonio was to receive one-half of Shylock's wealth and it is that portion that Antonio refashions into a trust in his own sentence proposal. If this is the case, Antonio's proposal would be no more appealing than the Duke's proposal in this regard. From Shylock's standpoint, what significant difference exists between ceding one-half of his wealth to Antonio straightaway and putting one-half of his wealth in a trust to benefit Antonio during Shylock's lifetime and to revert to Lorenzo, his despised son-in-law, upon Shylock's death?

The beneficiary of the trust during Shylock's lifetime might be Lorenzo and/or Jessica. Again, such an arrangement is not a significant advance over the Duke's initial sentence proposal. In effect, under these terms, one-half of Shylock's wealth would go to his despised son-in-law and/or traitorous daughter instead of flowing to Antonio. Perhaps this is a minor improvement from Shylock's perspective: his daughter remains his blood and even if she has forsaken his authority better that she receive Shylock's wealth than it enrich his enemy Antonio.

Still, this, at best, minor improvement in sentencing terms is unlikely to lead Shylock to be "content" with Antonio's sentence after Shylock had already rejected the Duke's proposal.

The other possibility is that Shylock is the beneficiary of the trust during his lifetime. Instead of relinquishing one-half of his wealth directly to Antonio, Shylock must place that amount in trust to be administered by Antonio (at an executive fee?) that will provide income to Shylock during his lifetime. This may well seem a significant improvement over the terms levied by the Duke. Although it impairs Shylock's liquidity, instead of forcing Shylock to yield one-half of his wealth to Antonio, this arrangement at least generates wealth for Shylock.

Assuming that this is the intent of Antonio's trust idea, is this amendment to the Duke's initial sentencing proposal enough to change Shylock's mind? Not obviously. After all, Shylock must also convert to Christianity which means that his usury business is history. Even brushing aside his personal humiliation and loss of self-esteem at having been broken by his Christian tormentors and having been coerced into joining their breed, Antonio's sentence has the overall result of diminishing Shylock's financial possibilities. The tradeoff between converting to Christianity and being named a lifetime beneficiary of a trust endowed with his own wealth is a significant net financial loss.

Readers with some sympathy for Shylock—and only the hardest of spirits can unequivocally cheer his plight—may well yearn for a different ending. I would prefer the following alternate version: "Duke, Antonio, and all you other sanctimonious citizens of Venice, hear me well. I reject your terms. I would prefer to die a rebellious Jew than to bend my knee in supplication to your bizarre legal system and your distorted reasoning. You invoke laws hitherto unknown; you conjure decrees that wrongfully discriminate against aliens in their relations with citizens; you violate every rule of law virtue that supposedly underwrites equality before the state. Worse, you dare make conversion to your twisted faith a condition of life itself—all in the name of Christian mercy! Does your God sanction such action? If so, is such a God worthy of worship? If not, are you posturing Christians worthy worshippers? You can take my wealth, you can kill my body, but you scurrilous, conspiratorial villains can never steal my spirit or corrode my soul. So do your business, you 'merciful Christians,' and execute the 'currish' Jew. But I say unto you now and forever: 'Fie upon your law. Fie upon you.'"

Unfortunately, Shylock does not go down with blazing defiance. From the available text, perhaps we must conclude that Shylock had simply been beaten down from the entire ordeal. His will had been overborne by cumulative events. Having gone from an apparent triumph in his civil case against Antonio to a devastating trashing in a criminal trial grounded in seemingly unknown laws, Shylock simply runs out of intellectual gas and rebellious energy. The thrill of anticipated victory degenerates into the agony of intractable defeat. At the end, the confused, broken moneylender resigns himself to his fate: "I am not well" (4.1.396).

9. Philosophical Interlude: Judicial Decision Making

The annihilation of Shylock is occasioned by his false understanding of judicial decision making. Shylock is convinced that equality before the law is sustainable only by simple decoding of statutory language and the mechanical application of the results. On that presumption, he sues for his forfeiture under the bond. On that presumption, Balthasar-Portia turns the law against Shylock and brings him to his knees. Throughout the early stages of the trial, the Duke of Venice, Balthasar-Portia, friends of Antonio, and prominent Venetian citizens beseech Shylock to extend mercy. But Shylock takes mercy to be a destabilizing element in law. As a discretionary factor bestowed episodically, mercy is external to law. As such, mercy jeopardizes equality before the law and threatens rule of law virtues. For a despised resident alien, such as Shylock, invocations of mercy invite discriminatory application of legal imperatives. In an explicitly biased social atmosphere, such as is ubiquitous in Venice, the parties most likely to benefit from pious pleas for mercy are the esteemed merchants such as Antonio; the parties most likely to be disadvantaged by such pleas are members of scorned minorities such as Shylock. Accordingly, to view Shylock as only a greedy, malicious litigant prepared to maximize his advantage over an enemy whom he has "upon the hip" is inaccurate and unfair. Shylock seeks equality in what he takes to be the only social forum in Venice capable of providing that value to him. To his dismay and personal annihilation, Shylock discovers that even the law can be an instrument of inequality and injustice. Even worse, his flawed understanding of judicial decision making can be turned to noxious purposes.

The critical question that Shylock asks during the trial—"Is that the law?" (4.1.314)— is never answered precisely. Is what the play takes to be "mercy" really external to law or is it internal to any nonprimitive judicial system? Is "mercy" always discretionary and bestowed episodically or is it required by the demands of judicial decision making? Why is Shylock's understanding of judicial decision making fatally flawed? I will examine such questions in the context of three contemporary theories of judicial decision making: H.L.A. Hart's Legal Positivism, Ronald Dworkin's Right Answer Thesis, and my Critical Pragmatism.

Hart concludes that judicial decision making involves "rules plus discretion:" The vast majority of cases are resolved by routine application of rules to particular facts, but "hard cases" are resolved by judicial discretion as adjudicators invoke social policy and in effect reach a legislative solution.[16]

According to Hart, at least three areas of indeterminacy pervade law. First, a statute may have unclear and contestable instances of application. Second, in certain situations determining and formulating the appropriate precedents to be applied may be problematic. Third, law often summons highly general standards, such as the standard of due care in negligence, the application of which often requires contestable judgments.[17]

Instead of lamenting the presence of indeterminacy in law, Hart accepts it as inevitable and desirable. Because of our need to make fresh choices, the flexibility of our current collective aims, and the impossibility of prior knowledge of future circumstances, a measure of legal indeterminacy has salutary effects.[18] He tells us that extreme formalists, such as Shylock, who aspire to eliminate indeterminacy fail to recognize the unwelcome consequences of doing so.

> [To end indeterminacy in law] is to secure a measure of certainty or predictability at the cost of blindly prejudging what is to be done in the range of future cases, about whose composition we are ignorant. We shall thus indeed succeed in settling in advance, but also in the dark, issues which can only reasonably be settled when they arise and are identified. We shall be forced by this technique to include in the scope of a rule cases which we would wish to exclude in order to give effect to reasonable social aims, and which the open textured terms of our language would have allowed us to exclude, had we left them less rigidly defined. The rigidity of our classification will thus war with our aims in having or maintaining the rule.[19]

Accordingly, questions of interpretation of meaning that arise in the penumbra—outside the settled core of paradigm instances—cannot be decided by logical deduction or any other alleged resort to formalism. Such questions, says Hart, must be resolved by the application of criteria purporting to support "what the law ought to be" on some social policy or purpose.[20] Laws often have gaps and judges must exercise creative choices to answer some legal questions. These creative choices can still be rational, although free. The choices are free in the sense that legal rules do not apply in a mechanical fashion, but rational in the sense that judicial decision making is constrained by numerous policies and principles which structure decisions by excluding most rationales. Judges address penumbra cases by confronting the purposes of the relevant statute in light of the interests of the respective litigants. Often, judges must weigh and balance conflicting factors in arriving at their decisions. In some cases, this weighing and balancing may not produce a uniquely correct answer to the case at bar.[21] In hard cases, judges must appeal to social purposes and goals that sometimes have and sometimes lack a moral component. Thus, penumbra cases are resolved through the exercise of judicial discretion and the application of considerations that are often extralegal. By this series of claims, Hart distances himself from all strictly formalistic or mechanical methods of judicial decision making.

Had Shylock the benefit of Hart's counsel, he would have had to reconsider whether his legal cause was the easy case he had imagined it to be. Surely, he would have intuited that if his cause was a hard case that background social purposes and goals would be unfavorable to the resolution he sought. Most important, Hart may have been able to dislodge Shylock from the false comforts of thinking that mechanical jurisprudence defined the application of law.

Ronald Dworkin's understanding of the distinction between easy and hard cases differs from that of Hart. In fact, Dworkin advances an ultra-sophisticated version of formalism, the right answer thesis: the duty of a judge is to discover the antecedent right answer and enforce the preexisting rights of litigants, not to legislate or create a new solution.[22] This concedes "discretion" to judges, but only in the unassailable and weak sense that it calls upon them to exercise judgment. Dworkin denies explicitly that judges have discretion in the strong sense that they are free to make decisions without a prior duty to decide in one way rather than another. Accordingly, for Dworkin, judges are rationally constrained by preexisting legal materials.[23] One of the unique aspects of Dworkin's position is the sophisticated reasoning judges must employ in order to discover the constraints on their decisions.

Judges must construct a scheme of abstract and concrete principles that provides a coherent justification for all common law precedents, as well as for constitutional and statutory provisions. His scheme, where applied to the United States, is ordered vertically into four levels: constitutional provisions, decisions by the United States Supreme Court, legislative enactments, and lower court decisions.[24] The justification for lower level principles must be consistent with the principles providing justification for higher level materials. The scheme is ordered horizontally in that the principles which justify a decision or act on one level must be consistent with the justification offered for other decisions and acts at that level. The resulting judicial theory, Dworkin assures us, will reflect only what the constitution, common law precedents, and statutes themselves require, and will ignore the judge's independent personal convictions about morality and optimum social policy.

At each vertical level of justification the judge's task is somewhat different. At the constitutional level she must develop a comprehensive theory of principles and policies that justifies the constitution as a whole. She does this by: (a) generating possible explanatory theories which justify different aspects of the scheme; (b) testing the resulting theories against the nature of more general political institutions; and (c) upon exhaustion of the effectiveness of that test, elaborating the successful theory's contested concepts.[25] At the statutory level, judges must decide which arguments from principle and policy could properly have convinced the legislature to enact particular statutes. Judges here are not trying to discern the original intent of the framers; instead, they are trying to discover the best justification of settled doctrine.[26] The actual intentions of the legislature are relevant only when necessary to choose between equally appropriate theories. At the common law level, judges must recognize that earlier decisions exert a "gravitational force" on later decisions insofar as arguments from principle justify such decisions.[27]

The best justificatory theory for existing law must furnish a more consistent fit with legal materials and must provide a more compelling moral justification in light of background morality than those accounts provided by competing theories.[28] Suppose, however, that one theory stigmatizes fewer aspects of legal doctrine as mistakes and thus provides the more consistent fit, while an opposing theory better meets the requirements and aspirations of background morality. Dworkin apparently suggests the following as a plausible, but probably too crude, answer: the consistent fit criterion is the threshold requirement; once two or more competing theories equally fulfill this requirement, background morality becomes the adjudicating criterion.[29]

Dworkin concedes straightaway that individual judges constituted by different backgrounds will construct different, mutually inconsistent theories. Also, it will often be impossible to demonstrate that only one of those theories is uniquely correct. Nevertheless, a judge must believe that there is some single correct justificatory theory which announces a single solution for each case. Dworkin rejects the notion that the truth of a proposition of law must be demonstrated on the basis of both physical facts and facts about human behavior. In his view, the presence of controversy among reasonable legal insiders acting reasonably is not logically sufficient to yield the inference that antecedent right answers do not exist.[30]

Dworkin, then, insists that Legal Positivists, such as Hart, make hard cases indeterminate because their jurisprudence concedes too easily that the law has run out in such cases and that judges must legislate an answer using policy and morality. Instead, Dworkin argues that virtually every legal question has a preexisting answer and denies that (strong) judicial discretion is required in so-called hard cases.

Had Shylock the benefit of Dworkin's counsel, he would have been even more wary of his chances to prevail than he would have been after listening to Hart. The good news for Shylock is that Dworkin insists that virtually every legal case has a right answer. The bad news for Shylock is that Dworkin's theory of jurisprudence requires an expansive review of background principles and policies that would, taken collectively, have been unfavorable to an alien such as Shylock.

My favorite theory of judicial decision making is Critical Pragmatism.[31] Using Dworkin's justificatory scheme as a springboard, Critical Pragmatism rejects his conviction that one best justificatory legal theory of law must emerge. Instead, several legitimate, sometimes conflicting, legal ideologies pervade rules, principles, and precedents. Judges will often differ as to which of these ideologies they invoke.[32]

Still, Critical Pragmatism insists that there are right answers in law in at least three senses of that phrase. There are right answers in the sense that the internal constraints and theoretical presuppositions of a particular ideology will demand certain specific answers to numerous legal questions.[33] Such answers are correct in the relativized sense: Once a judge adopts the requisite presuppositions and recognizes the internal constraints of a particular ideology, certain conclusions will follow in concrete legal situations. Furthermore, there are also right answers in the sense that otherwise divergent ideologies will nonetheless converge on some matters. Although ideologies such as Socialism, Feminism, Liberalism, Conservatism, and Economic analysis are unquestionably distinct, they still share some common prescriptive presuppositions; they often agree on the validity of numerous legal rules and extant doctrine; and thus their conclusions converge on many issues. Finally, there are right answers in the sense that antecedently existing doctrine on a specific legal question may overwhelmingly reflect one particular legitimate legal ideology.

It must be admitted, however, that these are limited senses of right answers which will strike some as odd or inadequate. These rights answers are not demanded by Reason itself, or immune from revision, or uncontaminated by conventionalism, or incontestable, or fully required by the one proper interpretation of extant legal doctrine, or demonstrably correct from a neutral vantage point. Critical Pragmatism acknowledges that the cat is out of the bag: law and judicial decision making are political in that judicial interpretations implicate descriptive and prescriptive world visions. But not just any world vision passes the tests for a legitimate legal ideology, nor are we committed to the simpleminded proposition that one vision is no better or worse than any other.

Recall also that the very distinction between easy and hard cases suggests that the phenomenology of judicial decision making includes more convergence than divergence. Indeed, such convergence is contingent: largely a result of the selection, education, and professional socialization of lawyers and judges, and on areas of agreement among otherwise disparate ideologies. Additionally, as an empirical matter, members of the legal profession and elected government officials, perhaps reflecting the dominant views of wider constituencies, are overwhelmingly political centrists.

By accepting the existence of easy cases, Critical Pragmatism does recognize and reinforce a limited conservative ("status quo preserving") bias in judicial decision making, and accepts a modest formalism. But this need not result in wholesale conservatism or in mechanical jurisprudence. Recall that Critical Pragmatism states that as a contingent reality legitimate legal ideologies will converge on numerous legal questions. The majority of legal questions are not even litigated.[34] Only interesting hard cases comprise the law texts that preoccupy legal academics, and this may give the erroneous impression that judicial divergence is more prevalent than it genuinely is. Usually, disparate ideologies agree on the appropriate legal doctrine that decides legal questions, and on its proper application. To agree, as Critical Pragmatism does, that legal language, logic, and normative reasoning are not fully determinate does not imply that easy cases are fictions.

Making this modest right answer claim is still important. First, it allows us to stigmatize as mistakes those judicial decisions that incorrectly apply the presuppositions, or incorrectly ignore the internal theoretical constraints of a particular ideology. Second, it permits us to account for the distinction between easy and hard cases, the predictability of most legal outcomes, and the convergence of otherwise divergent ideologies. Third, it grants us a way to fashion a deeper notion of the institutional and social constraints on judicial decision making. Fourth, it is compatible with the formal aspirations of the Rule of Law. Fifth, because it incorporates a merely modest formalism it is able to recognize concrete social reality: the contingency and political sources of legal conclusions; the continuing presence of class, gender, and racial oppression; and the economic and social pressures from which the judiciary is not immune.

The Critical Pragmatism in jurisprudence sketched here implies the following: (1) legal theory yields a rational, although not fully determinate, structure to open-ended legal concepts; (2) in a pluralistic culture the presence of several legitimate legal ideologies will preclude any single all-embracing theory from being able to account for the complex set of legal materials; (3) despite the lack of an all-embracing theory, the legitimate legal ideologies presuppose at least a thin, common normative framework; (4) this common framework prevents arbitrary, unremitting ideological conflict; (5) right answers (in the senses explicated previously) exist to most legal questions; (6) hard cases should be subject to a judicial discretion bounded by the values of fallibilistic pluralism,[35] and by the independent tests a justified legal theory must pass; and (7) judicial decision making implicates ideological vision and is thus political all the way down, but it does not follow that it is irrational, merely subjective, or unconstrained.[36]

Had Shylock the benefit of my counsel prior to suing Antonio in court, he would have been at least as wary of bringing suit against Antonio as he would have been after listening to Dworkin. The appeals to wider normative considerations than merely decoding of contractual language and to legitimate legal ideologies do not augur well for Shylock's cause.

In fact, under all three of these theories of judicial decision making, the civil trial of Shylock v. Antonio is an easy case to adjudicate: clear principles of contract law determine that Antonio has breached his bond with Shylock and the appropriate remedy is expectancy damages—an award of 3,000 ducats plus interest. From the standpoints of Legal Positivism, Legal Interpretivism, and Critical Pragmatism neither judicial discretion, nor an external appeal to equity, nor a bestowal of mercy is required to reach the correct result.

Independently of anyone's favorite theory of judicial decision nmaking, courts have recognized a host of principles of legal interpretation which, in effect, underscore that the law is much more than Shylock's simple decoding of statutory language. Here are a few:

Rule of Lenity. In construing ambiguous criminal statutes, the judiciary should resolve the ambiguity in favor of the defendant.[37]

Appeal to Legislative Purpose. Where a statute's language is not sufficiently plain or clear to establish that statute's meaning, a determination of the legislative purpose of the statute should be undertaken. What ultimate purpose did the ruling body intend this statute to facilitate or attain? In answering this question, the legislative history of the statute is commonly examined.[38]

Appeal to the Spirit of the Act. Even where a literal rendering of a statute, based on the plain meaning of the text, is available, courts have held that "where a literal rendering will lead to a result not in accord with the essential purpose and design of the act, the spirit of the law will control the letter."[39] At times, the words of a statute "may be expanded or limited according to the manifest reason and obvious purpose of the law. The spirit of the legislative direction prevails over the literal sense of the terms."[40]

Avoid Absurdity. Assume that the legislative body did not intend absurd or manifestly unjust outcomes. Thus, statutes must not be construed to lead to absurd results.[41]

Once employed by judges and incorporated into case law, such principles are not external to law. Instead, they are part of the law and judges are required to invoke them when appropriate. Doing so, of course, requires that judges must use their judgment when identifying and applying law. Not all judges embody equally sound judgment. Mistakes will occur, but that is inevitable. Accordingly, Shylock's dream of mechanical jurisprudence as the avenue of achieving equality and justice before the law is unwise and, happily, impossible in any legal system that is more complex than a code of tribal primitivism. In any reasonably sophisticated legal system, much of what is termed "mercy" in the play is itself part of the law.

One might conclude that *The Merchant of Venice* should end in utter exhaustion. Balthasar-Portia has domesticated the formerly wolfish will of Shylock and reduced him to complying meekly with a procedurally flawed and substantively unjust outcome. Portia has thereby rescued Antonio and seemingly cleared all obstacles preventing the sexual consummation of her marriage with Bassanio. What more is to be done?

A few loose ends must be resolved. Although the law is in repose, love must now be reconciled. Portia has more intrigue in her arsenal: Bassanio will be lured into malfeasance and then held accountable, all in the name of effective midwifery and marital harmony.

Three

THE MERCHANT OF VENICE: BONDS REPAIRED

The Christians of Venice and Belmont are thrilled by the siege of Shylock. The Duke, impervious to the substance and appearance of judicial impropriety, instructs Antonio to "gratify" the judge. On Antonio's behalf, Bassanio offers the esteemed jurist 3,000 ducats. Balthasar-Portia magnanimously declines what is, after all, her own money (4.1.406-420).

1. Broken Vows

But Portia needs to test Bassanio's resolve. As Balthasar, she asks for his gloves and his ring. At first, Bassanio tries to talk his way out of yielding the ring. He calls it a "trifle" and offers, instead, to bring the "dearest ring in Venice" to the jurist (4.1.430-435). As always, Balthasar-Portia far exceeds Bassano intellectually and persists in her request. Finally, Bassanio admits that he has made a vow to his wife that he would never part with the ring. Balthasar-Portia dismisses the vow and argues that she "deserves" the ring for exemplary services rendered (4.1. 441-446). (*The Merchant of Venice* has already schooled the audience that claims lodged on the basis of personal desert are often unreliable.)

The jurist departs, but Antonio takes up her cause:

> My Lord Bassanio, let him have the ring:
> Let his deservings and my love withal
> Be valued 'gainst your wife's commandement (4.1.449-451).

Always inclined to please the person nearest him at the moment, Bassanio weighs the moral power of his marital vow against the force of Antonio's love and the personal desert of Balthasar-Portia. He instructs Gratiano to deliver the ring to the jurist. Can anyone doubt that the scales of decision would have answered differently had Bassanio weighed the alternatives in the presence of his wife?

Gratiano scurries after Balthasar-Portia to deliver Bassanio's ring and to invite the jurist to dinner at Antonio's home. Balthasar-Portia accepts the ring, declines the diner invitation, and asks Gratiano to show her law clerk, the disguised Nerissa, to Shylock's house where the converted Christian is to sign the final legal papers (4.2.4-11). Along the way, the disguised Nerissa convinces Gratiano to give her his ring as payment for her services to Balthasar-Portia, which directly benefited Antonio. Ignoring his marital vow, Gratiano gives the law clerk the gold hoop.

The parties reconvene at Belmont. The no-longer-disguised Nerissa takes Gratiano to task for relinquishing the ring and what it represented. Gratiano makes the mistake of trivializing the worth of the ring. Nerissa stresses that Gratiano has broken its oath to her: he had promised to wear it until his death and carry it to his grave as symbolic of their unshakeable love (5.1.146-158). Portia scolds Gratiano, disingenuously adds that Bassanio made a similar vow to her, and she expresses her conviction that Bassanio would not part with his ring for all the money in the world. Pleased to indict another promise-breaker, Gratiano informs Portia that Bassanio "gave his ring away / Unto the judge that begg'd and indeed / Deserv'd it too" (5.1.179-181) (Another reference to the principle of personal desert as a problematic criterion of distribution.)

Portia turns on Bassanio. She will not share his bed until he produces the ring. Nerissa gives the same ultimatum to Gratiano. Predictably, Bassanio tries to sweet talk his way out of trouble: if Portia could know why and to whom Bassanio relinquished the ring and how reluctantly he did so, Portia's displeasure would soften. Just as predictably, Portia will not let Bassanio off easily:

> If you had known the virtue of the ring,
> Or half her worthiness that gave the ring,
> Or your own honour to contain the ring,
> You would not then have parted with the ring (5.1.199-202).

Bassanio explains that he did not bestow the ring on another woman, but on the distinguished judge who saved Antonio's life. The jurist requested the ring as a token of Bassanio's gratitude. As he was honor-bound to grant the request, Bassanio reluctantly parted with the jewelry. Portia retorts that should the jurist travel near her home she would mimic Bassanio and refuse him nothing, including her body and her husband's bed. Nerissa follows suit and suggests the same to Gratiano should the law clerk who has her ring wander to Belmont (5.1.209-235).

With no other arguments or reasons available, Bassanio throws himself upon Portia's mercy: "Pardon this fault, and by my soul I swear / I never more will break an oath with thee" (5.1.247-248). Emboldened by the results of his trial with Shylock, Antonio enters the proceedings and agrees, once again, to stand as Bassanio's surety: "I dare be bound again, My soul upon the forfeit, that your lord / Will never more break faith advisedly" (5.1.251-253).

So Antonio, again, offers to stand as surety for Bassanio. As such, he now stands between Bassanio and Portia just as he had earlier stood between Bassanio and Shylock. Does his position as middleman in the marriage portend the same disaster that ensued when he was Bassanio's surety with Shylock? Or will Portia be better able to control the situation with Antonio near at hand ("Keep your friends close and your enemies closer")? The best situation might well be for Antonio to abate his intermeddling, acknowledge his relationship with Bassanio as only one of friendship (not unrequited lover or mentor-protégé), and search for salutary intimacy and love elsewhere in Belmont as he is unlikely to stumble upon it in Venice. As the center of commerce and trade, Venice requires and reinforces individualism, self-pride, and cordiality in contrast to intimacy, community, and love.

Still motivated to torment Bassanio further, Portia produces a ring, hands it to Antonio, and instructs him to give it to Bassanio and order him to take better custody of it than he did the first ring. Bassanio recognizes the ring as the original. Portia turns the screws: she retrieved the ring through sexual congress with the jurist to whom Bassanio gave it. Of course, Nerissa takes the cue and informs her husband that she retrieved his ring by sexually engaging with the law clerk to whom Gratiano gave his ring (5.1.258-262).

Gratiano invokes the principle of personal desert one final time:

Why, this is like the mending of highways
In summer, where the ways are fair enough:
What, are we cuckolds ere we have deserv'd it? (5.1.263-265)

By setting the contractual terms of her relationship with Bassanio, Portia stakes her place on the individual-community continuum. She makes it clear that her sexual fidelity—always especially valued in patriarchal societies—depends on Bassanio's understanding that Venetian commercial values must yield to Belmontian communal values. So, too, Antonio pledges his soul as surety for Bassanio's future compliance with his marital oaths. The three characters highlight the inadequacy of arm's length bargaining and commodified arrangements for sustaining robust, intimate relationships. The sanctity of freedom of contract must be adjusted to the imperatives of intimacy. Still, contracts may not require love, but love cannot ignore contracts. Contractual understandings are still required for friendship and love, although they remain insufficient: Venice may be able to prosper materially without Belmont, but Belmont requires a dose of Venice to flourish emotionally. Accordingly, in Belmont, Portia reinstates the power of oaths, promises, and vows. Although the bonds she venerates are those of intimacy and not commerce, she makes clear that future breaches will be dealt with harshly.

Finally, Portia relents. She produces the letter from Doctor Bellario of Padua. She reveals that she was the judge and Nerissa was her clerk. She welcomes Antonio and in a fantastic finish unveils the glorious news that three of his ships have returned safely to port laden with riches. Not to forget Lorenzo and Jessica, Portia informs them that they are Shylock's legal heirs. The couples retreat to their bedrooms, while Antonio is presumably left to total his accounts (5.1.266-307). We must imagine that everyone lives happily ever after (Even Shylock?).

2. Philosophical Interlude: *The Symposium*

Plato's most evocative and beautifully imaginative dialogue is *The Symposium*.[1] Symposia in ancient Greece were all-male, after-dinner parties hosted by aristocrats. Centered on intellectual matters, these parties invariably offered sexual opportunities as young women and men—courtesans and musicians—served the guests. The importance of Plato's dialogue is undeniable. *The Symposium* includes moving speeches about the god, Eros, that reflect how educated Athenians understood love. Strikingly, all of these speeches can be interpreted to contain messages about love that glisten with contemporary relevance. Furthermore, each report on love mirrors the nature of its speaker's soul. Plato's overall lesson resonates: Each of us is in large measure constituted by whom and what we love. The things we value and the people with whom we are intimate reflect and sustain our characters.

Phaedrus is a modest, handsome young man who is the beloved of Eryximachus, a medical doctor. He extols Eros for giving human beings their greatest gift. For him, love centers on physical, homosexual relationships. Homosexual lovers fight more courageously than is typical because they do not want to dishonor themselves in the perception of their beloved. Eros, thus, nurtures certain virtues in the lover. Excellence resides in the lover, not the beloved; but the beloved has higher status than the lover because the beloved is pursued. In general, the lover's pursuit of the beloved affirms the higher status of the beloved (178a-180b).

Phaedrus demonstrates the meagerness of his soul through his theory of love. First, his understanding of love is narrow and one-sided. He speaks of lovers and those beloved, not of mutuality and reciprocity. Second, his notion of love is mainly or solely physical and focuses on the relative statuses of the parties. Third, he locates the value of love in the purely instrumental: how lovers are emboldened in battle lest they shame themselves in the eyes of the beloved; how the beloved gains social status through being an object of desire. Phaedrus shows little or no awareness of how intimate relationships extend our metaphysical boundaries or why communal bonds are critical for human flourishing. Still, we can tease out of Phaedrus's speech a contemporary lesson: Genuine, worthy love will elevate the parties. In crucial respects, the parties in a loving relationship should be better human beings than they would otherwise have been. If parties claiming to be in love are not elevated then they either are not in love at all or their version of love corrupts their spirits and is thereby unworthy.

Thus Phaedrus highlights a major concern about the pairing of Portia and Bassanio. Will they bring out the best in one another? Will Portia elicit Bassanio's ideal possibilities or will she micromanage his character counterproductively? Will Bassanio nurture Portia's independence and free spirit or will he unwittingly drain her of her transcendent trajectory?

The next speaker is Pausanias, longtime lover of the poet, Agathon. Pausanias is a pupil of the sophist, Prodicus. Pausanias speaks of base, earthly loves and glorious, celestial loves. Base loves center on physical, sexual relations that are heterosexual or homosexual involving young boys. Women in Athens did not receive formal education so some male aristocrats were convinced that heterosexual relations could be grounded only in the pursuit of physical pleasure. Likewise, young boys were too immature spiritually and mentally to inspire anything other than physical lust. For Pausanias, physical lust was an unworthy motivation. Inspired by a profound commitment to dualism, Pausanias was convinced that the mind or soul was the locus of personal identity and thus the higher part of human beings. Glorious, celestial loves concentrate on nurturing the fulfillment of our higher desires. Cultivating excellent character—centering concern on the soul and intellect—is the identifying mark of the best loves. The beloved, invariably a young man (not a young boy), sexually gratifies the lover, who reciprocates by teaching his beloved how to acquire virtue. Undoubtedly trying to advance his own self-interest with Agathon, Pausanias adds that the beloved should grant any sexual gratification requested by the lover (Are you listening, Agathon?) so that in return the beloved may learn more about virtue (180c-185c).

Pausanias advances our understanding of love by adding the notions of reciprocity and spiritual refinement to the earlier account. Although his idea of the substance of reciprocity is self-serving and mirrors the aspirations of his social situation, Pausanias reminds us that the merely physical is an inadequate basis for love: Genuine love must be reciprocal and it must energize our most valuable desires and capabilities.

Again, the question for Portia and Bassanio: Will the two lovers be equal partners in the joint project of mutual self-improvement? Or will the deficiencies in their respective characters post insurmountable obstacles to reciprocity and mutuality?

The third speaker is Eryximachus, a medical doctor and the lover of Phaedrus. Plato was not fond of medical practitioners. He was convinced that those who diagnosed and tended to only the physical would lack understanding of the spiritual and intellectual. In addition, medical doctors typically overestimated their intellectual talents. Predictably, Eryximachus seems overly self-important and smug. His theory of love emphasizes the harmony of opposites within individuals and the world. Genuine love facilitates virtue, self-restraint, moral action, and internal harmony. Ersatz love encourages self-indulgence and self-destruction. Genuine love nurtures a healthy body, while ersatz love results in sickness. The contemporary lesson: Genuine, worthy love moderates internal conflict and promotes health (186a-188e).

Lacking a refined conception of the mind-body connection, Eryximachus stresses the physical results of worthy loves. But his account is simplistic and exudes limited explanatory power. *Why* do genuine loves produce such effects? Is health really just a matter of reconciling opposites? Could not a valuable love exacerbate internal conflict but thereby promote intellectual and moral growth?

For Portia and Bassanio can a genuine harmony be attained? Or will ersatz compromise thinly veil seething incompatibility? At its best, love promotes high creativity and personal growth by transforming the inner conflicts of the parties to practical advantage.

The comedian, Aristophanes, is next on the docket. Historically, Aristophanes had caricatured Plato's mentor, Socrates, in several of his plays. Surprisingly, Plato allows Aristophanes to take the discussion in a more sophisticated direction. The comedian invokes an ancient allegory in order to illustrate truths about love. At an early point in our existence, human beings were colossal creatures. We each had four legs, four arms, two heads, with double the strength and intelligence we now embody. Unfortunately, we were also arrogant and our hubris upset Zeus. To once and forever put us in our place, Zeus severed us in half, which produced the relatively feeble creatures we now are. As a result, each of us is now searching for our missing half. For Aristophanes, the point of the allegory is that love is the pursuit of completeness. Instead of following the understandings of the prior speakers, the comedian moves away from instrumental views of love to the presumed nature of love, its animating obsession for wholeness (189c-193e).

However, the major problem in this account is evident: Our search is ill-fated. If we are literally searching for the other half that will make us whole then our chances of success are, in a practical sense, zero. To form literally two hearts beating as one is impossible. However zealously we pursue love in the name of attaining unity, we must remain separate. For Aristophanes, love is an exercise in self-transformation, but one doomed to failure. Love is an admission of profound vulnerability, but its results cannot match its aspirations.

Aristophanes points us the way to derive a host of modern lessons about love. First, genuine, worthy love is a paradox—it aspires to completeness but cannot attain it. Second, the pursuit of love is both a necessary and frustrating human endeavor. Third, the quest for perfection of the human spirit is impossible; at best, we can hope only to amplify satisfactorily our identities and mollify the more terrifying aspects of the human condition. Fourth, pursuing love both exposes and exacerbates our vulnerability. Fifth, instead of completeness, in pursuing love we might well seek (in my terminology) an enhanced sense of community: in love we enhance self-discovery, find in others a way to expand our subjectivities, and, if we are fortunate, forge connections with another person whom we come to regard as unique and irreplaceable. Aristophanes understands keenly that the pursuit of love has its source in a need and lack that can never be fulfilled once and forever. Yet, it is in the pursuit of love that we manifest what is most human about us.

Contrary to the aspirations of the casket test, Portia and Bassanio must understand that their union cannot be a fixed serenity or final completion. Their love is an ongoing negotiation of spirit, body, and mind that must not be taken for granted.

The poet, Agathon, fresh off a stirring victory in a verse competition, is the next speaker. The beloved of Pausanias and a student of the sophist, Gorgias, Agathon praises the qualities of the god, Eros. Coincidentally, all of the attributes that Agathon extols are traits that he is convinced he embodies: youth, fluidity, beauty, delicacy, and utter magnetism. As always, Plato is suspicious of poets whom he regards as mere imitators of an inferior reality. Agathon's apparent encomium to Eros is in fact a narcissistic ode to himself. He also praises the deeds of Eros: moderate and fair dealing, courageous and wise actions. So beautiful is Eros that he bestows attractiveness and goodness upon others (194e-197e).

The message is unsubtle: the other aristocrats at the symposium are elevated simply by basking in Agathon's presence. By exalting fixed attributes, Agathon suggests that love seeks final serenity—a perfected individual who is self-sufficient. As such, Agathon's speech is a step backward in our progression of understanding. Instead of recognizing that love begins in lack and in need, Agathon imagines that the triumph of love is in self-sufficiency. Do the best among us love only ourselves? Can love really attain a set of fixed, perfecting properties? Or is Agathon's soul deluded and arrogant? Agathon's soliloquy recalls the exaggerated self-regard exemplified by Portia's failed suitor, Arragon. Bassanio, too, must guard against the allure of his own intoxicating rhetoric and self-image.

Socrates then offers an exquisite mystical vision of love that he claims to have learned from the priestess, Diotima. Contra Agathon, love is not a fixed, glorious state or a static condition. Love demands ongoing change and adaptation; it is a process. Love is a desire; we desire that which we do not have or that which we have insufficiently; if love is the desire for beauty then love cannot be beauty. Indeed, love is a process by which we reveal and get closer to our deepest yearnings. We begin by recognizing and appreciating the beauty of a particular object or person in the world. This instance of physical beauty allows us to abstract and recognize all physical beauty; it permits us to go beyond the particular to the general. We then come to recognize and appreciate the beauty of the soul and spiritual beauty in general. We continue by recognizing the beauty of just laws, social institutions, and salutary customs and activities. We rise to the appreciation of the beauty of math, science, and knowledge in general. Finally, we may glimpse the most profound source of our yearning: a vision of Absolute Beauty, the Form of Beauty, Beauty as such (199c-212c).

As we climb Socrates's ladder of love—which is a journey toward higher degrees of reality, truth, and knowledge—we travel from the derivative reality of immediate experience to the foundational Reality in a timeless realm. Socrates assumes that if we love an object or person we do so for a reason and it is that reason that is the deepest object of our love. If I love Marcia because she is beautiful and good, then Beauty and Goodness are the true objects of my love, not any particular instance of beauty and goodness. Accordingly, loving particular people and things in the world directs me to the most fundamental source of my yearning: to attain my destiny in the eternal world of Forms. That is, genuine human fulfillment is impossible in this world; only in a disembodied condition can the human soul reunite with Absolute Truth, Absolute Beauty, and Absolute Goodness. The actual beloved in an intimate relationship is Truth, Beauty, and Goodness as such. Socrates unravels the paradox of love so brilliantly articulated by Aristophanes—that our deepest desires in pursuing love are never completely fulfilled, however fervently we undertake the quest. Socrates answers that because our true desire is for reunification with Forms in a transcendent realm, any earthly love will point us in that direction, but fall short of fulfilling our most profound aim. Hence, we will simultaneously be elevated yet be somewhat unfulfilled by even the most genuine earthly loves. We will always yearn for more.

Under the Socrates-Diotima rendering, love is a process through which we express and strive mightily to fulfill our longing for eternity and the divine. The pursuit of love by human beings is as inevitable as it is disappointing.

Socrates does not appear to be advising us to dismiss interpersonal love in deference to the philosophical love of Forms that he sketches. Interpersonal love is instrumentally valuable to our quest for eternal fulfillment in the transcendental realm. But is that the only value of interpersonal love? To serve as an energizing marker for or signpost to what we truly desire? If so, Socrates, at best, can tell us *why* we love, but he does not help us understand *whom* to love. Surely, we might pursue the person whom we were convinced best exemplified the general attributes which we allegedly desire—the best embodiment of truth, beauty, and goodness. But that suggests that we might legitimately seek to "trade up." If Marcia is a grand exemplifier of truth, beauty, and goodness, but later I meet Linda who exhibits those traits even more gloriously, should I then seek Linda's love and cast Marcia aside? If this is a consequence of Socrates's position then he loses an indispensable aspect of salutary, interpersonal love—how the other person comes to be viewed as unique and irreplaceable even when we recognize that someone else possesses more excellences. In healthy loves we do not seek to trade up as a strategy for deeper fulfillment. On the other hand, Socrates might advise us that it is not necessary to identify and court the person we are convinced is the *best* exemplifier of the excellences for which we allegedly pine. If so, the problem of trading up evaporates. But, still, we seek guidance about whom we should love. Will *any* person whom we regard as somewhat beautiful, good, and true be suitable? Should the degree of beauty, goodness, and truth embodied by particular persons have any bearing on our selection?

My point is that Socrates's underlying assumptions—that the reason we love is the genuine object of our love; that we seek the purest form of that object; and that love is therefore of excellent properties and attributes—reduce interpersonal love to a passionate, intellectual exercise. Our passion in love is not really directed toward another concrete person, but, instead, is centered on philosophical abstractions that allegedly subsist in a transcendental realm accessible to us only after we die. For Socrates, the world of everyday experience is never enough and earthly loves are merely instrumentally valuable.

Portia seems more grounded in this world than is Bassanio. Among his numerous possibilities, Bassanio's romantic soul might be lured to the pursuit of abstract absolutes. To the extent that it is, Bassanio might be trading a deep interpersonal connection for a passionate, but impersonal, intellectual exercise.

In the Platonic dialogues in which Socrates is the main character, he always gets the last word; except in *The Symposium*. An uninvited guest, the notorious Alcibiades, staggers in off the street. Drunk and loud, he offers the final depiction of the nature of love. He begins by alternately praising and berating Socrates. Physically ugly and emotionally indifferent to Alcibiades's romantic overtures, Socrates is an enigma. Alcibiades credits Socrates as a brave soldier who could endure hardships uncommonly well. Having ignored bodily pleasures, Socrates was less likely to feel physical pain acutely. He had distanced himself from the bodily sensations in order to fulfill his spiritual mission of philosophical contemplation and purity of the soul. Yet, Alcibiades, who was desired by so many, remained obsessed with Socrates. As Alcibiades deepens his account and underscores his attraction to Socrates, an alternate understanding of the nature of love emerges (213e-223a).

On Alcibiades's account, love is not directed to abstract properties and perceived excellences taken to their highest forms. In Alcibiades's eyes, Socrates's view of love is inaccurate. Instead, love centers on particular, concrete people. Often irrational and even obsessive, love is a specific relationship, not simply a longing for the eternal. Never conducted properly at a distance, love requires a merger of identities. Aristophanes suggested that love is unstable; it both exposes and heightens our vulnerability. Socrates has rejected Alcibiades's romantic overtures. For Alcibiades, love is thoroughly temporal and it focuses on the uniqueness of the other person. Genuine love is not fungible—we cannot substitute one person's praiseworthy properties for another person's praiseworthy properties. Instead of pointing us toward the eternal and to a transcendental realm, love immerses us fully in the specific, non-duplicable characteristics of a particular person. Accordingly, that Linda embodies more beauty, goodness, and truth than does Marcia cannot imply that I should try to trade up. Linda cannot duplicate Marcia's unique way of expressing those excellences. Marcia's unique way of exemplifying quite common excellences is critical to our love. Furthermore, we have a relationship that defines a shared identity. Where that relationship is healthy, we lack incentive to sever our bonds and incur painful transition costs to our sense of self.

The dialogue ends unresolved. The two concluding theories of love compete for our souls. Socrates offers a philosophical love of abstraction linked to virtue and knowledge. His view resonates today with religious believers who understand earthly love as preparation for what we most deeply seek: reunification with God. Alcibiades suggests an utterly earth-bound love that centers on concrete, particular people—a love that is often irrational, even obsessive. Such love is self-sustaining and does not point beyond itself. Whereas the Socratic view speaks to our urges to go beyond ourselves, to transcend our humanness and climb toward the divine, the view of Alcibiades reminds us that, for better or worse, we are immersed completely in this world.

Is there a difference in *The Symposium* between what Socrates argues and what Plato believes? Might Plato be revealing his misgivings about the metaphysical structure of the Forms and the nature of the transcendental realm? Might Plato be using Alcibiades as his mouthpiece to call into question some of Plato's earlier philosophical commitments? The possibilities suggested by such questions are uncommonly interesting.

In another dialogue, *Phaedrus*, Plato uses Socrates to unveil a different notion of love.[2] In several of his dialogues, Plato celebrates reason, self-sufficiency, and the superior values of the intellect, while denigrating passion and poetry. Surprisingly, in the *Phaedrus*, Socrates delivers two speeches, the last of which describes philosophy informed by passion and personal love. Certain kinds of passion are depicted as necessary for deep insight and the development of salutary character. Most important, intimate human relationships are critical to the good life. The most profound philosophy requires poetry and passion. Passions that are inspired by the gods, in contrast to those arising from mental defect or uncontrolled desire, bestow the gifts of prophecy, poetry and love. Now the self-sufficient and self-possessed person is perceived as embodying a narrow, deficient soul. The passions motivate robust action and the quest for the good; they respond to beauty and enhance understanding; and they inspire glorious self-transformation. In this dialogue, to love another person is not merely to seek a means to scale Diotima's ladder of love. Instead, to love another concrete individual is to be intoxicated with that person's character, and with mutual memories and shared aspirations. Here love is more than preoccupation with perceived excellences that the other person may well lose in the future. Passion fuels appreciation of the other for the person's own sake, not simply as a means to the world of Absolutes. In the *Symposium*, we were left with a choice of understanding love as either Alcibiades's obsessive, unexplainable madness for another person or Socrates-Diotima's portrayal of earthly love as an instrument for the soul's intellectual ascension to direct apprehension of the highest Good. In the *Phaedrus*, we are presented a fuller alternative: a vision of mature love that elevates both parties, that is defined by passion, and that focuses on relationships between concrete individuals that are valued for their own sake. Here lies the greatest hope for the marital union of Portia and Bassanio.

In any event, *The Symposium* and *Phaedrus* challenge us to test the vitality of our own souls by assessing what and whom we love. To begin that exercise, let us examine the main characters in *The Merchant of Venice*, evaluate the things they love, and describe what that tells us about the condition of their souls.

3. Love, and the Condition of Souls

The Merchant of Venice constructs obstacles to romantic love such as the casket test devised by Portia's father and Shylock's resistance to the relationship of Jessica and Lorenzo. Earthly love is analogized to divine grace. Human salvation depends on embodying the theological virtues of faith, hope, and charity, as well as opening one's soul to saving grace. So, too, earthly fulfillment depends on intimate relationships that welcome mutual risk, vulnerability, and sacrifice.

What does Shylock love? He seems to love wealth, but is that because circumstances dictate that the accumulation of material resources is his only path to a measure of security and a dose of external validation? He loves his daughter, but he loses her largely because patriarchal control is the manner in which he awkwardly expresses that affection. Jessica is another valuable piece of property under Shylock's domain. He seems to have loved his wife, Leah, or at least his memories of her. Unlike the Christian husbands, he values the ring she gave him and what it represents. Shylock apparently loves his friends, Tubal and Chus, and his religion; yet at the final reckoning he discards his principles as easily as yesterday's trash and converts to Christianity to save his life.

The things and people whom Shylock loves and the manner in which he loves them tells us that Shylock's soul is utterly confused. He is struggling mightily to establish a coherent personal identity in a hostile social environment. What he most cherishes is equality. He places his faith in the law because its underlying virtues uphold human equality even in the face of personal animus. Or at least so Shylock thought. Instead of seeking personal vengeance against Antonio or his other Christian tormentors, he seeks social validation of his equality under law. If the law grants his judgment then Shylock's cause and by extension Shylock's equality are ratified. Lawless, personal vengeance lacks social ratification. Vengeance could render Shylock an outlet for his malice, but could never bestow the social imprimatur he craves. In the end, Shylock is loveless: much of his wealth has been placed in a trust under the control of Antonio; his right to control what happens to his material resources at his death has been usurped; he can no longer operate his usury business; he has converted to Christianity, which strips him of his identity as a Jew; and the law has explicitly rejected his assertions of equality—instead, he is an alien. Granted, *The Merchant of Venice* is a fairy tale and moral parable, but do we have any basis to believe that Shylock will be warmly received within the Christian community, flourish as a true believer, and live happily ever after? Unless Shylock discovers new things and people to love, or unless he reconnects to Jessica and forges new bonds with Lorenzo—on a basis other than having been forced to make Lorenzo beneficiary of the trust and Jessica and Lorenzo his legal heirs—Shylock will remain loveless and his soul, once confused, will remain empty.

Antonio loves Bassanio specifically and he craves a deeper sense of community generally. On my reading, Antonio's homosexual love must remain unrequited by the heterosexual Bassanio. Antonio's pervasive melancholy arises from his understanding of that fact and his dissatisfaction with the commercial community of Venice. Other merchants and traders appreciate Antonio, they prize his company, and he apparently flourishes in the atmosphere of superficial banter and facile camaraderie. But Antonio yearns for more. His soul longs for deeper intimacy and enduring bonds. Antonio's soul is frustrated in Venice. When Shylock calls for the forfeiture under the terms of his bond, dozens of prominent, well-meaning citizens of Venice rise to Antonio's cause (or in outrage as to Shylock's design). Antonio, however, never pleads on his own behalf. At times, he instructs the others to stop wasting their time trying to transform Shylock's obdurate heart; in that vein, he advises the court to simply render a judgment for Shylock and be done with the dog-and-pony show; and he confesses to the bond immediately, never advancing feeble excuses or invoking extenuating circumstances. Unlike the others in the play, Antonio was willing to "give and hazard all he hath" to benefit his beloved Bassanio. Antonio risked his life and was willing to consummate the sacrifice right up to the point when Balthasar-Portia pulled the plug on Shylock by invoking legal legerdemain and obscure statutes. Antonio wanted only to die for what he took to be a glorious cause—his love of Bassanio—and to be remembered thereby as the consummate lover. Even at the end, Antonio is once again willing to stand surety—pledging his very soul as collateral—for Bassano's vow to never again break his oaths to Portia.

Although, prior to his forfeiture of his bond with Shylock, Antonio was a success when judged by the conventional standards of Venice, his soul was trapped by and unfulfilled in that city. His sense of "otherness" in Venice—grounded in that city's inadequate understanding of intimacy and community—is less explicit than that endured by Shylock but no less devastating in its effects. It is Antonio who most closely exemplifies the slogan of the lead casket and who bestows unconditional love. Antonio has a Belmont-soul that resides in a contractually-driven Venice community.

At the end of the play, Antonio is sometimes described as the odd man out. Portia and Bassanio have each other, presumably enjoying sounder contractual bonds and deeper mutual affections than they had forged earlier. Likewise, Nerissa and Gratiano have each other, now on a firmer basis. Meanwhile, Jessica and Lorenzo have a more promising future grounded in the trust and their status as Shylock's legal heirs. And Antonio tags behind with only the solace that his ships have miraculously and lucratively returned from the sea. But should Antonio liquidate his assets in Venice and return permanently to Belmont might he not attain the intimate community his soul craves? Might he not discover and create a salutary love that is requited? Might he not reimagine and re-create himself, and thereby transcend the pervasive melancholy that has afflicted him? We can only hope.

Bassanio loves sensuality, beauty, and pleasure. He seems to be, for better and worse, an irredeemable romantic. Bassanio loves the idea of being in love, curries the affections of those nearest to him at the moment, and genuinely means what he says when he says it—even if it contradicts what he said at an earlier time. At first blush, Bassanio strikes us as all form and little substance. As a man of mere appearances, he was able to pierce through the appearances of the casket test. Bassanio embodies a hedonistic soul. Yet, we must assume that there is more to Bassanio than first strikes the eye. After all, Portia loves him and she is the most intelligent, perceptive character in the play.

The existential philosopher Søren Kierkegaard sketched three life stages, processes by which we make choices, act, and define ourselves.[3] Kierkegaard's first stage, the aesthetic, fits Bassanio more crisply than does one of Bassanio's custom-tailored paeans to love. The person in the aesthetic stage basks in the immediacy of the moment. The pursuit of sensations and feelings rooted in particular pleasures define this stage of life. Detached from firm commitment to the extent possible, governed by sense, impulse, and emotion, Kierkegaard's aesthetic person recognizes no fixed, universal moral standards. Instead, the aesthetic person strives for the absence of all limits, except those imposed by his or her own taste. Boredom is taken to be the worst evil. Immersing themselves in pleasure, whether sensual or intellectual, aesthetic people live overwhelmingly for the moment, in search of yet another self-gratifying experience.

When we met Bassanio he stands as a glowing exemplar of Søren Kierkegaard's aesthetic stage of human development. Driven by the craving for pleasure and beauty, he lives in the present and seeks increasingly intense stimulation. Bassanio fears boredom, the mundane, and the commonplace. Sensuality drives his spiritual engine. As such, he appears to be the worst possible candidate for enduring commitment. He has squandered his money, permitted Antonio to pledge his flesh as surety for a loan, and seeks marriage with Portia at least in part for financial security.

For Kierkegaard, aesthetic people, such as Bassanio, cravenly flee from boredom, despair, and the burden of self-creation. Continually pursuing more intense pleasures, the aesthetic person is doomed to collapse back into boredom and despair. Living in the present can, at best, provide only a partial attitude toward life. By never forging bonds, by weakly committing to projects, and by making only transitory choices, the aesthetic person is a spectator of the world and fails to define his own life sharply. His chosen end is his own beginning: vague dissatisfaction, a sense of no remedy, no salvation, a foreboding of nothingness. Kierkegaard insists that the aesthetic person's choices are either to remain in despair at this stage or to make a transition to the next stage—the ethical—by choice and self-commitment. The ethical stage, among other things, involves embracing universal moral standards and is exemplified by congenial family life.

The critical question is whether Bassanio can transcend to Kierkegaard's ethical stage of human development. Can Bassanio embrace universal moral prescriptions, forge enduring relationships, and realize fulfillment in family life? Portia is betting that he can. Bassanio passed the casket test (with Portia's help?) and one of the premises of that exercise was that the man who did so would thereby reveal both the correct understanding of love and his capability of loving. Presumably, Bassanio understands that love is grounded in heightened mutual vulnerability, willing sacrifice, and emotional risk. Apparently he can exemplify those qualities and enact the requisite deeds. Yet, despite his consistent flowery rhetoric—Bassanio always knows how to please with words—he badly failed the ring test. After pledging to retain for all time and at all costs the ring that Portia bestowed upon him, Bassanio relinquished it to a judge he barely knew after being urged on by Antonio.

Yes, Portia perceives accurately Bassanio's ideal possibilities; she sees that he has the potential to transcend to Kierkegaard's ethical stage. But nothing guarantees that he will. As a capable teacher, Portia should be able to lead him in the right direction. Indeed, after the trial and upon their return to Belmont, she gives Bassanio a stern lesson in the fidelity of vows and oaths. Portia also makes explicit some contractual terms in their marriage: should Bassanio renege on any future pledges, Portia will be released from her marital obligations. Bassanio will get what he deserves. Despite her occasional boilerplate utterance of submitting to her lord, no careful reader of the play can reasonably conclude that Portia will embrace the role of obedient wife. Clever, manipulative, and often deceptive, Portia will run emotional circles around Bassanio. She will use his compulsion to please those around him to her advantage. Portia may well be able to lead Bassanio to Kierkegaard's ethical stage and achieve the blissful union to which she aspires.

But love offers no guarantees. As a connoisseur of the aesthetic, Bassanio perceives the beauty in intelligence, in moral virtue, and in other human excellences. In part, he is drawn to Portia for that very reason. Bassanio has a poetic-philosophical soul. (Despite Socratic-Platonic rants to the contrary, poets and philosophers exude many similarities.) Just as he potentially can transcend to Kierkegaard's ethical stage of development, he also can potentially descend into Agathon's narcissistic delusion. More strikingly, Bassanio can potentially ascend the Socratic-Diotima ladder of love in search of the divine. Bassanio's soul can turn toward its animating impulse: Absolute Beauty. If so individual exemplifiers of excellences on earth, such as Portia, will embody instrumental value for Bassanio's genuine quest: union with Absolute Beauty in a transcendental realm. The natural or supernatural consequence of Bassanio's infatuation with the aesthetic is the search for Beauty as such. This, too, is one of Bassano's idealized possibilities.

Our original question deepens. Which is more likely to be Bassanio's end: sinking into Agathon's sterile self-sufficiency or attaining serenity with Portia in Kierkegaard's ethical stage of development, or transcending passionately to a Socratic commitment to the contemplative and spiritual life? If Bassanio takes the latter course then Portia's importance fades to the merely instrumental, a diminishment that she is not likely to welcome. From the available evidence, I must conclude that Bassanio is least likely to climb the ladder of love. While he has the requisite passion, deep aesthetic appreciation, and the magnanimity of soul to begin the ascent, he lacks profound philosophical insight. Without keen cognitive awareness, even if he begins the climb he is likely to fall off the ladder. Also, Bassanio is unlikely to descend into Agathonian narcissism: he is never genuinely self-sufficient; he needs an audience to appreciate his gifts; and his soul more expansive than that of Agathon. In all probability, Portia will abide. Still, there are no guarantees and Portia's workload will be heavy.

What of Portia's soul? She loves Bassanio, in large measure because she perceives his idealized possibilities. She, too, is a sensualist and an aesthetic. But she is well- prepared for Kierkegaard's ethical stage of development. Although she is acutely intelligent she has no inclination to ascend the Socratic-Diotima ladder of love. Portia is more in tune with Alcibiades's understanding: love is of a concrete, particular person whose qualities, ways of exemplifying those qualities, and idealized qualities are unique and irreplaceable. She loves Bassanio in all of his particularity; no substitutes will do. However, Portia knows better than to think that love is *only* heightened mutual vulnerability, willing sacrifice, and emotional risk. Love is also an enduring relationship that involves mutuality and reciprocity. In part, love is contractual. You can take the lovers out of Venice, but you cannot completely remove Venice from the lovers. In their relationship, Portia and Bassanio will extend their metaphysical boundaries. But mutual agreements—codified in vows, oaths, and pledges—remain critical to that relationship. We hope mightily that Bassanio now understands all of this and remains true to his marital faith. We shudder as we imagine to what Portia will reduce him should he forget.

4. Human-All-Too-Human

In the 1950s, westerns pervaded television. Invariably, a squeaky-clean paragon —such as Roy Rogers, Gene Autry, The Lone Ranger, The Cisco Kid, Rex Allen, or Hopalong Cassidy— battled irredeemably sinister characters with appropriate identifying monikers such as Black Bart, Dead Beat Dick, or the Dastardly Daltons. Just in case viewers were too dim-witted to distinguish the heroes from the villains, the former typically wore white hats while the latter donned black hats. The color of the hats signified metaphorical truth: the plots of these shows lacked moral ambiguity; everything was black or white, no shades of gray or ethical complexity intruded on the message.

Of course, life is rarely packaged so tidily. Unlike the stars of early television, the major characters of *The Merchant of Venice* exude many shades of moral color and are not easily categorized. Antonio knows how to love and craves for more than the conventional success defined by Venetian commercialism. Although his love is unrequited, he is willing "to give and hazard all he hath" in service to his affection. Antonio is generous to his fellow Venetian traders and gracious to foreign businessmen. As a result, he is held in high esteem and enjoys a splendid reputation. But Antonio is a poor candidate to wear the white hat of moral purity. He is also gratuitously and relentlessly abusive to aliens within the Venetian community. Antonio routinely physically and verbally abuses Shylock for no other reason than he is a Jew, a designated outsider living within Antonio's geographical community. Even after Shylock brings Antonio's abuse to his attention and extends an interest-free loan to him and Bassanio, Antonio's heart is unmoved: he assures Shylock that he will continue to spit on him and verbally assail him in the future. At the end of the trial, Antonio's "mercy" consists of his making himself the administrator of one-half of Shylock's wealth, usurping Shylock's right to name his own legal heirs, and compelling Shylock's conversion to Christianity. Can we reasonably imagine that thereafter Antonio will embrace Shylock as a full-fledged member of his community?

Antonio's communitarian leanings have a dark underside: he is intolerant of aliens living within his geographical boundaries. Foreigners pose no threat; they are by definition outsiders and can be treated civilly under the etiquette of arm's-length contractual bargaining. Venetian Christian traders are kinsmen by both blood and religion; they can be treated warmly under the facile conviviality of Venetian societal mores. Even though Antonio finds those social codes fulfill his emotional needs inadequately, less passionate souls in Venice are grateful to interact with those who are convivial but not intimate. However, aliens residing within the Venetian community jeopardize Antonio's sense of order. They are quasi-citizens in that they live within the city's boundaries, but they are not kinsmen by either blood or religion. They thereby threaten the identity of Antonio's community. A communitarian soul, such as Antonio's, should resist the urge to marginalize as unworthy those who are geographically included but emotionally excluded from membership. Civility, mutual respect, and equal rights under law can mark the dealings of community members and alien residents. However, instead of resisting the urge to marginalize resident aliens as unworthy, Antonio unrepentantly goes out of his way to underscore difference and to attack those whom he regards as inferiors because of birth or religion. His is the communitarian soul run off the rail of genuine intimacy and expansive caring. Sadly, Antonio's community must stigmatize outsiders as a way to partially define and energize itself.

Furthermore, Antonio's unrequited love of Bassanio lures him into ungracious scenes involving Portia. For example, when he is convinced that Shylock will have his forfeiture under the bond, he melodramatically instructs Bassanio to "Commend me to your honourable wife:/Tell her the process of Antonio's end; /Say how I love'd you, speak me fair in death; /And, when the tale is told, bid her be judge/Whether Bassanio had not once a love" (4.1.273-277). This leads Bassanio, predictably armed with florid rhetoric designed to please the audience at hand, to declare that Antonio's life is of such high esteem that Bassanio would sacrifice his own life, his wife's life, and the entire world to save Antonio. Also, recall that it is Antonio who convinces Bassanio to part with his ring. He convinces Bassanio by inviting him to weigh the judge's "deservings" and Antonio's love against the importance of Portia's "commandement" (4.1.451-452). Undoubtedly, Antonio senses a competition with Portia for Bassanio's deepest affections and his zeal for victory sometimes manifests itself unworthily. Antonio is best suited for a gray fedora.

Shylock is malicious, vengeful, and rabidly materialistic. He runs his household tyrannically. Shylock lodges claims on the suspicious bases of his desires and deserts. In one sense, uncharitable readers may conclude that in the end he gets precisely what he deserves: judgment grounded in decoding the words of legal statutes and bright-line application of the results. In fact, perhaps he gets better than he deserves as Antonio's sentence spares his life. Shylock seems a suitable candidate for a black hat. But, surely, such a conclusion is hasty and incomplete. Shylock has been repeatedly abused without cause; he has been relegated to a third-rate existence in Venice; and he is scorned for practicing one of the few career paths open to him. True, as existentialists would insist on reminding us, he bears responsibility for the person he is becoming. To simply cast all responsibility upon his tormentors would be existentially inauthentic. But Shylock's craving for equality exudes nobility. He places his faith in the law, the most powerful instrument of social control. Shylock reasons: where there is law, there is equality; where there is equality, there is justice.

The Merchant of Venice is not merely or fundamentally a tale of the Old Testament ethic (Shylock's version of *lex talionis*) versus the New Testament ethic (Christian mercifulness mirroring the Sermon on the Mount). It is not merely or fundamentally a tale of Antonio exemplifying a latter day Christ in redeeming Bassanio from his profligate sins. More important, the play is a parable about the devastating effects of social inequality. Shylock, no less so than does Antonio, yearns for salutary community. Shylock, much more so than does Antonio, longs for social equality. His rigidity and inflexibility mask an utterly confused soul. Shylock is convinced that equality can be purchased only through mechanical jurisprudence that will delete bias and prejudice against minority groups.

Antonio and Shylock share another concern: the desire to control their posthumous fate to the extent possible; to help shape their legacy. Antonio aspires to do this through Bassanio, both by leaving a surviving beloved in whose heart Antonio will continue to resonant and by assigning Bassano the role of his eulogizer and biographer. Antonio, along with Portia's father, explicitly understands that although a person's biological life ends his biographical life typically continues.[4] Shylock, too, intuits this. When Jessica runs off with Lorenzo and converts to Christianity, Shylock is acutely aware that his flesh and blood, a constitutive of his personal identity, has abandoned him. As such, his living legacy has evaporated. At trial's end, when Antonio "mercifully" usurps Shylock's right to dispose of his goods at death, Antonio has driven another stake into Shylock's desire to shape this legacy and to control his posthumous fate to some extent. We can also reasonably construe this as the childless Antonio's attempt to replace Shylock as Jessica's (and Lorenzo's) father. Finally, Antonio's role in Shylock's conversion to Christianity under duress not only destroys Shylock's business practices but also eviscerates Shylock's sense of personal identity. Shylock's recurrent refrain at trial, "I'll have my bond" (4.1.37, 87, 207, 242) suggests not merely his contractual arrangements with Antonio, but his hereditary bond with Jessica, his own treasured personal identity, and his connection to equality before the law. By the end of the trial, Shylock has lost or failed to establish or regain all of these bonds.

Shylock's call for simple decoding of statutory language and bright-line application of the results arises from his understanding that judicial interpretation on any other grounds will discriminate against aliens such as himself; thus, his naïve identification of law, equality, and justice. Shylock's personal rigidity, inflexibility, and black-and-white understanding of the world flow from his passionate yearning for social equality. Once Shylock's world view is thunderously and permanently shaken—as Balthasar-Portia's legal magic demonstrates resplendently that no theory of judicial decision making can immunize minority groups from bias—his confusion surfaces. Balthasar-Portia has seemingly used Shylock's mechanical jurisprudence against him. His belief in the connection between law, equality, and justice having been destroyed, Shylock is broken. His aspiration for social equality crushed, he even resigns himself to conversion to Christianity under duress. Without his underlying quest for equality, Shylock is reduced to nothing. How can such a pathetic man be fitted for the black hat of moral reprobates?

Bassanio knows what to do but often fails to do it. He exemplifies Portia's caution that "If to do were as easy as to know what were good to do, chapels had been churches and poor men's cottages princes' palaces" (1.2.13-15). His shortcomings arise from weakness of will and an inordinate inclination to please his immediate audience. Bassanio is never explicitly venal. Even in his descriptions of and approach to Shylock he is less strident than are his crony Gratiano and his dear friend Antonio. His poetic-philosophical soul yearns to see beauty and experience pleasure. Despite his loose ways with money and women (prior to his marriage to Portia), Bassanio is well-received on the Rialto. If anyone is an expert in facile conviviality it must be Bassanio. Venice's breezy collegiality is suited for Bassanio's personality: long on flowery rhetoric, short on selfless acts. Accordingly, uncharitable interpreters are tempted to conclude that Bassanio is all show and little substance.

However, Bassanio is more complicated than he first appears. His is the journey from Kierkegaard's aesthetic stage hedonism to Kierkegaard's ethical stage universalism. Possessing only modest intellectual gifts, Bassanio embodies an expansive soul with great potential. Recall that he passed the casket test with flying colors; the man of appearance was not deceived by appearances. Embracing the premise of the test, we must conclude that Bassanio not only *knows* how to love but that he *will* love in accordance with the slogan of the lead casket. But was he not aided by Portia? Could he have passed the test if left only to his own devices? My reading is that Portia's subtle aid was necessary for Bassanio's success. Although he was inclined to choose the lead casket, he would have remained in a quandary but for Portia's push over the top. Bassanio is the soul of great but-as-of-yet-unrealized potential. He needs an able teacher, a skilled Socratic midwife, to help extract the higher good that lies within him. Bassanio needs Portia's continued teaching in this decidedly Socratic sense: he does not need a teacher who imparts wisdom or fills his empty soul with truths; he needs a midwife who can facilitate his coming to know what already resides within him.

Accordingly, Portia did not straightaway give Bassanio the correct answer to the casket test. Instead, she helped make explicit what was already implicit within Bassanio's soul. Likewise, in order for Bassanio to fully realize his idealized possibilities he will require Portia's continued midwifery talents. Portia's skills in that vein are apparent during the post-trial scene in Belmont wherein she makes Bassanio come to understand the full significance of relinquishing his ring, the enduring contractual elements in marital vows, and the paramount importance of keeping faith with sacred oaths.

Again, no guarantees underwrite love and marriage. Bassanio could relapse into Agathonian narcissism; he might transcend wildly into Socratic-Diotima mysticism; or he may continue to wallow in Kierkegaard's aesthetic stage. But under Portia's clever midwifery, he has a strong possibility of rising to Kierkegaard's ethical stage and enjoying marital bliss. We can only hope that Portia's influence is self-consciously understood as Socratic midwifery and not as her creation of a new Bassanio from her own design. A more domineering approach—say, one of creator to product—will result in Bassanio relapsing into one of the three less productive images of love cited above.

Portia begins from well-recognized excellences: intelligence, virtue, and beauty. She emerges as a feminist heroine: outsmarting the men at their own games, subterfuges, and conspiracies. Laboring under patriarchal oppression, she manages to impose her will at all critical junctures and control all crucial action.

Still, she falls short as a candidate for the white hat of moral purity. Portia is racially-biased against Morocco. She tells Nerissa, "if he have the condition of a saint and the complexion of a devil, I had rather he should shrive me [act as my confessor] than wive me" (1.2.142-144). After Morocco flunks the casket test, Portia sighs, "A gentle riddance. Draw the curtains, go. /Let all of his complexion choose me so" (2.7.78-79). Also, her assessments of her other suitors are unnecessarily harsh. She would rather "be married to a death's head with a bone in his mouth than to either" (1.2.54-56) the County Palatine or the Neapolitan prince. Her kindest remark about the French lord is that "God made him, and therefore let him pass for a man" (1.2.60-61). The young baron of England fares no better: "who can converse with a dumb-show?" (1.2.77-78). The German nephew of the Duke of Saxony rates even lower: "when he is best, he is worse than a man, and when he is worst, he is little better than a beast" (1.2.94-95). When evaluating her potential suitors Portia might well consult her own recommendations about the quality of mercy.

Also, despite her beautiful paean to the qualities of mercy, Portia better exemplifies her own admonishment that knowing the good is easier than doing the good. She is anything but merciful to Shylock. She knows that she "has him upon the hip" and she shrewdly manipulates the situation. First, she lures him into thinking that his mechanical jurisprudence will produce a judgment in his favor. Accordingly, Shylock rejects all judicially-crafted settlement offers. Second, she uses mechanical jurisprudence against Shylock and informs him that should he shed even one drop of Antonio's blood or extract even a fraction of an ounce more or less than one pound of Antonio's flesh, Venice will confiscate all of his wealth and execute him. When Shylock is too stupefied to question Portia's interpretation and thus offers to settle the case, Portia insists that it is too late: that door has closed. Finally, Portia pulls the Alien Statute out of her hat and informs Shylock that he is already subject to execution for contriving to murder a Venetian citizen. She warmly embraces, as do Antonio and all other noble Venetian citizens, the Alien Statute, which is substantively discriminatory, overly broad, often imposes a disproportionate penalty, and is procedurally flawed in that it is invoked without appropriate notice. At this point, the "tender mercies" of the Duke of Venice and Antonio seal the deal against Shylock.

In general, Portia tends to dominate situations with a velvet glove. She first entraps Bassanio into ceding his ring; she then uses the occasion as a teaching exercise. She accepts the premise of the casket test as understood by her father, but then aids Bassanio during his exam. At the end of the play, Portia faces her own test: Will she be content to operate as a midwife and nurture the birth of Bassanio's higher potentials? Or will she become impatient and assume a more dominant role, acting as creator and molder of Bassanio's reimagined soul? Upon this decision will rest the success of their love and marriage.

The major characters of *The Merchant of Venice* are not plausible candidates for either white or black hats: they are neither morally pure nor morally despicable. Instead, they are psychologically and morally complex, and thereby reflect the human condition more genuinely than the television westerns of my youth. Commentators throughout history have spilled much ink describing the "Christian hypocrisy" depicted in the play. I have followed that path to some extent. But we should be cautious about brandishing the charge of "hypocrisy." Much like repeated use of multiple exclamation points in comic books, indicting characters by calling them hypocrites can quickly lose its intended effect. Portia has instructed us that, contra Socrates's view, it is much easier to know the good than to do the good. If "hypocrisy" is the response every time a person fails to live up to his or her ideals then we are all hypocrites. If we are all hypocrites then stigmatizing a particular person as a "hypocrite" is utterly banal. Perhaps we could elude the charge only by ratcheting down the aspirations of our ideals. Such a strategy, however, would diminish our lives. A better approach is to reserve the charge of hypocrisy for those who consistently and systematically fail to fulfill their ideals, for those who on balance are more likely than not to betray their most deeply-held principles. In this way, we can retain a vibrant sense of the indictment that a particular person is a hypocrite and remain true to the reality that we are all morally fallible and flawed.

Today, we would say that the Christians are in denial: they do not perceive their own shortcomings or recognize their numerous failures to live up to their professed ideals. Thus, Bassanio tells Gratiano that, "Thou art too wild, too rude and bold of voice; / Parts that become thee happily enough/And in such eyes as ours appear not faults" (2.2.189-192). The recent convert to Christianity, Jessica informs Lorenzo, "But love is blind and lovers cannot see/The pretty follies that themselves commit" (2.6.36-37). Christian commitment is especially lacking: Bassanio, encouraged by Antonio, and Gratiano quite easily renege on their vows to their wives to cherish their rings; assurances, oaths, and promise flow readily but compliance is problematic. Christian charity fares even worse: Antonio is gratuitously abusive to Shylock; Portia is stunningly ungenerous to her suitors; at trial, the Venetian citizens, especially Gratiano, taunt Shylock once Balthasar- Portia snares him in her legal trap; in the end, Shylock is deprived of his livelihood, his right to control much of his wealth, his right to name his heirs, and even his identity. Christian Venice requires moneylenders such a Shylock to advance its commercial interests, yet relegates them to low social status, and applies discriminatory criminal laws against them when expedient. Worse, Venice warmly embraces the institution of slavery.

Are the main characters in the play hypocrites on my understanding of the term? While they all fail at times to live up to their most cherished ideals, I would prefer to follow their lives for a longer period of time before indicting them on that charge in the court of morality.

5. Summary of Philosophical Lessons

The Merchant of Venice explores natural, biological bonds, such as the flesh-and-blood bonds of Shylock and Jessica, and Portia and her dead father; conventional bonds that define social position, such as those between citizens and resident aliens in Venice; commercial contractual bonds that are voluntarily crafted, such as those between Shylock and Antonio; bonds of friendship, such as those between Antonio and Bassanio, and Shylock and Tubal; and marital contractual bonds, such as those between Portia and Bassanio, Nerissa and Gratiano, and Jessica and Lorenzo. Understood as a parable and as folklore, *The Merchant of Venice* embodies a host of philosophical lessons.

A. Beware of Claims Lodged in the Name of Desire and Desert

That claims grounded in desire are suspicious is not newsworthy. We must distinguish worthy from unworthy desires; not all of our desires ought to be pursued. Even among our worthy desires, we must take into account intensity. We want some things much more than we want other things. Even if our weaker desires are fulfilled we will be unsatisfied if some of our stronger desires remain unfulfilled. In that vein, we must distinguish between needs and wants. The way in which our desires are fulfilled is paramount: if our desires are satisfied through simulated instead of real accomplishments, a worthwhile happiness cannot result. Finally, even if all and only our worthy desires are satisfied we will be unhappy. Our life would be inhuman. We would have nothing further toward which to strive, no unsatisfied projects to address, no future toward which to aspire. We would be only a saturated sponge of desire. Unless we could quickly devise new desires, boredom and anomie would result. Part of the human condition is ongoing striving that animates our energies, enthusiasms, and zest for the future.

Accordingly, claims lodged in desire are problematic for a host of reasons. First, that I want something falls far short of implying that I should receive that something. Second, I may confuse worthy and unworthy desires. Third, even if I lodge claims based only on worthy desires it may not serve my overall interests to fulfill those desires. Fourth, fulfilling my worthy desires in appropriate ways is more important to my well-being than is satisfying those desires as such. The process of fulfillment is critically linked to my self-development.

The notion of personal desert is more complicated. Virtually every time a character in the play appeals to the notion of personal desert, a suspect conclusion follows. Shakespeare's message may well be that claims based on personal desert are typically overblown and arrogant. If we got what we truly deserve we would be radically dissatisfied. Shylock gets what he deserves, doesn't he? How did that turn out? Arragon spurned the desires of the masses as unworthy and placed his faith in receiving what he deserved. He was rewarded with the "portrait of a blinking idiot" (2.9.55). Antonio implores Bassanio to give Balthasar-Portia his ring partially because the judge deserved it for services rendered. Bassanio complies, betrays his vow to Portia, and trouble ensues. In addition, Shakespeare underscores that our personal merit—what we deserve— is insufficient for salvation; we need grace and God's mercy.

As explained earlier, the notion of personal desert is an inadequate basis for the distribution of social goods. Unraveling what we deserve based on our personal merit and distinguishing it from how much of what we accomplish is traceable to luck and our results in the genetic lottery is a daunting task. Even if we could do so, other principles of justice such as entitlement must be factored into the equation.

For example, a simple reading of Shylock may well conclude that he deserved precisely what he received: "justice" grounded in decoding of statutory language and mechanical application of the results. At first blush, Shylock is the architect of his own destruction; he receives what he desired and deserved. But if we ask a further question, "Why did Shylock have such desires and deservings?" the matter may be clouded. He is a victim of systematic oppression in Venice; he is often gratuitously abused by Antonio; he craves not lawless vengeance, but equality grounded in law. Shylock's socialization plays a major role in what he desires, what he desires molds what he thinks and does, and thus what he deserves. If we go more deeply into Shylock's motivations, and how and why they were formed, we may draw different conclusions about what he, all things considered, deserves.

My point is that the principle of desert is not everything, but it is something. That the principle of desert is insufficient for personal salvation; that arrogant people often think they deserve more than they genuinely do; that satisfying claims based on desert can sometimes ignore other principles of justice and nurture unwholesome results should not fool us into concluding that the principle of desert is an utter sham. Shakespeare overplays his hand a bit.

By stressing that human beings are morally fallible and flawed, Shakespeare can caution us about levying claims based on what we deserve. But our human condition, including our necessary moral imperfection, can be factored into what we deserve. That is, evaluating our personal merit should include the understanding that we must all fail the test of complete moral purity. The best of us can do only the best we can do given our natural constitution. A fair rendering of the principle of desert must include our inherent moral imperfection; we should not bear responsibility for what is beyond our control. Accordingly, despite its limitations, the principle of desert retains normative currency and should not be eliminated from our moral calculus.

B. Beware of Rigidity and Inflexibility

Shakespeare surely cautions against relying upon bright-line rules, inflexible judgments, and rigid codes of behavior. He revels in complexity and ambiguity. The reality of things often belies first appearances: "all that glitters is not gold" serves as a metaphor throughout the play. Furthermore, decoding statutory language and mechanically applying the results often offends our sense of justice and equality: the trial of Shylock amply illustrates the point. Human beings do not emerge from the womb with white or black hats, nor do they earn such chapeaus during their lives: I have sketched the moral complexity of the main characters above. Overly strict reliance on cherished principles will often be counterproductive: Shylock loves Jessica but his tyrannical rule leads her to run off with Lorenzo, pilfer part of her father's wealth, and convert to Christianity. Compassion for human weakness is recommended: Under the call for "mercy," the play advises us to both recognize the fact and empathize with the condition that we are human-all-too-human. In that vein, we will fail to live up to our most cherished ideals: we will break solemn vows, forge hypocritical deeds, and mean what we say when we say it only to soon betray it. In sum, reality cannot be captured accurately through rigid and inflexible interpretations. Our world is inherently imperfect and dotted with gray tones. *The Merchant of Venice* recalls the words of Aristotle: "Friendship unites the state. When men are friends, there is no need of justice, but even if men are just, friendship is still necessary. Friendship is not just necessary, but also noble."[5] Expand "friendship" to "love" and Aristotle's sentiments resound throughout the play.

C. To Know the Good is Easier Than to Do the Good

Plato famously uses Socrates to argue that virtue is knowledge: to know the good is to do the good. All evil-doing, then, flows from ignorance: miscreants wrongly believe that following the path of vice will benefit them. But, Socrates insists, the greatest human good is the cultivation of a healthy soul. Our souls are healthy when they are in balance, structured harmoniously, and in tune with virtue. Only when reason controls desire and spiritedness can this occur. The life of an evil person is out of tune in that desire dictates to reason. Evil people do not understand that performing virtuous actions is always in their self-interest. For such action reflects and nurtures the healthy soul. Also, the condition of a person's soul does not depend on his or her subjective evaluations. As is the case with physical health, the condition of souls is an objective matter. We in fact can be physically healthy but wrongly believe ourselves to be ill, or we in fact can be physically ill but wrongly believe ourselves to be healthy; so, too, with the health or illness of our souls. Accordingly, for Socrates, wrongdoing is grounded in ignorance as miscreants miscalculate their self-interest. In fact, virtue is its own reward and vice is its own punishment, all of which is recorded upon and constitutes the objective condition of our souls. Embracing this truth would remedy most if not all evil deeds.[6]

Shakespeare disagrees. Portia's musing, "If to do were as easy as to know what were good to do, chapels had been churches and poor men's cottages princes' palaces" (1.1.13-15), sounds a recurrent theme in the play. Throughout the fable, the main characters profess one thing, but too often practice its opposite. Although I hesitate to brandish the charge of "hypocrisy" facilely, there is no doubt that Portia's conviction is often illustrated. Why might people know the good but not practice it? Sometimes our wills are weak: we are inclined toward taking the easy path instead of the more difficult but correct path. Often we are unconvinced that virtue is its own reward and punishment its own vice: we are disinclined to accept Platonic-Socratic metaphysics about the nature and health of the soul. Frequently, strong emotions cloud our judgments: the picture of the perfectly just person whose reason always moderates desire and spiritedness is untrue to human experience. In the case of the Christians in the play, their sense of ethnic and religious tribalism too often stymies them from practicing the creeds of their faith when confronting resident aliens. In any event, the reasons why knowing the good is not enough to ensure that we practice the good are numerous and compelling.

D. Both Communities and Individuals Reap What They Sow

Antonio and Shylock deserve each other in that their mutual loathing sets the stage for the disconcerting events that befall them. Antonio's gratuitous abuse of Shylock and his ethnic and religious tribalism are unrestrained even by the possibility that Shylock seeks a rapprochement during the negotiations surrounding their bond. Antonio assures Shylock that the cruelty will continue and fashions the bond as an agreement between enemies. As a result, Antonio comes very close to achieving the martyrdom to Bassanio's cause that he apparently seeks.

Shylock ends up destroyed, both materially and spiritually, by his single-minded quest to wreak vengeance upon Antonio and the state of Venice. Balthasar-Portia mercilessly turns his theory of jurisprudence against him, refuses to allow Shylock to revisit the earlier settlement offers he had rejected, invokes esoteric statutes against him, and leaves him a broken man.

The state of Venice played a major role in creating the monster of revenge that Shylock became. By not merely marginalizing resident aliens, but virtually pushing them off the city's page, Venice nurtured Shylock's alienation, estrangement, and unquenchable thirst for vengeance. By celebrating ethnic and religious tribalism, Venice nourished Antonio's overly acute sense of difference. By embodying a commercial ethic that prized arms-length bargaining and mercantile collegiality, and that underplayed genuine intimacy and robust community, Venice thrived materially but misfired spiritually.

Accordingly, the Shylock v. Antonio trial can be viewed reasonably as an indictment of social injustice. Shylock sought equality before the law; the only institution in Venice that he thought compelled to render it to him. His aspiration, however, was fueled by a flawed theory of jurisprudence that wrongly concluded that rule of law virtues were both necessary and sufficient to ensure his cause. Social injustice, then, was a primary source of Shylock's vengeful motivation and the ultimate weapon of his destruction at the trial.

At the end of the play, Venice is not rehabilitated; Shylock is a falsely converted Christian; and Antonio is magically restored financially, but still emotionally ambiguous. Social injustice is a merciless master.

E. We Find Solace, but Not Salvation, in Love

Love can ease our pain, elevate our spirits, and soften our pretensions. Although we can take the love out of contracts, we cannot take the contract out of love. Love is on ongoing process, a negotiation between the respective current attributes and idealized possibilities of the parties. Love is not won once and forever, but must be renewed constantly without guarantees. On my reading, although *The Merchant of Venice* is a moral parable, we should not conclude that Portia and Bassanio must live happily ever after. I would clock the probability of that occurring at no more than 60 percent. Portia must serve as a midwife to Bassanio's higher potentials and avoid the temptation to be a more active molder of his future self. They both must find a higher purpose than the pursuit of *la dolce vita* and reveling in the idea of love. Portia and Bassanio must discover higher, sustaining tasks. Antonio must avoid trying to be the third wheel in their relationship, transcend his unrequited love of Bassanio, and seek a healthier relationship, preferably in Belmont. His commercial life in Venice was unsuited for his yearning spirit. Antonio has lost his faith in Venice's communal life, but kept his ships. Lorenzo and Jessica have a secure financial future—thanks to the "mercy" of Antonio's sentencing terms to Shylock—but what of their present? Gazing at the stars and exchanging sweet nothings can go only so far. They, too, must find suitable life tasks. We know less about Gratiano and Nerissa, but he is the most mean-spirited among the Venetian citizens we encounter. Can Gratiano soften his rough edges to accommodate a wider union with Nerissa? Can Nerissa emerge as more than Portia's echo? And what of Shylock? What community will embrace him? Will he have nothing more than a portion of his wealth, his memories of Leah, and the pain of betraying his deepest principles and his own identity in order to salvage his biological life?

Accordingly, realizing salutary love is a paramount aspect of attaining a robustly meaningful life. But love of itself cannot redeem an otherwise desolate soul. Although the desire for love arises from a sense of lack and insufficiency, if we approach love from desperate need we will be unlikely to achieve our ends. An individual standing alone is rarely fulfilled, but extremely needy people, who can derive a sense of self only from thorough absorption into a collectivity, are equally ungratified. We must heed the lessons of the individual-community continuum.

F. Love Requires Sacrifice, Risk, and Heightened Mutual Vulnerability

The unsuccessful suitors of Portia fail because of their lack of understanding and substance. They do not recognize that love requires grave sacrifice and risk; that desiring someone else fervently or deserving to be loved based on one's past meritorious deeds are insufficient. In the context of the moral parable, failing to understand these truths implies that they lack the personal attributes required to love well. Antonio, on the other hand, illustrates the moral lesson. He loves Bassanio, risks his life to benefit his beloved, begs no mercy from Shylock or the Venetian court, and is willing to sacrifice his life right up until the time that Balthasar-Portia springs her legal trap on Shylock. Antonio is rewarded: he retains his life, his ships are miraculously saved, and he journeys to Belmont where he may well find the community able to remedy his melancholy.

We must assume that Bassanio understands the nature of love because he passed the casket test. But in the play he sacrifices and risks little. He is the beloved of Antonio and of Portia. They benefit him significantly. At best, Bassanio demonstrates only that he has the potential for risk and sacrifice in service of love. He can sing the correct tune, but will his deeds match his crooning? Again, Portia midwifery will be crucial.

Portia risks much in marrying Bassanio. He arrives with even fewer guarantees than most spouses. She sacrifices her time, efforts, and skills—not to mention her wedding night—to rescue Bassanio's friend from legal disaster. She even tolerates Antonio on the periphery of her marriage, knowing well that he had in the past positioned himself as her rival for Bassanio's affections.

Jessica risks much in service of her love to Lorenzo: she flees her father's home, severing her parental bond; she converts to a religion that her father has taught her to despise; she has no solid plan for the future other than gazing at the skies with Lorenzo. Luck, a fraudulent jurist, and a victorious litigant conspire on behalf of Lorenzo and Jessica. Still, only their financial future is secure.

Despite all the surface celebrations of sacrifice and risk in love, we must remember that oaths, vows, and trust remain crucial to intimate relationships. The vestiges of the realm of contract remain. Portia makes this resplendently clear to Bassanio when they return to Belmont after the trial.

G. Money Cannot Buy Happiness

Notice how both Antonio and Portia enter the play by announcing their melancholy and world-weariness, respectively. Antonio laments, "In sooth, I know not why I am so sad (1.1.1). On my reading, Antonio is sad generally because he lacks the robust community for which he yearns; the commercial camaraderie of Venice is insufficient to fulfill his needs. Antonio is sad specifically because his homosexual love for Bassanio is unrequited, and Bassanio intends to court Portia, a wealthy maiden of Belmont. Thus, Antonio's wealth and mercantile success inadequately sustain his personal fulfillment.

Portia laments, "By my troth, Nerissa, my little body is aweary of this great world" (1.2.1). World-weariness at such a young age is stunning. Portia is wealthy but lacks a higher purpose beyond personal gratification. Not yet connected to love and consumed almost exclusively with suitors contemplating taking the casket test, Portia has not connected to a project larger than herself. Also, the casket test is the vestige of her father's patriarchal domination reaching out from the grave. Nerissa notes that, "they are as sick that surfeit with too much as they that starve with nothing. It is no mean happiness therefore, to be seated in the mean: superfluity comes sooner by white hairs, but competency lives longer" (1.2.6-10). Portia, too, is inadequately nourished by her inherited wealth.

As an empirical matter, Shakespeare was correct: money cannot buy happiness. Aristotle insisted that human beings are social animals. If living for extended periods in isolation, we are either gods or beasts, but not human beings. Although we need, especially in Western cultures, a keen sense of our individuality, uniqueness, specialness, and autonomy, we also require a measure of community. We seek bonds, connections, and extended subjectivity through family, friends, and lovers. We need to transcend ourselves and to feel part of something larger. We need to enlarge our sphere of concern from ourselves to others and sense that others have enlarged their sphere of concern to include us. Intimacy, sharing, and social belonging are paramount ingredients for happiness.

A popular self-help book of recent vintage advised us to imagine what we might regret on our deathbed as we were evaluating the life we led.[7] It is unlikely we would regret not spending more time at the office, not viewing yet another episode of *Friends*, not having met Donald Trump, or not owning a Rolls Royce automobile. Instead, we are most likely to regret not having been a better parent, spouse, child, sibling, or friend. If this observation is correct, then the health of our relationships is more important than we commonly think and act.

Social scientists estimate that around 70 percent of our happiness hinges on the number and quality of our friendships, the closeness of our families, and the health of our relationships with neighbors and co-workers.[8] Social support, a sense of mutual appreciation, and the ability to share are crucial to happiness. These depend upon and are nurtured by communication. Telling others who are important to us that they are, deepens our mutual bond. In adverse times, sharing our problems with those closest to us softens the sting of tragedies.

Extending ourselves through volunteer and charitable work also increases the likelihood of happiness because we alleviate boredom, heighten our sense of purpose, and foster feelings of mutual appreciation. Developing and pursuing common projects and interests deepen our social connections. Extroversion is part of the process. People who are introverts are less likely to share themselves, to forge salutary communities, and to be happy.[9]

Our salaries and income, educational levels, social and marital status, gender, and race are less important factors for attaining happiness than commonly assumed.

> People who go to work in their overalls and on the bus are just as happy, on the average, as those in suits who drive to work in their own Mercedes. Although men still retain a perilous grip on most of the reins of power in our society, they are not happier than are women. In spite of racism and relative poverty, African Americans enjoy on average the same feelings of subjective well-being as do white Americans.[10]

In sum, spending more time and effort fostering healthy relationships is the most important ingredient for attaining happiness. Antonio understood this subconsciously and Portia eventually leaves the stage happily because she (wrongly) believes that her relationship with Bassanio is settled well once and forever. The lie in fairy tales is that our heroes "live happily ever after." On the contrary, neither happiness nor love is a fixed state achievable at the resolution of a particular crisis. They are both processes subject to negotiation throughout our lives. Accordingly, Portia's apparent happiness and Antonio's seeming contentment at the end of the play are only temporary. As do we all, they must continue to immerse themselves in the processes of happiness and love, without any guarantees and with considerable emotional risks.

H. The Power of Feminism

At first, Portia appears to be a classic victim of patriarchal oppression. She is subject to her dead father's will even in so fundamental a choice as whom to marry. She is unhappy, apparently imprisoned by her own wealth, lack of agency, and failure to connect with projects beyond herself. But, as always, first appearances are deceiving in the play. Soon enough, Portia becomes the master architect of events. First, she finesses the casket test by facilitating Bassanio's choice. She does not give him the right answer to the test, but employing her best midwifery, she elicits from Bassanio the answer that lay within him. Portia nurtures and actualizes the idealized possibility—a proper understanding and practice of love—that Bassanio embodies. Second, Portia masquerades as a jurist and weaves the result reached at the trial of Shylock v. Antonio. She lures Shylock into thinking he has a winning case, which convinces him that he need not seriously consider settlement offers, and then springs the trap that jeopardizes his own life. To accomplish his subterfuge, Portia invokes laws of which no other character in the play is aware. While she begins with a tear-jerking paean to the virtues of mercy, she ends by remorselessly eviscerating Shylock's very identity. Third, she entraps Bassanio into relinquishing his ring, thereby breaking his solemn oath to her, and then verbally tortures him prior to forgiving him and setting firm contractual terms for their marriage. Unquestionably, Portia is the paramount agent in the play.

On the one hand, she is blazingly intelligent, uncommonly resourceful, and passionately sensitive; but, on the other hand, she is coldly manipulative, unrepentantly fraudulent, and morally cruel. Granted, in the Shakespearean context, women gain empowerment only through subterfuge and scheme. In a patriarchal context, female agency must be won by any means available. But Portia virtually turns deception into a way of life. Still, she wins contemporary sympathies: She should be able to choose her own spouse; she accurately perceives Bassanio's idealized possibilities and must serve as his Socratic instructor if he is to actualize them; and giving birth—bringing forth the possibilities that lie within one—is not painless.

We must, however, judge her more harshly for her role in the resolution of Shylock v. Antonio. A sympathetic teacher would not have manipulated Shylock so coarsely. While readers of the play may conclude unsympathetically that Shylock ultimately received what he desired and deserved—"justice" meted out according to simple decoding of statutory language and mechanical application of the results—surely that conviction is unpersuasive. Portia denied Shylock procedural and substantive justice in that she was a fraudulent jurist with a vested interest in the case; she manipulated Shylock into assuming an uncompromising position from which she later refuses to release him; she plucked obscure statutes seemingly out of a jurisprudential vacuum and invoked them to turn a civil dispute into a criminal trial against the plaintiff; and then, with the compliance of the Duke, permitted the civil defendant to craft the criminal sentence. In so doing, Portia was the primary designer of Shylock's demise. Portia's will glistens resplendently in the casket test, the trial of Shylock v. Antonio, and the aftermath in Belmont regarding Bassanio's broken oath. Portia is able to set the terms of her bond with Bassanio, refashion the terms of Shylock's bond with Antonio, and finesse the terms of her bond with her dead father. Her will is indomitable and supreme.

But we know better than to believe in fairy tales. Portia's future is far from secure. Again, she will need to confine herself to a midwifery role in teaching Bassanio how to realize his higher possibilities. To believe that Bassanio could act as an effective counterforce against Portia is unreasonable. Portia's own self-restraint will be necessary lest she dominate the relationship in ways that are counterproductive to it. Bassanio has it within him to exemplify the highest spirit of the aspirations expressed in the lead casket, as does Portia. Whether they can mutually attain that ideal is far from clear. The specter of Agathonian narcissism and Kierkegaardian aestheticism will haunt Bassanio, as will the allure of Socratic mysticism; while Portia must resist the urge to impose her will directly. Furthermore, even if Bassanio and Portia realize marital bliss, they must both connect to higher purposes and projects to sustain meaningful lives. Will they rear children? Become marriage counselors? Direct their efforts toward helping the less fortunate? Will Portia join a law school faculty? Will they endow The Shylock Foundation to support needy aliens seeking higher education?

In less patriarchal societies, the power of feminism can exert itself more openly and healthily than it could in Shakespeare's Elizabethan age. Portia is neither an enlightened, free-thinking icon nor a hypocritical, manipulating fraud. Instead, she is human-all-too-human. Like the rest of us, her most detestable vices are merely her most glowing virtues exaggerated and misapplied.

The themes of law and love are expertly intertwined in *The Merchant of Venice*. As we leave Belmont and Venice, we take with us Shakespeare's lessons on life. We will dearly need them. Mischief is brewing in Vienna.

Four

MEASURE FOR MEASURE: LAW AND ORDER

Vienna is teeming with sexual excess and resulting disease. Although the city is located in Austria, many of the citizens identified in *Measure for Measure* bear Italian or Roman names. (Perhaps a mass emigration from Venice took place after the Shylock v. Antonio trial.) Laws are harsh, but enforcement has been lax. The ruler of the city, Duke Vincentio, is generally highly respected and admired, but his overly permissive stewardship has unwittingly promoted corruption among citizens. The glory of individual freedom has amplified and then burst into the anarchy of unfettered license; general lawlessness has ensued. The Duke is aware of the problem and must fashion a solution.

1. The Delegation of Authority

The Duke is convinced that a temporary change of leadership is the remedy. He will go off on an executive sabbatical; in his stead, he will deputize Angelo as supreme authority and appoint Escalus as Angelo's counselor. The moral rectitude and logical precision of Angelo are well known. In the words of Escalus: "If any in Vienna be of worth/ To undergo such ample grace and honour, / It is Lord Angelo" (1.1.22-24). The Duke describes Angelo as "A man of stricture and firm abstinence" (1.3.12).

The Duke accepts responsibility for the deterioration of social conditions in Vienna: he recognizes that he has been excessively merciful for fourteen years. The result has been the collapse of respect for law, the trumping of justice by anarchy, and the corrosion of the social order. After deputizing Angelo, he confides to Friar Thomas at a monastery:

> We have strict statutes and most biting laws,
> The needful bits and curbs for headstrong steeds,
> Which for this fourteen years we have let sleep;
> Even like an o'ergrown lion in a cave,
> That goes not out to prey. Now, as fond fathers,
> Having bound up the threat'ning twigs of birch,
> Only to stick it in their children's sight
> For terror, not to use, in time the rod
> Becomes more mock'd than fear'd; so our decrees,
> Dead to infliction, to themselves are dead;
> And liberty plucks justice by the nose;

The baby beats the nurse, and quite athwart
Goes all decorum (1.3.19-31).

But why does the Duke not simply assert his power, reverse his overly permissive policies, and reinstate the rule of law? Vincentio is firmly convinced that if he is the architect of a radical reversal of city policies, he will be viewed as a tyrant and thereby lose his sterling reputation. Better that a new, temporary executive, such as Angelo, wield power and do what must be done.

Sith 'twas my fault to give the people scope,
'Twould be my tyranny to strike and gall them
For what I bid them do; for we bid this be done,
When evil deeds have their permissive pass
And not the punishment. Therefore indeed, my father,
I have on Angelo, impos'd the office:
Who may, in th' ambush of my name, strike home,
And yet my nature never in the fight
To do it slander (1.3.35-43).

But the Duke will not go to Poland on a holiday, as he has told Angelo and Escalus. Instead, he asks Friar Thomas for a monk's habit and instructions on how to impersonate a friar. Duke Vincentio cannot trust law and order in Vienna to chance. As a false friar, he will lurk within the city, monitor the actions of the primary agents, and manipulate events behind the scenes as necessary. Surreptitious surveillance will replace permissive law enforcement in Vienna.

2. Philosophical Interlude: The Art of Delegation

The classical example in philosophical literature of delegating political power is found in Machiavelli's *Prince*.[1] Convinced that ineffective nobles had exploited their subjects, and that internal corruption and destructive conflict—led by hordes of robbers, bandits, and criminals—were pervasive in Romagna, Duke Cesare Borgia acted decisively. He bestowed complete power over the region to the cruel, effective, Remiro d'Orco: "He was a man of some fifty years of age, violent and domineering, feared by all, and the dispenser of a harsh justice which had at least the merit of an impartiality that took no account of persons."[2]

D'Orco, then, adopted Shylock's theory of jurisprudence: simple decoding of statutory language and mechanical application of the results. Also, he was not above going outside the law when he concluded that the ends justified the means. Unsurprisingly, d'Orco's moral and political calculus rarely had trouble arriving at that conclusion.

Quickly, d'Orco established order through pitiless legal and extralegal means. Fearing that the inhabitants were coming to hate d'Orco, Borgia named a civil court of justice to investigate complaints against him. The people received the message that Borgia could be tough—he had appointed d'Orco—and he could be just—as he named a court to examine d'Orco's excesses. To prevent the people from wrongly concluding that Borgia was not completely in charge, Cesare had d'Orco killed. For theatrical and symbolic effect, he had d'Orco sliced in two and the bodily halves placed in the corners of the town piazza, with a chopping board and a bloody knife beside them. The citizens of Romagna were at once pleased, awed, and shocked (P 7).[3]

The conventional interpretation of this horrifying deed is that Borgia used d'Orco, then disposed of him when convenient and advantageous for Borgia: the autocratic governor was merely following Cesare's orders and murdered when he was no longer required for Borgia's purposes. The more charitable rendering is that d'Orco grossly exceeded what was necessary to pacify Romagna, expropriated and sold food for his own profit, and was also part of the conspiracy against Borgia: the tyrant of Romagna was properly slain for offending Borgia's sense of justice and for plotting against him.[4]

Borgia anticipated the strategy of Duke Vincentio: instead of being the front man for the stern political measures deemed necessary to reform a corrupt social order, he delegated the task. Borgia did not want to be associated directly with the radical reversal of political and legal policies. After that task was completed or exceeded, Borgia eliminated his appointed agent to the benefit of the state and, more important, to the enhancement of his own reputation. Borgia, then, intentionally exploited d'Orco, using him as a mere means to Borgia's purposes. When those purposes were realized, d'Orco was, again, objectified—slaughtered and displayed more gruesomely than would be a common beast. Perhaps d'Orco reaped what he had sown; perhaps, on one level, he received what he deserved—measure for measure. But Borgia's icy, premeditated exploitation was as menacing as a freshly honed stiletto.

While the initial stages of their respective strategies bear similarities, Duke Vincentio is no Duke Borgia. Vincentio is not setting up Angelo to do his dirty work and then dispose of him mercilessly. We should first be clear that Vincentio, unlike Borgia with d'Orco, does not instruct Angelo to simply turn the screws on the populace. Yes, he understands Angelo to be "precise" and a man of "stricture and firm abstinence." Surely, he anticipates that Angelo will serve as a counterweight to the Duke's fourteen years of overly indulgent leadership. But Vincentio is careful to avoid giving Angelo specific instructions; he never demands that Angelo adopt Shylock's theory of jurisprudence. Instead, he stresses that Angelo will have absolute power: "Mortality and mercy in Vienna/Live in thy tongue and heart" (1.1.44-45). He adds that "your scope is as mine own, /So to enforce or qualify the laws/As to your soul seems good" (1.1.64-66). In short, Angelo has absolute authority in the absence of the Duke, but he is to use his judgment in enforcing law. A reasonable reading of the Duke's instructions is that Angelo is to use his best judgment as chief executive and judicial officer to counterbalance the Duke's excessive mercy over the past fourteen years. But the Duke does not order Angelo to embrace simple decoding of statutory language followed by mechanical application of the results. Should Angelo adopt such a jurisprudence he will do so because he concludes independently that that version of judicial decision making is the most appropriate way to enforce the law; and Angelo will be thus responsible for the results.

Despite the esteem with which he apparently regards Angelo, Duke Vincentio harbors suspicions. He decides to masquerade as a friar and skulk about Vienna because, among other reasons, he is unsure how Angelo will respond to the corrupting influences of absolute power. The Duke mentions to Friar Thomas that Angelo is rigidly upright, acts cautiously with envy, and is oddly dispassionate: "Lord Angelo is precise;/Stands at a guard with envy; scarcely confesses/That his blood flows, or that his appetite/Is more to bread than stone; hence shall we see,/If power change purpose, what our seemers be" (1.3.50-54).

Throughout the first scene, Vincentio's wandering, awkward speech reflects his doubts and insecurities. That the Duke has governed Vienna carelessly is best explained by his lack of deep convictions, which mirror and sustain the confusion of the city. Vincentio is most concerned with maintaining his own reputation; unlike Borgia, he cherishes his reputation not as a means to brandish more effectively his political power, but for its own sake. Vincentio yearns for the approval of others.

Unlike Antonio's Venice, Vienna lacks the superficial mercantile camaraderie that at least produced a patina of facile community. Unlike Portia's Belmont, Vienna does not aspire to romantic love and personal transcendence. Instead, Vienna is a city where individualism runs amok; citizens assert their freedom without fully recognizing the impoverishment of their souls. The tragedy of Vienna is that its citizens do not even acknowledge what they lack: a sense of robust community that could nourish personal identity and elevate the spirits of citizens. As a result, communication in Vienna is often fractured; political anarchy and moral nihilism thrive; yet laws are clear and harsh. That Duke Vincentio has enforced these laws permissibly reflects and reinforces his personal confusion as well as that of the city.

Machiavelli would remind Duke Vincentio that statesmen should embrace this advice: *It is better to be feared than to be loved, but avoid being hated.* The prince should strive to be considered merciful and not cruel. But being merciful is trickier than it may seem. Cesare Borgia was thought cruel but his methods united and reformed the Romagna. A more squeamish prince, desiring a reputation for mercy, would have been gentler. The result would have been continued disorder and corruption which would be more harmful to the state in the long run. Cruelty and mercy, then, are not always what they initially appear to be. Being considered cruel will not jeopardize the prince's authority if in so doing he advances the order and security of the state, and the well-being of the people (P 17).

For a prince, being both feared and loved by the people is the best situation. But accomplishing both simultaneously is uncommon. If the prince cannot join these two emotions in his people, it is better to be feared than to be loved.

This is the case because of human nature. People are generally ungrateful, cowardly, selfish, deceptive, greedy, and inconstant. As long as the prince serves their interests, they pledge loyalty and offer extravagant promises. They talk grandly during high times, but act pettily in adverse situations. Love is an emotion that binds people through obligation. People, who are basically wicked and self-interested, will renege on such a duty when expedient. Fear has a greater hold because it includes dread of punishment. Love, then, appeals to the better angels of our natures, making it thoroughly discretionary and unreliable. Fear addresses our consistent aversion to coercion, suffering, and physical harm, making it completely reliable and predictable. Also, whether citizens fear the prince is more under his control than whether they love him. Accordingly, the fear of his subjects, again, is more predictable, reliable, and controllable than is the love of his subjects (P 17; P 18).

At all costs, a prince must avoid being hated (P 17; P 19). The people will hate a prince only if the ruler confiscates their property or their women. When the prince has to kill he should be able to articulate persuasive reasons and to make a clear case. Above all, he must not seize the property of citizens: "Men forget more quickly the death of a father than the loss of a father's estate" (P 17).

Military leaders, following the example of Hannibal, must be cruel in order to cement discipline and to instill useful fear. Those who praise the loyalty of Hannibal's troops but stigmatize Hannibal for his harsh measures, says Machiavelli, miss the mark badly. Hannibal's cruelty is what made his troops loyal, disciplined, and effective. Anticipating the words of Immanuel Kant, Machiavelli suggests that to will the end is to will the means necessary to achieve it (P 17).

Here Machiavelli offers his coldest, narrowest, most unequivocal and cynical assessment of human nature. Especially in terms of a prince who has just risen to power, Machiavelli claims to hold a mirror to people as they are and when he asks, "who is the fairest of them all?" the glass shatters. He goes so far as to accept that people value property rights over human rights to the extent that they cherish their possessions more than the life of a parent. In these passages, unlike other parts of his work, he offers no hope for transformation or redemption. If human beings are so desolate and intractable, one wonders, what is the worth of the glory those with *grandezza d'animo* (noble souls) seek? Who should bother to aspire to a fine reputation and an historical legacy among such pathetic specimens? Are they even worthy of Machiavelli's imagined prince of robust military and political *virtù* (excellence)?

A wise prince might rejoin that the alternatives posed are false. There is much room between being feared and loved, as there is between being loved and hated. A respected prince may be neither feared nor loved nor hated. Duke Vincentio is overly concerned with his self-image. As a result, he too often allows law to be ignored with impunity. The Duke unwittingly sacrifices the conditions of robust community of Vienna to his own preoccupation with currying favor with the masses. The result is a ruler who is neither loved nor hated nor feared. The Duke is liked, but not well liked enough to be loved. We can alter Machiavelli's dictum: *It is better to be respected than to be fancied lightly.* Respect flows from jurisprudence administered by a person of practical moral wisdom, one who neither invokes the false security of mechanical jurisprudence nor cowers in the face of perplexing moral and legal decisions.

3. The Crime

The loquacious, street-wise, Lucio, exchanges banter with two soldiers. In the mocking, one-upmanship, repartee we might term trash-talk, they exchange one-liners centered on sexual diseases, war, and personal worth. The madam of a house of prostitution, Mistress Overdone, enters their company. After being subjected to barbs from the merry trio, she informs them that Claudio, a well-bred gentleman, has been arrested and is scheduled for decapitation within three days. His offense: violation of the fornication statute which decrees that extramarital sex is a capital offense. Claudio has apparently impregnated his girlfriend, Juliet (often referred to as "Julietta" in the play). Lucio remarks that Claudio was supposed to meet with him two hours earlier but failed to show up. Mistress Overdone complains that war, poverty, plague, and the hanging of her customers have jeopardized the business of her brothel (1.2.59-84).

As Lucio and the soldiers depart, Overdone's pimp and tapster, Pompey, emerges. He informs Overdone that not only is Angelo strictly enforcing the fornication statute but he has also proclaimed that all brothels in Vienna must be abandoned and those in the suburbs will be razed (1.2.95-103). This signals that Angelo is no Duke Vincentio: he will enforce the law impartially and avidly.

Meanwhile, upon orders from Angelo, the prison Provost is publicly parading Claudio as an example for other potential wrongdoers. Throughout the play, the Provost has a sincere concern for the welfare of his prisoners, but he, too, must accede to the absolute authority of Angelo. Lucio asks Claudio to explain his plight. Claudio castigates his own sexual desire and excessive freedom:

> From too much liberty, my Lucio, liberty;
> As surfeit is the father of much fast,
> So every scope by the immoderate use
> Turns to restraint. Our natures do pursue,
> Like rats that ravin down their proper bane,
> A thirsty evil, and when we drink we die (1.2.125-130).

Claudio sadly admits that his impending death is the consequence of his indulgence of individual freedom. Rats greedily devour poison, which promotes their thirst for water, the satisfaction of which activates the toxic chemicals that destroy the rodents. Claudio eagerly embraced liberty, which stimulated his sexual lust, the satisfaction of which violated the fornication statute that triggers his upcoming death.

Notice that Claudio does not offer a beautiful soliloquy on love; he does not impugn the disproportionality of being executed for one extramarital sexual liaison; nor does he question Angelo's sudden crackdown on a law that has lain dormant for years. Instead, despite some self-pity, Claudio appears prepared to take responsibility for his actions and accept his fate. But as we know, first impressions, like fish resting in supermarkets and visiting in-laws, are not always what they seem.

The Provost instructs Claudio that they must leave. Claudio requests and is granted a few moments alone with Lucio. At this point, Claudio reveals his inner self. First, he makes clear the nature of the sexual liaison: He and Juliet acted upon a "true contract" (1.2.144-145). Claudio refers to a type of betrothal contract. Under English common law, this informal action sometimes constituted a legally valid marriage, but the Church required a formal religious ceremony before such a contract could be sexually consummated without being subject to ecclesiastic penalty. Claudio adds that only Juliet's lack of a dowry prevented the couple from engaging in the formal religious ceremony. He refers to their sexual intercourse as "mutual entertainment" (1.2.154). Juliet's pregnancy has stymied his plans for a better dowry and subjected him to legal recourse. (Claudio assumes that had Juliet not become pregnant their sexual rendezvous would have remained secret, and that absent the pregnancy a more suitable dowry was a genuine possibility.) Again, we observe no strong professions of love. Claudio talks only in contractual and material terms; his language of commodities intrudes upon the phenomena of intimacy: mutuality and expansion of identity. He is no Bassanio, uttering rhetorical flowers to the beauty and power of love. Claudio does profess to love Juliet, but we are hard-pressed throughout the play to grasp his meaning precisely.

Second, Claudio complains bitterly about Angelo's enforcement of the fornication statute. He is unsure whether the fault lies with Angelo or the office he temporarily holds. But he is stunned that he has been singled out as a victim of a law that has lain dormant for nineteen years (1.2.157-169). (Recall that Duke Vincentio stated that the law had not been enforced for fourteen years. The difference may be explained by simple copyediting error; or by the different reckonings of the Duke and Claudio about the enforcement of this particular law; or perhaps the Duke is referring to fourteen years of generally lax enforcement of law, while Claudio is referring to nineteen years of lax enforcement of the fornication law specifically; or maybe the discrepancy is symbolic of the breakdown in communication and shared understandings in Vienna.)

Claudio suggests that Angelo's insistence on justice may be "the fault and glimpse of newness" (1.2.158), or to show that "He can command" (1.2.162), or perhaps it is merely "for a name" (1.2.171), to establish himself in authority. All of these suggestions obliquely hint at Angelo's inadequacy as a ruler, but miss the true motive for his unreasonable stance, revealed by the Duke: Vienna is in its present state of disorder because the "strict statutes, and most biting laws"

(1.3.19) have long ceased to be enforced. A different approach to political leadership is required to elevate Vienna from pervasive chaos.

Interestingly, Claudio suggests that Angelo's caprice in sentencing him for violating the fornication statute mirrors the arbitrariness of God when choosing whom to save and whom to condemn (1.2.120-123). Here Claudio alludes to the notoriously problematic doctrine of predestination in Christian theology (Romans 9: 13-18). If some souls are predestined for eternal reward and others for eternal punishment then what becomes of final judgment grounded upon the principle of desert? What are we to say about the ultimate rationality and justice of the Divine Mind?

Lucio suggests that Claudio appeal to Duke Vincentio. Claudio has tried to do so, but no one can find the absent ruler. Instead, Claudio begs Lucio to go to the convent and ask Claudio's sister to plead his case to Angelo. She is about to become a nun and Claudio suspects that she will prove to be a compelling advocate for his cause. He is convinced that her optimism, intelligence, and earnestness will win the day. Lucio agrees to assume the task (1.2.177-191).

Claudio, thus, reveals his deeper mindset. He is not prepared to die; he views himself as wrongly charged; he feels neither contrite nor personally responsible for his predicament; he is puzzled by and outraged at Angelo; he claims to be in love with Juliet, but seems utterly self-absorbed; and, finally, he holds out hope that his sister, Isabella, can turn the legal tide in his favor.

4. Philosophical Interlude: The Doctrine of Desuetude

In 1996, motivated by his desire to deter teenage pregnancy and thereby lessen medical and welfare costs to a rural area of 12,000 residents, the County Attorney of Gem County, Idaho, prosecuted pregnant, unmarried teenage women and their teenage male partners under a 1921 Idaho statute prohibiting fornication.[5] The enabling statute read as follows:

> Any unmarried person who shall have sexual intercourse with an unmarried person of the opposite sex shall be deemed guilty of fornication and, upon conviction thereof, shall be punished by a fine of not more than $300 or by imprisonment for not more than six months or by both such fine and imprisonment; provided, that the sentence imposed or any part thereof may be suspended with or without probation in the discretion of the court (Idaho Code, 18-6603).

An unmarried fifteen-year-old female, Amanda Smisek, was prosecuted under the statute. After confessing to her act of fornication, which was amply confirmed by her pregnant condition, she was convicted in juvenile court. Her sentence was levied only a few days prior to the birth of her child: a fine of $10 and thirty-day suspended detention sentence with three years' probation. Furthermore, she was required to attend parenting classes, complete high school, and refrain from using drugs, alcohol, and tobacco. The sixteen-year-old father of her child was also convicted and sentenced to three years probation and forty hours of community service.[6] The prosecuting attorney and judge stated their rationales for enforcing the statute: because of the costs of illegitimate children to taxpayers and the greater risks of being involved with delinquency, drug abuse, and truancy that children born to unmarried teenage mothers posed, a deterrent to such pregnancies was necessary. The prosecuting attorney and judge denied that policing sex or morals motivated their actions.

A host of considerations supported Smisek's claim that she had been wrongly prosecuted: the fornication law had not been enforced for years even though violations had been frequent (desuetude); only teenage offenders were now being charged (denial of equal protection); her medical condition was the basis of the state's claim as other sexually active teenagers who did not become pregnant and sexually active adults were not prosecuted (lack of notice and procedural unfairness).

The doctrine of desuetude holds that a law is nullified through disuse. In Roman law, statutes were renounced not only by legislative action, but also by desuetude which implied the tacit consent of everyone.[7] Where a statute is not enforced over the course of years even though violations are well known, to conclude that its original purpose is outdated and that neither citizens nor state officials are concerned about it is reasonable.

The underlying justification of the doctrine involves procedural injustice: if for numerous years a statute has not been enforced while it has been openly violated then to apply it suddenly to a particular offender transgresses the rule of the law and is thereby unfair. That is, the offender had a legitimate expectation that given years of past practice his conduct would not be subject to prosecution. To indict him under such circumstances cuts to the heart of providing citizens fair notice of the requirements of law. Furthermore, the enforcement of desuetude statutes is often arbitrary and capricious; legal officials may be singling out an offender on grounds other than his transgression of the desuetude statute, which may in fact serve only as a convenient pretext. As such, legal officials would have overly broad discretion that would result in uneven enforcement.

Also, desuetude statutes underscore the dissonance between the law as written and the law as applied. Where the gap between the two is significant, the entire system of law is brought into disrepute. Accordingly, even if a desuetude statute is substantively fair, its random application would violate the principle of treating like cases alike. The doctrine of desuetude, then, is concerned with procedural fairness in the administration of law.

In Vienna, Claudio makes such an appeal to Lucio: The fornication law has not been enforced for nineteen (or fourteen) years; he had no antecedent reason to suspect that the law would be enforced against him; additionally, he and Juliet were married in the eyes of the common law. Oddly, Claudio accepts the substantive fairness of the law and even its draconian penalty. His protest is entirely procedural.

Arising from Roman law, desuetude is a civil law doctrine that has gained little traction in the United States with its common law tradition. However, the Supreme Court of Appeals of West Virginia has adopted the doctrine and held that certain laws abrogate their binding force when citizens openly and frequently violate them over a long period of time with the implicit consent of law enforcement officials.[8] Under such circumstances, judges may renounce the law. The Court devised a three-part test to determine when the doctrine of desuetude applies.

First, only statutes prohibiting crimes that are *malum prohibitum* are subject to being abrogated. The relevant distinction is between laws that prohibit conduct that is evil in itself (*malum in se*)—naturally evil actions as judged by the common sensibilities of a civilized community—such as murder; and laws that prohibit conduct that is wrong because it is deemed so by a statute (*malum prohibitum*)—such conduct, for example, speeding along the highway, is not inherently evil, does not involve moral turpitude, but may endanger the community and is thereby prohibited. The assumption is that where natural evil is at play the lack of fair notice is obviated because everyone is aware of the wrongness of the conduct even if it has not been prosecuted. (But, then, why has the statute prohibiting the conduct not been enforced? If that is because the offense is rare and knowing violations are infrequent then the condition of "open and frequent" transgressions over a period of years has not been satisfied and the doctrine of desuetude would not be triggered anyway.)

Second, "there must be an open, notorious, and pervasive violation of the statute for a long period."[9] Obviously, that a statute has been violated often cannot by itself render that statute void. Otherwise, most of criminal law would evaporate. This is a necessary not sufficient condition of the doctrine of desuetude.

Third, most important, the statute must go unenforced, conspicuously and over a long period of time. Citizens and state officials alike must have been aware of frequent violations of the statute and the consistent failure to prosecute them over numerous years. As such, the community has expressed its consensus that the underlying purposes of the statute in question are not important enough to justify prosecution of violations.

The West Virginia version of the desuetude doctrine has the effect of not only dismissing prosecutions brought under a statute, but also declaring that statute void, thus eliminating it from the written law. Under judicial systems, such as that of the United States, that are grounded in the separation of powers between executive, legislative, and judicial branches of government, this can cause serious concerns. Critics will clamor that the desuetude doctrine—by permitting judges to strike statutes from the written law—promotes wrongful judicial intervention into the legislative process.

To mollify the separation of powers objection to adopting the desuetude doctrine, some advocates of the doctrine argue that invoking desuetude is appropriate only as an exculpatory defense to prosecution. Defendants might base their desuetude claim on the fact that they either could not know that their conduct was criminal or they were lured into believing that the relevant statute would not be used. Such a claim might be advanced as an exculpatory defense that is akin to mistake of law, which consists of one's ignorance of the legal consequences of one's conduct, although one is fully cognizant of the facts and substance of that conduct. If successful, a court could hold that the defense negates the culpable mental state (for example, intent or knowledge) required by a criminal statute for one to be guilty of the crime at issue: "A belief that conduct does not legally constitute an offense is a defense to a prosecution for that offense based upon such conduct when the defendant acts in reasonable reliance upon a clear practice of non-enforcement of the statute or other enactment defining the offense by the body charged by law with responsibility for enforcement, unless notice of intent to enforce the statute or other enactment is reasonably made available prior to the conduct alleged."[10]

The alleged advantage of a mistake of law defense is that the case of defendants would be rightfully dismissed, yet judges would not be empowered to declare the desuetude statute void and strike it from written law. Thus, judges could not be plausibly faulted for usurping legislative functions. The alleged disadvantage of a mistake of law defense is that the discord between the law as written and the law as enforced would remain. (Of course, a legislature might be moved to repeal a desuetude statute in light of the judicial response.)

In Shakespeare's Vienna, no governmental separation of powers is in place. Duke Vincentio apparently has full executive and judicial authority. Furthermore, an independent legislative body does not appear in the play. The Duke, then, may simply be the sole governing power in the city. (Strangely, although the Duke acknowledges that the laws are harsh, the possibility of moderating, eliminating, or otherwise changing the laws never arises.) As such, no separation of powers principle stands as an objection to applying the doctrine of desuetude directly in Vienna.

Given the apparent immutability of law in Vienna, the mistake of law defense is appealing. Claudio could argue that he was relying reasonably on the past practice of non-enforcement of the fornication law. That he was given clear notice of a new intent to enforce the statute prior to his sexual liaison with Juliet is highly unlikely. Although a new judicial authority presides, Angelo, who is eager to impose the letter of the law, the play offers no evidence that a proclamation heralding the strict enforcement of the fornication (and all other) laws preceded Claudio's sexual congress with Juliet. In fact, Juliet was already showing her pregnancy when Claudio was arrested. The timeline does not support the argument that Claudio was given adequate notice of the new policy of enforcement prior to his alleged transgression of the fornication law. Thus, a mistake of law defense is possible for Claudio.

Of course, the problem is that what passes for a legal system in Vienna is not receptive to excuses for or justifications of legal transgressions. In the light of this, Duke Vincentio simply refused to enforce the law, while Angelo will enforce it strictly. As Claudio's hypothetical mistake of law defense will be offered to the judge of his case, Angelo, he is unlikely to succeed.

A third way of handling desuetude statutes is through Constitutional provisions enforcing procedural fairness. For example, following a line of cases that struck down desuetude statutes because they violated liberty interests protected by the Due Process Clause, a Virginia court in 2005 abrogated a statute that prohibited fornication (extramarital sex). In this manner, the court was able to reach the same result as would have been reached under a desuetude doctrine but by invoking already well-established Constitutional principles. No direct appeal to desuetude doctrine was required. Other constitutional means, such as the equal protection prohibition on arbitrary and capricious enforcement of law or procedural due process protections focused on fair notice might also be invoked. The disadvantage of invoking Constitutional provisions in this way is that doing so would at times be over-inclusive and at other times under-inclusive when compared to the aims of desuetude doctrine.[11]

In Vienna, appeals to constitutional principles would be futile because whether the city even has a well-defined constitution is doubtful. Furthermore, in the case of Vienna v. Claudio, the interpreter of any constitutional principles would be Angelo, the precise embodiment of the law as written.

5. Comic Relief

Officers are setting up the courtroom. Angelo and Escalus discuss the case of Vienna v. Claudio. Escalus suggests that Angelo is too rigid in prosecuting Claudio. He offers two considerations. First, Claudio has a "most noble father" (2.1.7). Spawned from worthy lineage, Claudio is neither a common criminal nor a threat to the community. Second, Claudio's offense is common. In fact, Escalus wonders if Angelo might not have been guilty of the same offense for which Claudio has been indicted: "Whether you had not sometime in your life/ Err'd in this point which now you censure him,/ And pull'd the law upon you" (2.1.14-16).

Clearly, Escalus has misread Angelo's political position and jurisprudential theory. Angelo had begun their conversation by insisting that "we must not make a scarecrow of the law" (2.1.1). That Claudio has a noble heritage and is known by Escalus is irrelevant to someone, such as Angelo, who is convinced that law requires simple decoding of statutory language and mechanical application of the results. Impersonality, generality, and universal application of law are at the core of Angelo's theory. Thus, in Angelo's eyes, the particular circumstances of a defendant's heritage or his otherwise felicitous character are legally irrelevant. In fact, that Escalus would advance such inappropriate factors in defense of Claudio—thereby seeking special favor for a perpetrator of a crime—may well seem insulting to Angelo.

In addition, Angelo assures Escalus that he has never violated the fornication law: "'Tis one thing to be tempted, Escalus, /Another thing to fall" (2.1.17-

18). One wonders why Escalus would raise this point given Angelo's impeccable reputation, especially in matters sexual. Angelo's alleged strong suit is his ability not to stray sexually where most men trod eagerly. More important, Angelo adds that the moral rectitude of those passing judgment is not a primary issue; applying the law impartially is paramount. The law intervenes only where transgressions are known. That some, even many, illicit sexual liaisons go unpunished is no justification for failing to punish those that are known. (Escalus did not raise explicitly the desuetude defense which is a stronger version of his claim that Claudio's offense is common and relatively minor.)

Finally, Angelo unsqueamishly and proudly proclaims that should he violate the fornication law, he, too, will subject himself to the same punishment as is about to befall Claudio: "When I, that censure him, do so offend,/ Let mine own judgment pattern out my death, And nothing come in partial. Sir, he must die" (2.1.29-31). True to his jurisprudential theory, Angelo refuses to make himself an exception to the imperatives of law. Accordingly, Angelo instructs the Provost to permit Claudio to see his confessor prior to being executed the next morning. The Provost departs and Escalus laments: "Well; heaven forgive him! And forgive us all!/ Some rise by sin, and some by virtue fall;/ Some run from brakes of vice and answer none, / And some condemned for a fault alone" (2.1.37-40).

The courtroom is prepared for the arrival of the miscreants of the day. Constable Elbow leads in Pompey, Mistress Overdone's pimp and bartender, and Froth, a foolish gentleman. Elbow quickly establishes himself as the master of malapropism, confusingly describing his prisoners as "benefactors" instead of "malefactors" (2.1.50). Throughout the scene Elbow misuses language, thereby exemplifying the disjointed communication that besets Vienna because of its fractured communal bonds. Mistress Overdone's brothel in the suburbs was razed, but she now operates another such enterprise that masquerades as a bath house.

The next passages amount to a confusing narrative wherein Pompey tries to evade charges by his own version of double-talk, which added to Elbow's naturally confusing discourse, and Froth's willingness to serve as Pompey's stooge, utterly exasperates Angelo. The violation centers on Elbow's pregnant wife wandering innocently into Overdone's establishment seeking prunes (a dish readily available in brothels because prunes were thought to ward off venereal diseases); but details are sketchy because the three interlocutors, for different reasons, are sultans of obfuscation. Angelo can take no more and departs. He leaves Escalus in charge and expresses his hope that "you'll find good cause to whip them all" (2.1.137).

Pompey continues the linguistic nonsense with Escalus. He asks the judge to peer into Froth's face. Given that Froth's face is the ugliest thing about him, he could not be responsible for anything uglier, including harming Elbow's wife. In the comic purpose of the scene, Escalus finds Pompey's argument compelling (2.1.147-160). Quips and puns, some sexual, along with more of Elbow's malapropisms plague the courtroom banter. Escalus dismisses Froth.

Pompey points out that if sexual laws are enforced in Vienna then all the young men will have to be castrated and the young women spayed (2.1.230-231). To shorten a tedious story: Pompey maintains his mocking, scornful attitude toward authority. Exhausted by Pompey's fatuous repartee, convinced that he is incorrigible, and perhaps preoccupied with Claudio's impending death, Escalus releases Pompey with a stern warning: should he appear before Escalus again on any charge he will be whipped (2.1.250).

The scene ends with Escalus expressing his grief to a court functionary about Claudio's fate. When the functionary points out that "Lord Angelo is severe" (2.1.282), Escalus notes that to extend mercy too frequently is to err in the long run in that wrongdoing is encouraged. Escalus is well aware of the social problems unwittingly nurtured by the Duke's past policies. Still, he laments that for Claudio "there is no remedy" (2.1.285).

Beyond providing comic relief, this scene underscores the rampant confusion, ruptured communication, sexual license, and shallow sense of community that ravages Vienna. Moral, political, and legal foundations no longer (if they ever did) constitute a justification for claims about truth, meaning and value. Vienna is enveloped by a nihilistic moment, a period when uncertainty reigns and the paramount social institutions sustaining culture are wavering.

6. Philosophical Interlude: The Threat of Nihilism

At your most despondent, have you peered into the cosmic abyss and felt the hot breath of nothingness caress your neck? Has paralyzing reflection lured you into thinking that our conventional notions of truth, meaning, and value are all shallow imposters, merely arbitrary sycophants of the supreme ruler: cosmic meaninglessness? Have you concluded that no substantive belief [12] genuinely warrants your deep allegiance? If so, you may have simply suffered the effects of consuming overly-spiced linguine and rancid Chianti. Or you may have sustained a frightening existential encounter with the nihilistic moment.

First appearing in popular literature in the mid-nineteenth century in Russia, "nihilism" bears numerous historical meanings.[13] Nihilism has been asserted in a host of existential, epistemological, political, and moral contexts.[14] Some of the uses detail the loss of cosmic meaning, some are reactions to that loss, some are mainly philosophical or theoretical doctrines, while others track psychological moods or movements. The most radical forms of nihilism capture a mood of despair over the emptiness of human existence and perceive no worldly solutions.

Frederick Nietzsche was concerned with the links between the conditions and fulfillment of culture and a tragic view of life. For Nietzsche, recognizing "the death of God" forces human beings to acknowledge the lack of objective foundations and justifications for their most important truth claims about meaning, value, and purpose. This introduces the "nihilistic moment" or stage when conclusions about these crucial dimensions of human life are up for grabs.

What did we do when we unchained this earth from its sun? Whither is it moving now? Whither are we moving now? Away from all suns? Are we not plunging continually? Backward, forward, in all directions? Is there any up or down left? Are we not straying as through an infinite nothing? Do we not feel the breath of empty space? Has it not become colder? Is not night and more night coming on all the while?[15]

Nietzsche cannot guarantee that human beings will respond energetically to the possibilities open in the nihilistic moment.[16] For him, the loss of a secure foundation for our dearest substantive beliefs suggests that we must ultimately choose under conditions of radical uncertainty. Human reason cannot redeem our predicament. Some of us will shrink back in horror. We will resign ourselves to bitterness and self-pity, and conclude that all is lost ("pathetic nihilism"). Some of us will refuse to relinquish the fantasy of a transcendent world and blissful afterlife ("passive nihilism"). Others of us will accept cosmic meaninglessness and use it as a point of departure for grand creativity ("active nihilism"). Having "killed" God by developing science and technology, and by creating the social conditions that provide compelling explanations for natural phenomena that in previous ages were explainable only by reference to God, we must now come to grips with the aftershock of our cultural accomplishment.

How shall we, the murderers of all murderers, comfort ourselves? . . . Is not the greatness of this deed too great for us? Must not we ourselves become gods simply to seem worthy of it? There has never been a greater deed.[17]

The most extreme nihilism is neither pathetic nor passive nor active. Deconstructive nihilists rage against the existing social order without any re-creative vision. They glisten with the worst attributes of obstreperous two-year-old children: an inflated sense of entitlement leavened by a deficient understanding of civilized life. Deconstructive nihilists are empowered by the nihilistic moment, but cannot transcend this stage because they lack the creativity required to re-imagine and re-make their social contexts. Instead, they invoke "nihilism" as an excuse to advance ineffectually their narrow self-interest.

Of course, Nietzsche is an unapologetic active nihilist. Embracing cosmic meaninglessness as the springboard to creative possibilities; reveling in radical contingency; relishing the human condition fully while recognizing its tragic dimensions; understanding the process of deconstructing, reimagining, and re-creating the self; and rejoicing in liberation from imposed values and meanings are at the heart of active nihilism. Active nihilism places paramount value on this life.

The difference between pathetic, passive, and active nihilism can be illustrated by the ancient Myth of Sisyphus.[18] Condemned by the gods to push a huge rock to the top of a hill from which it fell down the other side, to be pushed again to the top from which it fell again, and so on forever, Sisyphus was doomed to futile, pointless, unrewarded labor. His immortality was part of his punishment. His consciousness of the futility of his project was his tragedy. Sisyphus's life is representative of human life: repetitious, meaningless, pointless toil that adds up to nothing in the end. The myth portrays the eternal human struggle and indestructible human spirit. Although Sisyphus is not mortal, that deepens and does not redeem the absurdity of his life. While human life bears more variety than Sisyphus's life, the matter is only one of small degree. While some human beings take solace in producing and raising children, reproduction can be viewed as more of the same: adding zeros to zeros.

When faced with Sisyphus's sentence, a pathetic nihilist would metaphorically skulk off into a corner; curl up into the fetal position; and despair. A passive nihilist would counsel Sisyphus to withdraw from his task of endlessly pushing the boulder up a hill, and, failing that possibility, to detach himself from the task as he performs it. Nietzsche would advise Sisyphus to affirm his fate, to desire nothing more than to do what he is fated to do eternally, to luxuriate in the immediate texture of what he does, to confer, through attitude and will, meaning on an inherently meaningless task.

Pathetic and passive nihilists fail to see that value and meaning need not be permanent to be real; that process renders fulfillments independently of attaining goals; that the attainments of great effort and creation do not instantaneously produce emptiness; and that suffering is not inherently negative but can be transfigured for creative advantage.

To what state do passive nihilists aspire? Do they secretly yearn for a condition of never-ending bliss? Does freedom from suffering require that we want nothing more? Many would find such a life deadening. A life devoid of new projects, adventures, journeys, and goals lacks creativity: bland contentment replaces vigorous thought and action. Perhaps suffering is produced not by the process of seeking fulfillment of new desires but by the taming of our desire-creating mechanism. Having unfulfilled desires need not be painful; it is often exhilarating. We imagine rewarding new situations and pursue them vigorously. We find fulfillments in the process and, often, in achieving the goal. Our insatiability ensures that we continue to imagine and pursue rewarding projects, rather than being limited to contemplating earlier fulfillments. Whether the new desires we create produce overall suffering depends on what they are and how we pursue them, not solely on their presence.

In contrast, Nietzsche embraces an active nihilism grounded in the criterion of power: exertion, struggle and suffering are at the core of overcoming obstacles, and it is only through overcoming obstacles that human beings experience, truly feel, their power.

Higher human types joyfully embrace the values of power, while "last men," Nietzsche's male-gendered notion of embodied banality, and utilitarian philosophers extol the values of hedonism.

"What is love? What is creation? What is longing? What is a star?" thus asks the last man, and he blinks . . . "We have invented happiness," say the last men, and they blink. They have left the regions where it was hard to live, for one needs warmth. One still loves one's neighbor and rubs against him, for one needs warmth . . . Everybody wants the same, everybody is the same; whoever feels different goes voluntarily into a madhouse.[19]

The highest ambitions of last men are comfort and security. They are the extreme case of the herd mentality: habit, custom, indolence, egalitarianism, self-preservation, and muted will to power prevail. Last men embody none of the inner tensions and conflicts that spur transformative action. They take no risks, lack convictions, avoid experimentation, and seek only bland survival. In Nietzsche's view, Utilitarian philosophers, although not last men, unwittingly fuel the herd mentality with their celebration of pleasure, happiness, and egalitarianism.[20]

Nietzsche's tragic view of life understands fully the inevitability of human suffering, the flux that is the world, and the Sisyphus-like character of daily life. Yet it is in our response to tragedy that we manifest either a heroic or a herd mentality. We cannot rationalize or justify the inherent meaninglessness of our suffering. We cannot transcend our vulnerability and journey to fixed security. We are contingent, mortal beings and will remain so.

We are free, however, to create ourselves: We bear no antecedent duties to external authority and we are under the yoke of no pre-established goals. We need not recoil squeamishly from the horrors of existence, instead, we can rejoice in a passionate life of perpetual self-overcoming. Art can validate our creativity, while laughter can ease our pain and soften our pretensions.

Unfortunately, Nietzsche would not evaluate the main characters in *Measure for Measure* favorably. For example, how might Nietzsche judge Angelo? He is a man who flees from his freedom and takes solace in absolute rules. His judicial theory of simply decoding statutory language and mechanically applying the results is a cover to ignore his own responsibility for decisions. Angelo is existentially inauthentic in citing the law as the sole author of his legal conclusions. We might well credit Angelo for being existentially authentic in that as a defendant he is willing to apply the same principles to his own case. But his overall response to the nihilism that pervades Vienna is to resurrect and reinforce absolutist understandings that arose from an earlier age. In effect, instead of reimagining and recreating his world and himself, Angelo denies the need to do either. Accordingly, he completely misunderstands the conditions of his time and wallows in received opinions and feckless traditions. As such, Angelo is oblivious to the transformative possibilities arising from the nihilistic moment in Vienna. Indeed, Angelo does not genuinely recognize the presence or implications of nihilism in the city. Instead, he sees only the surface manifestations—lawlessness—and offers mechanical jurisprudence as a remedy to restore the *status quo ante*.

Isabella withdraws from the wider community and seeks the comfort of a cloistered convent. She, too, seeks the solace of absolutist understandings and a transcendent order. Although she forcefully special pleads the case of her brother, she is by disposition as deeply committed to his judicial theory as is Angelo. However, unlike Angelo, she is inclined toward forgiveness and willing to suspend harsh punishments when confronted by sympathetic victims. As such, Isabella is a passive nihilist par excellence: withdrawal from this world, indifference to the nihilistic moment, and faith in a blissful afterlife dominate her life.

Duke Vincentio has the authority to deconstruct, reimage, and recreate the social community of Vienna, but he lacks the courage and resolve to act decisively. At the end, he is reduced to brokering piecemeal deals to solve a series of personal crises. The Duke concedes his own responsibility in promoting the nihilism that infects Vienna, but is unwilling to rectify the situation because he is hostage to his own favorable reputation. His preoccupation with the opinions of his subjects renders him a peculiar hybrid of passive-pathetic nihilist.

In fairness, I should add that the play predates Nietzsche by over 250 years and to hold the characters to Nietzsche's standard may be anachronistic and thus harsh. Still, the localized nihilism infecting Vienna is undeniable and to indict the main characters of the play for their reactions to and responsibility for it is appropriate.

The *Übermensch* (overman) is Nietzsche's male-gendered symbol of human beings overcoming themselves to superior forms. Nietzsche does not give us a definite description, but the overman represents a superhuman exemplar that has not yet or has rarely existed.[21] Nietzsche's desiderata for higher human types include a host of general attributes:

(1) *Luxuriating in Contingency and Ambiguity*: the ability to marginalize but not eliminate negative and destructive impulses within oneself, and to transfigure them into joyous affirmation of all aspects of life; to understand and celebrate the radical contingency, finitude, and fragility of ourselves, our institutions and the cosmos itself; to regard life itself as fully and merely natural, as embodying no transcendent meaning or value.

(2) *Cultivating a Pure Spirit and Appreciation of Process*: to harbor little or no resentment toward others or toward the human condition; to confront the world in immediacy and with a sense of vital connection; to refuse to avert our gaze from a tragic world-view and, instead, to find value not in eventual happiness, as conceived by academic philosophers, but in the activities and processes themselves.

(3) *Pursuing Excellence*: to refuse to supplicate oneself before great people of the past but, instead, to accept their implicit challenge to go beyond them; to give style to our character by transforming our conflicting internal passions into a disciplined yet dynamic unity; to facilitate high culture by sustaining a favorable environment for the rise of great individuals; to strive for excellence through self-overcoming that honors the recurrent flux of the cosmos by refusing to accept a "finished" self as constitutive of personal identity; and to recognize the

Sisyphus-like dimension to human existence: release from the tasks described is found only in death. Given the human condition, high energy is more important than a final, fixed goal. The mantra of "challenge, struggle, overcoming, and growth," animating and transfiguring perpetual internal conflict, replaces prayers for redemption to supernatural powers. Part of our life struggle is to confront and overcome the last man within each of us, to hold our internal "dwarf" at bay.

The thrust of Nietzsche's thought is that we can formulate entirely new modes of evaluation that correspond to new, higher forms of life. The value of humanity is established by its highest exemplars and their creations. The overman, then, embodies the virtues of the active nihilist. Nietzsche warns readers not to view the overman as an evolutionary necessity or as an idealistic type to which many of us can genuinely aspire. His is an unapologetically aristocratic ideal. To live beyond yourself in self-creation is to forge a complex, subtle character that is worthy of "strutting its hour upon the stage" many times, even eternally.

Nietzsche's highest value of *amor fati*, a maximally affirmative attitude toward life, is not achieved through rational argument. Instead, it focuses on the rapture of being alive. *Amor fati* is an experience animated by faith, not cognitive discovery. *Amor fati* demands active response. While lower human types adopt passive nihilism, higher human types embrace the entirety of life. They view the lack of cosmic meaning and infinite redemption as liberation from external authority. Unlike the Stoics, Nietzsche glorifies the passions as robust manifestations of the will to power. To become who you are, to self-overcome, and to destroy, re-imagine, and re-create the self recurrently require an active nihilism that elevates the present into a fated eternity.

Of course, Nietzsche, by his own general philosophical framework, cannot prove or rationally establish the superiority of his vision. He can provide only aesthetic images of human types and ask us to which we are drawn. When Zarathustra describes the overman and the last man to the crowd, the masses yell back, "Give us the last man; turn us into these last men! Then we shall make you a gift of the overman!"[22] As always, the masses prefer the easier, less threatening, more comfortable alternative. They are unmoved by Zarathustra's artistry.

In his dialogue, the *Laws,* Plato's main character, the Athenian Stranger, chronicles the degeneration of the state through the democratization of judgment: excessive freedom in musical forms breeds contempt for established musical laws and emboldens the masses to think that they are competent judges of value; as the sovereignty of the best qualified to judge yields to the sovereignty of the audience, excessive freedom generally in the arts infects the polity; as the judgment of the masses is further amplified a general imprudence ensues, including contempt for statutory law; more and more citizens refuse to submit to magistrates and the authority of parents and elders is undermined; and soon obedience to law, loyalty to one's oaths, and reverence for religion pass from the scene. In this manner, beginning with license in the arts and continuing down the slippery slope of more individual freedom and less faith in expert judgment, the foundation of a society crumbles from within (700a-701c).

In *Measure for Measure*, the route to societal corruption is more direct: lax application of law encourages excessive individual freedom in sexual and other matters; excessive freedom in sex undermines robust community in the city; the loss of robust community signals the evaporation of shared values and common causes; the disappearance of these joint understandings corrodes the notion of a common good; the lack of a shared concept of the good undermines transparent communication; the result is a gaggle of voices often speaking past one another, class division between established authorities and the obstreperous purveyors of street life, and stark conflict between the vestiges of rectitude and abject cynicism. What is undeniable is that the nihilistic moment envelops Vienna.

In Vienna, last men abound. Agents of social change and higher human types who might lead the city out of the nihilistic moment by transcending received opinion and reconstructing values are missing in action. Sadly, Duke Vincentio may be Vienna's last best hope. But the Duke's will to power seems turned in other directions.

7. The First Plea

Isabella is discussing the liberty enjoyed by nuns with Sister Francisca. She asks whether nuns have any more privileges than those Sister Francisca has sketched. Sister Francisca is surprised that Isabella would want more. Isabella corrects her and expresses her desire for even stricter restraints than those imposed on the famously austere order of Saint Clare (1.4.1-5). Is Isabella's remark evidence that her soul, like Angelo's, is wound so tightly that arrogance in rectitude has effaced internal harmony? Or does it indicate that Isabella fears that her soul harbors sinful desires that require additional restraints lest they emerge?

Lucio visits the convent to inform Isabella about her brother's predicament and to convince her to plead his case to Angelo. After teasing her about her virginity, Lucio gets to the point. He apprises Isabella of the type of man with whom she will be dealing: Angelo has melted snow for blood; he does not experience the passions of normal men; he sublimates his instincts through intellectual pursuits; and he now seeks to make an example of Claudio to demonstrate that henceforth laws will be strictly enforced.

> Governs Lord Angelo, a man whose blood
> Is very snow-broth; one who never feels
> The wanton stings and motions of the sense;
> But doth rebate and blunt his natural edge
> With profits of the mind: study and fast.
> He (to give fear to use and liberty,
> Which have for long run by the hideous law,
> As mice by lions) hath pick'd out an act,

Under whose heavy sense your brother's life
Falls into forfeit; he arrests him on it,
And follows close the rigor of the statute,
To make him an example (1.4.57-68).

Although Isabella doubts that she can alter the course of events, Lucio assures her that when maidens "weep and kneel" men "give like gods" (1.4.80-81). They go off to petition the iron Lord Angelo.

Prior to meeting Isabella, Angelo parries with the Provost, who is squeamish about executing Claudio. Angelo suggests that the Provost can always resign if he finds his work distasteful. Angelo greets Isabella. She begins slowly: Isabella condemns Claudio's sin as the vice she most abhors (Are lust and premarital sex genuinely the worst vices—Dante did not think so—or merely the one that is especially repellant to a person such as Isabella who has taken a vow of chastity?) and admits that hers is a case of special pleading. Isabella implores Angelo to condemn Claudio's act but to pardon Claudio. This is a variation on the Christian theme of loving the sinner but hating his sin. Angelo responds that acting in such a way would renege on his administration function. Isabella admits that the law is just even if severe. Clearly, she is drawn to the Shylock-Angelo theory of jurisprudence, but feels that it is her sisterly duty to special plead on behalf of Claudio. Both the Provost, who implores the heavens to strengthen Isabella's persuasive powers, and Lucio, who suggests that Isabella is too cold and should kneel before Angelo while clutching his clothes, sense that the proceedings are not going well (2.2.26-47).

Isabella next makes a straightforward appeal to mercy. She points out that Angelo has the power to pardon Claudio should he so desire. Although Angelo does technically have precisely that authority—after all, we know that the Duke exercised such discretion too frequently—Angelo takes cover behind his jurisprudential theory and informs Isabella that it is too late for such consideration. As Lucio instructs Isabella, again, that she is "too cold," Isabella recites a short poem on how mercy is a crucial virtue of the powerful. She thereby distances herself from the Shylock-Angelo theory of jurisprudence with which she had flirted. (2.2.49-63).

In the next breath, Isabella tries a version of the Golden Rule: "If [Claudio] had been as you, and you as he,/ You would have slipp'd like him, but he, like you,/ Would not have been so stern" (2.2.64-66). Of course, Angelo, the prince of sexual propriety, would never have succumbed to premarital sex. Even if he had he would not have pleaded for mercy or favoritism if convicted of violating the fornication law. The problem with invoking Golden Rule arguments is that they depend too heavily on all parties embodying the same antecedent desires ("Do unto others as you would have them do unto you"). If, as here, one party is susceptible to lawlessness and yearns for mercy if indicted, while the other party is virtually invulnerable to vice but accepts the full force of law if caught straying, appeals to the Golden Rule are woefully ineffective. Angelo advises Isabella to withdraw.

Isabella persists. She tries another plea: What if she was Angelo and Angelo was Isabella? Lucio senses that Isabella is making headway. She appeals to God's mercy and suggests that Angelo is placing himself in God's place on earth. God redeemed the condemned souls of all those on earth. If God judged Angelo as he was, surely Angelo would seek mercy.

Angelo, though, characteristically retreats into his jurisprudential theory: it is the law, not Angelo, who condemn Claudio. All who are guilty of violating the law, regardless of their individual characteristics and relationships, must suffer as the law decrees (2.2.79-81). Of course, we know better. Angelo has the authority to render mercy and extend pardons as he deems appropriate. Furthermore, Duke Vincentio underscored this fact in his instructions to Angelo upon granting him temporary sovereignty.

Isabella tries a scattergun approach: Claudio is not prepared to die, give him more time; a quick execution offends heaven; and the crime he committed is common yet no one has been executed in the past for transgressing against the fornication statute. Although Lucio cheers her address, Angelo is less sanguine: Yes, the law has not been enforced, but it was only asleep not dead. The law has been aroused and will be enforced strictly henceforth (2.2.82-98). Isabella beseeches Angelo to show pity. Angelo responds sharply that mercy is best shown by strict enforcement of law. Unless future potential lawbreakers are deterred by observing how the force of law will now be strictly applied, sin will continue to be rampant in Vienna. Thus, if Claudio is not punished Angelo would not be showing mercy to those who will be tempted in the future to break the law.

Isabella retorts that "it is excellent/ To have a giant's strength; but it is tyrannous/ To use it like a giant" (2.2.107-108). Angelo's power will be brief and it is he, not the law, who sentences Claudio; it is Claudio, not abstract, unidentifiable people in the future who will thereby suffer. As the Provost and Lucio rejoice, Isabella stresses the difference between the theory and practice of exercising political and legal power.

Angelo is caught between utter befuddlement and a gradual recognition of his own desire for Isabella. He tells Isabella that he will ponder what she has said and she should come back tomorrow to discuss the matter further. Isabella closes by offering Angelo a bribe: her passionate and sincere prayers (2.2.143-155). As the Provost, Lucio, and Isabella depart, Angelo is stunned: he who has never been seriously tempted by garish prostitutes, now feels himself sexually drawn to this novice from a convent. He is unsure who is more to blame— Has she wittingly or unwittingly seduced him? Or is he at fault for yielding to the vice of lust? In any event, he is torn between self-loathing for the depraved thoughts circling his mind and the instinctive passion that has sprung so unexpectedly but naturally within his soul (2.2.162-186). He will have less than twenty-four hours to resolve his conflict.

8. Who is Angelo?

The other characters in the play agree that Angelo embodies high moral rectitude, although they also note his unusual lack of passion. They describe him as "worthy," "virtuous," a man "of stricture and firm abstinence," "precise," "unenvious," a person whose "soul seems good," "dispassionate," "severe," having "melted snow" for blood, " a person who "never feels the wanton strings and motions of the sense," and whose natural instincts are "blunted."

In the play, we *hear* several reports about Angelo's virtue, but we do not see actions that support the reports. The best we can do is cite his impartial administration of justice and expressed willingness to be governed by the same principles that he exerts: he refuses to allow others whom he might know or even himself to stand as exceptions to the imperatives of universal law. (Although even on this precept we will soon learn he will buckle.)

Worse, we will later discover that five years prior to assuming the role of temporary sovereign of Vienna, Angelo and Mariana had entered into a betrothal contract. However, Mariana's brother, Frederick, died at sea in a shipwreck that also destroyed Mariana's marriage dowry. Of course, Mariana was distraught. Angelo's response was to break off the engagement while falsely alleging that Mariana was dishonorable because she was unchaste. Despite this treachery, Mariana continued to love Angelo (3.1.213-230).

Accordingly, to reconstruct Angelo's presumed virtue is no small task. What separates Angelo from commonplace reprobates in Vienna? First, dismissing his treatment of Mariana, he apparently follows moral and legal rules precisely and consistently. Second, in that vein, Angelo has never broken the fornication law. His sexual ethics (again, ignore his cruelty to Mariana for the moment) are above reproach and Angelo is not even tempted by the painted hussies who stroll Vienna's streets. The textual evidence suggests that Angelo is a virgin. Third, Angelo has steadfastly served Duke Vincentio. He has "always been obedient to [the Duke's] will" (1.1.25).

Fourth, to the best of everyone's knowledge, Angelo has never broken any other Viennese laws.

Fifth, in comparison to the rampant individual license that infects Viennese social life, Angelo is controlled and disciplined. His personal comportment is much different, for example, from that of the loose-tongued Lucio and the self-promoting Pompey. While they stand as the troublesome products of a community fractured by excessive individual liberty, Angelo represents the stability, order, and predictability of restored government.

The problem, though, is clear. The case that can be advanced in support of Angelo's virtue is scanty. We never see Angelo exercising *sound judgment*, a cornerstone of Aristotle's person of practical moral wisdom: "The mark of a man of practical wisdom [is] to be able to deliberate well about what is good and expedient for himself [in terms of] what sorts of things conduce to the good life in general . . . wisdom must be intuitive reason combined with scientific knowledge . . . virtue makes us aim at the right mark, and practical wisdom makes us take the right means . . . it is not possible to be good in the strict sense without practical wisdom."[23]

Unlike the person of practical moral wisdom, Angelo takes refuge in conventional rules then inauthentically evades personal responsibility by claiming that the rules compel his actions. Can Angelo weigh competing normative claims? Can he adjudicate between the imperatives of conflicting moral principles? Can he confront fresh cases with resolve? Can he promote the common good when doing so is not spelled out explicitly in a prioritized set of commands?

Also, Angelo may well obey conventional negative duties, those requiring that we refrain from harming others and from violating other moral rules such as those prohibiting force, fraud, duress, and coercion; but we find no evidence that he recognizes moral positive duties, those requiring that we aid those in distress and render assistance to those in need.[24] When does Angelo show generosity? When does he extend himself to those less fortunate than he? When does he manifest compassion, caring, and love? So repressed is Angelo that he is content to do no wrong while neglecting his obligation to promote proactively the good.

Finally, Angelo lacks self-knowledge. Socrates and Plato overstated the case when they concluded that virtue is knowledge, but, surely, knowledge is a necessary (although not sufficient) condition of virtue. Angelo is a spring coiled too tightly; steel tempered too hard; instinct repressed too immaculately. Because he lacks an acute sense of self, Angelo takes refuge in traditional covenants and received normative opinion. As a result, his presumed "virtue" is starkly limited and subject to explosive transformation. When the internal tension overwhelms, high combustion must ensue.

At best, Angelo is a supercilious prig—an obsessive, anal-retentive moral grind who prefigures the glory days of Cotton Mather and Myles Standish. At worst, Angelo is a toady to authority who has ceded his existential transcendence on the altar of the conventional understandings constructed by the powerful. If he is the best Vienna can unveil when asked to divulge its moral paragon then the city is in even worse peril than first imagined by Duke Vincentio.

Angelo's major vice is arrogance: he is overly prideful in his alleged virtue. At first glance, pride is an odd inclusion among the seven capital vices.[25] Justified pride in our accomplishments animates the quest for excellence. Yes, if exaggerated, pride amplifies into arrogance and vanity: an unjustified sense of superiority that exalts the self by diminishing others. But if justified and measured, pride is seemingly the basis of self-respect that is presupposed in our ability to love self and others. Is not pride, understood charitably, merely a justified sense of self-worth? Furthermore, even from a Christian standpoint, pride seems necessary to maximize our highest potentials and thereby glorify God's bestowed gifts. Without pride and the desire to excel, we court passivity and slothfulness. Indeed, pride ignites heroism and underwrites most great accomplishments in the world. In short, a healthy pride spurs our best efforts, vivifies our quest for meaning and purpose, and protects us from resignation when adversity stings us.

The case against pride is primarily biblical (Proverbs 16:18–19; Luke 4:1–11; Luke 18:9-14; Romans 5:6). Pride corrodes judgment and facilitates sin. By luxuriating in our attainments and savoring our development, we jeopardize our connection to wider community and to the divine. We set ourselves apart, regarding ourselves as special or even unique, while evaluating others as less capable. We incline toward excessive love of self and objects that glorify the self—such as honor, awards, and social station—instead of focusing on spiritual goods. The most horrifying human acts bloom from the soil of pride. Wars, murders, rapes, terrorism, and the like, are perpetrated not by the self-effacing and apathetic, but by those fueled by an inflated sense of entitlement and excessive self-worth. Worse, pride supplies an unworthy motivation for performing deeds that seem from an external standpoint to be virtuous. We are all familiar with the charity worker who benefits the disenfranchised more from a sense of superiority than from genuine concern for their welfare: "Hey, look at me, I am doing what the better people always do, helping my social inferiors."

From a Christian vantage point, pride is love misdirected away from the divine and toward only the self. We wrongly idolize ourselves as we should be worshipping God. We become what we idolize. To focus on the self is to distort our identities. In sum, Christian tradition casts a wary eye on those aspiring for greatness. Behind every would-be hero stands the mythical Odysseus, gifted but preening and negligent in higher duties. The more prideful and self-sufficient we become, the more we withdraw from healthy human and spiritual communities. Additionally, one of the more destructive features of sin is its tendency to rupture the communities required for earthly and heavenly well-being.

The tricky part is that we can be prideful in our humility: "Hey, look at me, I am more self-effacing than most." We can take pride in our ability to ignore the temptations and glitters that lure the masses. Again, internal motives are often obscure; only external deeds are apparent and they bear ambiguous meaning.

Still, the indictment against pride is flawed. Christian tradition instructs us to love our neighbor as ourselves. This presupposes that self-love as such is not sinful, but a requirement of fulfilling our duty to love others. Accordingly, pride, insofar as it is self-love, is necessary for discharging moral obligation. Pride, as justifiable appreciation of the self, would appear to be unavoidable and even recommended. Pride requires robust communal connections to secure its value. What justifies pride is personal excellence, stellar achievements, and uncommon worth. Such achievements need not be historic. Small tasks done with exceptional skill and diligence give rise to justified pride. Intelligence, creativity, determination, imagination, overcoming significant obstacles, and maximizing one's highest potentials help constitute that skill and diligence. Recognition by others and the acclaim of the masses often accompany such skill and diligence, but are unnecessary to their existence.

The spectacular problem is that pride so easily amplifies to arrogance, which I take to be a more precise rendering of the capital vice. Arrogance is excessive, idolatrous, misdirected, and inaccurate. Arrogance is love of self wrongly diverted to contempt and hatred of others. Arrogance is redolent with the stench of epistemological and moral error, and scoffs contemptuously at community. Arrogance shuns moral duty as unworthy of pursuit. Arrogance struggles mightily to make the self-invulnerable. Arrogance is unreasonable, inaccurate, excessive, and narcissistic. As such, arrogance hardens our hearts to intimacy, spiritual and earthly, and celebrates self-aggrandizement as an intrinsic good. As with all sins, arrogance corrodes the self and eviscerates human relationships. Arrogance persuades us that we are more than we are; that we must demean those who may seem more exalted; that others are less worthy and deserve our scorn and condescension; that we are exceptions to the supposed moral law; that the good life is relentless striving for ever more recognition and status; that victories in zero-sum contests are the measure of greatness. The citadel of the self becomes impenetrable and supreme. As such, arrogance denies the need for community and thereby reneges on moral duties to others: the arrogant are selfish in that they ignore the interests of others when they should not. Herein lies the weakness of Angelo.

Arrogance flows from the desire to excel. But other people are seen as obstacles. We must strive mightily to diminish them in order to elevate the self. Also, arrogance is rebellion against rightful superiors, including the divine, as the self amplifies to become, in Nietzsche's words, its own God. As with all sin, arrogance is its own punishment. The more desperately we struggle for self-sufficiency the more empty and self-absorbed we become. Socrates whispers in our ears that evil-doing is its own punishment as our internal psyches reflect our wrongful actions.

The adage is by now a cliché: our vices are merely our virtues exaggerated. Pride so easily grows into arrogance that we must be ever vigilant and self-assessing. Perhaps arrogance is unavoidable, from a practical standpoint, and we must yet again admit to being sinners. We must supplicate ourselves in the knowledge that pride, as a condition of fulfilling moral duty, will perhaps inevitably fatten into arrogance, which threatens our humanity and contaminates our relationships. Although we cannot extinguish the problem, which lies at the core of the human condition, we can minimize its deleterious effects and remain resolute (and humble) in our predicament. These are the lessons that Angelo must learn.

Beyond the vice of arrogance, Angelo, that hitherto paragon of sexual propriety, finds himself beset by lust during Isabella's lengthy first plea that he spare her brother's life. His inner sexual coil, torqued so tightly, is about to burst.

Lust is wrongful or inordinate sexual desire. Advancing a strict morality of motivations and intentions, Jesus asserts: "I say to you that everyone who looks at a woman with lust has already committed [adultery] with her in his heart." (Matthew 5:27). The lust of the heart proposition indicts most of the human race for multiple sins. Lust can also be understood more generally to be inordinate desire for material goods. In any form, lust betrays excessive desire for improper objects. Sexual perversions, at least in part, flow from lust. Lust focuses not on the other person but on the satisfaction of its own desire. Intimacy, bonding, and establishing a wider subjectivity are tossed aside, only immediate craving reigns.

A complicating matter is the extent to which lustful feelings and thoughts are autonomic responses and reflexes, not considered judgments. In a strikingly non-Stoical account, John Medina reports that

> [T]here are aspects of sexual responsiveness that lie outside our conscious control. For us to consciously experience such impulses, they must be brought into our awareness, i.e., to our brains, and from that awareness we may experience the subjective feelings of arousal. However, since these reflex arcs occur independently of even the most rudimentary comment from the brain, we can say an astonishing thing. Sexual feeling (perhaps even the emotion itself) is something that *happens* to us. There is a certain amount of processing of our responses that occurs outside our conscious control.[26]

If lust of the heart is punishable as sin and lustful feelings and thoughts are often autonomic responses and reflexes outside our conscious control, then the principle of moral desert seems to be violated. If our sins do not arise from our free acts of choice then no moral culpability results. In the absence of moral culpability, punishment cannot rightfully be levied.

Perhaps returning to an old Stoic distinction can soften the puzzle. For Stoics, forming judgments involves perception, evaluation, and understanding. Impressions, whether sense perceptions caused by observations or products of reasoning flowing from the mind, imprint themselves on the soul. The Stoics called these impressions "first movements," We turn the impression into a proposition and then we either accept or reject the proposition. For example, we look in a certain direction and gain sense perceptions. We turn the sense perceptions into the proposition that "there is a dog relieving itself against a tree." We then either accept or reject the proposition depending on, in this case, how certain we are that there truly is a dog relieving itself against a tree. Sometimes the propositions we form may contain a value judgment such as "that a dog is relieving itself against a tree is a good (or bad) event." Such conclusions are considered judgments.

The impressions we get, the sense perceptions, are beyond our control. They imprint themselves on us. However, whether we accept or reject the propositions accompanying those impressions are within our control. Even Stoics are often overcome by the force of first impressions or instinctive reactions. My spontaneous reaction is essentially involuntary and natural. But I need not assent to the proposition that, say, lusting after another person is worthy. I still have time to reconsider my initial impression and affirm Stoic wisdom that only that which benefits my soul is genuinely good. From a Stoic standpoint, yearning for and even loving another person is merely a preferred indifferent (an event I antecedently desire, but one that is irrelevant to the health of my soul, the only personal good).

Brushing aside Stoicism's view of what constitutes good and evil, the distinction between first movements (immediate impressions) and considered judgments bears currency. If lustful feelings are only autonomic responses and reflexes then they should engender neither moral culpability nor punishment. Only when we form a lustful judgment—which involves rationally assenting to various propositions—do moral culpability and punishment come into play. If persuasive, we can accommodate the science of how lustful feelings arise with Christian commitment to punishment for sin and the principle of moral desert.

During the next twenty-four hours, prior to Isabella's next appearance, Angelo must confront his vices of arrogance and lust. The initial stage of "first movements" has passed. On the following day, Angelo will be responsible for the considered judgments that he derives and the actions pursuant to those judgments that he undertakes. He has no excuses.

Five

MEASURE FOR MEASURE: LUST AND DEATH

Angelo is tormented by his newly aroused lust. Prior to Isabella's return, he muses about his ambivalence: he accepts rationally the need for sexual propriety, but he longs for Isabella. Angelo is at war with himself; or, more precisely, he is torn between his past allegiance to sexual abstinence and what he now desires fervently. Angelo is consumed by Kierkegaardian dread: he is at once disgusted and tantalized by his newfound passion. Although he appreciates his past aloofness, he is tiring of the law and political authority. The basic instincts of human beings simmer beneath even those external postures that deny them. The tightly torqued coils that energize Angelo's psyche are struggling among themselves; they are about to explode (2.4.1-17).

1. The Second Plea: The Proposition

As Isabella enters, Angelo is reluctant to proposition her directly. Much of the initial dialogue consists of Angelo alluding to the possibility that Claudio might be spared, his trying to lure Isabella into offering herself as a bribe to that end, and Isabella misunderstanding the mating dance to which he aspires (2.4.30-49).

Angelo understands that he must be more explicit. He offers a hypothetical: Would Isabella give up her body, as did Juliet for Claudio, if doing so would redeem her brother? Isabella assures Angelo that she values her soul over her body: "I had rather give my body than my soul" (2.4.56). Angelo downplays the value of Isabella's soul and suggests that she would not be morally guilty for sinning under these circumstances. Isabella thinks Angelo is speaking of the possible sin in pardoning Claudio and assures Angelo that doing so would be merciful. Confusion pervades the conversation. Angelo verbally retreats and claims he was only testing Isabella. Isabella asserts that the only sin that is pardonable is her pleading for Claudio's life (2.4.57-73).

Isabella's apparent innocence and virtue excite Angelo further. The more pious Isabella appears, the greater lust stirs within Angelo. Like a deranged Socrates desperately yearning for direct apprehension of Absolute Good and Absolute Beauty, Angelo is aroused by Isabella's continually more intense approximations of the Good. Angelo tries the syllogistic approach: (1) Claudio is about to be executed; (2) He has been justly convicted and sentenced under law. Isabella agrees to both propositions. Angelo reaches for the deal clincher: Would Isabella have sex with a person who had the authority to pardon her brother (because he had "credit" with Angelo) if doing so was a condition of that pardon? (2.4.83-98). Isabella's response is curious. She proclaims emphatically that she would rather be stripped naked on a bed and whipped than accept such a proposition. The lurid sexual imagery contrasts with her apparently virtuous refusal. Angelo reiterates that her brother must then die. Isabella retorts that it is "Better it were a brother died at once, / Than that a sister, by redeeming him, /Should die for ever" (2.4.106-108).

When Angelo suggests that Isabella's stance is as cruel as she has alleged is the sentence imposed on Claudio, Isabella distinguishes "lawful mercy" from "foul redemption" (2.4.112-113). For Angelo to pardon Claudio would be a legitimate exercise of his prosecutorial discretion; for Isabella to secure such a pardon on illicit grounds would be doubly wrong: both the means used and the end attained would be morally contaminated.

Angelo inauthentically tries to shift blame to Isabella: it is her fault that he so desires her. Isabella confesses that she is in the uncomfortable position of pleading for mercy for the perpetrator of a sin she detests, but notes that sibling love is also in play. Angelo reminds Isabella that she had asked him to peer into his soul to discern whether he shared Claudio's vice. Becoming more aggressive, Angelo suggests that Isabella embodies the same vice (2.4.114-138).

Isabella tries to sooth Angelo with flattering words. Angelo expresses his "love" for her. Isabella counters that Claudio loved Juliet with disastrous results. Angelo assures her that Claudio will not die if Isabella has sex with him. Isabella first suspects that Angelo is only testing her, but then threatens him: if he does not pardon Claudio straightaway she will reveal his vile offer and true character to the world. Angelo replies haughtily that no one would believe her; his pristine reputation and lofty office mark his higher credibility (2.4.139-159).

His internal coils have snapped. Angelo now gives free rein to his sexual appetites. He aggressively declares that should Isabella refuse his demands, her brother will be tortured prior to being executed (2.4.160-167). She must answer his proposition on the following day. Angelo is both angered and aroused by Isabella's virtue. Isabella is convinced that her chastity cannot be bartered—not even for her brother's life. She will explain Angelo's proposition to Claudio. Surely he will understand and prepare himself for death.

2. Who is Isabella?

We must understand the high value Isabella places on her chastity in the context of Christian doctrine: she is a novice preparing to become a nun; as such, she has taken or will take a vow of chastity; and nuns are understood to be the brides of God. To violate her oath is not only to break her abstract promise but also to impair her relationship to God. The reason that extramarital sex is the vice that Isabella most abhors is grounded in these considerations.

Furthermore, as a Christian novice, Isabella would view earthly death as the inevitable prelude to final judgment. A human being's measly "three score and ten" years on earth (or less) are hardly comparable to an infinite residence in heaven or hell. Although tragic, Claudio's earthly death is far less lamentable than the commission of a sin that would jeopardize Isabella's standing in the afterlife.

But notice the jurisprudential theory in play. Isabella is very much drawn to the Shylock-Angelo position: normative law is best understood as simple decoding of statutory language and mechanically applying the results. However, she adjusts that position when she special pleads for Claudio. There the invocation of mercy and judicial discretion serve the crucial function of moderating the effects of harsh statutes. But Isabella is never fully comfortable with that adjustment. She recognizes the element of special pleading because it is her brother whose life is at stake and she continually reaffirms her faith in the law as written.

Suppose she accepted Angelo's offer. Isabella is convinced that her soul would be eternally doomed and that Claudio's life—having been redeemed ignobly—would be forever tainted. Does this mean that she imputes the Shylock-Angelo jurisprudential theory to God? Despite her earlier poems of praise to the virtue of mercy and to God's redemption of human beings from the stain of original sin, Isabella is convinced that sex under these conditions will automatically consign her soul to eternal damnation: better that a brother should die at once than a sister in redeeming him ignobly should die forever. But, surely, God cannot subscribe to the Shylock-Angelo jurisprudential theory; mercy and forgiveness are at the core of the Christian message. Furthermore, under Christian doctrine, sincere repentance prior to death presumably elevates a sinner from the clutches of hell. That Isabella would be eternally damned should she accept Angelo's offer is far from clear.

Ironically, Isabella implicitly attributes to God a mechanical jurisprudence (her having sex with Angelo to secure a pardon for her brother will be automatically condemned), while special pleading with Angelo to relax his own mechanical jurisprudence when dealing with Claudio. Perhaps we can soften the apparent contradiction by noting that if Isabella accepts Angelo's offer not only will she be a party to morally illicit sex, but she will also be conspiring with Angelo in an abuse of political authority: the granting of pardons on such grounds is morally wrong under mechanical and every other plausible theory of jurisprudence.

In fairness to Isabella, the interrelationship of repentance, divine mercy, and mortal sin is not clear-cut in Christian doctrine. Should Isabella harbor an antecedent desire to sin, knowing that she will later repent and thus be forgiven, her scheme is unlikely to be rewarded. Should she assume antecedently that God will be merciful and submit to Angelo's offer in that light, her anticipated pardon may not be forthcoming. The moral difference between sincere remorse for sins and calculated transgressions designed for future pardons is striking.

Isabella does, however, share some character traits with Angelo. Lucio indicts her as "cold." She, like Angelo, is wired tightly. Proud of her virtue, single-minded in her purpose, and at least somewhat emotionally repressed, she fears the basic passionate instincts that human beings share. Her reaction to the nihilistic moment in Vienna, is to withdraw from what passes for communal life. Keenly aware of the impoverishment of intimacy in Vienna, she takes refuge in an inner circle of devout religious believers who insulate themselves from the depravity of the city. Isabella, then, aspires to the Socratic-Diotima theory of love, but eliminates the middle man. That is, she recognizes the deepest yearnings of her soul—for Absolute Goodness, Truth, and Beauty personified in God—but bypasses the erotic love of another human being as a liaison to that end. For Isabella, the transcendent journey of the Socratic-Diotima pilgrim up the ladder of love can be undertaken directly, at least by a few human beings with a special religious avocation. For such specially-called spiritual travelers, the intercession of earthy, erotic love is unnecessary to the primary quest.

3. Philosophical Interlude: Is Premarital Sex Morally Wrong?

Morality may be understood in at least three ways. First, morality can be understood as *objective*, as consisting of normative principles that human beings do not create but can discover through the use of natural reason. Such principles are transcendent in that they arise from the dictates of a Supreme Being or are otherwise embedded in nature or emerge as conclusions of the single best application of human reason. Second, morality can be understood as *conventional*, as consisting of the normative principles and practices of a particular society; or, less likely, the normative principles and practices of the world as a whole. Such principles and practices are created by human beings and are identified empirically: by examining the actual principles and practices that govern a particular society's moral conduct. No claim is made on this conception that the moral code in place has transcendent, objective standing. Typically, this version of morality asserts that objective morality either does not exist or if it does its findings are inaccessible to human beings. Third, morality can be understood as *adjusted conventional*, as consisting of the normative principles and practices of a particular society that are refined by reason, in tune with certain requirements of logic, and compatible with human well-being. Here the starting point is conventional morality, but the actual normative principles and practices of a society are not taken as self-ratifying. On this account, we must filter out the biases, unwarranted instinctive reactions, and unreasoned prejudices that contaminate a society's principles and practices. Accordingly, normative principles and practices must meet certain logical and practical criteria: coherency; consistency; fit with physiological, psychological, and social conditions; and correlation with an independent standard of human flourishing. Numerous versions of adjusted conventional morality are available with somewhat different, but overlapping, independent criteria of evaluation.

Claudio has been indicted and found guilty of violating the fornication statute that prohibits, among other things, premarital sex. Three questions arise: Is premarital sex genuinely morally impermissible? If so, should such a moral wrong be prohibited by law? Is so, should violators of such a law be subject to capital punishment? I'll address each of these questions in turn as this work proceeds.

One contemporary version of morality understood as adjusted conventionalism would conclude that premarital sex is not morally impermissible as such. Libertarian contractualism attracts much initial acceptance in those cultures that are that venerate the right of contract as necessary for the sanctity of human freedom.[1] Starting from the axiom that persons are ends in themselves, possessors of rights, and the bearers of inherent dignity, libertarian contractualists are wary of moral theories that promote paternalistic measures to protect individuals from their own alleged poor judgment. Libertarians argue that each of us thus has a series of natural rights which correlate to a set of natural negative duties: to refrain from harming, defrauding, coercing, and stealing from other human beings. No external source, whether governmental or religious or social, has the right to decide what is in the self-interest of individuals. Such decisions are unwarranted paternalisms that condescendingly deny the exercise of individual freedom and mock individual autonomy.

Applying libertarian philosophy to sexual relations results in the view that sex is morally permissible if and only if it is consummated with mutual and voluntary informed consent. Rather than focusing on a particular conception of the marriage institution, or a specialized understanding of the proper function of sex, or a natural law perception of the necessary link between sex and human personality, this view highlights the importance of human autonomy as reflected in the agreements we choose to undertake. Proponents insist that the paramount values are individual freedom and autonomy. Thus it is tyranny to insist on a particular kind of sexual interaction or to prescribe a specific domain for acceptable sex. The test of morally permissible sex is simple: Have the parties, possessing the basic capabilities necessary for autonomous choice, voluntarily agreed to a particular sexual interaction without force, fraud, and explicit duress? Accordingly, sex is impermissible only where one or both parties lack the capabilities for informed consent (for example, they are underage, or significantly mentally impaired) or where there is explicit duress (for example, threats or extortion), force (for example, coercion), or fraud (for example, one party deceives the other as to the nature of the act or the extent of his or her feelings as a way of luring the other to accepting the liaison). Accordingly, under this view, the premarital sex of Claudio and Juliet did not violate moral imperatives.

The libertarian contractualist rendering of adjusted conventional morality, however, does not capture fully our contemporary understanding. The most glaring weakness of this position is that it ignores numerous moral distortions that occur in the realm of contract: parties to a contract may have radically unequal bargaining power; they may embody prominent differences in psychological vulnerability; one of the parties may bargain under the oppression of destitute circumstances; or the contract may treat important attributes constitutive of human personality as if they were mere commodities subject to market bartering. Such distortions call into question whether a particular contract is truly morally permissible. The mere existence of a contract that has been transacted according to libertarian guidelines does not establish its moral credentials: contracts are not morally self-validating. That is, once we know that a contract, arrived at through voluntary consent, exists there is still the further question: Are the terms of that contract morally permissible? The libertarian position can succeed only if voluntary contractual interaction comprises the totality of morality. But we have already observed that contemporary contract law, following our sense of morality, denies that view. Numerous contracts that would pass libertarian muster are legally unenforceable because their terms violate public policy or are substantively unconscionable (both of which imply moral judgments) or because the contract is procedurally unconscionable (which sometimes involves moral judgments as to the presence of unequal bargaining power or wrongful exploitation of a contracting party's desperate situation).

A more persuasive version of adjusted conventional morality is recommended. I call it "sexual morality in five tiers."[2] The first tier of evaluation is libertarian consent: Has the sexual liaison occurred under conditions that pass the test of libertarian contractualism? Under my view, libertarian consent is a necessary but not sufficient condition of morally permissible sex. At the second tier of evaluation we must examine general considerations which are applicable when evaluating all moral decision making. There are a number of moral principles commonly acknowledged in our culture: keep promises; tell the truth; return favors; aid others in distress when doing so involves no serious danger or sacrifice to oneself or innocent third parties; make reparation for harm to others that are one's own fault; oppose injustices when doing so involves no great cost or sacrifice to oneself; promote just institutions and facilitate their continuation and refinement; assume one's fair share of societal burdens and thus avoid being a "free rider"; avoid causing pain or suffering to others; avoid inexcusable killing of others; and avoid stealing or otherwise depriving others of their property. Obviously, this is not an exhaustive litany of our moral duties, but the above does constitute the general framework from which we derive other specific obligations. The principles listed above are *prima facie*, not absolute. Their respective imperatives often conflict and thus it is often impossible to fulfill all of their dictates in every moral context. Additionally, appeals to consequences and the real effects of actions will often compel the overriding of a *prima facie* moral principle.

At the third tier of moral evaluation we examine the possibility of wrongful exploitation. Paradigm cases of exploitation involve one party taking advantage of another party's attributes or situation to exact gain for the former or the former's compatriots.[3] The various types of exploitation display various degrees of coercion. At times, exploitation is explicitly coercive, which destroys the possibility of mutually informed consent and libertarian agreement. At other times, exploitation is subtly coercive: the exploiter may capitalize on the victim's relatively inferior bargaining power or special vulnerabilities. At still other times, exploitation may not seem coercive at all: the victim may render fully informed libertarian agreement to the victim's misuse by the exploiter. In cases of noncoercive exploitation, the victim's consent is relevant to, but not dispositive of, moral assessment. That Jones renders fully informed consent to Smith's mutilation of Jones's body, for example, does not entail that Smith's act is morally permissible. Thus, the victim's consent may prevent *the victim* from lodging a credible claim that the victim has been personally wronged by the exploiter's opportunism, but it does not by itself exonerate the exploiter from charges of wrongful exploitation: "What we must mean by (unfair) exploitation is 'profitable utilization of another person that is either on balance unfair to him, or which in virtue of its other unfairness-producing characteristics would be unfair on balance to him but for his voluntary consent to it.'"[4]

At the heart of exploitation is the profit exacted by the exploiter from his or her use of the victim: the victim either suffers an overall setback to his or her interests, or no gain, or a disproportionately meager gain. All this yields the flavor of exploitation as one person 'using another as a mere means' for her own ends. The images here are those of a victim being regarded as less than she is: not as an equal subject of experience, but as a mere instrument for the advance of the exploiter's purposes and profits.

In this vein, the paradigm of subtly coercive exploitation consists of an exploiter with relatively strong socio-economic bargaining power; a victim with special vulnerabilities, needs, or deep wants; a proposition, initiated by the exploiter and formulated for the exploiter's advantage and at the victim's loss or disproportionately small gain, which has the effect of narrowing or closing the victim's overall opportunities.[5] Such exploitation is "subtly coercive" because the force used to secure "consent" is not so obvious as to trigger a violation of libertarian agreement, yet not so benign as to translate clearly to fully informed, mutual consent.

That brings us to the special problems raised by the third type of exploitation, consensual exploitation. Here the victim renders fully informed consent to her misuse by the exploiter. One might be tempted to argue that so long as the victim consented it is presumptuous of others to deem the interaction a "misuse." For who is a better judge of the victim's interests and references than the victim? But a person's perceptions of her best interests and what would advance them are not incorrigibly correct. There are moral limits to what we may do to others even with their consent. The key here is to distinguish different sorts of risks that others are willing to take which we would refuse. When is consent to an uncommon action rash and foolish and thus likely to set back the victim's interests? When is it mere risk-taking that reveals nothing more than the victim's adventuresome and unrestrained nature? The answers are found when we assess the prospects of the victim's gain relative to the exploiter: Will the exploiter realize significant profit, while the victim suffers loss, no gain, or disproportionately paltry gain? Does the victim's consent betray her vulnerabilities, negative self-image, misfortune and destitute circumstances, or human weaknesses? Has the exploiter manipulated the victim by appealing to such vulnerabilities, circumstances, and weaknesses? Has the exploiter thus pandered to the worse aspects of the victim's self? It becomes clearer that to establish "exploitation" we must attend not merely to the foreseeable effects on the victim's interests but also to the exploiter's motives, intentions, and expected gain. Accordingly, the totality of circumstances surrounding the victim's consent is paramount.

Tier four reminds us that sexual acts can be immoral despite the presence of libertarian agreement, the absence of exploitation, and compliance with general moral considerations between the consenting parties. This is the case because sometimes sex acts morally wrong third parties such as innocent children of adulterous parents. We are concerned here mainly with the reasonably foreseeable and actual consequences of the sexual acts in question on the immediate circle of people affected by the acts. Of course, the mere presence of harmful or offensive effects to others by a sexual act is insufficient to establish that the act in question is morally flawed when judged by tier four. At times, third parties, because of their own biases or prejudices, are offended by sexual actions that are morally permissible (for example, the racist who is highly offended by interracial dating). The paramount questions, then, are whether the rights of third parties have been violated and whether their interests have been transgressed unjustifiably.

Tier five assesses wider social context: there are times when sexual activity accompanied by libertarian agreement nevertheless has detrimental social effects. Such acts might reflect and reinforce oppressive social roles, contribute to continued social inequality, gestate new forms of gender oppression, or otherwise add to the contamination of the wider social and political context surrounding sexual activity. Sex acts are not always merely discrete interactions between consenting parties.

Although I am presenting the theory in discrete levels of analysis, sexual morality in five tiers is not so easily categorized. Often the questions implicated at one level of analysis replicate themselves at another level, or require answers supplied at least partly from analyses at other levels. Here I have provided only a sketch of sexual morality in five tiers. Elsewhere I have worked out its implication in detail.[6]

Under this account, *Measure for Measure* provides no evidence that Claudio and Juliet violated moral imperatives during sexual intercourse. Their liaison was involved mutual consent, did not transgress any general moral considerations, lacked exploitive elements, did not wrongfully trample upon the rights or interests of immediate third parties, and produced no wrongful effects on the wider social context.

But, of course, the (imaginary) Viennese morality that informs the play is much different from our own. Instead of invoking a particular version of adjusted conventional morality, the Viennese subscribe to an objective morality grounded in Christian religion. As such, they would never address the distinctions or struggle with the calculus that informs sexual morality in five tiers. Instead, they would assert confidently that all sexual activity outside the confines of marriage is morally wrong as such. The basis of that judgment would be well-established interpretations of Christian scripture and doctrine. From all accounts, despite this grounding, the moral theory and moral practice of the citizens of Vienna diverge widely from Christian dogma. Unfortunately for Claudio, under the version of morality that underwrites the play, he is morally guilty. The questions whether the law should be used to enforce this moral judgment and whether the prescribed punishment fits the crime remain to be examined.

4. Downbeat Consolation

Angelo had granted Claudio the privilege of consulting a confessor prior to his execution. The confessor who appears is none other than Duke Vincentio disguised as a friar. The Friar-Duke asks Claudio if he hopes for a pardon from Angelo. Claudio responds that "I have hope to live, and am prepar'd to die" (3.1.4).

The remainder of the session consists of the Friar-Duke instructing Claudio to be certain that he must die and orating drearily against the value of life. Life is an attribute that only fools would keep. Life is insubstantial, gravely frustrating, riddled with diseases, corrupted by painful aging, and irredeemably base.

> If I do lose [life], I do lose a thing
> That none but fools would keep. A breath thou art,
> Servile to all the skyey influences,
> That dost this habitation where thou keep'st
> Hourly afflict. Merely, thou art death's fool,
> For him thou labor'st by thy light to shun,
> And yet run'st toward him still. Thou art not noble,
> For all th' accomomodations that thou bear'st
> Are nurs'd by baseness (3.1.7-15).

The Friar-Duke's soliloquy on the value of life continues and grows bleaker with every line. He paints a portrait of life without consolation, deeper meaning, and larger significance. So dispiriting is the speech that we expect the Friar-Duke to advise Claudio to send Angelo a bouquet of roses in gratitude for ordering his executing and thereby releasing him from the pitiless suffering that defines human life. Notice that the Friar-Duke never broaches the topics of divine forgiveness, personal redemption, and infinite reward. However, Claudio is overtaken by the Friar-Duke's downbeat eloquence, thanks him, and pledges that he is now prepared to die (3.1.42-44).

5. Philosophical Interlude: The Specter of Pessimism

The Duke refocuses Claudio's attention from death to life. If life is not as precious as commonly thought then death is far less frightening a deprivation. Human beings are impelled toward the future; we in effect chase after death which may befall us at any moment. We seek respite in sleep and what is death but an infinite sleep? Human beings are but specks of universal dust; even our sense of individuality is but illusion; we are discontented in our strivings; subject to inevitable disease and the maladies of aging; and pursue our goals mightily then find the rewards of success insufficient to our efforts. The only certitudes of human life are frustration, insecurity, and disappointment, followed by death.

Duke Vincentio's oration on death anticipates the work of Arthur Schopenhauer. The German philosopher was deeply skeptical that attaining happiness was even possible.[7] Schopenhauer observed that human life is beset with universal, unavoidable suffering which prevents fulfillment of basic needs and wants. Life itself, not merely mortality and fear of death, renders human existence problematic. Striving is the basic nature of the will, and no finished project can end striving. Schopenhauer envisions human beings as fastened to a punishing pendulum: Sensing a lack or deficiency we conjure, subconsciously or consciously, a desire. We pursue that desire and either attain it or fail to do so. If we fail, we become frustrated, disappointed, angry, and may even indulge in self-pity. If we attain our goal, we experience a brief period of elation, followed swiftly by boredom. Attaining our goal never brings the glorious transformation we had imagined. Because striving is incapable of final serenity, we alternate between the lack of fulfillment we feel when not achieving temporary goals and the sense of letdown and boredom we feel when we attain them. In either case, we soon thereafter pursue new goals, obtusely hoping for a different result while repeating the same futile process.

Schopenhauer claims, then, that human desire is unquenchable. Much like Plato's tyrannical man, we create new desires soon after we fulfill earlier desires. We always want more regardless of how many desires we fulfill. Worse, a few "decoy birds" that seem to be happy, lure us into mindlessly remaining on this self-defeating pendulum of desire. Schopenhauer concludes, along with the Buddhists, that we should minimize our attachments to this life and withdraw as much as possible from it. Our existence is cheeriest when we perceive it least. Philosophical contemplation, music, and art elevate us by allowing us to be disinterested spectators of life. But only specially gifted human beings can pursue such lofty activity and they will pay a price for their talents: They are more vulnerable to suffering and are estranged from the masses.

But we should not jump aboard Schopenhauer's pessimistic bandwagon nor purchase a ticket on Duke Vincentio's epigone express. Schopenhauer fails to see that value and meaning need not be permanent to be real; that process renders fulfillments independently of attaining goals; that the attainments of great effort and creation do not instantaneously produce emptiness; and that suffering is not inherently negative but can be transfigured for creative advantage.

What is the state to which Schopenhauer aspires? Does he secretly yearn for a condition of never-ending bliss? Does freedom from suffering require that we want nothing more? Many would find such a life deadening. A life devoid of new projects, adventures, journeys, and goals lacks creativity: bland contentment replaces vigorous thought and action. Perhaps suffering is produced not by the process of seeking fulfillment of new desires but by starving our desire-creating mechanism. Having unfulfilled desires need not be painful; it is often exhilarating. We imagine rewarding new situations and pursue them vigorously. We find fulfillments in the process and, often, in achieving the goal. Our insatiability ensures that we continue to imagine and pursue rewarding projects, instead of being limited to contemplating earlier fulfillments. Whether the new desires we create produce suffering depends on what they are and how we pursue them, not solely on their presence.

A crude dualism infects Schopenhauer's analysis. He separates human experience into desires and results. But human life is not experienced as a series of discrete pursuits of isolated goals. The process of striving itself yields satisfactions independently of attaining its goals. Upon being attained, goals propel us to new projects. Boredom results from inactivity, a loss of faith in life, and a lack of imagination. But human beings live in a continuous process of desires, finding appropriate means of satisfying those desires, and failing to achieve or attaining the ends we seek. As a continuous process, the categories of desires, means, and ends are fluid. What is called an end in relation to a particular means is itself a means to another end. What is an end with respect to a particular desire is itself a desire leading to pursuit of another end. The continuous process, at its best, energizes our spirit, manifests our faith in life, and reveals our imagination.[8]

Schopenhauer talks of our incessant striving as if it were a disease to be eradicated through withdrawal. But human beings are not static characters trying to find a fixed point called "contentment." If contentment suggests inactivity, a final termination, or a mere savoring of the past then it does conjure terminal boredom or retreat from the world. If we understand contentment more robustly we will underscore its compatibility with continuous activity and self-creation. Contentment is not a final resting point, but a positive self-appraisal: an acknowledgment that we are on the proper course, a savoring of the past seasoned with hope for the future, a satisfaction with the self we are creating. Schopenhauer failed to understand that if we create an endless supply of rewarding projects, our lack of final satisfaction bears joyous tidings. Life, after all, is far from as dreary as it is depicted by Schopenhauer and in Duke Vincentio's speech to Claudio. The Duke may have stunned Claudio for the moment, but more vigorous human instincts will reappear. For better and for worse, Claudio's desires to continue living and resist death will regenerate.

6. The Family Feud

Isabella enters and alludes to the possibility that Claudio may live because of Angelo's "devilish mercy" (3.1.64). As always, in the context of the play, allusion, foreshadowing, and innuendo enjoy privilege of place over direct speech. Isabella instructs Claudio that six or seven years of continued life (Is that all the time that remains for Claudio should he evade the executioner's scythe?) is less valuable than perpetual honor: an honorable death is preferable to a life dishonorably redeemed. Furthermore, anticipating the astuteness of Franklin Delano Roosevelt, Isabella assures Claudio that the only thing we have to fear about death is the fear of death itself (3.1.75-77). Isabella's convictions are grounded in her fervent Christian belief in a perfectly just afterlife. She wants Claudio to take her off the ethical hook; she seeks and expects that Claudio will firmly reject Angelo's despicable proposition. Isabella yearns to cast off moral responsibility for the decision. Still savoring the Friar-Duke's counsel, Claudio assures Isabella that "If I must die, / I will encounter darkness as a bride,/ And hug it in mine arms" (3.1.81-83). We shall soon discover that Claudio's Christian commitment to a perfectly just afterlife is far less robust than that of Isabella.

Having engaged in the obligatory windup and preliminary parrying, Isabella comes to the point: Angelo is a devil in saint's clothing; he will grant Claudio a pardon if and only if Isabella has sex with him. On cue, Claudio is shocked at the overture and instructs Isabella that she must not accept Angelo's vile terms. As ever, drawn to the drama of martyrdom, Isabella says she would gladly give her life (but presumably not her chastity) to redeem the life of her brother: death before dishonor. She advises Claudio to prepare for death the following day (3.1.88-102).

Suddenly, Claudio forgets the Friar-Duke's lessons on life and his own earlier resolutions to Isabella. He begins to recognize his stark fears. Whether he loves life or whether he fears death, Claudio is not prepared for his execution. He begins his retreat: familiar with Dante, Claudio argues that lust is morally wrong, but, after all, it is the least of the seven deadly sins; Angelo is too wise to risk eternal damnation for only one sex act. Claudio suggests that God would not punish this act under these circumstances as harshly as Isabella first suspected. Isabella is puzzled as she has not yet captured fully the drift of Claudio's discourse (3.1.109-114).

Claudio then offers a soliloquy on the horrors of death that mirrors the darkness of the Friar-Duke's speech on the shallowness of life. Unlike Isabella, Claudio is uncertain as to the nature of death. Our bodies may rot in gloom and cold. Again recalling Dante, our spirits may "bathe in fiery floods," or "reside in thrilling region of thick-ribbed ice" to be "imprison'd in the viewless winds" and "blown with restless violence round about" (3.1.117-124). Claudio imagines frightening "howling" and a most loathsome afterlife that by comparison renders any life a "paradise" (3.1.127-131): any life is preferable to death. Isabella cries out in grief and Claudio finally expresses his point: "Sister, sister, let me live./ What sin you do to save a brother's life,/ Nature dispenses with the deed so far,/ That it becomes a virtue" (3.1.131-134).

Less religious than his sister, Claudio fears that death may be utter annihilation. If an afterlife does await him, he can conjure only the horrors of Dante's

Inferno.[9] Perhaps Claudio feels guilty because he knows his past much better than do readers of the play. Perhaps Claudio reflects his noble birth and places too much importance on his own existence. In any case, Claudio implores Isabella to advance his cause.

Spurred by self-interest and stone cold terror of death, Claudio, the wavering Christian, invokes a merciful God. Surely, such an infallible judge would not eternally condemn Isabella for sex under these circumstances. Yes, to describe the act as "virtue" is a moral stretch on Claudio's part, but human beings often confront conflicts between seemingly absolute moral rules; we often must select the lesser of two competing evils or the greater of two competing goods. Regardless of the dubious source of his conclusion, Claudio does express a pertinent moral point.

Undoubtedly frightened by sex as such, appalled that her brother would barter her sexuality as if it were a mere commodity, and acutely aware of her novice oaths, Isabella's tightly-wound moral coils explode. She calls Claudio a "beast," a "faithless coward," and a "dishonest wretch" (3.1.135-136). Those are the kindest remarks she offers her cowering sibling.

She is stunned that Claudio would cling to life by requiring her to sin. She suggests that Claudio could not have issued from her father's blood and must be illegitimate. She curiously characterizes the redeeming of life through a sister's shame as "incest" (3.1.137-138). Claudio has cast the moral responsibility for the decision back upon Isabella and the maneuver horrifies her. Isabella closes cruelly, "I'll pray a thousand prayers for thy death, /No word to save thee. / . . . 'Tis best that thou diest quickly" (3.1.145-150). Desperately, Claudio cries out to her.

7. Philosophical Interlude: Life & Death

The Friar-Duke's dismal assessment of life and Claudio's lament on death reflect common themes, sometimes claimed to include an Epicurean flavor.[10]

Epicureanism was an influential version of hedonism. Epicurus (341-270 BC) and Titus Lucretius Carus ("Lucretius") (95-50 BC) were the most important Epicurean philosophers.[11] Liberating human beings from fear and maximizing their prospects for happiness motivated Epicurus. On his view, pleasure, which defined happiness, was the greatest good. But not just any pleasure, only simple, sustainable ones. Worthy pleasures, those that define happiness, do not include the tortured trinity of wine, women or men, and song. The best pleasures preclude pain and produce a serene spirit. Epicurus's recipe for happiness was health, self-control, independence, moderation, simplicity, cheerfulness, friendship, prudence, intellectual and aesthetic values, and peace of mind. The calm, tranquil, harmonious life is the happy life. He explained why this is so by appealing to the conditions of the world, to human nature, and to the natural order.

The recipe for Epicurean acquisition was sparse: friendship is critical for self-validation and to nurture gentleness and sympathy; freedom is crucial and defined by liberation from the anxieties and imprisonments of social and political affairs; philosophical contemplation is required to ease irrational fears and to vivify pleasures of the mind; and simple food, clothing, and shelter are necessary to satisfy basic physical needs. This quartet and the means required to attain them are the only *natural and necessary* human desires.

Natural but unnecessary human desires would include sex, lavish banquets, private baths, spacious homes, special foods and drinks, and the like. Human beings should regard the satisfaction of such desires with indifference. *Unnatural and unnecessary* human desires, which are not grounded in reality, include fame, power, wealth, and the like. We should repudiate such desires. For Epicurus, the satisfaction of these two categories of desires can never bring human fulfillment; whereas the satisfaction of natural and necessary desires both guarantees and is required for human fulfillment. The greatest good is Epicurean pleasure. Moral virtue has instrumental value as a means of attaining that pleasure, but remains subordinate to the greatest good.

Epicurean prescriptions are few, but powerful: live kindly and sympathetically among friends; live quietly and avoid the troubles of competition and aggressiveness; live with few material possessions—you'll have less to lose and fewer responsibilities; live moderately and avoid excesses. Such imperatives may require common sense and practical wisdom to apply, but they do not demand esoteric understanding or deep intellectualism. Unlike the Friar-Duke, Epicurus did not portray life as irredeemably frustrating and pointless. We can transform our lives through philosophical insight.

One aspect of living a full Epicurean life is the alleviation of fear. Epicurus devised a powerful strategy. First, he identified the beliefs and actions that caused human beings unnecessary pain and suffering: Fear of the gods, anxiety about death and an afterlife, and the pursuit of self-defeating pleasures. Then, he reimagined and re-created a vision of human life that eliminated the main causes of human pain and suffering. Finally, he and his followers embodied and acted on this vision, and drew supporters attracted to the charismatic exemplars of the Epicurean lifestyle.

If fear of the gods is a problem then what is the solution? Epicurus might have simply denied that gods exist: No gods, no fear. This solution, though, would have been unpersuasive to a Greco-Roman world that acknowledged and paid tribute to numerous, anthropomorphic deities with carefully circumscribed spheres of influence. Epicurus was convinced that the universal belief in the gods could be explained only by their objective reality. The gods, then, existed.

Epicurus, though, rejected the common view that celestial bodies were deities. The sun, moon, and stars are inanimate, whereas gods must be animate; celestial bodies are destructible, whereas gods are immortal; and celestial bodies are insensitive, whereas gods enjoy pleasurable lives. Anticipating an enduring, theological problem, Epicurus was puzzled by the amount of evil and suffering in the world. How could such enormous, unexplainable evil persist if divine providence ruled? Epicurus concluded that divine providence was a myth, a misunderstanding of the nature of the gods. Although the gods existed, the nature of their existence differed from the prevalent understanding. Epicurus brought forth the good news that the real nature of the existence of the gods should not engender fear. The gods exist as beautiful, happy, calm, merry, and indifferent to human life. The gods, fortuitously, are Epicureans! Indeed, they serve as divine ideals for the proper human life. Accordingly, human beings should not fear the gods because the gods do not punish or reward us. Instead, we should look to the lives of the gods as exemplars toward which to strive while on earth.

Having eliminated to his satisfaction the fear of gods, Epicurus took on his next target: Fear of death and an afterlife. He observed that fear of death and anxiety over an afterlife disabled numerous human beings from full engagement in this world. Such suffering was unnecessary and grounded on philosophical errors.

Epicurus rejected mind-body dualism and belief in personal immortality. Subscribing to the atomic theory developed by the pre-Socratic philosopher, Democritus, Epicurus argued that the world is eternal and composed of atoms that produce everything by their infinitely variable combinations. Each human being is composed of atoms that disperse entirely after the death of the body. No afterlife waits us.

Epicurus held that death is not an evil. He argued that death is irrelevant to us. For Epicurus, all good and evil consists in sensations: Pleasure is good, pain is evil. However, death is the end of all sensations, so death is nothing to us. We have no good reason to fear what is nothing to us.

Having eliminated to their satisfaction the fear of death and an afterlife, Epicureans took on their final target: Dissatisfaction caused by pursuit of self-defeating pleasures. Epicurus, following the Socratic-Platonic tradition, disparaged physical and material pleasures as enslaving: The more we get the more we want *ad infinitum*. Here part of the Friar-Duke's message to Claudio resonates. We too easily become addicted to pleasures over which we have too little control and which jeopardize a well-ordered, harmonious internal condition. Such pleasures produce, at best, transitory pleasure that transforms into more enduring suffering. Epicurus, though, goes further. He disputes several of the projects that Aristotle thought necessary for *eudaemonia*. Epicurus observed that politics, marriage, family relations, and most passionate pursuits too often produced anxiety and ended badly. Avoiding pain, especially mental suffering, is even more important than pursuing pleasure. The absence of passion facilitates contentment. We must discard many of our desires or, at least, not act on them. The Epicurean program is explicitly for personal development, an egoistic hedonism grounded in withdrawal from public life. Thus,

Epicurus anticipates Isabella's strategy of self-exile from the corruptions of the city.

Lucretius reinforced and refined Epicurean doctrine. His *De Rerum Natura* includes a rejection of religious superstition and its fear-inducing consequences; a contrast between Epicurean serenity and the hyper-aggressive, ultra-competitive, zero-sum game afflicting Roman politics; a parody of people who desperately hold on to life from their misguided fear of death; a critique of the alleged benefits of sexual desire; and an effusive eulogy to Epicurus as the potential rescuer of mankind if only more people would heed his counsel.

Lucretius indicted traditional Roman competitiveness and relentless striving as the source of the republic's political and social predicament: "The quietism that Lucretius advocated could not sit well with most members of the Roman elite. They had been raised on an ideology that placed a premium on military achievement and political renown. Lucretius's poem, however, coming at the collapse of the Roman Republic was a remarkable challenge to traditional Roman values."[12] In contrast to Stoicism, which supported some of Rome's cherished political, religious, and social traditions, Epicureanism seriously resisted several Roman fundamental beliefs.

For Lucretius, nonphilosophical political and military strivers are akin to insignificant insects, hopping from task to task without reflecting on the meaning of anything. Only wisdom, which demands conversion to Epicurean philosophy, can lead human beings to their highest fulfillment. The relentless striving seeks more and more, but realizes less and less (DRN 2.7-2.14).

Lucretius concluded that the fear of death was the source of the Roman zero-sum contests for wealth, power, and honor. Horrified by their looming mortality, citizens desperately clung to life in the forms of economic security and the celebrity of military and political victories. Although such unnatural, unnecessary pursuits could not provide enduring satisfaction—even if their goals were achieved—men were drawn to them as a puny, self-defeating defiance of their finitude (DRN 3.59-3.86). However, unnatural, unnecessary desires are built around fantasies; they cannot be satisfied or bring fulfillment.

Lucretius also argues against the transmigration of the soul and personal immortality. For those subscribing to transmigration theory—the view that the soul is immortal and at death passes into another body—Lucretius poses a question. If one argues that a human soul always passes into a human body, then why is an infant not as learned as an adult? If the reply is that the soul grows young in a young body, then the soul is mortal because it loses some of its former properties. The soul must be, then, corporeal. The union of soul and body brings forth human life. The belief that an immortal soul changes with its change of body is inconsistent: If the soul can change then it can also be disaggregated and perish. Composed of atoms, the human soul is destined for disaggregation. At death, the body dies and can no longer meld the soul together, so the atoms composing the soul must scatter. What comes into being with the body will pass from existence with the body. Death, in the sense of annihilation, holds no terror for us. By rejecting dualism, embracing monism, and appreciating our mortality, we eliminate the fear of punishment after death (DRN 3.323-3.369; 3.417-3.829).

Lucretius placed no stock in claims of antecedent natural law or the divinity of the universe. The constitutive elements of the universe are inappropriate havens for life and human thought. The laws of the universe emerge only after atoms randomly collide, form bodies, and develop structure. Also, because neither the universe as a whole nor its constitutive parts are animate, they cannot be divinities (DRN 5.110-5.145). The gods lack a conception of the world prior to its actual existence; no convincing account can be offered for the god's alleged change before and after creation; and the flaws in our world deny divine providence (DRN 2.167-2.183; 5.156-5.234). The gods exist not to impose upon or punish human beings, but to permit them to pursue pleasure, which is also the chief concern of the deities. The world is free from divine intervention. Human beings have no need to fear the gods (DRN 2.646-2.651). Human beings were led to believe in the gods because of dream visions and their inability to explain celestial activity. True piety, though, does not reside in rituals, sacrifices, and currying favor with divinities, but in peaceful contemplation of the universe (DRN 5.1169-5.1203).

The only entities as such are atoms and the void. Time is a feature of the universe, not an independent dimension governing it. Atoms form combinations that comprise nature and the natural process; there are no controlling agents above the atoms and the void. The swerve of atoms falling allows them to stray from a perfectly downward course, contact one another, and form the requisite pacts that constitute the world. But for the swerve, atoms would fall straight through space into the void and our world would not exist. Our world, then, developed empirically, through trial and error, and the purposeless play of atoms, not teleologically, through a grand design, master creator, or inherent design.

Lucretius also develops Epicurus's remarks on fearing death. Life is finite. We are not anxious or upset because we did not exist prior to our actual births, so we should not fear a comparable nonexistence after death. Put in a modern context: the year 1505 was nothing to us and conjures no anxiety in the year 2008; so, too, the year 2099, by which we will all be dead, should cause us no anxiety now. The reality of being dead—nothingness—will be no better or worse for us than the expansive period prior to our births (DRN 3.830-3.869).

Lucretius's argument is simple but challenging: Human beings are untroubled by prenatal nonexistence; posthumous nonexistence ("death") is the mirror image of prenatal nonexistence; accordingly, human beings should be untroubled by their upcoming deaths. The core of the argument is that prenatal nonexistence was an indefinitely long experiential zero that held no terror for us. Death is an indefinitely long experiential zero the prospects of which should also hold no terror for us. Neither prenatal nonexistence nor death harms us; we have no persuasive reason to fear that which does not harm us; thus we have no persuasive reason to fear death.

Epicureans, then, unlike the Friar-Duke, offer a way to attain happiness in life: eliminate or ignore the urge to satisfy unnecessary desires; focus only on pursuing natural and necessary desires; and eliminate irrational fears. Unlike Claudio, they offer a way to soften or eliminate the terror of death: accepting the annihilation thesis that holds that death brings the end of our existence; and understanding that death is neither a good nor an evil.

We all can benefit from a dose of Epicurean advice. But like all medicines, if we consume too much we will aggravate our illness. If we take Epicureanism too seriously we dehumanize ourselves. My general objection to Epicureanism is that it fails to capture the subtlety of the antinomies generated by the individual-community continuum. Epicureans deny our existential condition by trying to extinguish our need for robust community. Even friendship is reduced to instrumental value, as its main Epicurean justification is benefit to the self, not the other person. Although it was a powerful philosophy in its historical setting, contemporary thinkers might well conclude that Epicurean austerity needs a measure of nineteenth-century romanticism for completion. Anesthetizing ourselves from social pain also prevents us from experiencing our greatest joys and triumphs. By denying the human need for transcendence, our quest to reimagine and re-create our selves and our contexts, the Epicurean version of egoistic hedonism severs us from paramount sources of human meaning and value: family, civic participation, grand social projects. Critics can cogently argue that steadfast devotion to Epicureanism offers much consolation but little growth. Accordingly, Epicureanism encourages human beings to settle for small enterprises and to be satisfied with mundane engagements. The romantic impulses toward robust context-smashing, self-transcendence, vigorous social engagement, and large-scale adventures wither away. Surely avoiding the dreary conclusions about life offered by the Friar-Duke does not require that we settle for Epicurean minimalism.

Regarding death, some human beings, including Isabella, take comfort in a belief in personal immortality. Energized, typically by theistic faith, they view earthly life as a preparation for an eternally blissful afterlife. Under this view, death is often seen as a separation of a self-subsistent soul from the body. Others deny the dualism—the separation of immaterial soul from material body—in the immortality thesis and take death to be the cessation of all experience, the irrevocable termination of consciousness. The denial of dualism and immortality can lead to personal despair and suffocating doubt about the meaning and value of life. What can it all matter if in a few years our lives will be coldly, cruelly, and efficiency snuffed out by an unfeeling cosmos to which no appeal for mercy is possible?

Epicurus and Lucretius rejected dualism yet maintained that death is not an evil. They argued that death is irrelevant to us. For Epicureans, all good and evil consists in sensations, death is the end of all sensations, so death is nothing to us. Death, reasoned Epicurus, must be nothing to us because death is not with us while we are living and when it arrives we no longer exist. Therefore, death does not concern either the living or the dead, because for the living death is not, and the dead are no more. For Epicurus, death is the cessation of all experiences, and at death a human decomposes and no sensations can persist because there is no physical object to sense anything.

The Epicurean view of death is unpersuasive, but annoyingly challenging. Both Epicurus and Lucretius accept a hedonistic assumption: the sensations of pleasure and pain define what is good and bad for us. This assumption is unacceptable. We are sometimes harmed by events because they violate our rights or transgress against our just entitlements. But such events do not necessarily hurt us—that do not cause us pain or suffering—if we are unaware of them. What we do not know may not hurt us, but it can still harm us. For example, if someone tells malicious lies about me to a third party behind my back, the lies may harm my reputation but I may never discover the betrayal. I am harmed because my interest in maintaining my deserved, high reputation is transgressed upon, but I am not hurt by the lies because I am unaware of them and thus I am not pained by them. The hedonistic assumption, then, defines good and bad too narrowly. Even if death does not hurt us from an Epicurean perspective, it may well harm us. Death often harms because it deprives us of the ongoing good that was our life.[13] Accordingly, the Epicurean pleasure principle cannot capture the entire truth about morality. Good cannot simply be identified with pleasant sensations, evil with painful sensations. Thus, we cannot conclude that death is nothing to us because it is the end of all sensations.

This also demonstrates why the pleasure principle is more widely flawed. By evaluating right and wrong only in terms of individual or collective pleasure and pain, we capture, at best, only part of our fixed moral judgments. At times, morality requires performing the proper act despite the fact that our or the collective pleasure is not served. Furthermore, heroic deeds are such because they sacrifice individual pleasure for wider, moral purposes that do not automatically increase collective pleasure.

Instead of being nothing to us, death makes us nothing, if we reject, with Epicurus, dualism and the immortality thesis. Death renders us incapable of enjoying pleasure and suffering pain. If death is an evil it must be because it is a deprivation, it ends those aspects of our lives that are meaningful, valuable, and good. Even if the hedonistic assumption was correct, death could still be considered a detriment. If a death cuts off a life that could have enjoyed a much greater balance of pleasurable over unpleasurable sensations if it had continued, then that death could reasonably be viewed as tragic, an unfortunate deprivation, even if we restrict, as do the hedonists, good and bad only to sensations. The person would have been better off if he or she had not died.

Those things of value in life—interpersonal relationships, projects, goals, aspirations, interests, and associations—end at death. And that is why death often seems so bad. Mere biological survival is not important to us. We do not hope for a permanent coma even if we are thereby kept biologically alive. A life completely lacking value and meaning would be a life not worth living, at least to the person in this condition. Death ensures, stipulating the rejection of dualism and the immortality thesis, that we are permanently deprived of the value, meaning, and good connected to our lives. While many of us also dread the process of dying and theists may fear eternal damnation, deprivation is the main reason we fear death and regard it as an evil.

Some deaths are more evil than others, even though the democracy of death commands we all die once. The evilness of a death is directly proportional to the actual and potential value of the life that has been terminated. Death is not always an evil because it is not always true that a meaningful and valuable life has ended. A meaningless and valueless life is one in which a person's crucial activities and aspirations cannot be engaged in, nor is there a potentiality for future participation. If life itself, or a particular life, is not a good then its termination is not an evil. When our dearest projects are complete, our creative energies exhausted, and our higher human capabilities evaporating, death can be timely.

Although death is inevitable this does not make the deprivation of life any less evil. Inevitability means the fact that we shall die is out of our control, but to acknowledge this need not make an occurrence any less evil. Suppose on every first Thursday all human beings would inevitably undergo severe stomach cramps, bleed profusely from the nose, and be afflicted with double vision, would the inevitability of these ills make them less evil or painful or bad? The inevitability of death may mean that worrying about whether we will die is pointless, but that is about all it means.

Isabella does not fear death because she is convinced that her virtuous Christian life will be infinitely rewarded in the afterlife. Having transcended the Friar-Duke's dire assessment of life, Claudio fears death because he believes that death is either utter annihilation that he tacitly regards as a deprivation; or death will initiate the parade of horribles described by Dante. Claudio has scant confidence that he has led a life that will be rewarded infinitely. Our evaluation of the lives we have led will greatly influence our perception of our impending deaths.

8. The Bed Trick

Having overheard the conversation between siblings, The Friar-Duke enters and assures Claudio that Angelo never intended to carry out the terms of his proposition to Isabella. Instead, he was only testing her virtue. The Friar-Duke claims to know this because he is Angelo's confessor. Thus, Claudio must prepare to die. The ever vacilating Claudio swallows the bait, "Let me ask my sister pardon. I am so out of love with life that I will sue to be rid of it" (3.1.171-172). In order to facilitate his nest of lies, schemes, and intrigues, the Friar-Duke keeps the siblings apart.

The Friar-Duke approaches Isabella, who has resolved to reveal Angelo's treacheries to the Duke when he returns to Vienna. The Friar-Duke observes that Angelo will claim that he was only testing her. But the Friar-Duke has an idea: Claudio can be saved and Isabella's honor preserved. Five years earlier, Angelo and Mariana had entered into a betrothal contract; however, a shipwreck had cost Mariana her brother's life and her dowry. Bereft of the material security he sought through marriage, Angelo reneged on his promise and spread false allegations that Mariana was unchaste (if these allegations were true they would have provided Angelo just cause to withdraw from their agreement). Despite Angelo's cruel mendacity and undeniable opportunism, Mariana continues to long for him. The Friar-Duke then unveils the scheme: Isabella will accept Angelo's proposition, but the Friar-Duke will convince Mariana to take Isabella's place. After the couple has sex, Angelo will fulfill his part of the arrangement and pardon Claudio. Thus, Claudio's life will be spared, Isabella will not sin, and Mariana, especially if impregnated during the liaison, will have a marital claim (3.1.189-255). The Friar-Duke adds that "the doubleness of the benefit defends the deceits from reproof" (3.1.257-258).

Suddenly, we have left the realm of absolute moral rules and entered the domain of means-ends utilitarian calculations. Does Isabella recoil at the deception, manipulation, and extramarital sex involved? Does she question the fate of those who violate critical moral rules?

Of course she does not. She has the assurances of one whom she believes to be a religious superior and Isabella readily complies with the dictates of religious management. Does she wonder if Angelo can be so easily duped so as to think his former girlfriend is Isabella? Of course she does not. This is a play and the bed trick is a staple feature of the genre and the period.

Prior to the Friar-Duke convincing Mariana to sign on to his intrigue, he comes upon Constable Elbow, Pompey, and some officers. Soon thereafter they are joined by Lucio. Pompey, the pimp-tapster, has been arrested for possession of a picklock. Lucio needles Pompey throughout and refuses to bail him out of prison. Lucio goes on a series of rants against Angelo, indicting his nonhuman repression of instincts and questioning his parentage. But then Lucio, who claims to know the Duke well and love him, slanders him: The Duke would not condemn men to death under the fornication statute because the Duke enjoys women himself; the Duke is superficial and ignorant; he frequents prostitutes; and he would "mouth with a beggar though she smelt brown bread and garlic" (3.2.183-184). Always preoccupied with his standing among citizens, the Friar-Duke seethes and stores the information securely in his memory. Lucio's promiscuous tongue will be dealt with at the appropriate time (3.2.1-188).

The Friar-Duke and Isabella meet Mariana. Isabella has agreed to Angelo's proposition and tried to set terms that will minimize the possibility that Angelo will discover it is Mariana with whom he copulates (4.1.28-39). Isabella convinces Mariana to accept her role in the intrigue. The Friar-Duke adds, "Nor, gentle daughter, fear you not at all. / He is your husband on a pre-contract:/ To bring you thus together 'tis no sin, / Sith that the justice of your title to him/ Doth flourish the deceit" (4.1.70-74). That the Friar-Duke misstates Church doctrine, which did not confer legitimacy upon extramarital sex between an engaged couple, whether undertaken voluntarily or through deceit, goes unexplored. As always, the women genuflect before what they take to be superior religious authority.

9. Philosophical Interlude: If Premarital Sex is Morally Wrong Should it be Legally Prohibited?

Under my preferred view, sexual morality in five tiers, premarital sex is not immoral as such. Of course, as are any sexual interactions, particular instances of premarital sex are immoral if they violate the standards of the five tiers. However, the Elizabethan age did not anticipate sexual morality in five tiers. At least in theory, premarital sex as such was judged immoral during this period because it presumably violated the law of God as interpreted by the Church.

Stipulating for the sake of argument that premarital sex is morally wrong, the next question is whether the law should prohibit these acts. As the domain of the moral and the realm of the legal overlap but are not identical, not all immoral actions are prohibited by the law. The case against legally prohibiting premarital sex is strong: suppressing premarital sex is not required for public security as such acts do not typically harm third parties; any harm that results from premarital sex is antecedently consented to by the parties; any harm that results is indirect and not the direct purpose of the act—unlike, say, a contract involving disablement or killing or slavery; laws prohibiting acts such as premarital sex are virtually impossible to enforce equitably—because the acts are private, detection will be random and enforcement will be capricious, thereby triggering compelling claims of procedural due process and fairness, as well as sapping respect for law generally; the existence of such laws invites state officials to target otherwise law-abiding people whom they desire to victimize for other reasons; and in societies that prize individual freedom the coercive powers of the state should be invoked only when prohibiting the act in question is much more important than honoring citizens' rights to privacy and autonomy.[14]

In spite of such considerations, Patrick Devlin famously offered an argument in favor of legally prohibiting certain sexual behavior.[15] Devlin based his argument on the relationship between private action and social harm. He began by claiming that the prevention of harm to society itself, not just prevention of harm to individuals, is an appropriate function of criminal law. A shared moral code, a web of beliefs binding individuals together, is a necessary condition for the existence of a community. To damage the shared moral code by, say, engaging in forms of sexuality that it emphatically proscribes, is to weaken, for your part, the fabric of the community and to harm society itself. Because of the dangers involved, society has as much right to safeguard its moral code as it does to protect its political institutions. Devlin underscores his argument by analogizing private morals offenses to treason: "The suppression of vice is as much the law's business as the suppression of subversive activities; it is no more possible to define a sphere of private morality than it is to define one of private subversive activity."[16]

Unsurprisingly, politically liberal theorists have not embraced Devlin's argument warmly. First, even if we concede that a shared morality is a necessary condition for the existence of a vibrant community, does it follow that the particular moral code in place is the only suitable candidate to fulfill that role?[17] So even if widespread private sexual behavior at variance with a society's processed moral code takes place and even if it has the effect of weakening the web of moral beliefs hitherto in place, it does not follow that the existence of the community is thereby jeopardized. Perhaps the community can evolve quite nicely by accommodating the adjusted moral code that ensues. Second, in that vein, the analogy between private sexual behavior and treason is strained. For example, will a host of people independently engaging in premarital sex really produce a threat comparable to a treasonous plot? Even if the effects are comparably small, do not the acts differ in intent and motivation? To engage in, say, premarital sex or a *ménage a trois* is rarely undertaken in the spirit of bringing down the commonwealth. Also, unlike the oaths citizens take to uphold the political institutions of their society and against treasonous action, we utter no vows that we will comply fully with the established sexual mores of our society.

Third, Devlin may be exaggerating how thick a shared moral code must be to bind the community. A marginal adjustment or incremental change to the sexual consensus of a community is unlikely to alter appreciably the shared moral code. More important than a few specific sexual practices to the shared moral code are the broad moral principles that inform the community. If the law enforces strict compliance with specific sexual practices it will jeopardize the aspirations of a pluralistic society. Exactly how much theoretical consensus and practical compliance with that consensus is required for a community to exist? Must all or the vast majority of citizens share all moral beliefs in order for a society to exist? Even where a society believes that its existence is threatened by aberrational sexual behavior it does not follow that the society's existence is actually in jeopardy. Does even widespread deviation from a society's professed sexual mores really threaten the very existence of that society? When Devlin talks about the survival of society hinging on a particular set of moral beliefs and practices, he must distinguish violations of those beliefs and practices that constitute a clear and present danger from violations that have no or little effect on the viability of society. Surely not every instance of deviant sexual behavior places society in imminent danger. The value of individual freedom to act sexually in ways not counseled by society when doing so does not harm others must be included in the equation. What principles can distinguish adequately private, consensual sexual behavior that poses an imminent threat to society from that which does not? Do we really want to sign on to the view that any deviant sexual behavior engaged in privately is automatically a threat to the very existence of society?

Fourth, as Devlin himself acknowledges, any assessment of social harm must balance the alleged public interest in a particular moral order with the rights of citizens to privacy and autonomy. Should the power of the state be exerted to influence the moral beliefs of citizens in any direction when harmfulness is not in play? Also, that calculus must also factor in the difficulty of fairly enforcing laws prohibiting private sexual conduct.

However, a society such as Vienna may rejoin on behalf of Devlin's argument as follows: Our state is not based on conventional or adjusted conventional versions of morality. Instead, we self-consciously subscribe to an objective morality, the one true version that is immutable and transcendent. Thus, we do not seek to maintain a moral code simply because it happens to be ours and it underwrites our society. Instead, we seek to enforce right conduct as such; even if violations of the moral law produce no tangible negative effects on other citizens other than the consenting parties to the acts, and even if such violations do not visibly jeopardize the existence of the state, they are inherently sinful and ought to be prohibited by criminal law. Accordingly, violations of sexual morality should be prohibited even when the parties act privately, with fully informed mutual consent, and when no visible harm ensues.

The hypothetical Viennese response avoids several of the reasons advanced against Devlin's argument and self-consciously renounces the values of a pluralist society. On this line of thought, the Viennese stake their community on values they take to be eternal and divinely-created. Appeals to individual freedom, robust social experimentation, and evolving standards of decency ring hollow in Vienna. Theirs is a self-consciously closed society, mutually bound by fervent commitment to precise, articulated moral rules codified into law. Of course, appeals to the one true objective moral code invite other questions. How do we know that such a code even exists? If we know such a code exists, how do we know when we have accessed its truths? Even if we can independently verify that we have discovered the moral truths of the objective code, should criminal law enforce sexual morality given the enormous problems of efficiency, fairness, and effectiveness in policing such consensual, private activity?

The Viennese may respond by citing the general breakdown in morals and in society that has occurred because Duke Vincentio has refused to enforce law strictly over the past fourteen (or nineteen) years. When we examine sexual matters, we find that houses of prostitution flourish, venereal disease is rampant, illegitimate births are rising, and a general licentiousness thrives in the city. The Duke has placed Lord Angelo in charge not to abrogate the law, but to remedy the breakdown in law.

Critics will be tempted to argue that laws will be ineffective in curbing natural sexual appetites and instincts; that widespread failure to comply with moral codes suggests that citizens do not take them to reflect the universal conclusions of objective morality; and that enforcing the fornication law will transform numerous, otherwise model, law-abiding citizens into common criminals. What end will be served by the existence and strict enforcement of such laws? Will strict enforcement really deter the conduct proscribed? Or will potential law-breakers find new ways to hide their conduct or cover up its effects—perhaps developing better methods of birth control, abortion, and disposing of unwanted infants?

The Viennese may try a more subtle maneuver. They might argue that in contemporary liberal societies such as ours the exculpatory defense of consent is permitted for only a few legal charges such as rape, false imprisonment, and theft. The defense of consent is not permitted for other crimes such as assault, battery, mayhem, and homicide that inflict harm on a person. If some private, consensual sexual activity harms one of the parties should not the perpetrator be held accountable? On this view, private, consensual sexual activity can produce harm and at least when it does it should be prosecuted and the exculpatory defense of consent should not be allowed. Accordingly, if we take an unwanted, illegitimate pregnancy to be a type of harm we might well prosecute the wrongdoer.

First, this approach will severely limit the number of violations of the fornication law that will be prosecutable. A showing that one or both parties were harmed as well as a clear definition of what constitutes harm in these circumstances would be required. However, this might not trouble those who subscribe to Lord Angelo's jurisprudence because these factors might correlate to how proof of violations is gathered. For example, an illegitimate pregnancy is indisputable evidence that premarital sex has occurred.

Second, who is the wrongdoer? Is it the sexually marauding male? Is it the willing female? Is it both parties—did they harm each other? Third, in cases of rape, false imprisonment, and theft that the acts in play were not consensual is a crucial part of the harm. That is why the exculpatory defense of consent is permitted. Round squares, four-sided triangles, consensual rape, consensual false imprisonment, and consensual theft are oxymorons. The nonconsensual element of certain acts—their coercive and involuntary properties—is necessary for their classification as crimes. That is, in such cases the presence of consent eliminates the harm: if the alleged victim consented to sex the act was not a rape; likewise with false imprisonment and theft. With crimes such as assault, battery, mayhem, and homicide the presence of consent does not eliminate the harm. Instead, in such cases the victim agreed for some odd reason to be harmed. The exculpatory defense of consent is not legally permitted in cases where harm persists despite mutual consent. The claim of consent in such cases must be filtered through the legal prisms of procedural and substantive unconscionability.

In sum, the legal case for enforcing prohibitions against alleged immoral sexual behavior such as private, consensual premarital sex is thin. Still, such laws graced the legal codes of Shakespeare's Vienna and their vestiges remain today; just ask Amanda Smisek. We will assume for argument's sake that some societies will find the case for prohibition compelling. We will later confront the question of what punishment is appropriate for prosecuted violations.

10. The Betrayal

Back at the prison, the Provost offers Pompey a way out of his sentence. Instead of being whipped and serving a stretch in prison, Pompey will serve as an apprentice to the executioner, Abhorson. On the following day, two hangings are scheduled: Claudio and Barnardine, a prisoner whose talents for drinking and sleeping are well-known, are penciled-in for extinction (4.2.1-67).

The Friar-Duke enters and in a discussion with the Provost defends Angelo from the charge of tyranny. Angelo subdues within himself that which he punishes in others. He thus obeys the rules which he imposes upon others; he does not make himself an exception to the imperatives of law. Furthermore, Angelo advances the rule of law by applying law impersonally and predictably; his consistency will relieve any potential anxiety citizens might otherwise endure (4.2.79-84). Of course, the Friar-Duke is reporting only Angelo's self-image and reputation to date. Soon, Angelo's sexual lust will fuel his descent into tyranny.

The Friar-Duke suggests to the Provost that Claudio may well be pardoned by Angelo. Thinking Angelo has staked too much of his authority in the execution, the Provost is unconvinced. As he anticipates Angelo's message to the Provost to release Claudio from custody, the Friar-Duke tacitly admits in a soliloquy that his advice to Isabella and Mariana was disingenuous: "This is [Claudio's] pardon, purchas'd by/such sin/For which the pardoner himself is in" (4.2.108-109). The Provost's doubts are ratified when he receives a letter from Angelo: "'Whatsoever you may hear to the contrary, let Claudio be executed by four of the clock, and in the afternoon Barnardine. For my better satisfaction, let me have Claudio's head sent me by five" (4.2.120-123).

The Friar-Duke is puzzled that Angelo has apparently betrayed the bargain that animated the bed trick. Again, the Friar-Duke tacitly confirms that he misled Isabella and Mariana: he remarks to the Provost that "Claudio, whom here you have warrant to execute, is no greater forfeit to the law than Angelo who hath sentenc'd him" (4.2.156-159). The Friar-Duke's bed trick, contrived to offset Angelo's sexual proposition to Isabella, has backfired. Perhaps the Friar-Duke's "the end justifies the means" moral calculation has gleaned what it deserved.

Thinking quickly, the Friar-Duke beseeches the Provost: "To make you understand this in a manifested effect, I crave but four days' respite; for the which you are to do me both a present and a dangerous courtesy" (4.2.159-162). The Friar-Duke's plan is for the Provost to execute Barnardine, who has been imprisoned for nine years but who has evaded execution because his friends have wangled reprieves, and then dispatch Barnardine's head to Angelo as a substitute for Claudio's. The Provost is concerned that Angelo will easily discover the ruse, but the Friar-Duke assures him that Barnardine's head can be disguised sufficiently to resemble Claudio's. The Friar-Duke clinches the plot by showing the Provost the signature and signet of the Duke as evidence of the Friar-Duke's authority (4.2.170-194).

However, one unforeseen snag foils the scheme: Barnardine refuses to cooperate. Neither Abhorson nor Pompey nor the Friar-Duke can convince Barnardine that today is his time to die. Sleepy, hung over, and irritable, Barnardine dismisses the trio. They will have to come to his cell and beat his brains out with clubs; but he will not stroll compliantly to the gallows: "I will not consent to die this day, that's certain . . . I swear I will not die to-day for any man's persuasion" (4.3.55-61). The embodiment of pure obstinacy and robust rebellion, Barnardine foils, at least temporarily, the Friar-Duke's intrigue.

11. Philosophical Interlude: What Punishment Fits the Crime of Fornication?

Angelo imposed the death sentence upon Claudio for his violation of Vienna's fornication statute. That execution as a punishment for premarital sex would now be considered unthinkable in our contemporary society is self-evident. But by examining the current state of our Eighth Amendment prohibition against inflicting "cruel and unusual" punishment we can understand better the relationship between crime and punishment.

In general, gradations of punishment are measured by two vectors: the perpetrator's degree of responsibility for the legal offense and the perpetrator's culpability for the legal offense as determined by motive and circumstances.

In *Furman v. Georgia*, the United Sates Supreme Court ruled in a 5-4 decision, that capital punishment as *then administered* was prohibited by the Eighth Amendment and thereby was unconstitutional.[18] The decisive ground for the majority judgment was that out of the relatively large number of people presumably deserving of the death penalty, only a few were selected in an apparently capricious fashion, without stated or justified criteria of selection. Some of the justices stressed selectivity and discrimination[19]—the seeming importance of irrelevant factors such as race and economic status in determining the severity of sentence—while others emphasized the "freakishness" and "wanton" nature of the punishment[20] as evidenced by its imposition on a tiny percentage of offenders who appeared no more deserving of death than those who were given lesser sentences.

The following three criteria emerged later from the Court's interpretation of the cruel and unusual punishment clause in *Gregg v. Georgia*:[21] (1) the phrase must draw its meaning from the "evolving standards of decency that mark the progress of a maturing society."[22] Thus, we must assess contemporary values by examining "objective indicia" that reflect current public attitudes toward given punishments. Such objective indicia include legislative judgments which presumable reflect the will of the people; historical attitudes, including the intent of the framers, toward the punishment at issue; and actual jury verdicts.[23] (2) A penalty must also accord with the "dignity of man."[24] This means, says the

Court, that the punishment must not be excessive."[25] The inquiry into excessiveness includes two considerations: the punishment must make a measurable contribution to acceptable goals of punishment, and thus not involve the "unnecessary and wanton" infliction of pain: and the punishment must not be grossly disproportionate to the severity of the crime.[26] (3) Finally, at least in the case of capital sentences, the punishment must not be imposed under sentencing procedures that create a substantial risk that the punishment will be inflicted "arbitrarily" or "capriciously." Nor can the penalty be imposed "discriminatorily, freakishly, and so infrequently" that any given sentence is cruel and unusual.[27]

United States v. Weems was the first United States Supreme Court case that held that the Eighth Amendment required a penalty to be proportionate to the offense.[28] Later decisions clarified the factors that must be considered when assessing the proportionality of a punishment to an offense: the gravity of the offense; the reasonableness of the legislative purpose supporting the punishment; a comparison of the petitioner's punishment with punishments imposed in other jurisdictions for similar offenses; and a comparison of punishments imposed for other crimes in the jurisdiction with the punishment at issue.[29]

The Court's demand in *Gregg* for "guided discretion" was intended to prevent the arbitrary application of severe penalties; ensure the imposition of the death penalty more frequently and reliably; and stress the importance of procedural safeguards. States complied generally with the Court's instructions through a combination of statutory refinements including bifurcated proceedings, which temporally separate the process of guilt determination from sentencing;[30] statutory specification of "aggravating circumstances,"[31] some of which must be found to exist beyond a reasonable doubt before a death sentence can be imposed, and consideration of "mitigating circumstances,"[32] which could lead to a recommendation of mercy; narrowing the categories of murder for which offenders become eligible for the penalty;[33] and instituting mandatory state appellate review of all death sentences.[34] However, the Court has not looked sympathetically upon state mandatory death statutes for specific crimes.[35] The need for "individuation" and "particularization" has been held paramount.

Accordingly, the death penalty must be administered "reliably," not "infrequently," with "guided discretion," and with concern for the "uniqueness" of each crime and criminal. Sentencers must distinguish rationally the "few who receive the penalty from the many who do not."[36] All relevant mitigating factors must be considered, while statutory aggravating factors must not be overly broad. The penalty itself must not be "grossly disproportionate" to the crime, but need not be the "least severe penalty" available to accomplish legitimate legislative purposes. The penalty, though, must not offend egregiously the prevailing societal sense of decency.[37]

The death penalty, then, must be imposed only where the uniqueness of each offender is examined; where all relevant mitigating circumstances are canvassed; where considerations of mercy are allowed; and only where it is deemed an "appropriate" punishment. However, it is well known that deterrent effects are best actualized by swift and certain punishment.[38] Yet the death penalty must also be applied reliably and consistently, not infrequently or discriminatorily, and only after the most careful and time consuming review process. The tensions among the requirements defining the process of capital punishment are striking.

For example, empirical studies suggest that guided discretion is an illusion.[39] Although juries and appellate judges must state the presence or absence of aggravating and mitigating circumstances, still there are no meaningful standards operating consistently in the system. Factors such as race, economic status, and the geographical locale of trial persistently play a large role in determining who receives the death penalty, and the stated criteria which are supposed to guide sentencers have failed to systematically divide groups of offenders by differing desert.[40] That racial and economic prejudice is so firmly established in our society that we can predict confidently that members of disadvantaged classes will be deemed to "deserve" the death penalty more frequently than others is highly probable. (Elsewhere I have offered an alternate interpretation of the Eighth Amendment that avoids most of the difficulties besetting the current legal understanding.[41])

Claudio and Juliet launched into premarital sex while they were engaged to be married. From the available evidence contained in the play, extramarital and premarital sexual liaisons were common in Vienna. Although a fornication statute graced the legal rulebook, it had not been enforced in at least fourteen years. Even if premarital sex was officially considered immoral and even if legal enforcement of that moral view is judged permissible to avoid tangible and intangible harm to society, levying the death penalty is disproportionate to the offense. First, on behalf of Claudio we can cite mitigating circumstances: he has no history of prior criminal activity; there is no individual victim as Juliet consented to the act; and prior to consummating the act, the parties were engaged to be married. Second, the sentencing procedures are arbitrary and capricious in that Claudio's offense, although frequently and openly committed by Viennese citizens, has suddenly and without notice been targeted. Third, if the underlying purposes of the fornication statute are to minimize tangible and intangible social harm then those purposes are not realized in the instant case. Being of noble birth, Claudio can easily support his newborn baby, who will not drain societal resources. No spread of social disease is in play. That engaged couples enter into premarital sex does not tear at the social moral fabric and jeopardize the viability of the community; indeed, sexual consummation by an engaged couple transformed some betrothal agreements into a common law marriage. Fourth, the penalty is disproportionate to the offense: the offense is not particularly grave as has been pointed out above; the reasonableness of the legislative purpose supporting the punishment is dubious, to say the least; and comparing the punishment for premarital sex and the punishment for murder in Vienna and finding them equal suggests that the response to premarital sex is vastly out of kilter. Fifth, if capital punishment is a mandatory sentence for violation of the fornication statute then the individuating and particular circumstances of the case at issue have not been considered.

In sum, the execution of Claudio would violate the prohibition against cruel and unusual punishment. Although this is obvious under current understandings, several considerations weighing against capital punishment for premarital sex by engaged couples were evident in Shakespeare's time. For example, the principle of proportionality is deeply rooted in common law jurisprudence. It was expressed in the Magna Carta, applied by the English courts for centuries, and repeated in the English Bill of Rights (which postdated Shakespeare) in language that was adopted in the Eighth Amendment.

Of course, the notion of disproportionate penalties evolves over time. What is obvious to us may have seemed less so in the Elizabethan age. In earlier centuries, death was a much more common sentence than it is today despite the existence of the Magna Carta. For example, more than fifty years prior to Shakespeare's composition, some English clerics proposed the penalty of death for adulterers. A few went even further and argued that those convicted of incest, fornication, and prostitution should also be executed. Those advocates of capital punishment who suspected the monarchy lacked the nerve to go that far offered a less harsh alternative: brand the word "God" on the cheeks or foreheads of perpetrators so they might be distinguished from upright Christians. The zealotry of these champions of strict rectitude was rewarded about one hundred years later: In 1650, Puritans enacted into law a statute decreeing mandatory death sentences for adulterers.[42]

Bear in mind, however, that Vienna is not subject to Anglo-American law. There strict Catholic religious imperatives seem embodied in secular law. Given the possibilities of sincere repentance and divine grace—staples of Catholic doctrine—that premarital sex should warrant the death penalty is highly doubtful.

In any event, Angelo has demanded Claudio's head as evidence of his execution. The Friar-Duke concocted a scheme with the Provost to substitute the dome of Barnardine, but the doughty felon refused to cooperate. The Friar-Duke must reconsider.

Six

MEASURE FOR MEASURE: LAW AND MARRIAGE

Having been thwarted by Barnardine's refusal to accept his fate, the Friar-Duke must conjure new arrangements to stymie Claudio's execution in the light of Angelo's betrayal of the agreement that energized the bed trick. However, fortune will smile kindly on the Friar-Duke this day and a suitable alternative arises immediately.

1. The Head Trick

The Provost informs the Friar-Duke that an imprisoned pirate, Ragozine, has contracted a fever and died. Coincidentally, his age, beard, and visage resemble those features of Claudio. His head will be substituted for that of Claudio's. The Friar-Duke instructs the Provost to hold Claudio and Barnardine safely and secretly. The Friar-Duke pledges to convince Barnardine to die willingly (4.3.69-90).

Isabella enters and the Friar-Duke continues his manipulations. He informs Isabella that Claudio has been executed and his head is being delivered to Angelo. Isabella cries out angrily and threatens to "pluck out" Angelo's eyes (4.3.115-119). The Friar-Duke must keep Isabella away from Angelo until the time is proper. Lucio appears and, again, gratuitously insults the Duke as a man of "dark corners" (secret lechery) and an accomplished "woodman" (hunter of women) (4.3.157, 162). He also reveals that he had once been brought before the Duke on charges of impregnating a woman, but he denied the allegation because he would otherwise have been forced to marry the wretched person. Lucio, though, now admits that he was guilty as charged (4.3.169-174).

Meanwhile, Angelo and Escalus receive word of the Duke's imminent return. After Escalus leaves, Angelo's soliloquy reveals that he refused to pardon Claudio because he feared he would take revenge against Angelo for his treachery. Angelo is now torn between the brute struggle to survive, enormous self-doubt and recrimination, lame efforts at justification, and utter confusion (4.4.20-34).

The head trick has convinced Angelo that Claudio is dead. Having been informed by the Friar-Duke, Isabella, too, believes that Claudio is dead. The Friar-Duke knows the truth: Claudio is alive. Angelo believes that he has had sex with Isabella. The Friar-Duke, Mariana and Isabella know the truth: Angelo copulated with Mariana. The Friar-Duke is returning to Vienna to adjudicate all affairs.

2. The Trial, Stage One: Isabella's Accusation

The Friar-Duke has shed his garments. As Duke he begins to preside over the confusions that remain in Vienna. He begins by disingenuously lauding Angelo's good work and praiseworthy desert (5.1.4-15). (As always, Shakespeare is suspicious about responding to people strictly on the basis of what they supposedly deserve.) Isabella and Friar Peter enter. Isabella pleads for "justice, justice, justice!" (5.1.25). Dripping with false sincerity, the Duke assures Isabella that Angelo will render justice once she relates her cause. Isabella calls Angelo "the devil." Angelo maintains his poise and suggests that Isabella has lost her wits; although she sought leniency for her brother, justice has decreed his death. Isabella accuses Angelo of being a "murderer," an "adulterous thief," a "hypocrite," and a "virgin-violator" (5.1.38-42). Knowing but concealing the truth for both dramatic and moral effects, the Duke pretends to believe that Angelo is correct: Isabella has gone mad. He orders her away. But Isabella persists, and beseeches him to hear her plea and bracket his preliminary view that she is deranged: "Even so may Angelo, / In all his dressings, caracts, titles, forms, / Be an arch-villain. Believe it, royal Prince, / If he be less, he's nothing, but he's more,/ Had I more name for badness" (5.1.55-59).

The Duke begins to shift gears. Still feigning conviction that Isabella is mad, he notes the logical order of her report. Committed to playing his role close to the vest, Angelo remains silent. Isabella tells her story: Lucio had sought her help in securing a pardon for Isabella's brother, Claudio, who was condemned to death by Angelo. (When Lucio begins to confirm Isabella's account, the Duke, obviously irritated, tells him to be still.) Isabella pleaded with Angelo on Claudio's behalf. Angelo sexually propositioned Isabella. After deep contemplation, Isabella's sisterly duty overwhelmed her sense of honor and she surrendered to Angelo. Angelo reneged on the deal and executed Claudio (5.1.60-103).

The Duke insists that Angelo's integrity is unimpeachable. He wonders who might have convinced Isabella to concoct such a fable. Isabella is gravely disappointed that justice is denied her and says a short prayer for the Duke, who promptly has her arrested. Upon questioning, Isabella says that Friar Lodowick (the name used by the Friar-Duke) knew of her intention to plead her case to the Duke. Lucio pipes up that Lodowick is a "meddling friar" who had slandered the Duke (5.1.107-130). Having himself slandered the Duke to the Friar-Duke, he now slanders the Friar-Duke to the Duke.

Collaborating in the Duke's intricate scheme, Friar Peter discredits Isabella and seemingly vouches for Angelo. As Isabella is taken away by prison guards, Friar Peter also praises Friar Lodowick. Finally, the Duke decides not to preside over the accusations. After making light of the charges, he orders Angelo to be judge in his own case (5.1.137-167). Angelo is in a precarious position: he believes that the charges against him are sound; he has apparently been assured of the Duke's confidence in him; and, despite the glaring conflict of interest, he has been given authority to preside over his own trial. Thus far, Angelo has been ill at ease, but has cagily held his tongue. He can no longer maintain that posture. Besides, a surprise witness will soon appear.

3. The Trial, Stage Two: Mariana's Confession

Friar Peter brings a veiled woman before the court. She refuses to reveal who she is until her husband bids her to do so. Upon questioning from the Duke, she claims that she is neither a wife nor a widow nor a maid. Brash as always, Lucio concludes she must be a prostitute, but is silenced by the Duke. The woman continues to speak in riddles: she has never been married, but she is not a maid because she has known her husband carnally, but her husband is unaware that he has known her carnally (5.1.169-187). Not wise enough to cut his losses, Lucio opines that her husband must have been drunk. After the Duke puts down Lucio again, the woman says that the person who accuses Angelo of fornication is accusing her husband. Momentary confusion evaporates when the woman makes it clear that Angelo is her husband, he does not think he has ever had sex with her, and he thinks he has had sex with Isabella. Angelo demands that she unveil her face. The woman says she will do so because her husband has bid her. Mariana shows herself, points out parts of her body, and declares that she, not Isabella, was Angelo's recent sexual partner (5.1.188-213).

Angelo admits he knew Mariana five years earlier; they had spoken of marriage, but her dowry was insufficient and her reputation was sullied. Since that time, Angelo claims neither to have seen nor spoken to her. Mariana provides details of the bed trick. Angelo's cool demeanor melts and desperation ensues. He has been set up by a mightier, dark force. He must discover what conspirators are afoot. The Duke pretends that Mariana and Friar Peter are slanderers. He demands that Friar Lodowick, who is the Friar-Duke, be summoned to clarify matters. The Duke leaves, Escalus take over the proceeding, and Angelo remains silent. Upon questioning from Escalus, Lucio charges that Friar Lodowick is a dishonest slanderer of the Duke (5.1.216-277). The Duke will soon return in the guise of Friar Lodowick, along with Isabella. The noose is beginning to tighten around Angelo's neck.

4. The Trial, Stage Three: Wedding Bell Blues

Escalus asks the Friar-Duke if he encouraged Isabella and Mariana to slander Angelo. The Friar-Duke points out that Angelo should not be adjudicating charges against himself. The Friar-Duke bemoans the corruption pervading Vienna and accuses Angelo of villainy (5.1.288-322). Lucio accuses the Friar-Duke of slandering the Duke as a "fleshmonger, a fool, and a coward" (5.1.333-334), precisely the allegations that Lucio had levied against the Duke to the Friar-Duke earlier. The Friar-Duke accurately points out that he loves the Duke as he loves himself and that it was Lucio who had spoken harshly of the Duke in their previous conversations. Losing patience, Escalus orders that the Friar-Duke, Isabella, and Mariana be taken to prison (5.1.336-347).

As the Provost takes control of the Friar-Duke, the ensuing commotion ends when Lucio pulls the hood from the Friar-Duke's head. The Friar-Duke is in reality the Duke. The mood of the court quickly changes: Lucio realizes he is in deep trouble; Angelo understands that he is finished; Isabella and Mariana are shocked; and Escalus begins to put the pieces of the puzzle together (5.1.350-366).

Aware that the Duke was managing events behind the scenes as Friar Lodowick and the Duke is aware of all relevant information, Angelo accepts his fate. Law must be applied impartially and universally. Angelo asks only for a speedy sentence and his swift execution: "No longer session hold upon my shame, / But let my trial be mine own confession. / Immediate sentence then, and sequent death, / Is all the grace I beg" (5.1.371-374). However, the Duke has a better idea. He demands that Angelo take Mariana, marry her immediately, and return to the court (5.1.377-379). One wonders whether the Duke is being merciful or harsh. Angelo does not want to marry Mariana. Mariana apparently wants to marry Angelo, but why?

5. Philosophical Interlude: The Paradox of Agapic Love

Prior to his ascent to the post of temporary governor of Vienna, Angelo was sexually repressed, rigidly rule-oriented, and generally faithful to his negative moral duties. But the play provides no evidence that he was generous, warm, loving, or proactive in fulfilling his positive moral duties. Furthermore, although engaged to wed Mariana, once her dowry was lost he dropped her faster than a soiled diaper, then slimed her reputation with false allegations of sexual misconduct. But five years later, Mariana still pines for the discredited Lord. In addition to his past transgressions and social limitations, she now knows that he condemned Claudio to death for premarital sex with his beloved Juliet and he sexually propositioned Claudio's sister, Isabella, a novice nun. Furthermore, after the bed trick, he reneged on his promise to pardon Claudio and took steps to have him executed. After all this, that Mariana remains eager to marry Angelo boggles the mind.

We might dismiss her ardor as the misdirected affection of a young woman victimized by patriarchal Vienna. Lacking self-esteem, wallowing in a community whose bar of moral propriety is set so low that even Angelo is praised as virtuous, and requiring connection to a powerful male to realize her value, Mariana weighs her unattractive options and concludes that marrying Angelo is her most prudent choice. Such an analysis, however, fails to account for Mariana's love. She is not merely choosing the least of a host of evils. Mariana genuinely loves Angelo.

Perhaps her love is agapic.[1] If Mariana loves Angelo agapically then his characteristics, properties, and actions are irrelevant to her affection. Angelo's perceived value as a human being would simply not be the ground or object of Mariana's love. On this conception, Mariana would love Angelo unconditionally. Her love would be unwavering: even if Angelo is ungrateful, even if Angelo does not love Mariana in return, even if Mariana has perceived Angelo's personal qualities inaccurately, Mariana would still love Angelo. As such, Mariana's agapic love would surmount all obstacles and persist through all vicissitudes. Regardless of how Angelo changes, Mariana's amorous motivations would remain constant. She desires the best for Angelo even if acting on those desires results in her self-denial. Instead, Mariana's love creates value in Angelo: by dint of her love, she bestows value upon the troubled Lord.

However, agapic love is more easily described than experienced. The genesis of the concept is Biblical. God presumably loves all of God's creations agapically. Even if some human beings stray from the moral law repeatedly in the vilest fashions, God loves the sinner while despising her sins. God's act of creation and ongoing affection bestow value upon us. Beyond resolute divine affection, parents often love their children agapically. Despite the disappointing actions or unworthy character development of their offspring, many parents remain thoroughly loving.

Still, the paradox of agapic love is undeniable: on the one hand, the object of agapic love is a distinct individual, not merely a set of properties. Mariana loves Angelo; she does not love everyone or anyone else agapically. But, on the other hand, if a person's properties are irrelevant how can we distinguish one person from another? Stripped of all constitutive and accidental properties, what remains of a person? And if we are all the same once we are divested of our individuating properties then why love Angelo instead of Zeke, Otto, or Fritz? How is Angelo genuinely the object of Mariana's love if none of Angelo's properties are relevant to her love?

This paradox is not a problem for God, who presumably loves all of God's human creations equally regardless of their individuating properties or moral worth. Here a general, relational property is crucial: being a human creation of God's presumably triggers God's unconditional love. The paradox is also less telling for parents. If they love their children agapically they can still differentiate them from all others whom they do not love agapically: He is my child; I helped create him; we are in the world together, we share one flesh; in a certain metaphysical sense, we are not fully separate and distinct. Again, a general relational property—this is my child—animates unconditional love. But sexual lovers must confront the thick paradox of agapic love. Is such a love based on the constancy of Mariana's nature and not at all on Angelo's nature? Must such a love be grounded in illusion or philosophical error? Is Mariana simply in love with the idea of being in love?

Furthermore, that we should want to be loved unconditionally by our spouse is unclear. Although such a love provides much consolation—after all, no matter what we do and how we act we will still bask in love—but provides little incentive for personal growth. Why strive mightily to realize our idealized possibilities when doing so presumably does not matter to our lover? Granted, we may have other reasons to actualize our highest potentials. But, typically, we would believe that some motivation to do so should arise from our love relationship. We do not have to be committed apostles of the Socratic-Diotima theory of love to suppose that erotic love should elevate us and spur our growth. Perhaps the solution is that the parties may strive for personal growth as a way of expressing their love for their lovers. Although my personal growth would not presumably increase love (as it is already unconditional), that I become a better human being might be better for my lover in other ways and thus I have reason within the love relationship to actualize my highest possibilities.

My lover may encourage my personal growth because she desires the best for me. Even though her continued unconditional love does not depend on my success, she may understand that my becoming a better person is valuable. We might conclude charitably that even though Mariana's love of Angelo is not hostage to whether he realizes his ideal possibilities, she still cares whether Angelo grows because doing so will enhance Angelo's well-being. On this reading, regardless of whether he attains his highest potentials or whether he descends to the dark side of his nature, Mariana will still love Angelo; but she can still urge Angelo toward self-improvement because, as always, she desires the best for him.

Still, if Mariana loves Angelo agapically, the basis and ground of her affection is murky. Does she really love Angelo, the concrete individual? Or is her embrace of agape simply another symptom of her oppressed psyche in a patriarchal society? We can imagine Alcibiades bursting upon the scene, discrediting agape in sexual contexts, and braying about love as obsession with a person in all of his or her particularity.

In sum, whether Mariana loves Angelo agapically is unclear. The case in favor of that conclusion is circumstantial: it would allow us to account for her affection for Angelo in the face of his past and present conduct toward her and others. The case against that conclusion is philosophical: it is difficult to sketch a coherent account of agapic love in sexual contexts; this is especially so when lovers are in the early stages of their relationship and cannot be said to have united metaphysically—as can be claimed after years of a successful marriage. Does Mariana love Angelo despite his shortcomings or because of them or are they irrelevant to her affections?

What can be said if we suppose, instead, that Mariana's love of Angelo is classically erotic.[2] On this account, Mariana loves Angelo because of a combination of his perceived excellences, his unique way of embodying those excellences, and his idealized possibilities. We could add to these considerations the relationship—presumably close—they once shared that led to their betrothal. Erotic love is neither unconditional nor automatically constant and faithful. By responding to the perceived merit and value of the other person, erotic love can evaporate if the beloved changes in ways radically incompatible with the lover's motivations for caring. Given that people inevitably change, erotic love should not be taken for granted. The Socratic-Diotima version of erotic love claims that love of particular people is an earthly reminder of our deepest yearnings for Absolute Truth, Beauty, and Goodness. Alcibiades's version of erotic love claims love is of the particular; we love concrete individuals, often irrationally and obsessively.

In the instant case, identifying the excellences of Angelo is not an easy task. From the available evidence, he never loved Mariana and we have no reason to think that has changed merely because the Duke has ordered their marriage. Angelo guards his privileges and prerogatives; he regards his own past reputation for virtue arrogantly; and, once vested with power, he has failed miserably to fulfill his political and legal obligations. A few readers of the play will be attracted to the unique way Angelo embodies his supposed excellences. If anything, he is a commonplace, rule-worshipping bureaucrat distinguished only by his extraordinary narrowness of purpose and lack of judgment: *pasta asciutta* (dried up macaroni) writ large. Finally, we must assess his idealized possibilities. Now that the pressure valve within his tormented psyche has exploded, will a new Angelo emerge?

Hegel described the dialectic as a process fueled by the clash (thesis and antithesis) of opposites, both of which are incomplete and inadequate.[3] The collision results in a new combination (synthesis) in which the conflicting elements are both preserved and reconciled at a higher level. Every synthesis will give rise to a new opposite as the process continues. Social and personal change, then, is fueled by the radical antagonisms, explosive transformations and temporary resolutions, and recurring conflicts between opposing vectors. Hegel saw the dialectic as a triumphant historical journey that tracks the inevitable progress of the Absolute as it struggles toward self-consciousness and maximum freedom. Stripped of Hegelian metaphysics, we can contrast the dialectic's dynamic with the marginal adjustments and incremental changes that constitute reform movements. For Hegel, when opposites reach their extreme points they become indistinguishable. Whereas reforms occur through a series of relatively minor alterations, the dialectical dynamic exudes dramatic swings and relentless conflicts that define historical and personal growth.

Once relieved of political power, perhaps Angelo will attain a psychological balance through the dialectical dynamic: his thesis was small-minded application of general rules and sexual repression; his antithesis was the capricious use of power to satisfy sudden lustful sensations; perhaps his synthesis will be domesticated sexuality within marriage, a wholesome family life, and the development of practical moral wisdom and judgment.

Shakespeare did not compose a sequel to *Measure for Measure* so we will never know for sure. But later in the play, Mariana will passionately state her case on behalf of Angelo: "They say best men are moulded out of faults, / And for the most, become much more the better / For being a little bad; so may my husband" (5.1.437-441). Perhaps she subscribes to the idea that a person's deficiencies are merely the exaggeration or misapplication of his or her virtues. On this reading, Angelo's moral implosion is the natural result of virtue wired too tightly and tempered too hard. On another reading, Mariana may be implicitly appealing to the dialectic dynamic: Having confronted his unexpurgated dark side, Angelo will emerge a better human being from the experience; he will attain a worthy synthesis. In either case, Mariana is invoking Angelo's idealized possibilities; but unlike Portia's assessment of Bassanio, Mariana's evaluation is built upon a flimsy foundation. To bank one's future, as does Mariana, on Angelo's perceived ideal possibilities would not seem to be a recommended marital strategy. Lacking a veridical lens, Mariana can filter her understanding of Angelo's possibilities for growth only through her own wishful eyes.

We have no evidence that Mariana takes her love of Angelo in the Socratic-Diotima fashion. She does not perceive Angelo as her instrument to climb the ladder of love and grasp for Absolute Truth, Beauty, and Goodness. That she loves Angelo for his own sake is clear. Accordingly, the best way to understand Mariana's love for Angelo is neither agapically nor erotically in the sense of Socratic-Diotima ascension. Instead, Mariana may well be an excellent case study for Alcibiades's theory of erotic love. She loves Angelo as a concrete, particular individual, not as an abstract repository of properties and excellences. From our vantage point, just as Alcibiades said love often is, her love is obsessive and irrational. Duke Vincentio provides confirming evidence when he describes Mariana's love for Angelo: his cruelty in breaking off their betrothal because her dowry was lost at sea and his spreading of false sexual allegations against her should have extinguished her love for him when judged by standards of rationality; instead, Mariana's love for Angelo became "more violent and unruly" (3.1.240-243).

Perhaps that obsessiveness and irrationality are the effects of Mariana's subordinate position in a thoroughly patriarchal society. Perhaps they reflect her lack of worthy, genuine alternatives. Perhaps they betray her inadequate self-esteem and masochistic subtext. Or perhaps they underscore the ineffability and magic of love, that dimension of affection that resists doctrinal analysis. Mariana has been in love with Angelo for many years. Her emotion is genuine even if unrequited. My practical side must conclude that she is making an error on stilts. My romantic side cheers the purity of her passion and anticipates that the dialectic dynamic will work its wonder and Angelo will attain his balanced psychological synthesis.

6. The Trial, Stage Four: The Grand Resolution

The Duke persists in part of his deception: he asks Isabella to pardon him for not being able to save the life of Claudio. He adds a weak consolation that Isabella laps up eagerly: "But peace be with him! / That life is better life, past fearing death, / Than that which lives to fear. Make it your comfort, / So happy is your brother" (5.1.396-399).

Bypassing a honeymoon, the newlyweds, Angelo and Mariana, return. The Duke starkly judges Angelo to be "in double violation/ Of sacred chastity and of promise-breach" (5.1.404-405). As Claudio has been executed, so should Angelo," 'An Angelo for Claudio, death for death!' / Haste still pays haste, and leisure answers leisure; / Like doth quit like, and *Measure* still *for Measure*" (5.1.409-411). Mariana immediately pleads for her husband's life. But the Duke is obdurate. Mariana should be satisfied that she will inherit Angelo's goods upon his death and be able "To buy you a better husband" (5.1.424). Mariana is stunned and kneels for effect. The Duke is unmoved. Mariana begs Isabella to kneel with her: "Sweet, Isabel, do yet but kneel by me. / Hold up your holds, say nothing; I'll speak all. / They say best men are moulded out of faults, / And for the most, become much more the better / For being a little bad; so may my husband (5.1.437-441).

Still believing that Claudio has died, Isabella not only kneels with Mariana; she speaks on Angelo's behalf: "I partly think/ A due sincerity governed his deeds, / Till he did look on me. Since it is so,/ Let him not die. My brother had but justice, / In that he did the thing for which he died; / For Angelo, / His act did not o'ertake his bad intent, / And must be buried but as an intent / That perish'd by the way. Thoughts are no subjects, / Intents but merely thoughts" (5.1.445-453). Isabella, once more, embraces the Shylock-Angelo theory of jurisprudence and accepts her brother's fate; but she argues that the Duke cannot legitimately execute Angelo for what amounted to only thoughts and intentions: Angelo may have lusted after Isabella but he never consummated his desires with her. She suggests further that Angelo's application of his jurisprudential theory was sincere. His lust and moral waywardness was triggered only after he set eyes on Isabella. Perhaps Isabella wonders whether her own manner lured Angelo toward the dark side. In any case, Isabella has uttered her final words in the play.

Mariana cheers Isabella's argument. The Duke commands her to stand. The Duke then shifts course and asks the Provost about Claudio's execution. The Provost plays along: he knew it was wrong and in reaction to Claudio's death he has not yet executed Barnardine. The Duke sends the Provost to bring Barnardine to him (5.1.454-469). Escalus and Angelo have a sidebar conversation. Escalus expresses his disappointment that Angelo erred so badly in morals and judgment. Angelo is resigned to his fate, which he considers his due: "That I crave death more willingly than mercy:/ 'Tis my deserving, and I do entreat it" (5.1.476-477). Once again, the notion of personal desert is invoked.

Barnardine, the Provost, Juliet, and a muffled prisoner enter. The Duke describes Barnardine as a "stubborn soul," pardons him of all past transgressions, and hopes he will turn his life around. Ostensibly, Barnardine is pardoned in place of Claudio. But the Duke asks the Provost about the muffled prisoner. The Provost unmuffles Claudio. The Duke springs even bigger surprises: he proposes marriage to Isabella, he pardons Angelo, and admonishes him to be a worthy husband!

> Give me your hand [Isabella], and say you will be mine,
> He [Claudio] is my brother too. But fitter time for that.
> By this Lord Angelo perceives he's safe;
> Methinks I see a quick'ning in his eye.
> Well, Angelo, your evil quits you well.
> Look that you love your wife; her worth worth yours (5.1.492-497).

The Duke then threatens Lucio. For his repeated slander, Lucio will be whipped and hanged. But first he must marry the prostitute, Kate Keepdown, whom he impregnated. Lucio ignores the whipping and hanging elements of his sentence, but begs that he not be forced to marry: "I beseech your Highness do not marry me to a whore. Your Highness said even now I made you a duke; good my lord, do not recompense me in making me a cuckold" (5.1.514-517). Lucio's position is clear even if unusual: Better to be whipped and hanged than to be forced to marry a prostitute. The Duke withdraws the whipping and hanging elements of Lucio's sentence, but insists that he will marry: "Slandering a prince deserves it" (5.1.524). Perhaps because the offense was personal to the Duke, he is willing to respond to Lucio based on what Lucio deserves.

The Duke ends by speaking to each of the major characters in turn. Claudio must restore the woman whom he wronged (Did he wrong Juliet by having consensual premarital sex? Did he wrong Isabella by urging her to trade her chastity to spare his life?). Angelo must love Mariana whose virtue should be rewarded with joy. The Duke thanks Escalus for his goodness and the Provost for his care and secrecy in facilitating the Duke's scheme. The Duke notes that Angelo must forgive the Provost for substituting Ragozine's head for Claudio's. Finally, the Duke repeats his marriage proposal to Isabella. Isabella remains silent.

Notice how the Duke sweeps in and "remedies" a situation that he had permitted to occur and even engineered. Although he had reservations about Angelo's suitability for power, he installed him as temporary sovereign. After he understood that Claudio had been condemned and Isabella sexually propositioned, he refused to intercede directly. Instead, disguised as Friar Lodowick he fomented intrigues, not all of which ended as planned. Then he presides over a kangaroo court that alternately deceives witnesses and savors skewering the guilty slowly. Finally, his only solution is to order several weddings and propose to Isabella. Duke Vincentio goes off to a round of applause. But is he prepared to take the next required steps to transform Vienna and resurrect it from the nihilistic moment?

In a decidedly theological interpretation, G. Wilson Knight concludes that,

> Thus Isabella stands for sainted purity, Angelo for Pharisaical righteousness, the Duke for a psychologically sound and enlightened ethic. Lucio represents indecent wit. Pompey and Mistress Overdone professional immorality. Barnadine is a hard-hearted, criminal, insensitiveness. Each person illumines some facet of the central theme: man's moral nature.[4]

The characters should not be so neatly drawn. Isabella is generally virtuous and admirable, but she is too harsh in condemning her brother for not relieving her of her moral responsibility of having to accept or reject Angelo's dastardly proposition. Part of her cruel diatribe arises from her visceral recognition that the alternatives posed by Angelo's offer make it difficult for her to assume full responsibility for her choice. Furthermore, her unquestioning acceptance of the Friar-Duke's assurances about the bed trick is another flight from moral responsibility: she is willing to trust Friar Lodowick even though his words do not consistently track established religious moral law. At her first meeting with Angelo, Lucio repeatedly accuses Isabella of being too cold. Isabella's pinnacle is her bestowal of mercy to Angelo at a time when she is convinced that he had ordered the execution of her brother. Mariana had not called upon her to speak, only to kneel in silent prayer. Despite the hollowness of her argument on Angelo's behalf, Isabella takes a Kierkegaardian leap of faith and beseeches the Duke to pardon Angelo. Isabella forgives Angelo, extends mercy toward him, and begs the Duke to bestow his mercy upon the discredited bureaucrat. This is precisely what she had told Angelo she would do in her first encounter with him. Isabella told him that she would grant mercy if she were in a position of authority such as his (2.2.68-71).

As for the Duke, although he allegedly knows himself much better than most of the other characters, his "psychologically sound and enlightened ethic" unwittingly nurtured the social chaos pervading Vienna. For all of his enlightenment, the Duke's jurisprudence style when confronted by miscreants was apparently "either hang them or liberate them" (4.2.132-134). If so, the Duke is not exactly a master of nuance. Perhaps the good Duke was overly concerned with his self-image and insufficiently attentive to the common good. Note at the end that the Duke forgives everyone except Lucio. He feigns forgiveness, but must admit that "slandering a prince deserves" the fate he levies on Lucio (5.1.519, 524). Of all the violations in the city, transgressions against restrictions on free speech sting the Duke most permanently, especially because the slanders were directed against him. Even if the dialectical dynamic has transformed the Duke in healthy ways, he retains his obsession with self-image.

The Duke's past leniency arose from his obsession with self-image—he would rather be loved than feared and he fears being hated—and his sensitivity to the darkness within his own soul. A generally upstanding and even insightful person, Duke Vincentio recognizes in the transgressions of other men the frailties of his own psyche. Their weaknesses are externalized instances of what he senses to be the worst potentials within himself. Having more self-knowledge than the self-righteous, obtuse Angelo, the Duke understands that under different circumstances he, too, might stray from goodness as have his subjects. The Duke bemoans the general lack of knowledge about human nature that plagues the efforts of most governments. Instead, ignorant arrogance and stentorian bravado masquerade as righteous exercise of power. The personification of that masquerade, Angelo, until his fall, is convinced that he is a cut above the average sinner and immune to common temptations. Grounded in arrogance, that self-deceit evaporates when his internal moral coil bursts from the unbearable pressure of his lust. Angelo, then, is victimized by his own self-righteousness: his lust for moral purity and spiritual asceticism triggers the pressure that explodes his tightly-wound inner spring. Angelo had tried to sacrifice his human instincts on the altar of his pride in rectitude, but human impulses proved too resilient for extinction.

Still, for all his supposed self-knowledge, the Duke was convinced that he was invulnerable to the passions of sex and love that beset younger people (1.3.2-5; 3.2.121-122). That proves not to be the case as Isabella later wins his heart. Furthermore, the Duke's preoccupation with learning more about the psychology of human nature may well have contributed to his negligent rule in Vienna. Had he attended to ruminations about human psychology less and directed his energies more to crafting a nuanced jurisprudence, Vienna would have been much better served.

Lucio, Pompey, Mistress Overdone, and Barnadine reflect different human reactions to the moral and epistemological nihilism swirling in the city. In the political background, we find the Duke's ambivalence and curious duality ("hang them or free them") and Angelo's dogmatic rectitude underwritten by mechanical jurisprudence. In the social foreground, we find Isabella's cloistered moral perfectionism; Claudio's naïve sensuality; the cynicism and acute intelligence of the hustler, Lucio; Pompey and Mistress Overdone plying the world's oldest profession in fertile territory; and Barnardine's single-minded refusal to comply with the dogs of execution.

Barnadine gives credence to the conviction that within the human spirit resides a defiant chord that resists supplication before bright-line rules. His determination to live on his own terms and to bend others to his design vivifies the will to survive in a disordered context. Barnardine has limited horizons and does not rise above concern for his own sensations, but retains a will to power. He refuses to comply with the penal system and willfully excludes himself from the last bastion of Viennese order.

Barnardine neither fears nor courts death. His indifference to both life and death marks him as a nihilist of a different stripe. He neither seeks consolation in the promise of a blissful afterlife; nor strives to transcend current understandings and establish new values; nor despairs after recognizing the collapse of epistemological and moral foundations; nor lashes out in self-serving destruction of the vestiges of culture. Instead, when peering into the abyss of meaning and value, Barnardine shrugs his shoulders and spews, "So what!" Having placed no faith in established cultural foundations, Barnardine experiences no sense of loss and no dread at their demise. Having little capability for reflection and introspective examination, he is a unique character: the nonchalant nihilist. As such, the Friar-Duke's preliminary assessment of Barnardine is squarely on the mark: "Unfit to live, or die" (4.3.64).

Each of the characters copes differently with the social dysfunction that permeates the nihilistic moment in Vienna. Some, such as Pompey and Mistress Overdone, seize commercial opportunity where it arises and hold deeper moral and social reflection in abeyance. Some, such as Lucio, seek pleasure in unpretentious self-indulgence and contemptuous evaluations of lesser minds. Lucio manifests keen wit severed from robust conviction, profound commitment, and refined moral conscience. Some, such as Claudio and Juliet, seek the solace of love as an oasis from the general dishevelment of their environment. Others, such as Isabella, exile themselves from the pandemonium of the wider community and cloister themselves within a circle of the faithful. While Barnadine escapes the social tumult through drunkenness and rebellion, Angelo encloses himself in a cocoon of inflexible obedience to the rules prescribing negative duties. But where are the social reformers? Where are the higher human types who might transcend the nihilistic moment by transforming values and social understandings? Is Duke Vincentio Vienna's last best hope for redemption?

7. What Type of Betrothal Agreements Did Claudio-Juliet and Angelo-Mariana Contract?

Informal marriages, grounded only in the mutual consent of the parties, were often recognized by English common law and by the early canon law of the Roman Catholic Church.[5] One such type of union, a *sponsalia per verba de praesenti*, was formed when two parties declared themselves spouses in the presence of witnesses or, in some cases, if the parties exchanged vows in secret. Under English common law, this informal action constituted a legally valid marriage, but the Church required that marriages be public and thus required a formal religious ceremony before such a contract could be sexually consummated without being subject to religious penalty. Another type, a *sponsalia per verba de futuro*, was formed when two parties promised to marry one another at some future date. They could live together as man and wife but the very act of sexual intercourse transformed the status of their agreement into a valid marriage at common law.

> In the irregular marriage, i.e., *sponsalia per verba de praesenti*, everything was presumed to be complete and consummated in substance, but not in ceremony, and the ceremony was enjoined to be undergone as a matter of order. In the *sponsalia per verba de futuro*, nothing was presumed to be complete or consummated either in substance or in ceremony, but if the parties who had exchanged the promise had carnal intercourse with each other, the effect was to convert the engagement into an irregular marriage.[6]

The Roman Catholic Church recognized such informal marriages until the Council of Trent, 1454-1563. They were still valid unions under English common law until the Marriage Act of 1753.[7]

Questions emerge as to the type of informal unions, if any, existed between Claudio-Juliet and Angelo-Mariana. Of course, we might conclude simply that trying to force a rational rubric on a piece of literature is folly from its inception. Shakespeare was not composing a documentary about real law or actual events. After all, *Measure for Measure* is only a *play*, not an instrument of social reform or a legal case study. Still, grappling with this problem is intellectually stimulating and helps cast light on possible interpretations of the main characters. Here are the pieces of the puzzle:

(1) Claudio states that he had sex with Juliet under a "true contract" and that she "is fast my wife" (1.2.144-145, 147).
(2) The Viennese fornication statute prohibited, among other things, premarital sex.
(3) When convincing Isabella to participate in the bed trick scheme, Duke Vincentio argues that "[Mariana] should this Angelo have married; was affianc'd to her by oath . . . her combinate-husband" (3.1.214, 222).
(4) None of the major characters disputes that Claudio is guilty of violating the fornication statute. Claudio himself is beset with guilt over his sexual liaison with Juliet (1.2.125-130). Juliet also feels guilty (3.1.20, 28, 35).
(5) Continuing the ruse that Claudio has been executed, Duke Vincentio decrees that Angelo, too should be executed because he criminally violated "sacred chastity" during his liaison with Mariana (whom Angelo thought was Isabella) (5.1.405, 409-411).
(6) Thinking that Claudio has been executed, Isabella, distinguishes his case from that of Angelo's and pleads with the Duke to be merciful to Angelo: she reiterates that Claudio received "justice," but claims that Angelo, despite his evil intentions, is not guilty because Isabella's chastity is intact (5.1.447-453).
(7) After finally revealing that Claudio is alive, Duke Vincentio pardons Angelo and Claudio. He had earlier ordered Angelo to wed Mariana and now orders Claudio to marry Juliet (5.1.496-498, 525-526).
(8) Prior to being pardoned, Angelo consistently admits that he is guilty; that he is deserving of death; and asks to be executed (5.1.370-374, 474-477).
(9) The play was written around 1600. Still affiliated with the Roman Catholic Church at that time, Vienna would recognize the Council of Trent doctrines, 1454-1563.
(10) Having split from the Roman Catholic Church, Elizabethan England would not have recognized Council of Trent doctrines at that time.

Given that both couples presumably have some form of contract, the possibilities are these: (a) Angelo-Mariana had a *sponsalia per verba de praesenti* ("present contract"), while Claudio-Juliet had a *sponsalia per verba de futuro* ("future contract"); (b) Angelo-Mariana had a future contract, while Claudio-Juliet had a present contract; or (c) Angelo-Mariana and Claudio-Juliet had the same type of contract—the couples both had either a present contract or they both had a future contract.

Let us first examine the case for possibility (a).[8] If Claudio is guilty of violating the fornication statute, as the main characters concede, then he had no legal right to have sex with Juliet. Claudio bemoans how excess liberty energized his lust, leading him to illegitimate sex that ends in death—just as rats are led to poison that kills them indirectly (1.2.125-130). Juliet, then, was not yet his wife at the time of sexual consummation; theirs must have been a future contract. Such contracts did not confer the legal right of sexual congress upon the parties. Sex under such circumstances resulted in an informal marriage; but, as Duke Vincentio instructs Claudio in his final speech, Claudio's premarital dalliance is a "wrong" which must be "restored" by means of a church ceremony that would sanctify the marriage (5.1.525). Thus, Angelo is technically correct that Claudio has violated the fornication statute, but his prosecutorial zeal is excessive because he ignores the extenuating circumstances: Claudio and Juliet intended to marry; their activity was consensual and mutual; and the punishment is disproportionate to the offense.

On this reading, Angelo-Mariana had a more-binding present contract. Future contracts could be rescinded for a host of reasons: mutual consent of the parties; if one of the parties entered in a present contract with someone else; if one of the parties had sex with someone else; failure to provide the promised dowry; contraction of certain diseases; and the like. But present contracts could be rescinded only on the basis of adultery or if one of the parties entered a religious order or under special papal dispensation. Only a present contract permitted sexual activity. When the Duke cajoles Isabella into participating in the bed trick scheme, he assures her that no moral violation will result. Only if Angelo-Mariana have a legitimate claim to sex can this be the case. Additionally, five years earlier, Angelo had (falsely) charged Mariana with sexual promiscuity as a way to wiggle out of his commitment to marry her. Had they a future contract the mere fact of her lost dowry would have been sufficient. Finally, Isabella distinguishes the cases of Claudio, whom she concedes was guilty, and Angelo, whom she argues is innocent. This is true only if Angelo-Mariana had some legitimate claim to sex that Claudio-Juliet lacked.

The case for reading (a) has strong plausibility, but several holes. First, on several occasions, Duke Vincentio equates the transgressions of Claudio and Angelo, which suggests that the two men had the same type of pre-contract with their partners: "This is [Claudio's pardon, purchas'd by such sin/ For which the pardoner [Angelo] is in (4.2.107-109); "Claudio whom here you [the Provost] have warrant to execute, is no greater forfeit to the law than Angelo who hath sentenc'd him" (4.2.156-159); " 'An Angelo for Claudio, death for death!'/

Haste still pays haste, and leisure answers leisure; / Like doth quit like, and *Measure* still *for Measure*'" (5.1.409-411).

Second, the Duke orders both Claudio and Angelo to wed their partners as part of the atonement (5.1.377, 525-526). The Duke thereby responds to the same offense with the same resolution. Third, although Isabella struggles mightily to distinguish Claudio's premarital sex from that of Angelo (5.1.448-453), the Duke is unconvinced by her entreaty: "Your suit's unprofitable; stand up, I say" (5.1.455). In all likelihood, by this time, the Duke had already decided to pardon everyone in the fashion that he eventually does. He undoubtedly was impressed by Isabella's gracious imploration for mercy for Angelo even though she still believed falsely that Angelo had ordered the execution of Claudio. But, clearly, Vincentio is not persuaded by Isabella's logic. The fact that Angelo intended to have sex with Isabella, but because he was deceived by the bed trick, he had sex with Mariana neither exonerates Angelo from his violation of the fornication statute nor does it relegate Angelo's offense to one only of "bad intent" and "thoughts" (5.1.451-453). That the precise object of his affections, Isabella, was not ultimately the subject of his lust does not entail that he did not knowingly and intentionally violate the fornication statute. Angelo's would be an offense merely of bad intent and thoughts only if he had not engaged in illicit premarital sex with anyone.

Let us now examine the case for possibility (b).[9] This view claims that Angelo-Mariana must have had a future contract because such contracts evolved into matrimony at common law once the parties sexually consummated their relationship. Sexual consummation did not alter the legal status of a present contract. The Friar-Duke connived to compensate Mariana ("advantage" her) through the bed trick and that seems to ensue only if the sexual encounter between Angelo-Mariana bears a felicitous legal consequence. Accordingly, Angelo-Mariana must have entered into a future contract. In that vein, Friar-Duke assured Isabella and Mariana that the bed trick was morally permissible.

Claudio-Juliet must have had a present contract because their vows were never severed. They await only the transfer of her dowry from the "coffer of her friends [relatives]" when time had convinced the relatives that Claudio and Juliet should be formally wed (1.2.150-153). The lack of a dowry was insufficient to dissolve a present contract. Claudio refers to their arrangement as a "true contract" and to Juliet as "my wife" (2.1.144, 147).

The case for reading (b) is also less than compelling. First, as mentioned above, the Duke on several occasions equates the sexual transgressions of Angelo with those of Claudio. One would think that the moral equation, reinforced by similar legal resolutions of the two cases by the Duke, provide evidence that the two couples transacted the same type of pre-contract. [Curiously, when the Duke reprimands Angelo he charges that Angelo is guilty of "being criminal, in double violation/ Of sacred chastity and of promise-breach" (5.1.404-405). The Duke does not indict Angelo for an abuse of public office—for offering to trade the pardon of a criminal for sexual favors from his sister.]

Second, if Claudio and Juliet had a present contract then a strong case can be made that they had legal rights to sex and Angelo's prosecution of Claudio, readily accepted by everyone in the play, becomes problematic.

Third, the Friar-Duke's assurances to Isabella and Mariana about the bed trick are dubious. Given his later condemnation, as Duke, of Angelo's sexual liaison with Mariana; his moral and legal equations of the respective acts of Claudio and Angelo; and his ultimate, similar resolutions of their situations, that Angelo's sexual relations with Mariana were morally permissible sounds a false note. Throughout the play, the Friar-Duke is a grand, if sometimes ineffective, manipulator who accepts the proposition that the ends justify the means: "by this [the bed trick] is your brother sav'd, your [Isabella's] honor untainted, the poor Mariana advantag'd, and the corrupt deputy scal'd [found morally deficient] . . . the doubleness of the benefit defends the deceit from reproof" (3.1.253-258). A plausible conclusion is that it is only the deceit involved in the bed trick that is morally justified by the results: Angelo is being duped as a means of saving Claudio's life, preserving Isabella's honor, and "advantaging" Mariana. Part of those means also include an apparently illicit act of sex for which Angelo will be at first skewered, then pardoned. However, when cajoling Mariana to participate in the intrigue of the bed trick, the Friar-Duke claims that her premarital sex with Angelo would not be sinful: "He is your husband on a pre-contract:/ To bring you thus together 'tis no sin, / Sith that the justice of your title to him/ Doth flourish [justify] the deceit" (4.1.71-74).

That the Friar-Duke misstates Church doctrine, which did not confer legitimacy upon extramarital sex between an engaged couple, whether undertaken voluntarily or through deceit (even if such sex, consummated pursuant to a future contract, sealed a valid common law marriage) goes unexplored. Why do Isabella and Mariana accept the Friar-Duke's assurances? Perhaps they wanted to believe what they heard as the Friar-Duke's proposition would seemingly resolve several problems. More important, the Friar-Duke is a religious figure whose interpretations supposedly bear theological imprimatur. They are unaware that Friar Lodowick counsels under false pretenses—that he is in fact only the Duke of "dark corners." As always, well-meaning women in a thoroughly patriarchal context genuflect before what they take to be superior religious authority. Notice that in the final trial scenes, Mariana, although she often refers to Angelo as her "husband" and extols his alleged virtues, does not argue as follows: "Angelo is innocent of the charge of sexual misconduct. I acted pursuant to counsel from Friar Lodowick. Legally, we had a present contract that permits sexual union. Morally, I was assured by the good Friar that no culpability attached to this action." Yes, Isabella struggled unsuccessfully to distinguish Angelo's transgression (only one of thoughts and bad intent) from Claudio's, but not even she invoked the assurances of Friar Lodowick. This is the case even though (or perhaps especially because) at the time of their final pleading on behalf of Angelo both women know that Friar Lodowick was none other than Duke Vincentio himself.

Fourth, if adultery was a legitimate ground for dissolving a present contract then Angelo's false allegations about Mariana attach to a reason. If they had a future contract then the failure to provide the promised dowry would have been sufficient to invalidate the arrangement. (Of course, that the couple had a future contract and Angelo's false allegations were merely piling on—giving him even more reason to invalidate the arrangement, a gratuitous cruelty concocted in order to underscore the reasonableness of his action—is possible. In spite of his pre-Claudio reputation, Angelo was certainly not above such chicanery.)

However, the most reasonable interpretation is (c): both couples had the same type of marital contracts. Beyond the considerations already cited, concerning the Duke's parallel treatment of the Claudio-Juliet and Angelo-Mariana cases, the entire play is directed toward setting up Angelo to commit the same transgression that led him to sentence Claudio to death. For example, early in the play, Escalus challenges Angelo to acknowledge his similarities to Claudio: "That in the working of your own affections, / Had time coher'd with place, or place with wishing . . . Whether you had not sometime in your life/ Err'd in this point which now you censure him,/ And pull'd the law upon you" (2.1.10-16). Isabella echoes this theme:

> Go to your bosom,
> Knock there, and ask your heart what it doth know
> That's like my brother's fault. If it confess
> A natural guiltiness such as is his,
> Let it not sound a thought upon your tongue
> Against my brother's life. (2.2.136-141)

As events conspire, both Angelo and Claudio engage in sexual intercourse with women to whom they are betrothed but not formally wed; the two contracts are described in similar ways and in both cases the formal wedding ceremony was derailed by considerations of dowry (1.2.144-150; 3.1.213-218; 5.1.209-210, 227-228). Additionally, Angelo is condemned to death for violating the same statute as had Claudio; responding to Escalus early in the play, Angelo assures him that should he commit the same legal offense as Claudio that he, too, should be condemned just as he has sentenced Claudio (2.1.29-31); later, when he recognizes their parallel legal infractions, Angelo is true to his word and he requests the same sentence that he had meted out to Claudio (5.1.474-477). As a result, Angelo's haughty sense of rectitude evaporates as he is, after all, vulnerable to the same moral excesses as that for which he condemned Claudio. That, of course, is one, if not the main, theme of the play. Thus, trying to distinguish the betrothal contracts of Claudio-Juliet and Angelo-Mariana obscures an important point of the work.

If the two betrothal agreements are the same then which are they more likely to be: present or future contracts. I must conclude that they are present contracts. The critical reason is that if Angelo-Mariana had a future contract then their bond was broken five years prior to the bed trick. On a future contract, the lack of a dowry was sufficient to void the agreement. As that occurred, along with Angelo's false allegations of Mariana's unchaste behavior, the future contract between the couple would have been nullified. Angelo offers uncontroverted testimony at trial that he has neither spoken to nor seen nor heard from Mariana in the five years following their break-up (5.1.222-223).

In the light of these facts, to argue that the main motivation of the bed trick is to sexually consummate the union between Angelo and Mariana, thus making their future contract legally binding is unpersuasive. If the original betrothal agreement between Angelo and Mariana was a future contract then at the time of the bed trick they had no contract. The lack of a dowry was sufficient to rescind a future contract. Angelo had played that card five years prior to the bed trick and also alleged that Mariana was unchaste. Thus, if their agreement was a future contract it was at the time of the bed trick without legal effect under common law. The couple had no contact in the five years after Angelo's rescission. Thus, under this theory, the bed trick promoted sexual intercourse between two people who lacked any active betrothal agreement. If so, the Friar-Duke's assurances to Isabella and Mariana that the bed trick was morally permissible are utterly implausible. Also, Mariana insists that she and Angelo were affianced "as strongly as words could make up vows" (5.1.227-228), which suggests a present, not a future, contract.

Accordingly, if their betrothal agreement was a future contract it would have been nullified five years prior to the bed trick, which would have eliminated the parallels between the cases of Claudio-Juliet and Angelo-Mariana, as well as invalidated the understandings among the Friar-Duke, Isabella, and Mariana that facilitated the bed trick. In sum, if the betrothal agreements between Claudio-Juliet and Angelo-Mariana were future contracts the coherency of the play is radically ruptured: the bed trick would not be contrived pursuant to any informal marriage contract as the only former bond between Angelo-Mariana would have been dissolved five years earlier. To argue that Angelo and Mariana had originally agreed to a future contract is incoherent given the countervailing evidence.

Concluding that the two betrothal agreements were present contracts validates the coherency of the general plot—luring Angelo into committing the same offense for which he has condemned Claudio—and confers plausibility on a specific device that advanced that end: the bed trick.

Still, we must answer several questions. First, if Angelo-Mariana had agreed to a present contract would not that bond have been broken by Angelo's allegations that Mariana was unchaste? If so, we are right back to the lack of parallels between the acts of Claudio-Juliet and Angelo-Mariana, and the problem of Angelo and Mariana lacking a betrothal contract at the time of the bed trick.

In rejoinder, I would think that mere allegations of adulterous behavior would be insufficient to invalidate a present contract. After all, anyone can allege anything; establishing truth is more taxing. Assuming that adultery was a legitimate ground for nullifying a present contract, all the relevant parties know that Mariana was not unchaste despite Angelo's false charges. Thus the present contract would not be considered voided by those with veridical understandings.

Second, why are Isabella, Mariana, and the Friar-Duke so willing to concoct the bed trick given that the result is the same type of offense that condemned Claudio, whose conviction for violating the fornication statute is overwhelmingly accepted? I have already sketched several of the possible answers: the trio wanted to resolve the dispute in the best possible manner by preserving Isabella's honor, saving Claudio's life, and softening the pain of Mariana's unrequited love for Angelo by resurrecting her relationship with him. Surely, expediency prevailed over rigid compliance with principle. (And is this not another recurring theme in Shakespeare?) The ladies were also susceptible to accepting the judgments of the Friar-Duke (Friar Lodowick), who is presumably a representative of God on earth. He may, indeed, know something that they do not. As for the Friar-Duke, he is throughout the play a master of expediency who is willing to sacrifice pure means to secure the best (or least evil) end. The bed trick will expose Angelo to the same offense for which he has condemned Claudio and ease the way for the Duke to order Angelo and Mariana to participate in an appropriate church wedding ceremony. Surely, we recognize that the Duke is neither a dogmatic legalist nor a dogmatic moralist.

A crucial confusing element pervades the play: the differences between early canon law, English religious law after the Reformation, Roman Catholic law after the Council of Trent, English common law, and (imaginary) Viennese law. Depending on which of these imperatives we apply in a particular situation we may well derive a different conclusion about moral rightness or wrongness, and about legality and illegality. Vienna is not subject to English common or ecclesiastic law. In my judgment, we must view the Viennese (imaginary) fornication statute as the codification of a Roman Catholic ecclesiastic principle into secular law: premarital sex is morally wrong. Thus, appeals to the existence of informal betrothal contracts, whether present or future, are irrelevant to whether that law has been violated. That explains why none of the characters makes a strong appeal to the existence of informal betrothal contracts as a defense to the charges levied against Claudio and later against Angelo. The fornication statute does not recognize the existence of an informal betrothal contract as an exculpatory defense. That explains why Claudio's guilt under the statute is widely accepted, even by his sister. Under English common law, the existence of a present contract would confer a legal right to sex. Under early canon law, sexual activity would be legally permitted under common law, but religiously prohibited; however, a religious wedding ceremony would remedy the offense. Thus, only if the Viennese (imaginary) fornication statute was based on either English common law or early canon law would an exculpatory defense or an obvious remedy (immediate marriage to Juliet) have been available to Claudio straightaway. But they were not. Even though they are committed to each other, both Claudio and Juliet feel guilty because they have clearly violated the Viennese fornication statute: they engaged in premarital sex which under that statute is illegal as such—because it is immoral in the eyes of the Roman Catholic Church and that religious principle has been codified in the secular law. Claudio believes that Angelo's prosecutorial zeal is excessive because he recognizes the disproportionality of the punishment to the moral gravity of the offense. After all, under Roman Catholic religious law, sincere repentance and petitioning for God's mercy soften the punishment of even a mortal sin.

Yes, several of the characters make oblique references to the existence of informal betrothal contracts—how they should at least mitigate the wrongfulness of premarital sex. I would explain this by the acknowledgment such contracts enjoyed under early canon law, which predates Roman Catholic law after the Council of Trent. Even in Vienna, there would have remained a tradition that respected informal marriage contracts. But after the Council of Trent that tradition does not have any moral or legal effect in Vienna. Consequently, Claudio is guilty as charged. Now, had Claudio been charged in England he would not have been found guilty. In 1600, English common law still recognized informal marriage agreements and the existence of a present contract, which I am concluding existed between Claudio-Juliet and between Angelo-Mariana, would have conferred sexual rights. Thus, England could not have enacted a fornication statute or could have enacted only one that provided several explicit exculpatory defenses, among which would be the defense of the existence of informal marriage by present contract.

Even under canon law, present contracts, although valid and legally binding under common law, were deemed morally wrong. Upon discovery, prelates typically demanded that the offending parties participate in a church wedding ceremony to rectify their wrongs. This, in fact, is the solution contrived by Duke Vincentio: Angelo must marry Mariana, Claudio will marry Juliet, and loose-lipped Lucio must marry the prostitute whom he impregnated. To tame his own growing lust, the Duke of dark corners proposes marriage to Isabella,

In my view, the Friar-Duke knew that premarital sex is always morally wrong under Roman Catholic ecclesiastic law after the Council of Trent. He also knew that this theological principle was codified into Viennese secular law. In terms of the settled moral and legal codes in Vienna, his advice to Isabella and Mariana while hatching the bed trick was deeply disingenuous. The ground of his advice was either early canon law or English common law or, less likely, English religious law after the Reformation—none of which underwrote behavior in Vienna at that time. He rendered his advice to Isabella and Mariana in order to secure what he took to be the best (or least evil) solution to a social predicament. Duke Vincentio was willing to sacrifice rigid adherence to principle in deference to what he took to be the common good. We know that the Duke never subscribed to the jurisprudential theory that energized Angelo (and Shylock).

As for Isabella, although she recognizes that Claudio is guilty of violating the fornication statute, she is not above special pleading on behalf of her brother. She is also not above accepting the bed trick after assurances from what she takes to be superior religious authority. Despite first appearances (which in Shakespeare are never infallible), Isabella, unlike Angelo, is willing at times to adjust her principles to pressing expediencies. She will not barter her sexuality; she had made an explicit vow to remain chaste, a cornerstone of commitment to her religious order. However, Isabella will rationalize her doubts about the bed trick away on consequential grounds—it produces the best or less evil consequences—and on deontological considerations—Angelo will be placed in precisely the predicament that he deserves. On my view, though, Isabella requires religious reinforcement, which is provided by Friar Lodowick.

For some of the same reasons, Mariana accepts the bed trick. But she has a deeper motivation: her irrational, but constantly growing unrequited love for Angelo might be validated. Not having seen him for five years, Mariana's aching heart begs for fulfillment. Under such circumstances, even a person of high virtue will adjust her moral principles. Remember, Shakespeare was never a fan of overly-rigid, dogmatic moralism or legalism.

Of course, once he heard that Angelo had condemned Claudio to death, the Duke might have returned to Vienna and set things right straightaway without having to resort to manipulations and machinations. But, then, we would not have much drama and we would have a short, dull play.

As always, I am not claiming that I have peered through the centuries and discovered Shakespeare's underlying intentions. Instead, as ever, I strive to place a rational understanding on events that are often confusing because they are conjured in large measure for their aesthetic and literary effects.

8. Theological Interlude: Religion and Jurisprudence

A host of biblical principles about judging others, supported by propositions sketched in scripture, underwrite events in the play:

> *Reciprocity of Judgment*: "Judge not, that ye be not judged. For with what judgment ye judge, ye shall be judged; and with what measure ye mete, it shall be measured to you again" (Matthew 7:1-2);
>
> *Recognition of One's Own Moral Limitations*: "Thou hypocrite, first cast out the beam out of thine own eye; and then shalt thou see clearly to cast out the mote out of thy brother's eye" (Matthew 7:5); and "He that is without sin among you, let him first cast a stone at her" (John 8:7);
>
> *Principle of Desert (Divine and Human)*: "whatsoever a man soweth, that shall he also reap" (Galatians 6:7); "revelation of the righteous judgment of God: Who Will Render To Every Man According To His Deeds" (Romans 2:6-6);
>
> *Avoid Violent Retaliation*: "Ye have heard that it hath been said, An eye for an eye, and a tooth for a tooth: But I say unto you. That ye re-

sist not evil: but whosoever shall smite thee on the right cheek, turn to him the other also" (Matthew 5:38-39);

Principle of Mercy: "Be ye therefore merciful, as your Father also is merciful. Judge not, and ye shall not be judged: condemn not, and ye shall not be condemned: forgive and ye shall be forgiven . . . For with the same measure that ye mete withal it shall be measured to you again" (Luke 7:36-38); "And forgive us our debts, as we forgive our debtors" (Matthew 6:12).

Duke Vincentio is reluctant to judge his subjects. As a result of his excessive leniency, Vienna degenerates into a cesspool of sexual license, fractured communication, and afflicted community. The Duke confused biblical guidelines for pious individuals assessing their neighbors with secular imperatives of judging for those exercising political authority. In his private life, the Duke's proclivity for forgiveness and reluctance to judge his fellowmen may well have been a productive or at least a workable strategy. In his public life, the Duke's inclinations sowed the seeds of social disaster. Furthermore, we can be confident that part of the Duke's diffidence was motivated by his obsession with public image: Vincentio wanted to be loved by his subjects. Much like an overly indulgent father who is frightened by the possibility that his children will not worship him if he disciplines them, Vincentio is overly lenient and he reaps what he had sown. By undermining the credibility of his own government, Vincentio unwittingly stimulates a disjointed, chaotic city that spawns the likes of Lucio, who slanders the Duke when he thinks he can do so without retaliation. The Duke learns that public officials cannot control totally the reactions and evaluations of their subjects. The Duke gets precisely what he deserves.

To his credit, Angelo at least understands that public officials must judge their subjects in order to fulfill their public duties. He understands keenly that public officials cannot "make a scarecrow of the law" (2.1.1) and that even though human beings lack the infallible knowledge and judgment of God, they must still do the best they can if civilization is to thrive: a city with too much official forgiveness and too feeble an application of law is doomed to chaos (2.1.18-27). In Vienna, only a few enclosed shelters provide safe oases from the general urban muddle: Mariana's moated grange, Isabella's cloistered nunnery, Angelo's brick-walled garden, even Barnardine's prison. Yes, human judging is thoroughly fallible, but in its absence we descend to the bestial. The only solution is the rule of law: applying the demands of statutes impartially, universally, and without the special considerations that advantage the instant defendant at the expense of the rest of the world (2.1.29-31).

Angelo's downfall is that he lacks self-knowledge and flees from his freedom. Angelo is existentially inauthentic in that he refuses to take responsibility for his judgments; instead, he hides behind the alleged imperatives of law. He claims that the law condemns Claudio, not Angelo. So lacking in the skills and sensibilities required for righteous adjudication, Angelo pulls himself inside the shell of mechanical jurisprudence: simple decoding of statutory language and robotic application of the results. Angelo refuses to consider mitigating circumstances. He does not address the disproportionality of penalty to offense. He does not examine the substantive fairness of the law itself. To enforce zealously overly-harsh statutes that permit or mandate excessive punishments brings no honor to law. He abrogates judgment in deference to the worship of bright-line rules. As such, Angelo's methods provide the antithesis to the Duke's thesis: mechanical jurisprudence unseats feckless laxity. Worse, when Angelo commits the same violation for which he has condemned Claudio, he underscores the lessons of the Biblical adages: he will be judged measure for measure; he was not in a position to cast the first stone; and he had not cast the beam out of his own eye prior to stigmatizing Claudio. He, too, will get what he deserves.

The synthesis of the process must result in judicial decision grounded in practical wisdom. Perhaps Escalus provides a glimpse of attending to the particularities of a case and assessing factors beyond the procedural legitimacy of statutes. In his final speech, the Duke praises Escalus: "Thanks, good friend Escalus, for thy much goodness, / There's more behind that is more gratulate" (5.1.528-529). Perhaps this augurs the day of balanced jurisprudence in Vienna. Perhaps the dialectic dynamic has worked its magic on the Duke and he has attained a personal synthesis that will translate into a revived jurisprudence to guide Vienna. Neither automatic mercy nor mechanical jurisprudence confers esteem upon judicial decision making.

9. The Aftermath

At the end of the play, Duke Vincentio struggles mightily to domesticate raging sexual passion in Vienna. At least (or maybe at most) the union of Claudio and Juliet exudes mutuality: both parties have expressed their love and desire to wed the other. Granted, Claudio is no Bassanio and Vienna is no Belmont (or even Venice). Claudio lacks the poetic soul and implicit understanding of love that Bassanio displayed however imperfectly. Vienna is a cesspool of miscommunication, individual license, and unbridled sexuality. Only Mariana's moated grange recalls the vibrant beauty, robust community, and teeming romanticism of Belmont. In a thickly patriarchal society with a fractured sense of community and growing epistemological chaos, the likes of Claudio may be the best an eager young matron can reasonably expect.

Prospects for the newlyweds Angelo and Mariana I have already sketched. A rational calculator would clock the success rate of their marriage at about twenty percent. Mariana seems too needy and too dependent on a prominent man whose reputation for virtue was always vastly overrated. Her growing, unrequited love, even five years after Angelo spurned her for lack of a dowry and cruelly slandered her good name, does not speak well for her sense of autonomy and self-worth. She strikes me as someone who sees love as her ticket for personal redemption—always a losing proposition.

Angelo's arrogant righteousness makes him especially vulnerable to temptation and sin. Lacking self-knowledge, his spirit was impoverished by rigid reliance on the prescriptions of negative duties and by lack of compassion for the human condition. Has Angelo repented? Although he claims to have a "penitent heart," the final words he utters in the play plea for his deserved death and eschew mercy (5.1.474-477). At that point, Angelo is still convinced that Claudio has died at his order. When Claudio is unmuffled, the Duke reports that he sees a renewal of life in Angelo's eyes (5.1.495).

If Angelo is remorseful for the proper reasons, does such repentance automatically imply that Angelo will love Mariana as he has been commanded by the Duke? The remorseful soul graciously accepts divine grace, mercy, and future opportunities of atonement. But must such a mindset—assuming Angelo possesses it—translate into earthly love for a woman he has treated so cavalierly in the past? Does Angelo's acceptance of Mariana as his bride augur his new self-knowledge, a salutary synthesis of his soul? Or is the union doomed because of the vast disparity between Mariana's need and Angelo's icy indifference?

The Duke masterminded the bed trick then later orders Angelo to marry Mariana because the couple engaged in sex. Given that the bed trick was a response to Angelo's abuse of power and submission to lust, the marriage is clearly punitive. Yet the Duke takes himself to be a dispenser of mercy. He apparently believes that Angelo can be ordered to love, not merely wed, Mariana.

That Angelo and Mariana can achieve a luxurious dose of equality, mutuality, and reciprocity is highly doubtful. That the Duke feels compelled to order Angelo to love Mariana speaks volumes (5.1.526). Still, if the dialectical dynamic has worked its magic, if Angelo can realize a personal synthesis that transforms his possibilities for domestic bliss, then the possibility of a serendipitous destiny remains. *Buona fortuna* to our seemingly mismatched couple.

The fate of Lucio and his "punk" is dismal. Lucio insists that his forced marriage is akin to being pressed to death by heavy weights, whipped, and hung (5.1.522-523). None of Lucio's assessments of his sentence are ambiguous. While the prostitute whom he impregnated undoubtedly has few exciting prospects, even under the best circumstances marrying the sarcastic Lucio cannot be judged as good fortune. Furthermore, unlike the possibility that Angelo's character has been transformed by the events chronicled in the play, Lucio remains the same throughout the work. As such, Lucio evades the transformative power of the dialectical dynamic.

Will Isabella marry the Duke? Shakespeare shrewdly invites our speculation. Given the conditions in Vienna, my guess is that Isabella is best served by trusting her first instincts: remove herself from the confusion, head for the convent, and serve God directly. Isabella knows the Duke only as the conniving Friar Lodowick. The Duke knows Isabella only as a compliant novice willing to accept his disingenuous counsel as authoritative because he masqueraded successfully as a servant of God. The Duke swells with lust in the presence of Isabella's earnestness and purity, qualities that are rare in Vienna. The Duke's reaction to Isabella recalls Angelo's emotional unraveling. As always, the Duke's solution is to domesticate dangerous, raging passion through marriage.

What will become of Vienna? At the end of the play is not the status of the law in the same place where we began? Does the return of the Duke mean only that lax enforcement will again plague the city?

We must imagine that progress has been made. The Duke, too, has undergone the dynamic of the dialectic. His thesis was lenient enforcement of law leavened by his obsession with personal image. His antithesis was stealthy, unevenly effective manipulation of events while posing as Friar Lodowick. His synthesis may well be more balanced judgment that reflects better the person of practical moral and legal wisdom. Being subjected to Lucio's slander while posing as Friar Lodowick, should awaken the Duke to the truism that most events are not fully under human control. Regardless of how the Duke acts some of his subjects will judge him unfavorably and unjustly. Better to do the right thing, maintain one's integrity, and not curry the favor of others than to be paralyzed by indecision and fear of what others may think of your actions.

How grave was Claudio's (and Juliet's) transgression of law? The establishment figures in Vienna, such as Angelo, Isabella, and the Friar-Duke judged it sternly, while the products of the fractured Viennese community, such as Pompey and Lucio, treat it lightly. Perhaps, this, too, suggests the dialectical dynamic: the antagonism between "violations of sexual propriety are serious moral wrongs" (thesis) and "premarital sex is mutual entertainment" (antithesis) may augur a new synthesis: "evaluate the wrongness, if any, of extramarital sex in the light of the totality of circumstances."

We must conclude that Vienna will emerge from its nihilistic moment with renewed resolve, led by the firm but fair decisions of Duke Vincentio. With time, the city will create salutary communal meaning and transcend its past. Or so we must believe.

10. Philosophical Interlude: Refashioning Viennese Jurisprudence

If mercy, as bestowed by the Duke was the thesis of jurisprudence in Vienna then mechanical jurisprudence, as applied by Angelo prior to his fall, was the antithesis. Neither method amounted to justice, which requires a synthesis of nuanced jurisprudence. But what, precisely, can be done to rejuvenate Vienna's jurisprudence? In large measure, the substantive lack of quality in the laws themselves is to blame for the vacillation between the Duke's overly permissive application and Angelo's mechanical jurisprudence. How, exactly, might the fornication statute be administered such that it neither falls into desuetude nor sweeps too many otherwise innocent citizens into its net? Only if the law is rewritten, amended, or nullified can a more refined jurisprudence be formulated. Surely, Vienna might declare prostitution illegal, but exclude premarital sex from prosecution (or at least, exclude premarital sex engaged in pursuant to a betrothal contract). However, the laws in Vienna are taken to be immutable. The Duke bemoans their harshness, but seems powerless to rewrite the rulebook.

Much like the Volstead Act in the United States—which was the enabling legislation for the Eighteenth Amendment, which prohibited the production, sale, and transport of intoxicating liquors—Vienna's fornication statute (and apparently many other of its laws) is impossible to enforce equitably.

Prohibition in the United States was a losing legal enterprise because there existed a high demand by otherwise lawful citizens for the prohibited product; the prohibited product had a host of legitimate uses centered on camaraderie, pleasure, and refined digestion; there existed a long tradition of use, especially among recent immigrant groups; the law was difficult to enforce widely and consistently; and because of all this, corruption of officials charged with enforcing the law was relatively easy. The problems arose from the substantive character of the law in the context in which it was enacted. Thus, the law was virtually impossible to enforce equitably. One of the unforeseen consequences was the promotion of several crime syndicates that eventually used the profits from bootlegging to infiltrate politics, organized labor, gambling, and a host of other aspects of American life.

The laws in Vienna bear similar problems. The fornication statute is apparently overly broad and may include a mandatory death sentence as the prescribed penalty. Although not stated explicitly in the play, the fornication statute and other Viennese laws probably include such a sentence. This would account for the Duke's admission that the laws are "strict" and "biting" (1.3.19), and that his own jurisprudence has been either to free or to execute offenders (4.2.132-134). The Duke's jurisprudence and that of Angelo's are two doomed solutions to an intractable problem: how to administer fairly laws that are substantively problematic.

Nietzsche heralded the death of God as signaling the rise of European nihilism, as that moment where the foundations for meaning, truth, and value had collapsed and everything was temporarily up for grabs. In Shakespeare's Vienna, the underlying substance of the laws promotes the same result. Law in Vienna lacks both its coercive and directive dimensions. Under the Duke, the lack of enforcement strips the law of its capability to inspire fear of punishment (the coercive dimension of law) and citizens no longer internalize the prescriptions of law and accept them as their own (the directive dimension of law). Angelo's mechanical jurisprudence might well resurrect the coercive dimension of law in Vienna, but the impossibility of administering the fornication statute equitably (as only a relatively few cases will be detected) and the grossly disproportionate penalty that attaches are unlikely to revive the directive function of law. The underlying problem, then, is not necessarily executive or judicial, but legislative.

Who enacts law in Vienna? We know that the Duke holds sole executive and judicial power. No mention of a separate legislative branch of government appears in the play. The most reasonable conclusion is that the Duke also enacts law. Yet the Duke seems to regard the law as immutable and fixed. Yes, I understand that *Measure for Measure* is only a play and the drama requires irresolvable conflicts. But the question concerns the future in Vienna.

Given that he is most probably the sole legislator, why would the Duke understand the laws in may subscribe to the view that human beings can discover natural law through use of instinct, fundamental reason, and careful attention to nature's messages Vienna to be immutable and fixed? One possibility is that he is a natural law theorist. Assuming that God created a natural order that is immanent in the universe, Vincentio. He would take the natural order to be not merely descriptive and scientific, but normative and action-guiding. Natural law is permanent and universal. Human beings cannot subtract from it, and compliance with it is necessary if we are to attain our appropriate function. Thus, natural law guides human beings to our earthly ends and is our participation in eternal law—law that exists in the Divine Mind and fixes the essences of all things. The fundamental principles of natural law, however, do not require the use of elaborate deductive or inductive logical processes. Instead, the basic principles are self-evident, universal, and beyond rational demonstration: God has presumably installed the basic principles of natural law into the minds of human beings.[10]

If Duke Vincentio is a natural law theorist then he must consider the laws of Vienna immutable and fixed insofar as they reflect the imperatives of God's natural order. Thus, even though in principle the Duke can amend, discard, or rewrite the laws in Vienna—he probably has the secular power to do so unilaterally—he lacks the normative authority to change laws that mirror God's imperatives. I have already argued that Vienna's fornication statute embodies the religious conviction that sex outside of marriage is immoral as such. Accordingly, Duke Vincentio could well understand that statute to be grounded in natural law; it is thus immutable and fixed. If most of Vienna's laws are understood in the same fashion then the pieces of the puzzle begin to come together: Vienna's laws are strict and biting because they mirror the exacting demands of a religion; these religious imperatives are presumably grounded in natural law; and human authorities lack normative standing to change that which mirrors natural law. We can then pinpoint the problem of the administration of law in Vienna: whether power is placed in the hands of the Duke, Angelo, Escalus, or anyone else, he must apply a strict moral imperative—which in fact requires the infallibility of the divine mind—to a secular context rife with epistemological and moral uncertainty. Escalus's point that human beings are inherently flawed, fallible judges has currency after all (2.1.10-16). Exacting moral laws when codified into secular law often are impossible to apply equitably due to the human limitations of judges. Lacking the ability to peer into the minds and souls of our fellow human beings, we cannot access the motives, intentions, and spiritual condition of alleged offenders adequately enough to mete out justice defined by strict religious imperatives. Yet, if I am correct, this is precisely what much of Viennese law requires.

The problem is not one of balancing the letter and spirit of the law. The fornication statute is simple; it does not exude a conflict between its letter and spirit. Sex outside of marriage is morally wrong as such. This includes not only prostitution, but pre-marital and extra-marital sex. Those administering this law have limited options: the Duke's negligence which leads to desuetude; Angelo's mechanical jurisprudence which is pitiless; or some selective application of the law that reneges on the commitment to natural law and jeopardizes the generality of the rule of law. Accordingly, enforcing morality that requires a God's-eye view is often impossible from a human vantage point.

That the textual evidence suggests that violators of the fornication statute and other Viennese laws face mandatory death sentences complicates matters. Religious imperatives are not so draconian. Traditionally, remorse and repentance on the part of sinners expunges at least some of the gravity of a moral transgression. Even mortal sins do not automatically consign an offender to eternal damnation. By established Catholic doctrine, repenting one's mortal sins and opening one's soul to divine grace redeems a person from eternal suffering. Thus, even if the Viennese fornication statute arises from natural law and mirrors an imperative of religious morality its mandatory death sentence conflicts with religious doctrine and exceeds rightful punishment under natural law.

The character of judges is crucial in Shakespeare. The art of judging is captured neither by automatic leniency nor by false alternatives ("hang them or free them") nor by mechanical jurisprudence. But the laws themselves must permit refined jurisprudence. Where law codifies strict religious mandates and requires mandatory sentences, the practical moral wisdom—grounded in self-knowledge and epistemological modesty—that defines refined jurisprudence is helpless.

Assume that the dialectical dynamic has worked its magic: whether he marries Isabella or not, Duke Vincentio arrives at a new personal synthesis and is prepared to adopt a refined jurisprudence; Angelo, too, is personally transformed and stands prepared to assist his Duke; having proven his worth, Escalus is also ready to accept more judicial responsibility. How can they possibly nurture the reformation of the city when the laws are so poorly crafted yet taken to be immutable? Although the play emphasizes the fornication statute as its point of departure, we can reasonably conclude that sexual license is only one of several maladies plaguing Vienna because of overly harsh laws that are impossible to enforce equitably. That formal law and righteous judgment are incommensurable and severed in Vienna is no accident. The solution to the nihilistic moment in Vienna must begin with rewriting the legal rule book. Only then can a synthesis in jurisprudence—emerging from the thesis of the Duke's leniency and the antithesis of Angelo's hard line—emerge. Personal transformation, enhanced self-knowledge, and recognition that past methods of jurisprudence have failed are not enough to revive the polity. The disorder in Vienna flows from the inevitably inequitable administration of religious imperatives translated into secular laws. The Duke must restore the conditions under which the directive function of law can flourish. Paradoxically, restoring the directive function of law may well require the scuttling of natural law theory. Even if Viennese laws continue to be understood as immutable and fixed, their sentencing provisions must permit judicial discretion. Mandatory death sentences are neither demanded by natural law nor consistent with religious teachings.

11. Summary of Philosophical Lessons

A. Judging Others Requires Self-Understanding and General Knowledge of Human Nature. Pretension and Arrogance Undermine Success

Human beings are prone to faulty judgment and to abuse their power. Angelo is unaware of the potentialities of his dark side. As a result, he is uncharitably narrow and flees from personal responsibility under cover of mechanical jurisprudence. His world is black and white, and he is self-deluded enough to think he wears the most pristine bonnet. His inexperienced zealotry divorced from human instinct is the leavening agent for a colossal abuse of political power.

The more we know about ourselves the more we will recognize the moral fallibility inherent in human nature; that recognition should spawn a profound appreciation for the necessity of forgiveness, mercy, and charity for human flourishing. When a single-minded, relentless man such as Angelo, who lacks self-knowledge and is ignorant of human nature, gains political power the horrors of mechanical jurisprudence are unleashed.

The Socratic paradox is well known: while being certified by the Delphic Oracle as the wisest person in Athens, Socrates nevertheless was convinced of his ignorance.[11] Finally, after undergoing countless hours in the marketplace interrogating the most successful people in the city-state, he concluded that his wisdom resided in his ignorance: Socrates knew that he did not know. His wisdom, then, arose from his awareness that the foundations of all understanding—Absolute Truth, Beauty, and Goodness—immutably subsisted in the transcendental world of Forms, but his use of earthly reason, logic, and experience could, at best, provide only images of those foundations. Understanding human limitation was the first step toward purification of the soul. The successful people of Athens whom Socrates had questioned were unaware of these conclusions and thereby grossly overestimated their own grasp of truth: they were convinced they knew much more than they in fact did.

Socrates's modest epistemological (and thus moral) self-assessment contrasts with the preening rectitude of Angelo. The temporary ruler of Vienna was convinced that he was invulnerable to the excesses of normal people. Having repressed several of his human instincts, Angelo embodied an unshakeable certitude that he could quite easily repel mundane temptations. But his thin, intellectual grasp of moral and legal rulebooks lacked the ballast of robust experience. Like the successful people in Athens, Angelo was arrogant in thinking that he knew more than he in fact did, and in concluding that such knowledge immunized him from common vices. The fall of Angelo is the deflation of arrogance, which, after all, is the final cause of most sin. Angelo reaped what he had sown. The moral of the story is simple yet too often forgotten: frailty, fallibility, and finitude define the human condition; do not overestimate your knowledge, goodness, or presumed superiority to other people.

B. The Interrelations of Opposites

In *Measure for Measure*, the strongest character traits of people bear within themselves the seeds of their opposites: when enflamed, the highest virtue can trigger vice. Witness the saga of Angelo, whose arrogant rectitude explodes from the pressures of sexual lust and degenerates into a stunning abuse of political power and cowardly breach of promise. Isabella, too, exemplifies this principle as evidenced by her stinging invective against her brother. Duke Vincentio's high level of self-knowledge and prudent sympathy for human weakness fuel his overly permissive jurisprudence which facilitates the nihilism and corruption plaguing Vienna. His extended deception of Isabella—even if required to elicit her mercy for and forgiveness of Angelo—seems harsh.

The problem is especially acute for those who are overly prideful in their virtue for, using the old Greek metaphor, the chords of their souls will be strung too tightly. Instead of attaining a felicitous harmony, equilibrium, and balance that distinguish people of practical moral wisdom, those who cherish their own virtue too dearly torque their souls too intensely and must eventually find release. The play underscores a related lesson: moral pretension is a source of much social evil. That the characters in the play who are most prominent in Vienna's social hierarchy are also the most morally pretentious and the ones who illustrate most vividly the emergence of vice from virtue is no accident. Minor characters such as Pompey, Mistress Overdone, Lucio, and Barnardine lack the moral pretension that augurs the onset of this type of evil.

Nietzsche was troubled by binary oppositions because they mock the complexity of life. They do not appreciate adequately the interdependence of human motives and the genealogy of our social practices. Instead of viewing so-called opposites as separate substances vying for supremacy, Nietzsche imagines them as points on a single continuum: morality arises from immorality; selflessness flows from selfishness; truth blossoms from illusion; and good emerges from evil. For Nietzsche, everything deemed valuable once depended on a seemingly opposed value. Things in general are interrelated, in flux, and derive their features from their interrelationships.[12] The Chinese theory of yin-yang is also supported by the law of unity of opposites: yin and yang are in conflict, yet mutually dependent. The opposites in all objects and phenomena are in constant motion and flux; some measure of its opposite is contained in anything that exists; the balance of Nature is always maintained.

Such thoughts may be at the core of Mariana's paradoxical assessment of Angelo: "They say best men are moulded out of faults, / And for the most, become much more the better / For being a little bad" (5.1.439-441). I do not take Mariana to be merely repeating the bromide that our faults are only our virtues exaggerated or misapplied. The solution to the problem rests in the dialectic dynamic: from a thesis of supercilious virtue and the antithesis of stunning vice the possibility exists for a synthesis of practical moral wisdom.

On some level, Mariana may subscribe to the notion that Angelo's renewed and higher morality—a synthesis of the clash between his thesis of supercilious rectitude and antithesis of lust and betrayal—may arise from his interlude of immorality. In that sense, Angelo will become better for having been bad and will be partially molded from his moral excesses. Furthermore, both his moral precision and his lurid transgressions are interrelated and spring from the same internal source. Should it occur, Angelo's personal transformation will depend upon his capability of "being a little bad." But for that capability Angelo would be unable to go beyond his arrogant self-image and mechanical compliance with and application of bright-line rules. If Angelo is to begin his ascent toward approximating Aristotle's person of practical wisdom—if he is to develop refined judgment—he must be molded out of his faults. This is the imploration of Mariana's faith.

Isabella, too, is subject to the dialectical dynamic. She begins as a cloistered paragon of virtue, who subscribes and complies with all conventional religious pieties (thesis). Later, she lashes out uncharitably at Claudio, who lacks the heroism to remove the moral responsibility of choice from her shoulders (antithesis). Removed from her comforting certitudes by her immersion in the messy world, Isabella cruelly evaluates Claudio by the lofty standards of the hero, martyr, or saint. When he fails that stringent test, Isabella condemns him mercilessly. Finally, Isabella, armed only with sophistical arguments and her own good will, beseeches the Duke to pardon Angelo, even though at that point she is convinced that he ordered the execution of her brother (synthesis). Will her synthesis now transform into a new thesis as she marries the Duke?

Angelo's dialectical dynamic begins from a thesis of the vantage point of a smug, complacent, arrogant self-image that vivifies mechanical jurisprudence. Like Isabella, Angelo distances himself from moral complexity. After his fall, he is confused, riddled with guilt, with an utterly destroyed self-image (antithesis). He resigns himself to being sentenced according to his personal desert. At the end, a new knowledge of events prefigures his possible synthesis: chastised, he is wed to Mariana, whom the Duke has ordered him to love. However, we lack the textual evidence required to conclude that Angelo is genuinely transformed. His sins are common among those of us who repress our instincts in the face of moral complexity and who take refuge in complying with simple, bright-line rules of conduct. Whether we will attain salutary personal transformation, even after stunning revelations, is an open question—just as it is for Angelo.

C. The Human Condition Merits Sympathy

Again, Shakespeare sends the message that personal desert is insufficient for salvation. Human beings require divine grace and mercy. We should extend mercy to other people in accord with being judged measure for measure. Angelo's request for death in the final scene reflects his commitment to mechanical jurisprudence: measure for measure as understood by simple statutory decoding and automatic application of the results. To his credit, Angelo is willing to be judged as he has judged. But does his consistency suggest an inflexibility that remains an obstacle to salutary personal transformation? If Angelo petitions or even accepts mercy would that eviscerate his self-understanding and thereby jeopardize his identity? Does Angelo reject that route because he resists those results? Although his self-righteousness has proved inadequate to the test of wielding political power, Angelo may still cling to the vestiges of his ersatz rectitude.

At one level, Angelo is a victim of the Duke's tinny social experiment. Placed reluctantly in a position of power and under circumstances that would foreseeably trigger his worst excesses, Angelo meets expectations.[13] Angelo does not seek supreme sovereignty in Vienna and must be encouraged to accept it; he follows the Duke's neglectful reign that encouraged the nihilistic moment in the city; although he is not instructed explicitly to enforce the laws mercilessly, the reasonable expectation is that he should be much sterner that the Duke has been; and his widely-known proclivity for endorsing and complying with simple bright-line rules precludes refined judgment. The Duke requests that Angelo assume temporary control because the Duke is fearful that his own reputation would be sullied should he become suddenly more diligent in enforcing the law. Although the Duke expresses reservations about his choice of Angelo, if he had even a portion of the self-knowledge and understanding of human nature attributed to him by literary critics the Duke would have known with certainty from the outset that Angelo was not the right person at the right time for this task.

Isabella's entreaties on Angelo's behalf reflect her faith in Christian judgment: measure for measure as understood by granting mercy on earth in recognition of our own shortcomings and our need for mercy in the afterlife. To open our souls to redemption requires repentance of our transgressions and a willingness to accept divine grace and mercy. Such receptivity is predicated upon the theological virtues of faith, hope, and charity. We must anticipate our final judgment by evaluating and responding to others on earth in that spirit. We shall be judged, at least in part, by how we judge others—both on earth and at final judgment. We shall be judged not merely by our shortcomings and our failures, but how we respond to those frailties and transgressions. Measure for measure, in this sense, is not reflexive permissiveness; Duke Vincentio has taught us that laxity is counterproductive. Nor is it inflexible application of harsh bright-line rules; Angelo has demonstrated that mechanical jurisprudence produces draconian results. Instead, the proper measure for measure requires evaluation and judgment by Aristotle's person of practical moral reason.

As I read it, the play is not a conflict between Justice and Mercy. Where laws are substantively or procedurally unfair or both, law cannot plausibly masquerade as justice. In any case, justice is not defined by the laws that happen to be in place. On the contrary, in a normatively sound society, the procedure and substance of the laws are designed to fulfill an independent standard of justice; they do not aim at defining justice. If the laws are completely congruent with the independent standard of justice then a felicitous union of law and justice ensues. One would be hard-pressed to argue that in Vienna such an alliance is in place. Accordingly, *Measure for Measure* is better interpreted as a clash between procedurally and substantively flawed laws and the virtue of charity: Given the inherently fallible human condition, how should secular authorities respond to our misdeeds?

In any event, cultivating the proper habits, nourishing valuable character, and refining our moral judgments will serve all of us, religious believers and nonbelievers alike.

D. Patriarchy Dehumanizes Women

Although Vienna is mired in the nihilistic moment, one constant remains: men call the shots. Thoroughly patriarchal, Vienna offers few possibilities for women. Mistress Overdone is the proprietress of a house of prostitution and has been married nine times; Kate Keepdown is a prostitute; Juliet has violated the fornication statute and escapes prosecution only because she is pregnant; Francisca is a nun who worries that new votaries might seek too much freedom and privilege; Isabella has sought refuge and security in a convent; after being jilted by Angelo, Mariana retreats to her moated grange. Only secluded enclosures can distance women from the confusions of the nihilistic moment and the oppressions of the patriarchy. During the course of the play, Isabella and Mariana are lured into participating in the bed trick by the disingenuous Friar-Duke, who furthers his social experiment under cover of religious authority. At the end, three marriages are ordered and the Duke proposes clumsily to Isabella. In all cases, women are defined through their sexual activity: either prostitutes or celibates by vow or impregnated law breakers or married domestics. Worse, sexual activity in a Vienna enveloped by the nihilistic moment is uncommonly dangerous.

That Mariana remains loyal to and declares her love for Angelo after his deplorable treatment of her and his treachery while temporary sovereign screams volumes about the power of patriarchal oppression. That the Duke feels entitled to propose marriage publicly to Isabella, while no relationship exists between them other than their discussions while he fraudulently posed as a Friar, underscores how entrenched patriarchy is in Vienna.

E. Beware of Existential Inauthenticity

Existential inauthenticity, in the sense of denying freedom and fleeing from personal responsibility for actions, haunts the play: Angelo claims he does not condemn Claudio, the law does ("I am doing only what my job demands"); Isabella wants Claudio to assume her burden of choice and take her off the moral hook—

when he vacillates, she explodes; the Duke transfers responsibility for setting Vienna straight from himself to Angelo; Angelo, baffled by the verbal confusion generated by Froth, Elbow, and Pompey, delegates the case to Escalus; Isabella too readily joins the Friar-Duke in plotting the bed trick as a way of avoiding moral choice; Lucio denies responsibility for impregnating Mistress Keepdown and for his slander of the Duke; and in the play's finale, Angelo marries Mariana and Lucio marries Keepdown not by choice but because of the Duke's order. When the Duke proposes or orders Isabella to marry him, she remains silent.

Existential authenticity is not enough to guarantee either a robustly valuable life or a morally sound path, but it is required for that quest. Products of and contributors to Vienna's nihilistic moment, the major characters of the play too often try to evade the anguish of moral choice, too frequently deny responsibility for their actions, and too readily make excuses for their roles in events. When cultural foundations for epistemological and normative standards collapse, existential authenticity is often the first victim. For the active nihilist, the time is ripe to begin the process of creating new values and the constructing of invigorating meaning: the nihilistic moment is liberating and opens the world to infinite possibilities. Unfortunately, Vienna is not replete with cultural transformers.

However, we can read Shakespeare and Nietzsche and derive a deeper lesson: relish the anxiety of moral choice as required for salutary personal transformation; take responsibility for choices and actions pursuant to them; and bask in the freedom to re-imagine and remake the self. There are no excuses.

F. Sex Can be Dangerous

Vienna bristles with rapacious sexual marauders, repressed sexuality masquerading as high rectitude, and bodily commodification. In Vienna, sex curries death (Claudio, later Angelo; Pompey becomes assistant executioner), social degeneration (the corruption of community), self-loathing (Angelo when facing his lust), venereal disease (rampant), uncharitable reactions (Isabella), corruption of virtue (Angelo, who also tries to debase Isabella), unplanned pregnancies (Juliet, Mistress Keepdown—Lucio's eventual wife), and unbridled cynicism (Lucio).

The moral degeneracy, excess license, and widespread venereal disease spawned by sex in Vienna are symptoms of a defective community promoted by warped jurisprudence. The two commonest responses to sex in Vienna have proved unsuccessful: wholesale indulgence, as exemplified by Lucio, Pompey, and a host of minor characters; and utter abstinence, as illustrated by Isabella, Angelo (prior to his fall), and Mariana (cloistered within her moated grange savoring her masochistic, unrequited love). Also, the "mutual entertainment" of Claudio and Juliet has proved disastrous.

The link between sex and death is unmistakable. Sex leads Claudio to be sentenced to death. Claudio describes his lust as leading to death as surely as a rat's longing for poison facilitates the rodent's end: we can die from securing what we most desire. Isabella expresses her preference for torture and death instead of sexual dishonor. Although he later pardons him, the Duke sentences Angelo to death for his sexual activity. Angelo broke his vows with Mariana because the death of her brother at sea resulted in the loss of her dowry. Lucio prefers death to marriage to a "punk." Pompey is transformed from pimp and tapster to executioner's assistant.

Commodification and the fungibility of bodily parts also pervade the play: Isabella's chastity is to be traded for Claudio's life; Mariana's body is substituted for Isabella's in the bed trick; Barnardine's head is to replace Claudio's in the head trick; and Ragozine's head does replace Claudio's in the head trick.

The Duke's negligent rule facilitated the sexual chaos defining Vienna. Angelo's mechanical jurisprudence sought to repress sex. Isabella's solution was to withdraw from social life to the safety of a nunnery. Mariana could only pine away for a reprobate within her moated grange. At the end, Duke Vincentio tries to salvage sex by domesticating it through forced marriages. I have sketched previously the problematic nature of most of those marriages: Lucio struggles to the altar kicking and screaming; Angelo is ordered to love Mariana; the Duke proclaims, instead of proposes, marriage to Isabella, who remains silent; only Claudio and Juliet seem compatible (at least if Juliet's dowry quickly emerges).

Where is love? Not in Angelo, even if he has repented his wrongdoing. Not in Lucio, whose heart is closed to deep affection and profound commitment. Yes, Mariana exudes an obsessive, perhaps masochistic, love of Angelo that more betrays her need than signals her well-being. Does Isabella suddenly love the Duke because he has expressed his desire? If so, the reed of her ardor is flimsy: she knows him only as the false Friar, whose counsel was aimed at expedient resolution of a growing social problem. Does the Duke love Isabella? He had earlier spoke of his invulnerability to love and the pangs of passion. But the alleged repository of self-knowledge in the play proves fallible. He desires Isabella and in a line worthy of the casket test in *The Merchant of Venice*, declares, "What's mine is yours, and what is yours is mine" (5.1.537). Is the Duke in love with Isabella, with her unique combination of excellences, shortcomings, unactualized possibilities, and way of manifesting that combination? Or is the Duke in love only with her excellences, either in themselves or as a way of scaling the Socratic-Diotima ladder to the world of Absolutes? Or is the Duke more of an Alcibiadean lover, one who obsesses over qualities he lacks and in desperation must possess? Because of the Duke's impulsive and surprising proclamation of marriage, we lack the textual evidence to draw a reasonable conclusion.

Constable Elbow seems to love his wife. But his malapropisms, after all, could be Freudian slips. A microcosm of the fractured social structure, his feeble communication skills do not permit a clear conclusion about the condition of his conjugal passion.

Prodded by the leading questions of the Friar-Duke, Juliet emphasizes the mutuality of her relationship with Claudio and states unequivocally that she loves him as much as she loves herself (2.3.24-27). Claudio also declares his love for Juliet, but in more somber tones. He describes their sex as "mutual entertainment" (1.2.154) and likens his lust to a rat hungry for that which will indirectly kill him (1.2.125-130). Those searching for a flowery, romantic poem to love are better advised to contact Bassanio.

Interpreted charitably, the message may be that sex and love are gravely problematic when pursued within morally polluted social conditions. Where the underlying social understandings that nurture mutuality, reciprocity, intimacy, and robust community are absent, salutary sex and love face daunting obstacles.

Sex is different from ordinary contractual exchanges of commodities and services. Sex in our culture (and in Shakespeare's) has a socially-charged meaning that in most cases implicates more of our constitutive attributes and thus puts more of our self-identity in jeopardy than do other mundane voluntary exchanges: we are more vulnerable in sex and love because we risk more emotionally. The fact that sex is different from ordinary contractual exchanges of commodities and services does not imply that sex must be different. That sex is different because of contingent historical and cultural reasons than because of underlying, immutable features of human nature is more likely.

The voluntariness of sex and love is often, but not always, impaired by economic reality and the imperatives of particular economic structures. The sexual domination of women by men is a particularly widespread and pernicious form of oppression, although not clearly the fundamental cause of all oppression. In a generally patriarchal context, it is still possible for a woman to exploit sexually a man. Specific women may have power advantages over specific men based on culturally defined physical attractiveness and seductiveness, as well as economic and political leverage. Furthermore, in a generally patriarchal context, it is still possible for women and men to create microcontexts that adequately expunge gender conflict and facilitate salutary sex and love. In Vienna, this may be illustrated by Claudio and Juliet.

The point is that sex and love do not operate in a social vacuum. In Vienna, general social confusion and disjointed sexual and intimate relations are mutually sustaining. Without a vibrant community that nourishes intimacy, sex and love become perplexing and even dangerous.

G. Fear of Death Can be Overcome

Death assumes several images in the play: Isabella alludes to heroic martyrdom in the face of moral compromise ("death before dishonor"). When counseling Claudio, Duke Vincentio conjures death as an endless respite and a comforting sleep. Claudio vacillates between death as annihilation—a serious deprivation of value—and death as followed by a horrifying afterlife. Angelo is prepared to accept death as appropriate retributive punishment for his moral transgressions; he thus understands death as the forfeiture of value. Barnardine perceives death as an untimely inconvenience to his primary purposes: drinking, sleeping, and intransigence.

Perhaps one of the lessons we can derive from of the play is that human existence is a process of amassing greater self-knowledge which nurtures successful living. A death that cuts off that process is unfortunate. We must repent our wrongs; extend mercy and even forgiveness to those who have wronged us; and learn to accept the fallible, flawed human condition. Part of the process is to accept death as our earthly end. We should neither be paralyzed by fear of death nor should we hasten its approach.

Sharpening our awareness of death can be one path toward more robust and authentic living; confronting death is connected to learning how to live; and tranquilized immersion in the everydayness of habit and diversion dulls our spirits and dishonors the narrative of our life. A healthy attitude toward death includes fully recognizing its inevitability, refusing to live less energetically, constructing our projects in ways compatible with viewing ourselves as part of a long generational chain, pursuing ideals that affirm life's possibilities, maintaining a zest for the adventures, triumphs, and failures that constitute life, and appreciating the chance to be part of human history.[14]

That slogan, "On their deathbeds people don't regret not having spent more time at the office," is useful because it gives us a sense of priorities. But the reason we might regret on our deathbeds failed relationships is that at that point we sense most sharply our isolation. We are about to die, we are scared, we are leaving the world, the others we know are staying, some of us are terrorized by eternal damnation. We need comfort. Extra time at the office, watching another episode of *Law and Order*, completing the cement work on our front porch steps, going to the racetrack one more time, none of these actions provide that comfort. Comfort can be supplied only by those who share our fate or by a benevolent Supreme Being willing to forgive and forget. Or we suppose they are our final best hope. Who but an unapologetic philosopher such as Socrates could sit about calmly speculating about the immortality of the soul while awaiting the hemlock that would consume his life?

Most of us are not so obsessed with death that we have only the obituary pages to highlight our days. We are not merely in chains awaiting our turn. We have opportunities to pursue meaning and value. We are not consumed with our demise every waking moment. We attend to projects, interests, and relationships that animate our spirits and brighten our days. We do, however, watch the physical deterioration and deaths of love ones, endure suffering, and inch closer to the turnstiles of doom with each passing hour.

From a personal perspective, my death is the end, as long as we do not adopt theism, of the world. My consciousness is obliterated; the planets and heavenly bodies evaporate. From a wider perspective, my death is part of the process of change, allowing another person the time and space to enjoy or to suffer. My death itself is insignificant. An intermediary perspective would deny both extremes. My biological death need not toll the end of my biographical life, nor the end of those projects, meanings, and values upon which my life centered. While permanence is denied me, lingering influence is not.

Our attitude toward death deeply influences our possibilities for maximally affirming life. The end of our existence is less significant than the effects our knowledge of mortality has on the way we live. A life does amount to what a person does, but that need not fuel an inveterate striver's winner-takes-all mentality. Against Nietzsche, the possibility of a robustly meaningful life is not restricted only to the greatest among us.

A healthy, adequate awareness of death can energize meaningful activities. Human beings often take a romantic-heroic path in trying to transcend death by participating in projects that endure beyond their deaths. We achieve a fragile immortality by raising children, sharing grand political and social causes, creating new technological and communication networks, making artistic contributions, and the like. We connect to value by extending beyond ourselves through relationships, projects, and creative endeavors upon which we stamp our identities. We can achieve a heroism that resists mortality by courageously struggling against a hard lot. An entire line of thinkers such as William James, Emerson, and Nietzsche sees the heroic quest as an attempt to transcend death by participating in projects of lasting worth.

We know, however, that we cannot transcend death, our projects do not last forever, the stamp of our identities smudges with time, and for all but a few our footprints are trampled upon, then obliterated. But the experiences, the stream of processes, the struggles, defeats and triumphs elevate our lives with meaning. The heroic quest may be a response to the terror of human vulnerability, limitation, and inevitable death. Perhaps an unearned narcissism fuels the journey. Perhaps human life is impossible to live robustly without illusions. Perhaps religious commitment, instead of being the vehicle by which dominant classes solidify power, or by which the herd minimizes the glory of potential nobles, or by which human beings project their need for a Great Father, is an especially seductive narrative of the heroic quest for personal immortality.

The struggle to triumph over life's limitations, the hunt for ersatz immortality, the yearning for connection with value and meaning, render us noble in the face of our terror. Confronting the Grim Reaper at the moment of ultimate Truth can itself crown the meaningfulness of our lives, or not.

This is, perhaps, what Nietzsche meant in celebrating *amor fati*. Embracing life fully means accepting its tragic dimensions including human limitation, individual estrangement, and inevitable death. A full acceptance of life and the surrounding world includes, for Nietzsche, the realization that prior to death our life has been fulfilling and is in need of no further acts to complete it. As the final curtain falls over our life, we savor the whole and wish only that it could be re-lived over and over, infinitely. Granted, this is a Nietzschean ideal, as death arrives on its own schedule and too often interrupts our best-hatched plans, but Nietzsche imagines a praiseworthy attitude toward death which sees mortality as neither necessary for a meaningful life nor necessarily depriving life of meaning. Mortality is our unchosen context, malleable within limits by our attitude.

Living with adequate recognition of mortality, yet responding zestfully, can vivify meaning in our lives and elevate death beyond meaningless termination. Mortality is our context, not necessarily our defeat. We need not glorify death, we need not pretend we do not fear death, but we should temper the Grim Reaper's victory by living and dying meaningfully.

The idea of biographical life revolves around human life as a narrative, a story.[15] We are a series of stories in that we understand and identify ourselves through a chain of events, choices, actions, thoughts, and relationships. Our biographical lives, including value and meaning connected to our death and events thereafter, extend beyond our biological lives. Many human beings recognize this by consciously nurturing legacies, images, creative works, children, and projects that flourish beyond their deaths. We are aware, however, that our projects cannot endure forever and we pursue them in that light. Death, then, does not supervene on life; it provides a context for life.

Admittedly, for most of us, our biographical story does not continue long after our deaths. Our fantasies to the contrary notwithstanding, we are not indispensable. At most, our departure would bring deep sorrow to those closest to us. Once those few who actually knew us and were influenced by us themselves die, most of us remain, at most, represented only by uncaptioned photos in web-covered albums stored in the corner of neglected attics. Most of our deaths will not be accompanied by massive displays of anxiety and gnashing of teeth. Beyond family, friends, and close associates, others will take note of our demise, perhaps attend a service, moan, "Too bad about Old Spike," or whisper, "No great loss," and get on with the mundane rhythms of life. Still, the question of what my future death means to me now is crucial. As Nietzsche insisted, the brio with which I live each moment of my life, the spirit of *amor fati*, is paramount. The meaning of my death hinges on the quality of my life. But we cannot maintain a lifelong giddiness. As we project toward the future we can, however, become more aware of the processes, not merely the outcomes that constitute our lives. To make our activities more fulfilling, to focus our creative interest in the act of creation instead of only on the result, speeds us toward the Nietzschean ideal.

Leaving a rich legacy is not a way of achieving immortality, even though the advice "plant a tree, beget children, build a house, write a book" is sometimes taken in that vein. We are finished at death if no afterlife awaits us. But generating a legacy is a way of enriching the meaning of our lives now. Some of our projects should reach beyond our lifetimes. Guiding the next generation, creating something that has a life and identity outside of ourselves, transmitting a culture and heritage, attending to enduring yet finite projects, and influencing the future are not ways of halting the Grim Reaper, but they are paths to meaning. Although our biological lives expire, our biographical lives continue through such legacies. Again, this is not immortality, but it does mark a life well lived. Generating rich legacies energizes faith in life, binds us to something beyond ourselves, and nurtures meaning above narrow self-fulfillment. Approaching our life and death in such a way may even ground the accurate, positive, self-appraisal of our lives that exudes worthwhile happiness.[16] This must be enough to stoke the fires of our hearts and rekindle the sparks of our souls.

At the end of the play, Claudio, Angelo, Barnardine, and Lucio evade execution. They are cast back into the fractured community that is Vienna—three of them with new brides. Will the events they endured bring them new self-knowledge that will translate into more robust living? Or will they revert to their past characters? Will greater understanding of living a meaningful life result in a sharper appreciation of the human context of finitude? Will they learn how to face their eventual, inevitable deaths with wisdom and resolve?

More important, how will those of us who have read Shakespeare's plays and pondered the lessons we might derive from them answer those questions for ourselves?

NOTES

Introduction

1. Harold Bloom, *Shakespeare: The Invention of the Human* (New York: Riverhead Books, 1998).
2. Ibid., 171-178.
3. See, for example, Stuart Hampton-Reeves, *Measure for Measure* (New York: Palgrave MacMillan, 2007), 107-140.

Chapter One

I derive citations to *The Merchant of Venice* from Hardin Craig and David Bevington, eds. *The Complete Works of Shakespeare* (Glenview, Ill.: Scott, Foresman and Company, 1973). The format is standard. For example, 1.1.161 = Act 1, Scene 1, Line 161.

1. See, for example, Raymond Angelo Belliotti, *Seeking Identity: Individualism Versus Community in an Ethnic Context* (Lawrence, Kans.: University Press of Kansas), ix-x, 157-158, 191-193.
2. See, for example, Hardin Craig and David Bevington, eds. *The Complete Works of Shakespeare* (Glenview, Ill.: Scott, Foresman and Company, 1973), 509 n.1; G. Blakemore Evans and J.J.M. Tobin, eds. *The Riverside Shakespeare* (Boston: Houghton Mifflin Co., 1997), 292 n.1.
3. This section has been informed by Joel Feinberg, *Doing and Deserving* (Princeton: Princeton University Press, 1970); John Kleinig, "The Concept of Desert," *The Philosophical Quarterly* 8:1 (January, 1971); David Miller, *Social Justice* (Oxford: Oxford University Press, 1976); Julian Lamont, "The Concept of Desert in Distributive Justice," *The Philosophical Quarterly* 44: 174 (1994); Brian Barry, *Political Argument* (London: Routledge & Kegan Paul. 1965); George Sher, "Effort, Ability, and Personal Desert," *Philosophy and Public Affairs* 8:361 (1979); Fred Feldman, "Desert: Reconsideration of Some Received Wisdom," *Mind* 104:413 (1995); John Rawls, *A Theory of Justice* (Cambridge, Mass.: Harvard University Press, 1971); Robert Nozick, *Anarchy, State, and Utopia* (New York: Basic Books, 1974); Michael A. Slote, "Desert, Consent and Justice," *Philosophy and Public Affairs* 2:323 (1973); Alan Zaitchik, "On Deserving to Deserve," *Philosophy and Public Affairs* 6: 370 (1977).
4. Feldman, "Desert," 418.
5. Rawls, *Theory of Justice*, 311-313.
6. Raymond Angelo Belliotti, *Dante's Deadly Sins: Moral Philosophy in Hell* (Oxford: Wiley-Blackwell Publishers, 2011), 138-139.
7. Martin Heidegger, *Being and Time*. Translated by John Macquarrie and Edward Robinson (New York: Harper and Row, 1962).
8. Non-existentialists take these values and their subordinate prescriptions as, at best, necessary but not sufficient conditions for leading a good human life. After all, we can easily imagine a person who is existentially intense and authentic, but still a thoroughly immoral person who causes much unjustified injury to others.
9. See, for example, Robert C. Solomon, *The Passions* (New York: Anchor Press, 1976); *Love: Emotion, Myth, and Metaphor* (New York: Anchor Press, 1981); *About Love:*

Reinventing Romance for Our Times (New York: Simon & Shuster, 1988); Robert Nozick, "Love's Bond" in *The Examined Life: Philosophical Meditations* (New York: Simon & Shuster, 1989), 68-86; Irving Singer, *The Nature of Love, Volume 3: The Modern World* (Chicago: University of Chicago Press, 1989).

10. Raymond Angelo Belliotti, *What is the Meaning of Human Life?* (Amsterdam: Rodopi, 2001), 73-91; *Happiness is Overrated* (Lanham, Md.: Rowman & Littlefield Publishers, Inc., 2004), 84-88, 120-122, 156-159.

Chapter Two

1. E. Allan Farnsworth, Contracts (New York: Wolters Kluwer Law & Business, 1999), 765-770.
2. See, for example, *P.C. Data Ctrs. of Pa, Inc. v. Federal Express Corp.*, 113 F.Supp.2d 709, 715 (M.D. Pa. 2000); *Guard v. P & R Enter., Inc.*, 631 P.2d 1068, 1071 (Alaska 1981).
3. For example, contracting parties incur unreimbursed litigation costs for attorneys' fees and can rarely recover prejudgment interest. Also, damages that were not reasonably foreseeable or not proven with certainty will be denied. Damages for emotional distress are also rarely awarded.
4. When proving expectancy damages with sufficient certainty is difficult, courts often award reliance damages which are expenditures incurred before the breach that were made in reliance on the contract.
5. *H.J. McGrath Co. v. Wisner*, 55 A.2d 793, 785 (Md. 1947).
6. *Wollums v. Horsley*, 20 S.W. 781, 781 (Ky. 1892).
7. See, for example, *United States Nursing Corp. v. Saint Joseph Medical Ctr.*, 39 F.3d 790, 792 (7th Cir. 1994).
8. Robert A. Hillman, "Debunking Some Myths About Unconscionability," 67 *Cornell Law Review* 1 (1981).
9. See, for example, Raymond Angelo Belliotti, *Posthumous Harm: Why the Dead are Still Vulnerable* (Lanham, Md.: Lexington Books, 2011), chapter five.
10. Raymond Angelo Belliotti, "The Rule of Law and the Critical Legal Studies Movement," 24 *University of Western Ontario Law Review* 67 (1986); A. V. Dicey, *Introduction to the Study of the Law of the Constitution* (Chestnut Hill, Mass.: Adamant Media Corporation, 2000), 188-196; F. Hayek, *The Road to Serfdom* (Chicago: University of Chicago Press, 1944), 124-129; *The Constitution of Liberty* (Chicago: University of Chicago Press, 1978), 210-215; H.W. Jones, "The Rule of Law and the Welfare State," 58 *Columbia Law Review* 143 (1958.
11. See, for example, Martha C. Nussbaum, "Equity and Mercy," 22 *Philosophy & Public Affairs* (1993), 83-125.
12. Andrew Brien, "Mercy Within Legal Justice," 24 *Social Theory and Practice* (1998): 83-110, 86. See also, John Tasioulas, "Mercy" 103 *Proceedings of the Aristotelian Society* (2003): 101-132; Lucy Allais, "Forgiveness and Mercy," 27 *South African Journal of Philosophy* (2008): 1-9; Carol S. Steiker, "Murphy on Mercy," 27 *Criminal Justice Ethics* (2008): 45-54.
13. Steiker, "Murphy on Mercy" 49-51.
14. Allais, "Forgiveness and Mercy."
15. "Shylock is perhaps the one person in the courtroom who does know how to cut the flesh without spilling the blood. Drain the blood first. Slaughter Antonio as if he

were an animal being ritually killed. It is this thought, and not what Portia literally says, that so horrifies Shylock. For once, he does not take things literally. When he at last sees that he is treating Antonio as an animal is treated, he wants nothing more to do with the pound of flesh he had so recently demanded. Both the Duke and Portia appeal to Shylock for mercy. But these appeals, rooted in claims of common humanity, were answered in advance by Shylock: Common humanity supports revenge as well as it supports mercy. Portia cannot reach Shylock until she appeals to a ground higher than mere humanity. For Shylock, that higher ground is Jewish law. Only after Portia has caused Shylock to see that he is a Jew and that as a Jew he cannot murder Antonio, does she appeal to the Venetian law that would have trumped the bond from the beginning." Christopher A. Colmo, "Law and Love in Shakespeare's *The Merchant of Venice*," 26 *Oklahoma City University Law Review* 307 (2001): 320-321.

While this is a refreshingly original interpretation of events, the simpler explanation is that Shylock requests monetary payment because he is moved by considerations of self-interest and desperation, not by a sudden epiphany of the implications of Jewish law. Balthasar-Portia's language, "Shed thou no blood" (4.1.325) is unlikely to permit the draining of blood as a prelude to cutting the flesh. The draining of blood would cause Antonio's death which Portia's decoding of contractual language would not permit. The crucial idea in the "you may cut your pound of flesh but only if you shed no blood" is to prohibit the lawful slaying of Antonio. Moreover, that this admonishment awakens Shylock to the realization that Antonio will almost certainly die when one pound of flesh is removed from nearest his heart is not credible. Shylock was keenly aware of that all along. Finally, that Jewish law would prohibit the slaying of Antonio should have been clear to Shylock from the outset.

16. H.L.A. Hart, *The Concept of Law* (Oxford: Clarendon Press, 1961), chap. 1; Raymond Angelo Belliotti, *Justifying Law* (Philadelphia: Temple University Press, 1992), p. 47.
17. Hart, ibid., p. 126 and chap. 5 generally.
18. Ibid.
19. Ibid., 126-127.
20. Ibid., chap. 5.
21. Ibid., 132 and chap. 5 generally.
22. Ronald Dworkin, *Taking Rights Seriously* (Cambridge, Mass.: Harvard University Press 1977), p. 28-31: Belliotti, Justifying Law, 75-107.
23. Dworkin, ibid. 31-39.
24. Ibid., 117-118. Judgments on each scheme will sometimes differ from judge to judge because each jurist proceeds from her own philosophical and intellectual convictions (118). However, her subjective judgments will have no force because "they will not enter [her] calculations in such a way that different parts of the theory [she] constructs can be attributed to [her] independent convictions rather than the body of law [she] must justify" (117-118).
25. Ibid., 107-109.
26. Ibid.
27. Roughly, if prior decisions are justified by a particular set of principles which act as reasons for those decisions, and those principles dictate a certain judgment in the instant case, and those principles have neither been "recanted nor institutionally re-

gretted," then that judgment applies to the instant case. This comprehensive scheme incorporates a theory of mistakes. That is, the scheme must limit the number and nature of events that can be stigmatized as mistakes, and outline for future decision making why such events are mistakes. To disparage an event as a mistake is to deny its continued gravitational force—its authority for future judicial decision making—but not its specific institutional authority—its authority to affect the particular institutional consequences the event encompasses. A mistake will be "embedded" when the event's specific institutional authority is situated firmly and outlives the loss of its gravitational force. A mistake will be "corrigible" when the event's specific institutional authority depends upon its continued gravitational force. Ibid., 111-115, 121-123; Belliotti, *Justifying Law*, 77-78.
28. Dworkin, ibid., 105, 106-123.
29. Ronald Dworkin, "Seven Critics," 11 *Georgia Law Review* 1201, 1252 (1977). Dworkin says that a jurisprudential question is raised when a theory based on one principle is a better fit with past doctrine and another theory with a contrary principle is morally preferable. Although he admits his answer is "crude," Dworkin suggests that the theory that is a better fit, the one that characterizes less of past doctrine as mistakes, should prevail if the morally preferable theory stigmatizes past doctrine too much. When two competing theories fit adequately, however, Dworkin contends that the theory that is morally preferable should prevail, even if it stigmatizes a greater amount of past doctrines as mistakes than does the rival theory.
30. Dworkin, *Taking Rights Seriously*, 280-283.
31. Belliotti, *Justifying Law*, 221-254; "Toward a Theory of Judicial Decision-making: A Synthesis of Ideologist Jurisprudence and Doctrinalism," 28 *The Catholic Lawyer* 28 215-252 (1983).
32. Belliotti, *Justifying Law*, 233-236.
33. Legitimate legal ideologies are produced from a complex method of reasoning that seeks to justify extant law. Belliotti, ibid., 238-240. These ideologies will roughly reflect general political philosophies such as centrist-liberalism, centrist-conservatism, socialism, economic-libertarianism, and the like. Trying to forge a master legal theory, ala Dworkin, by taking principles and policies from each legitimate legal ideology and assigning relative weights in accordance with their embodiment in extant legal doctrine, is unlikely to be successful. Except in homogeneous societies, such a project is doomed to interminable confusion and conflict. Thus, no single, demonstrably best, legal ideology is likely to emerge from the analysis, but the field will have been narrowed.
34. Ibid., 244.
35. "[Engaged fallibilistic pluralism] means taking our own fallibility seriously—resolving that however much we are committed to our own styles of thinking, we are willing to listen to others without denying or suppressing the otherness of the other. It means being vigilant against the dual temptations of simply dismissing what others are saying by falling back on one of those standard defensive ploys where we condemn it as obscure, wooly, or trivial, or thinking we can always easily translate what is alien into our own entrenched vocabularies." Richard Bernstein, "Pragmatism, Pluralism, and the Healing of Wounds," 63 *American Philosophical Society Proceedings* 5, 15 (no.3 1989); Belliotti, ibid., 206-207, 218, 219, 236, 241-242, 243, 250-251.

"Critical Pragmatism recognizes a measure of objectivity emerging from internal constraints, from community agreements and practices, and from behavioral restraints, but it spurns arid conventionalism because it does not take societal conventions as timeless givens or as incorrigible foundations. We must test extant societal conventions by internal criteria of coherence with other conventions, compatibility with fundamental theories of the person, and the role of morality in a diverse society; by the methods of immanent critique; and by their ability to facilitate our professed principles and goals." Belliotti, ibid., 238. For the independent tests a justified legal theory must pass, see Belliotti, ibid., 240-242.

36. Belliotti, ibid., 241-242; Critical Pragmatism concludes that a judge is obligated to decide easy cases in accord with their respective right answers, but the scope of this obligation is bounded. Judges are under the relevant obligation if and only if affirming the right legal answer would not generate inordinate substantive injustice that cannot be justified on other institutional grounds. The acknowledgment that the judicial obligation to apply what are clearly the law's requirements is bounded, does not open the doors to wholesale judicial civil disobedience. Judges are justified in not applying the law only after making the determination that substantive injustice would occur; no other institutional justifications can be persuasively offered for applying the law (e.g., the rules/principles/policies which support applying the law are morally justified and ignoring them in the extraordinary instant case will do them significant damage; the legal system as a whole is morally justified and will be damaged more by ignoring the law's requirements than the good that is produced, or harm prevented, in the instant case); there is no less drastic means of resolving the problem (e.g., negotiation, alternate dispute resolution). Ibid., 248.

37. *Adamo Wrecking Co. v. United States*, 434 U.S. 278, 285 (1978); *McNally v. United States*, 483 U.S. 350 (1987); Jared Tobin Finkelstein, "In Re Brett: The Sticky Problem of Statutory Construction," 52 *Fordham Law Review* 430, 435 (1983).

38. *Potomac Electric Power Company v. Director, OWCP*, 449 U.S. 268, 273-80 (1980); Finklestein, ibid., at 40-42.

39. *New Jersey Builders, Owners & Managers Assoc. v. Blair*, 60 N.J. 330, 338, 288 A.2d 855, 859 (1972); Donald J. Rapson, "A 'Home Run' Application of Established Principles of Statutory Construction: UCC Analogies," 5 *Cardozo Law Review* 441, 442 (1984).

40. *New Capitol Bar & Grill Corp. v. Division of Employment Sec.*, 25 N.J. 155, 160, 135 A.2d 465, 467 (1957); Rapson, ibid.

41. *Green v. Bock Laundry Machine Co.*, 490 U.S. 504 (1989); *State v. Provenzano*, 34 N.J. 318, 322, 169 A.2d 135, 137 (1961); Rapson, ibid., 450. The principles of interpretation sketched in the text accompanying notes 37-41 do not always rest together easily. For example, the appeal to legislative purpose, the invocation of the spirit of the act, and the principle of applying the plain meaning of a statute (not sketched here) will sometimes produce conflicting judgments. To soften such conflict, philosophers have advanced numerous theories to guide and to justify judicial decision making. See, for example, the text accompanying notes 16-36.

Chapter Three

1. Plato, "The Symposium," trans. by Michael Joyce, *Plato: Collected Dialogues*, ed. by Edith Hamilton and Huntington Cairns (Princeton, N.J.: Princeton University Press,

1973), 526-574. All parenthetical references in the text reflect the standard Stephanus pagination.
2. Plato, "Phaedreus," trans. by R. Hackforth, *Plato: Collected Dialogues*, ibid., 475-525.
3. Søren Kierkegaard, *Either/Or*, trans. by Alastair Hannay (London: Penguin Books, 1992).
4. See, for example, Raymond Angelo Belliotti, *Posthumous Harm: Why the Dead are Still Vulnerable* (Lanham, Md.: Lexington Books, 2011), chapter five.
5. Aristotle, *Nicomachean Ethics*, trans. by Martin Ostwald (Indianapolis, Ind.: Bobbs-Merrill, 1962), Bk. 8, sec. 1.
6. See, for example, Plato, "The Republic," trans. by Paul Shorey, *Plato: Collected Dialogues*, ed. by Edith Hamilton and Huntington Cairns (Princeton, N.J.: Princeton University Press, 1973), 575-844, especially Books 8 and 9.
7. Stephen R. Covey, A. Roger Merrill, and Rebecca R. Merrill, *First Things First* (New York: Simon & Schuster, 1992), 17-31.
8. David Niven, *The 100 Simple Secrets of Happy People* (New York: HarperCollins Publishers, 2000), 22; Raymond Angelo Belliotti, *Happiness is Overrated* (Lanham, Md.: Rowman & Littlefield Publishers, Inc., 2004), 99-123. Dr. David Lykken, *Happiness* (New York: St. Martin's Press, 1999), 17.
9. Niven, *The 100 Simple Secrets*, 22-23.
10. Lykken, *Happiness*, 17.

Chapter Four

I derive citations to *Measure for Measure* from G. Blakemore Evans and J.J.M. Tobin, eds. *The Riverside Shakespeare* (Boston: Houghton Mifflin Co., 1997). The format is standard. For example, 5.1.439 = Act 5, Scene 1, Line 439.

1. Niccolò Machiavelli, *The Prince in Selected Political Writings*, ed. and trans. by David Wootton (Indianapolis: Hackett Publishing Company, 1994. Parenthetical citations to Machiavelli's *The Prince* indicate chapters. For example P 17= *The Prince*, Chapter 17.
2. Rafael Sabatini, *The Life of Cesare Borgia* (Teddington, UK: The Echo Library, 2006), 159.
3. Raymond Angelo Belliotti, *Niccolò Machiavelli: The Laughing Lion and the Strutting Fox* (Lanham, Md.: Lexington Books, 2009), 111.
4. Sabatini, op.cit., 187-188, 193-194.
5. See, for example, Heidi Meinzer, "Idaho's Throwback to Elizabethan England: Criminalizing a Civil Proceeding," *Family Law Quarterly* 34 (1) (2000): 165-175; Robert Misner, "Minimalism, Desuetude, and Fornication" *Willamette Law Review* 35 (1999): 1-55.
6. Misner, ibid., 5-6.
7. Note, "Desuetude," *Harvard Law Review* 119 (2006): 2209, 2211.
8. *Committee on Legal Ethics v. Printz*, 416 S.E.2d 720 (W.Va. 1992) (laws lose their binding force when citizens openly and notoriously violate them over a long period of time with the tacit consent of law enforcement officials). *State v. Donley*, 607 S.E.2d 474 (W.Va. 2004) (applying the doctrine of desuetude in a case involving felony concealment of a minor child). A Connecticut appellate court discussed desuetude doctrine *in dicta* but issued no ruling on that question because the matter had

not been raised by the defendant at trial level. See *State v. Linares*, 630 A.2d 1340, 1346 n.11 (Conn. App. Ct. 1993). *Hill v. Smith,* Morris 70 (Iowa 1840), 1840 WL 2834 at 7 (Iowa Terr.) ("We pronounce it contrary to the spirit of Anglo-Saxon liberty which we inherit, to revive, without notice, an obsolete statute, one in relation to which long disuse and a contrary policy had induced a reasonable belief that it was no longer in force."), overruled by *Pearson v. Int'l Distillery*, 34 N.W. 1, 5-6 (Iowa 1887).
9. *Committee on Legal Ethics v. Printz*, 416 S.E.2d 720, 726 (W.Va. 1992).
10. Erik Encarnacion, "Desuetude," *Columbia Journal of Law and Social Problems* 39 (2005): 149, 160.
11. Ibid., 162-163.
12. By "substantive belief" I mean a belief centered on meaning, purpose, value, or significant truth. Of course, even the most skeptical human beings will accept a host of beliefs focused on mundane conventional truths (for example, what day of the week today is, what time of the day it is, what my name is, whether I own a dog, and the like).
13. See, for example, Ivan Turgenev, *Fathers and Sons* (1862), trans. Richard Freeborn (New York: Oxford University Press, 2008).
14. See, for example, Raymond Angelo Belliotti, *Stalking Nietzsche* (Westport, Conn.: Greenwood Press, 1998), 62-63; Max Stirner, *The Ego and His Own* (1845) ("political nihilism") in Daniel Guerin, *Anarchism: From Theory to Practice* (New York: Monthly Review Press, 1970); Fyodor Dostoevsky, *The Brothers Karamazov* (1880) ("existential nihilism") trans. Richard Pervear and Larissa Volokhonsky (New York: Farrar, Straus, and Giroux, 2002); John L. Mackie, *Ethics: Inventing Right and Wrong* ("moral nihilism") (New York: Penguin Books, 1977); Richard Rorty, *Contingency, Irony, and Solidarity* ("epistemological nihilism") (Cambridge, UK: Cambridge University Press, 1989).
15. Friedrich Nietzsche, *The Gay Science*, trans. Walter Kaufmann (New York: Random House, 1967), Section 125.
16. Ibid.
17. Ibid.
18. Albert Camus, *The Myth of Sisyphus*, trans. Justin O'Brien (New York: Vintage Books, 1991); Raymond Angelo Belliotti, *What is the Meaning of Human Life?* (Amsterdam: Rodopi, 2001), 51-71.
19. Friedrich Nietzsche, *Thus Spoke Zarathustra*, in *The Portable Nietzsche*, trans. Walter Kaufmann (New York: Viking Press, 1954), Part 1, "Zarathustra's Prologue," Section 5.
20. Ibid.
21. Nietzsche, ibid., Sections 3-4; "On Priests."
22. Nietzsche, ibid., Section 5.
23. Aristotle, *Nicomachean Ethics* in *Selections*, ed. W. D. Ross (New York: Charles Scribner's Sons, 1955), 1140a24-1144b32.
24. See, for example, Raymond Angelo Belliotti, "Negative and Positive Duties," *Theoria* 47 (1981), 82-92; "Negative Duties, Positive Duties, and Rights." *The Southern Journal of Philosophy* 16 (1978), 581-588.
25. Raymond Angelo Belliotti, *Dante's Deadly Sins: Moral Philosophy in Hell* (Oxford: Wiley-Blackwell Publishers, 2011), 127-129.

26. John Medina, *The Genetic Inferno: Inside the Seven Deadly Sins* (Cambridge: Cambridge University Press, 2000), 28-29.

Chapter Five

1. Raymond Angelo Belliotti, *Good Sex: Perspectives on Sexual Ethics* (Lawrence, Kans.: University Press of Kansas, 1993), 87-96.
2. Ibid., 175-227.
3. See, for example, Joel Feinberg, *Harmless Wrongdoing* (New York: Oxford University Press, 1988), 176-210.
4. Ibid., 200.
5. Ibid., 178-179.
6. Belliotti, *Good Sex*, 175-227.
7. Arthur Schopenhauer, *The World as Will and Idea*, 3 vols., trans. R.B. Haldane and J. Kemp (London: Routledge & Kegan Paul, 1948); Raymond Angelo Belliotti, *What is the Meaning of Human Life?* (Amsterdam: Rodopi, 2001), 33-36.
8. Irving Singer, *Meaning in Life* (New York: The Free Press, 1982).
9. See, for example, Raymond Angelo Belliotti, *Dante's Deadly Sins: Moral Philosophy in Hell* (Oxford: Wiley-Blackwell Publishers, 2011), 19-47.
10. Phoebe S. Spinrad, "*Measure for Measure* and the Art of Not Dying," in *Measure for Measure*, ed. Harold Bloom (New York Chelsea House Publishers, 1987), 114; Harold Bloom, *Shakespeare: The Invention of the Human* (New York: Riverhead Books, 1998), 369.
11. Epicurus, "Letter to Menoeceus," in *The Stoic and Epicurean Philosophers*, ed. Whitney J. Oates, trans. C. Bailey (New York: The Modern Library, 1940), 31; Lucretius, "On the Nature of Things," in *The Stoic and Epicurean Philosophers*, ed. Whitney J. Oates, trans. C. Bailey (New York: The Modern Library, 1940), 131; Raymond Angelo Belliotti, *Roman Philosophy and the Good Life* (Lanham, Md.: Lexington Books, 2009), 98-107.
12. A.A, Long, "Roman Philosophy," in *The Cambridge Companion to Greek and Roman Philosophy*, ed. David Sedley (Cambridge: Cambridge University Press), 2003), 196.
13. Raymond Angelo Belliotti, *Posthumous Harm: Why the Dead are Still Vulnerable* (Lanham: Md.: Lexington Books, 2011).
14. See, for example, Joel Feinberg, *Social Philosophy* (Englewood Cliffs, N.J.: Prentice Hall, Inc., 1973), 36-40; Louis B. Schwartz, "Morals Offenses and the Model Penal Code," *Columbia Law Review* 63 (1963): 669; Martin Golding, *Philosophy of Law*, (Englewood Cliffs, N.J.: Prentice Hall, Inc., 1975), 59-68.
15. Patrick Devlin, *The Enforcement of Morals* (London: Oxford University Press, 1965).
16. Ibid. 13-14.
17. Feinberg, *Social Philosophy*, 38-39.
18. *Furman v. Georgia*, 408 U.S. 238 (1972).
19. Justices Douglas, Brennan, and Marshall.
20. Justices Stewart and White.
21. *Gregg v. Georgia*, 428 U.S. 153 (1976).
22. See, also, *Trop v. Dulles*, 356 U.S. 86, 101 (1958).
23. *Gregg v. Georgia*, 176-182.
24. *Trop v. Dulles*, 100.

25. Id.
26. *Furman v. Georgia*, 392-393; *Wilkerson v. Utah*, 99 U.S. 130, 136 (1879); *United States v. Weems*, 217 U.S. 349, 381 (1910); *Trop v. Dulles*, 100.
27. *Gregg v. Georgia*, 194-195.
28. *United States v. Weems*, 217 U.S. 349 (1910); A.F. Granucci, "Nor Cruel and Unusual Punishments Inflicted: The Original Meaning," *California Law Review* 57 (1969: 839.
29. See, for example, *Hart v. Coiner*, 483 F.2d. 136, 140-142 (4th Cir. 1973), cert. denied, 415 U.S. 983 (1974).
30. *Gregg v. Georgia*, 190-191.
31. The *Model Penal Code* Section 921.141 (Supp. 1976-1977) lists a host of aggravating circumstances including the capital felony was committed by a person under sentence of imprisonment; the defendant was previously convicted of another capital felony or of a felony involving the use or threat of violence to the person; the defendant knowingly created a great risk of death to many persons; the capital felony was especially heinous, atrocious, or cruel; the capital felony was committed to disrupt or hinder the lawful exercise of any governmental function or the enforcement of laws; the capital felony was committed for pecuniary gain; and the like.
32. The *Model Penal Code* Section 921.141 (Supp. 1976-1977) lists a host of mitigating circumstances including the defendant has no significant history of prior criminal activity; the capital felony was committed while the defendant was under the influence of extreme mental or emotional disturbance; the victim was a participant in the defendant's conduct or consented to the act; the age of the defendant at the time of the crime; the capacity of the defendant to appreciate the criminality of his conduct or to conform his conduct to the requirements of law was substantially impaired; and the like.
33. See, for example, *Jurek v. Texas*, 428 U.S. 262 (1976).
34. See, for example, *Proffitt v. Florida*, 428 U.S. 242 (1976); *Woodson v. North Carolina*, 428 U.S. 280 (1976).
35. See, for example, *Woodson v. North Carolina* (mandatory death penalty for first degree murder is unconstitutional); *(Stanislaus) Roberts v. Louisiana*, 428 U.S. 325 (1976) (same); *(Harry) Roberts v. Louisiana*, 431 U.S. 633 (1977) (mandatory death penalty for first degree murder of police officers is unconstitutional).
36. *Furman v. Georgia*, 313.
37. *Gregg v. Georgia*, 175. Subsequent developments in Eighth Amendment interpretation include the following: *Estelle v. Gamble*, 429 U.S. 97 (1976) (deliberate indifference to a prisoner's serious medical needs constitutes "unnecessary and wanton infliction of pain" proscribed by the Eighth Amendment); *Farmer v. Brennan*, 511 U.S. 825 (1994) (deliberate indifference to a prisoner's serious medical need occurs where a prison official knows that inmates face a substantial risk of serious harm and disregards that risk by failing to take reasonable measures to abate it); *Enmund v. Florida*, 458 U.S. 782 (1982) (the Eighth Amendment does not permit the imposition of the death sentence for the crime of felony murder); *Atkins v. Virginia*, 536 U.S. 304 (2002) (the Eight Amendment succinctly prohibits excessive sanctions such as the imposition of the death sentence for crimes committed by mentally retarded people); *Roper v. Simmons*, 125 S.Ct. 1183 (2005) (the Eighth Amendment guarantees individuals the right not to be subjected to excessive sanctions such as the imposition of the death sentence for crimes committed by juveniles); *Kennedy v.*

Louisiana, 128 S.Ct. 2641 (2008) (death is a disproportionate punishment for the crime of rape where the victim, even if a child, does not die); *Baze v. Rees*, 128 S.Ct. 1520 (2008) (plurality opinion) (the risk of pain from improper administration of three-drug lethal injection as an execution procedure and the failure to implement proposed alternatives to that protocol does not constitute cruel and unusual punishment).

38. See, for example, Ernest Van Den Haag, *Punishing Criminals* (New York: Basic Books, (1975).
39. See, for example, Charles Black Jr., *Capital Punishment: The Inevitability of Caprice and Mistake* (New York: Norton & Co., 1981); Stephen Nathanson, "Does it Matter if the Death Penalty is Arbitrarily Administered?" *Philosophy & Public Affairs* 14 (1985): 149-164.
40. Black, *Capital Punishment*, 20.
41. Raymond Angelo Belliotti, "Gloom and Doom: Executing the Eighth Amendment," *The International Journal of Applied Philosophy* 3 (1986): 43, 44-52.
42. Hunter, Robert Grams, *Shakespeare and the Comedy of Forgiveness* (New York: Columbia University Press, 1965), pp. 210-212. "Legislation enacted in 1285 by Edward I granted English ecclesiastical courts jurisdiction to try its parishioners for adultery and fornication. Punishments were very lenient. Sexual lapses not resulting in pregnancy 'were usually described as incontinence or suspicious life.' While punishing fornication fell exclusively under the jurisdiction of the ecclesiastical courts, only public incontinence or lewdness, consisting generally of either keeping or frequently bawdy houses, or of public indecency, was indictable in the secular courts. Although the American colonies maintained both ecclesiastical and secular courts, the colonies imported almost all of English law into the secular courts . . . colonial enforcement of fornication concentrated on 'empowering the magistrates to enjoin the parties to marriage.' England, however, took a more practical approach, with the 'English justices of the peace being primarily concerned with the economic problem of fixing responsibility for support of a bastard child upon its reputed father'. . . A 1576 Elizabethan statute granted justices of the peace the authority to punish the reputed parents of bastard children. Although the statute did not stipulate any punishment, 'contemporary exposition was that a corporeal punishment was intended.' In 1609, Jacobean legislation stipulated a specific punishment of commitment to a house of correction to be inflicted only on 'lewd' women who had delivered bastards chargeable to the parish. In 1834, an amendment to the Poor Laws decriminalized bastardy." Heidi Meinzer, "Idaho's Throwback to Elizabethan England: Criminalizing a Civil Proceeding," *Family Law Quarterly* 34 (1) (2000): 165, 166-167, 168.

Chapter Six

I derive all biblical citations from *The Holy Bible*: King James Version (1611) (Nashville, Tenn.: Thomas Nelson Publishers, 1990). The format is standard. For example, Matthew 7: 1-2= Book of Matthew, Chapter 7, Verses 1 to 2.

1. See, for example, N.K. Badhwar, "Love" in Hugh LaFollette, ed., *Practical Ethics* (Oxford: Oxford University Press, 2003), 42-69.

2. See, for example, Robert C. Solomon, *The Passions* (New York: Anchor Press, 1976); *Love: Emotion, Myth, and Metaphor* (New York: Anchor Press, 1981); *About Love: Reinventing Romance for Our Times* (New York: Simon & Shuster, 1988); Robert Nozick, "Love's Bond" in *The Examined Life: Philosophical Meditations* (New York: Simon & Shuster, 1989), 68-86; Irving Singer, *The Nature of Love, Volume 3: The Modern World* (Chicago: University of Chicago Press, 1989).
3. G.W.F. Hegel. *The Logic: Part One of the Encyclopedia of the Philosophical Sciences* (1830), trans. William Wallace (Oxford: Oxford University Press, 1975).
4. G. Wilson Knight, *The Wheel of Fire* (Oxford: Oxford University Press, 1930), 74. Knight also assures us that the marriage of the Duke and Isabella "is to be the marriage of understanding with purity; of tolerance with moral fervor . . . we may expect her in future to learn from him wisdom, human tenderness, and love" (95-96). Knight's identification of the Duke with Christian justice strikes me as simplistic given the Duke's proclivity for expediency, his disingenuous manipulation of the bed trick, his obsession with his public image, his masquerade as a friar during which he even heard confessions, and his whimsical proposal to Isabella. Moreover, the trajectory of the play treats law and political power harshly, both of which are embodied in Duke Vincentio. Harold Bloom asks us to consider the possibility that Lucio is not a slanderer, but a truth teller. If so, Duke Vincentio, contrary to his self-reports, is a womanizer, a superficial fool, a coward, and a drinker. So depicted, the Duke is a low-level Machiavellian prince absent the violent rhetoric. Harold Bloom, *Shakespeare: The Invention of the Human* (New York: Riverhead Books, 1998), 370-372.
5. See, for example, Margaret Scott, 'Our City's Institutions': Some Further Reflections on the Marriage Contracts in *Measure for Measure*." *English Legal History* 49 (4) (1982), 790-804; S. Nagarajan, "*Measure for Measure* and Elizabethan Betrothals," *Shakespeare Quarterly* 14 (2) (1963), 115-119; Harriet Hawkins, "What Kind of Pre-Contact had Angelo?" *College English* 36 (2) (1974), 173-179; Ernest Schanzer, "The Marriage-Contracts in *Measure for Measure*," *Shakespeare Survey* 13 (1960), 81-90; Davis P. Harding, "Elizabethan Betrothals and *Measure for Measure*," *Journal of English and Germanic Philology* 49 (1950), 139-158.
6. *Encyclopedia Britannica*, 9th Edition, Volume XV, 567.
7. Scott, "Our City's Institutions," 795.
8. Nagarajan, "*Measure for Measure* and Elizabethan Betrothals."
9. Schanzer, "The Marriage-Contracts in *Measure for Measure*."
10. See, for example, Raymond Angelo Belliotti, *Justifying Law* (Philadelphia: Temple University Press, 1992), 17-43.
11. Plato, "The Apology," in Edith Hamilton and Huntington Cairns, eds. *Plato: Collected Dialogues* (Princeton: Princeton University Press, 1961), 3-26.
12. Friedrich Nietzsche, *Beyond Good and Evil*, trans. Walter Kaufmann (New York: Vintage Books, 1966), sec. 2, 229; *The Gay Science*, trans. Walter Kaufmann (New York: Random House, 1967), sec. 112, 121; *On the Genealogy of Morals*, trans. Walter Kaufmann and R. J. Hollingdale (New York: Vintage Books, 1967), bk. I, sec. 8.
13. See, for example, F.R. Leavis, "The Greatness of '*Measure for Measure*'," *Scrutiny* 10 (1941), 246.
14. Raymond Angelo Belliotti, *What is the Meaning of Human Life?* (Amsterdam: Rodopi, 2001), 152-156.

15. Raymond Angelo Belliotti, *Posthumous Harm: Why the Dead are Still Vulnerable* (Lanham: Md.: Lexington Books, 2011).
16. Raymond Angelo Belliotti, *Happiness is Overrated* (Lanham, Md.: Rowman & Littlefield Publishers, 2004), 120-123, 160-166.

BIBLIOGRAPHY

Ajzenstat, Samuel. "The Ubiquity of Contract in *The Merchant of Venice*," *Philosophy and Literature* 21 (2) (1997), pp. 262-278.
Allais, Lucy. "Forgiveness and Mercy," *South African Journal of Philosophy* 27(1) (2008), pp. 1-9.
Andrews, J.A. "The Common Law Marriage," *The Modern Law Review* 22 (1959), pp. 396-407.
Aristotle. *Nicomachean Ethics* in *Selections*. Edited by W. D. Ross. New York: Charles Scribner's Sons, 1955.
_____. *Nicomachean Ethics*. Translated by Martin Ostwald. Indianapolis, Ind.: Bobbs-Merrill, 1962.
Barry, Brian. *Political Argument*. London: Routledge & Kegan Paul. 1965.
Belliotti, Raymond Angelo. *Justifying Law*. Philadelphia: Temple University Press, 1992.
_____. *Good Sex*. Lawrence, Kans.: University Press of Kansas, 1993.
_____. *Seeking Identity*. Lawrence, Kans.: University Press of Kansas, 1995.
_____. *Happiness is Overrated*. Lanham, Md.: Rowman & Littlefield Publishers, 2004.
_____. *What is the Meaning of Human Life?* Amsterdam: Rodopi, 2001.
_____. *Stalking Nietzsche*. Westport: Greenwood Press, 1998.
_____. *Niccolò Machiavelli*. Lanham, Md.: Lexington Books, 2009.
_____. *Roman Philosophy and the Good Life*. Lanham, Md.: Lexington Books, 2009.
_____. *Posthumous Harm*. Lanham Md.: Lexington Books, 2011.
_____. *Dante's Deadly Sins: Moral Philosophy in Hell*. Oxford: Wiley-Blackwell Publishers, 2011.
_____. "Gloom and Doom: Executing the Eighth Amendment," *The International Journal of Applied Philosophy* 3 (1986), pp. 43-57.
_____. "The Rule of Law and the Critical Legal Studies Movement," *The University of Western Ontario Law Review* (24) (1) (1986), pp. 67-78.
_____. "Billy Martin and Jurisprudence: Revisiting the Pine Tar Case," *Albany Government Law Review* 5 (2012), pp. 210-239.
_____. "Negative and Positive Duties," *Theoria* 47 (1981), pp. 82-92.
_____. "Negative Duties, Positive Duties, and Rights," *The Southern Journal of Philosophy* 16 (1978), pp. 581-588.
_____. "Toward a Theory of Judicial Decision-making: A Synthesis of Ideologist Jurisprudence and Doctrinalism," *The Catholic Lawyer* 28 (1983): 215-252.
Bernstein, Richard. "Pragmatism, Pluralism, and the Healing of Wounds," *American Philosophical Society Proceedings* 63 (3) (1989), pp. 5-18.
Black, Charles, Jr. *Capital Punishment: The Inevitability of Caprice and Mistake*. New York: Norton & Co., 1981.
Bloom, Harold. *Shakespeare: The Invention of the Human*. New York: Riverhead Books, 1998.
_____, Ed. *Measure for Measure*. New York: Chelsea House Publishers, 1987.
Brien, Andrew. "Mercy Within Legal Justice," *Social Theory and Practice* 24 (1) (1998), pp. 83-110.

Camus, Albert. *The Myth of Sisyphus*. Translated by Justin O'Brien. New York: Vintage Books, 1991.
Carpi, Daniela. "Failure of the Word: Law, Discretion, Equity in *The Merchant of Venice* and *Measure for Measure*," *Cardozo Law Review* 26 (2005), pp. 2317-2329.
Colmo, Christopher A. "Law and Love in Shakespeare's *The Merchant of Venice*," *Oklahoma City University Law Review* 26 (2001), pp. 307-324.
Covey, Stephen R., A. Roger Merrill, and Rebecca R. Merrill. *First Things First*. New York: Simon & Schuster, 1992.
Craig, Hardin and David Bevington, Eds. *The Complete Works of Shakespeare*. Glenview, Ill.: Scott, Foresman and Company, 1973.
Craig, Leon Harold. *Of Philosophers and Kings*. Toronto: University of Toronto Press, 2001.
Devlin, Patrick. *The Enforcement of Morals*. London: Oxford University Press, 1965.
Dicey, A.V. *Introduction to the Study of the Law of the Constitution*. Chestnut Hill, Mass.: Adamant Media Corporation, 2000.
DiMatteo, Anthony. "'Our Sovereign Process': Reading Shakespeare's Politics," *College Literature* 38 (2) (2011), pp. 161-170.
Dollimore, John and Alan Sinfield, Eds. *Political Shakespeare*. Manchester: Manchester University Press, 1994.
Dostoevsky, Fyodor. *The Brothers Karamazov* (1880). Translated by Richard Pervear and Larissa Volokhonsky. New York: Farrar, Straus, and Giroux, 2002.
Dworkin, Ronald. *Taking Rights Seriously*. Cambridge, Mass.: Harvard University Press, 1977.
_____. "Seven Critics," *Georgia Law Review* 11 (1977), 1201-1267.
Encarnacion, Erik, "Desuetude," *Columbia Journal of Law and Social Problems* 39 (2005), pp. 149-184.
Evans, G. Blakemore and J.J.M. Tobin, Eds. *The Riverside Shakespeare*. Boston: Houghton Mifflin Co., 1997.
Farnsworth, E. Allan. *Contracts*. New York: Wolters Kluwer Law & Business, 1999.
Feinberg, Joel. *Social Philosophy*. Englewood Cliffs, N.J.: Prentice Hall, Inc., 1973.
_____. *Harmless Wrongdoing*. New York: Oxford University Press, 1988.
——. *Doing and Deserving*. Princeton: Princeton University Press, 1970.
Feldman, Fred. "Desert: Reconsideration of Some Received Wisdom," *Mind* 104 (1995), pp. 63-77.
Finkelstein, Jared Tobin. "In Re Brett: The Sticky Problem of Statutory Construction," *Fordham Law Review* 52 (1983), 430-440.
Geckle, George L., Ed. *Measure for Measure*. Englewood Cliffs, N.J.: Prentice Hall, Inc., 1975.
Golding, Martin. *Philosophy of Law*. Englewood Cliffs, N.J.: Prentice Hall, Inc., 1975.
Hamilton, Edith and Huntington Cairns, Eds. *Plato: Collected Dialogues*. Princeton: Princeton University Press, 1961.
Hampton-Reeves, Stuart. *Measure for Measure*. New York: Palgrave MacMillan, 2007.
Hapgood, Robert. "Portia and *The Merchant of Venice*: The Gentle Bond," *Modern Language Quarterly* (28) (1) (1967), pp. 19-32.
Harding, Davis P. "Elizabethan Betrothals and *Measure for Measure*," *Journal of English and Germanic Philology* 49 (1950), pp. 139-158.

Hart, H.L.A. *The Concept of Law.* Oxford: Clarendon Press, 1961.
Hawkins, Harriett. "What Kind of Pre-Contact had Angelo?" *College English* 36 (2) (1974), pp. 173-179.
Hayek, F. *The Road to Serfdom.* Chicago: University of Chicago Press, 1944.
_____. *The Constitution of Liberty.* Chicago: University of Chicago Press, 1978.
Hazlitt, William. *Characters of Shakespeare's Plays.* Lexington, Ken.: Maestro Publishing Group, 2011.
Heffernan, William C. "Constitutional Historicism." *American University Law Review* 54 (2005), pp. 1355-1448.
Hegel, G.W.F. *The Logic: Part One of the Encyclopedia of the Philosophical Sciences* (1830). Translated by William Wallace. Oxford: Oxford University Press, 1975.
Heidegger, Martin. *Being and Time.* Translated by John Macquarrie and Edward Robinson. New York: Harper and Row, 1962.
Heilman, Katie Roth. "Contemplating 'Cruel and Unusual.'" *American University Law Review* 58 (2009), pp. 633- 663.
Hillman, Robert A. "Debunking Some Myths about Unconscionability," *Cornell Law Review* 67 (1981), 1-49.
Holy Bible: *King James Version* (1611). Nashville, Tenn.: Thomas Nelson Publishers, 1990.
Hunt, Maurice. "Being Precise in *Measure for Measure*," *Renascence* 58 (4) (2006), pp. 243-267.
Hunter, Robert Grams. *Shakespeare and the Comedy of Forgiveness.* New York: Columbia University Press, 1965.
Jones, F.H.W. "The Rule of Law and the Welfare State," *Columbia Law Review* 58 (1958): 143-156.
Joughin, John J., Ed. *Philosophical Shakespeares.* London: Routledge Publishers, 2000.
Kierkegaard, Søren. *Either/Or.* Translated by Alastair Hannay. London: Penguin Books, 1992.
Kleinig, John. "The Concept of Desert," *The Philosophical Quarterly* 8:1 (1971), pp. 71-78.
Knight, G. Wilson. *The Wheel of Fire.* Oxford: Oxford University Press, 1930.
Kornstein, Daniel J. *Kill All the Lawyers?* Lincoln, Neb.: University of Nebraska Press, 2005.
Kottma, Paul A., ed. *Philosophers on Shakespeare.* Stanford: Stanford University Press, 2009.
LaFollette, Hugh, Ed. *Practical Ethics.* Oxford: Oxford University Press, 2003.
Lamont, Julian. "The Concept of Desert in Distributive Justice," *The Philosophical Quarterly* 44 (1994), pp. 45-64.
Leavis, F.R. "The Greatness of '*Measure for Measure*'," *Scrutiny* 10 (1941), pp. 234-242.
Lee, Randy. "Who's Afraid of William Shakespeare?" *University of Dayton Law Review* 32 (2006), pp. 1-28.
Lucretius. *De Rerum Natura.*, Translated by Rolfe Humphries. Bloomington: Indiana University Press, 1968.
Lykken, David. *Happiness.* New York: St. Martin's Press, 1999.
Machiavelli, Niccolò. *The Prince in Selected Political Writings.* Edited and translated by David Wootton. Indianapolis: Hackett Publishing Company, 1994.

Mackie, John L. *Ethics: Inventing Right and Wrong.* New York: Penguin Books, 1977.
McGinn, Colin. *Shakespeare's Philosophy.* New York: HarperCollins Publishers, 2006.
McWhirter, Robert J. "Baby, Don't Be Cruel," *Arizona Attorney* 46 (2009), pp. 13-28.
Meinzer, Heidi. "Idaho's Throwback to Elizabethan England: Criminalizing a Civil Proceeding," *Family Law Quarterly* 34 (1) (2000), pp. 165-175.
Miller, David. *Social Justice.* Oxford: Oxford University Press, 1976.
Misner, Robert. "Minimalism, Desuetude, and Fornication," *Willamette Law Review* 35 (1999), pp. 1-55.
Morss, John R. "'Desperately Mortal': Exclusion in Shakespeare's Legal Plays," *Deakin Law Review* 12 (1) (2007), pp. 181-191.
Nagarajan, A. "*Measure for Measure* and Elizabethan Betrothals," *Shakespeare Quarterly* 14 (2) (1963), pp. 115-119.
Nathanson, Stephen. "Does it Matter if the Death Penalty is Arbitrarily Administered?" *Philosophy & Public Affairs* 14 (1985), pp. 149-164.
Nietzsche, Friedrich. *Thus Spoke Zarathustra.* Translated by Walter Kaufmann. In *The Portable Nietzsche.* New York: Viking Press, 1954.
———. *Twilight of the Idols.* Translated by Walter Kaufmann. In *The Portable Nietzsche.* New York: Viking Press, 1954.
———. *Beyond Good and Evil.* Translated by Walter Kaufmann. New York: Vintage Books, 1966.
———. *The Birth of Tragedy.* Translated by Walter Kaufmann. New York: Random House, 1967.
———. *Ecce Homo.* Translated by Walter Kaufmann and R.J. Hollingdale. New York: Random House, 1967.
———. *The Gay Science.* Translated by Walter Kaufmann. New York: Random House, 1967.
———. *On the Genealogy of Morals.* Translated by Walter Kaufmann and R. J. Hollingdale. New York: Vintage Books, 1967.
Niven, David. *The 100 Simple Secrets of Happy People.* New York: HarperCollins Publishers, 2000.
Noonan, John T. *Bribes.* New York: MacMillan Publishing Company, 1984.
Note. "Desuetude," *Harvard Law Review* 119 (2006), pp. 2209-2229.
Nozick, Robert. *The Examined Life: Philosophical Meditations.* New York: Simon & Shuster, 1989.
———. *Anarchy, State, and Utopia.* New York: Basic Books, 1974.
Nussbaum, Martha C. "Equity and Mercy," *Philosophy & Public Affairs* 22 (2) (1993), pp. 83-125.
Nuttall, A.D. *Shakespeare: The Thinker.* New Haven: Yale University Press, 2007.
Oates, Whitney, Ed. *The Stoic and Epicurean Philosophers.* Translated by C. Bailey. New York: The Modern Library, 1940.
Olsen, Chad. "How the Tenth Circuit's Ruling in *Martinez v. Beggs* Affects the Deliberate Indifference Standard for Eighth Amendment Claims," *Brigham Young University Law Review* 2010 (2010), pp. 199-214.
Olson, Trisha. "Pausing Upon Portia," *Journal of Law & Religion* 19 (2) (2003), pp. 299-330.
Posner, Richard A. Law & Literature. Cambridge, Mass.: Harvard University Press, 2009.

Rapson, Donald J. "A 'Home Run' Application of Established Principles of Statutory Construction: UCC Analogies," *Cardozo Law Review* 5 (1984), pp. 441-453.
Rawls, John. *A Theory of Justice*. Cambridge, Mass.: Harvard University Press, 1971.
Rorty, Richard. *Contingency, Irony, and Solidarity*. Cambridge, UK: Cambridge University Press, 1989.
Sabatini, Rafael. *The Life of Cesare Borgia*. Teddington, UK: The Echo Library, 2006.
Schanzer, Ernest. "The Marriage-Contracts in *Measure for Measure*," *Shakespeare Survey* 13 (1960), pp. 81-90.
Schopenhauer, Arthur. *The World as Will and Idea*, 3 vols. Translated by R.B. Haldane and J. Kemp. London: Routledge & Kegan Paul, 1948.
Schwartz, Louis B. "Morals Offenses and the Model Penal Code," *Columbia Law Review* 63 (1963): 669-686.
Scott, Margaret. "'Our City's Institutions': Some Further Reflections on the Marriage Contracts in *Measure for Measure*," *English Legal History* 49 (4) (1982), pp. 790-804.
Sedley, David, Ed. *The Cambridge Companion to Greek and Roman Philosophy*. Cambridge: Cambridge University Press, 2003.
Shakespeare, William. *The Complete Pelican Shakespeare*. Edited by Stephen Orgel and A. R. Braunmuller. New York: Penguin Books, 2002.
_____. *The Oxford Shakespeare: The Complete Works, 2nd Edition*. Edited by Stanley Wells, Gary Taylor and John Jowett. Oxford: Oxford University Press, 2005.
Sher, George. "Effort, Ability, and Personal Desert," *Philosophy and Public Affairs* 8:4 (1979), pp. 361–376.
Singer, Irving. *Meaning in Life*. New York: The Free Press, 1982.
_____. *The Nature of Love, Volume 3: The Modern World*. Chicago: University of Chicago Press, 1989.
Slote, Michael A. "Desert, Consent and Justice," *Philosophy and Public Affairs* 2:4 (1973), pp. 323 - 347.
Solomon, Robert C. *The Passions*. New York: Anchor Press, 1976.
_____. *Love: Emotion Myth, and Metaphor*. New York: Anchor Press, 1981.
_____. *About Love: Reinventing Romance for Our Times*. New York: Simon & Shuster, 1988.
Steiker, Carol S. "Murphy on Mercy: A Prudential Reconsideration," *Criminal Justice Ethics* 27 (2008), pp. 45-54.
Stewart, Stanley. *Shakespeare and Philosophy*. New York: Routledge Publishers, 2010.
Stirner, Max. *The Ego and His Own* (1845). In Daniel Guerin, *Anarchism: From Theory to Practice*. New York: Monthly Review Press, 1970.
Tambling, Jeremy. "Law and Will in *Measure for Measure*," *Essays in Criticism* 59 (2009), pp. 189-210.
Tasioulas, John. "Mercy," *Aristotelian Society* 103 (1) (2003), pp. 101-132.
Tiffany, Grace. "Law and Self-Interest in *The Merchant of Venice*," *Papers on Language & Literature* 42(4) (2006), pp. 384-400.
Turgenev, Ivan. *Fathers and Sons* (1862). Translated by Richard Freeborn. New York: Oxford University Press, 2009.
Van Den Haag, Ernest. *Punishing Criminals*. New York: Basic Books, 1975.
Van Doren, Mark. *Shakespeare*. New York: New York Review of Books, 1939.
Weisberg, Richard, Ed. "*The Merchant of Venice*," *Cardozo Studies in Law and Literature* 5 (1) (Spring 1993).

_____. "Antonio's legalistic cruelty," *College Literature* 25 (1) (1998), pp. 12-20.
Willson, Michael Jay. "A View of Justice in Shakespeare's *The Merchant of Venice* and *Measure for Measure*," *Notre Dame Law Review* 70 (1995), pp. 695-725.
Yachnin, Paul and Desmond Manderson. "Shakespeare and Judgment," *The European Legacy* 15 (2) (2010), pp. 195-213.
Yoshino, Kenji. *A Thousand Times More Fair*. New York: HarperCollins Publishers, 2011.
Zaitchik, Alan. "On Deserving to Deserve," *Philosophy and Public Affairs* 6:4 (1977), pp. 370–388.
Zamir, Tzachi. *Double Vision*. Princeton, N.J.: Princeton University Press, 2007.

ABOUT THE AUTHOR

Raymond Angelo Belliotti is SUNY Distinguished Teaching Professor of Philosophy at the State University of New York at Fredonia. He received his undergraduate degree from Union College in 1970, after which he was conscripted into the United States Army where he served three years in military intelligence units during the Vietnamese War. Upon his discharge, he enrolled at the University of Miami where he earned his Master of Arts degree in 1976 and Doctorate in 1977. After teaching stints at Florida International University and Virginia Commonwealth University, he entered Harvard University as a law student and teaching fellow. After receiving a Juris Doctorate from Harvard Law School, he practiced law in New York City with the firm of Barrett Smith Schapiro Simon & Armstrong. In 1984, he joined the faculty at Fredonia.

    Belliotti is the author of twelve other books: Justifying Law (1992); Good Sex (1993); Seeking Identity (1995); Stalking Nietzsche (1998); What is the Meaning of Human Life? (2001); Happiness is Overrated (2004); The Philosophy of Baseball (2006); Watching Baseball Seeing Philosophy (2008); Niccolò Machiavelli (2008); Roman Philosophy and the Good Life (2009); Dante's Deadly Sins: Moral Philosophy in Hell (2011); and Posthumous Harm: Why the Dead are Still Vulnerable (2011). Good Sex was later translated into Korean and published in Asia. What is the Meaning of Human Life? was nominated for the Society for Phenomenology and Existential Philosophy's Book of the Year Award. He has also published 70 articles and 25 reviews in the areas of ethics, jurisprudence, sexual morality, medicine, politics, education, feminism, sports, Marxism, and legal ethics. These essays have appeared in scholarly journals based in Australia, Canada, Great Britain, Italy, Mexico, South Africa, Sweden, and the United States. Belliotti has also made numerous presentations at philosophical conferences, including the 18th World Congress of Philosophy in England, and has been honored as a featured lecturer on the Queen Elizabeth-2 ocean liner.

    While at SUNY Fredonia he has served extensively on campus committees, as the Chairperson of the Department of Philosophy, as the Chairperson of the University Senate, and as Director of General Education. Belliotti also served as United University Professions local Vice President for Academics. For six years he was faculty advisor to the undergraduate club, the Philosophical Society, and he has served that function for *Il Circolo Italiano*. Belliotti has been the recipient of the SUNY Chancellor's Award for Excellence in Teaching, the William T. Hagan Young Scholar/Artist Award, the Kasling Lecture Award for Excellence in Research and Scholarship, and the SUNY Foundation Research & Scholarship Recognition Award. He is also a member of the New York State *Speakers in the Humanities* Program.

INDEX

Abhorson, 154, 155
absurdity, appeal to avoid, 70
Aesop's fables, 5
Aesthetic stage:
    and Bassanio, 83–84
    and Kierkegaard, 83, 88, 89
Agathon, 74, 75, 77, 84, 85, 89
Alcibiades, 79–80, 165, 166, 194
Alien Statute, 59–61, 90
    and justice, 59–60
    and rule of law, 59–61
    and Balthasar–Portia, 59–61, 90
    and Shylock, 59–61
Allen, Rex, 85
Amor fati, 119, 185, 197, 198
Angelo:
    and arrogance, 124–26
    and Claudio, 106–109, 111–114, 120–122, 132, 137, 139, 154, 158, 171
    and condition of his soul, 123–128, 169, 170, 181–190
    and delegation of authority, 101, 103–104
    and Duke Vincentio, 101– 103,106, 152, 190–191
    and Isabella, 121–122, 129–130, 131, 139
    and jurisprudence, 111–114, 121–124, 129–131, 140, 153, 162, 167, 180–181
    and lust, 126–128
    and marriage contracts, 123, 171–180
    and Nietzsche, 117
    and the Trial of Vienna, 160–162,166–171
    anger, contrasted with wrath, 21–22
Antonio:
    and Bassanio, 6–7, 41, 50–51, 62, 81–82, 86–87, 97
    and condition of his soul, 81–82, 98
    and love, 41, 50–51, 85–86
    and melancholy, 6, 7, 97
    and mercy, 60–62, 86
    and Portia, 6, 72, 73, 86–87, 97
    and Shylock, 8–10, 18, 21, 23, 33, 38–40, 85–87, 91, 95

Aristophanes, 76
Aristotle, 21, 31, 94, 97, 123–24, 143
arrogance, contrasted with pride, 124–126
authenticity:
    and existentialism, 22–23, 192–193
    and Shylock, 18–19, 20, 23, 87
Autry, Gene, 85
avarice, and Shylock, 20–21, 50

Balthasar-Portia, 36, 48–52, 56–59, 59–64, 71
    See also under Portia as Balthasar
    and fraud, 59–64, 89–90
    and justice, 56–59
    and mercy, 58–72
    and Shylock, 48–52, 56–59, 59–64
Barnardine, 154, 155, 158, 167, 170, 194, 195, 199
Bassanio, 182
    and bonds, 8–10
    and condition of his soul, 82–84
    and ethical stage, 83–84
    and human condition, 88–89
    and love, 29, 31, 71–73, 75, 82–84, 95–97
    and Portia, 26–28, 29, 31–32, 71–73, 75, 79, 83–85, 88–89, 95–97
bed trick, the, 148–150, 154, 177, 180, 194
Bellario, 36, 42, 48, 73
Belmont, 24, 100, 104, 182
    and Venice, 5–6
Bible, 180–181, 182
Bill of Rights, English, 158
biographical lives, 196, 198–199
biological lives, 196–198
Bloom, Harold, 1
bond:
    between Shylock and Antonio, 8–10, 38–40, 85–86, 91, 95
    between Portia and Bassanio, 26–28, 71–73, 83–84, 88–89, 95–97
    between Gratiano and Nerissa, 58, 71–72, 82, 91, 96
Borgia, Cesare, 102–103, 104

Buffalo Bills, 12

capital punishment:
    and Eighth Amendment, 155–157
    and pre–marital sex, 155, 157–158, 187
casket test, 24–28, 194
Cassidy, Hopalong, 85
Christians:
    and aliens, 59–61, 90
    and hypocrisy, 8–10, 17–18, 19, 21, 56, 62–63, 93
    and mercy, 58–72
    and Shylock, 8–10, 17–18, 19, 21, 56, 62–63, 93
Cisco Kid, 85
Claudio:
    and Angelo, 106–109, 111–114, 120–122, 132, 137, 139, 154, 158, 171
    and condition of his soul, 182, 195
    and Duke Vincentio, 159–199
    and Friar-Duke, 137, 139, 143, 148–149
    and Isabella, 139–141, 158, 190, 194
    and Juliet, 106–108, 111, 132, 136, 157–158, 171
    and marriage contracts, 171–180
    and Trial of Vienna, 16–62, 166–171
community and individualism, 7–8, 17, 146
contract, 36, 40
    and equity, 36–39
    and equity redemption, 38
    and law, 36–40
    and specific performance, 38
    and unconscionability, 38
    between Shylock and Antonio, 38–40
    damages for breach of, 37–40
    freedom of, 38
contracts, marriage, 107, 149
    and Angelo and Mariana, 123, 149, 161, 171–180
    and capital punishment, 155–157
    and Claudio and Juliet, 107, 149, 171–180
    and dowry, 123, 149, 171–180
    and *sponsalia per verba de futuro*, 171–180
    and *sponsalia per verba de praesenti*, 171–180
    and the Trial of Vienna, 166–171
cosmic meaninglessness, 114–115, 170, 197–198
critical pragmatism, 64, 67–69

Dante, 140
death:
    and Claudio, 137, 139, 140–141
    and Epicurus, 142–143, 146–148
    and fear, 142–143, 195–199
    and fear of gods, 142–143
    and Isabella, 146, 148
    and Lucretius, 144–148
death penalty, 155–157
    and premarital sex, 155, 157–158
    and Shylock, 59–61
delegation of authority:
    and Duke Vincentio, 101, 103–104, 105
    and Machiavelli, 102–106
Democritus, 143
desert, principle of, 10–17
    and Shakespeare, 28, 92–93, 190–192
    and Shylock, 92–93
desuetude, doctrine of, 108–112
    and rule of law, 109–111
    and Virginia, 112
    and West Virginia, 110
Devlin, Patrick, 150–152
Diotima, 77–78, 80
D'Orco, Remiro, 102–103
dowry, 149
    and marriage contracts, 123
Duke of Venice, 39, 40–42, 59, 60–64
    and mercy, 60–61, 62
Duke Vincentio, 138, 139
    See also under Lodowick, Friar
    and Angelo, 101, 102, 103, 106, 152, 190–191
    and condition of his soul, 169–170
    and delegation of authority, 101, 103–104, 105
    and Isabella, 149–150, 192
    and jurisprudence, 152, 181–182, 184–88

Duke Vincentio, *cont'd*
    and Nietzsche, 118, 120
    and refashioning Viennese law,
        136–137, 152–153, 184–188
    and Trial of Vienna, 16–62, 166–171
    as Friar-Duke, 137, 139, 140–143,
        148–150, 154–155, 158,
        160–162
Dworkin, Ronald, 64, 66–67

Eighth Amendment, 155–157
Elbow, Constable, 113, 149, 193, 194
Emerson, Ralph Waldo, 197
entitlement, principle of, 12–13
Epicurus, 141–144
equality, concept of:
    and rule of law, 42
    and Shylock, 42–47, 51–52
    formal, 42–48
    substantive, 45–48
equity, concept of, 52–53
Eryximachus, 75–76
Escalus, 102, 112–114, 158, 161, 167,
    176, 182, 186, 187, 193
ethical stage:
    and Bassanio, 83–84
    and Kierkegaard, 83–84, 88, 89
existentialism, 16–17, 22–23, 146
    and authenticity, 22–23, 192–193
    and Heidegger, 22–23
    and Shylock, 18–19, 20, 87

feminism, 99–100
    and *Merchant of Venice*, 94–100
    and *Measure for Measure*, 162, 192
    and patriarchy, 162, 192
forgiveness, concept of, 55–56
formalism:
    and judicial decision-making, 68
    and rule of law, 43–48
fornication statute, Viennese, 106–109,
    111–113, 123, 132, 157–158,
    172, 178–179, 186–187
Froth, 113, 193
Francisca, Sister, 120
Furman v. Georgia, 155

Gabbo, Launcelot, 17
gods, pagan, and fear of death, 42–43

Golden Rule, 121–122
Gorgias, 77
Gratiano, 36, 48, 51, 57, 60, 71–72, 91
    and Nerissa, 58, 71–72, 82, 91, 96
Gregg v. Georgia, 155, 156

Hannibal, 105
Hart, H.L.A, 64, 66–67
    and legal positivism, 66–67
head trick, the, 159
hedonism, 116, 147
Heidegger, Martin, and existentialism,
    22–23
human condition:
    and Antonio, 81–82, 98
    and Bassanio, 82–84
    and Portia, 94–95
    and Shylock, 87

individualism and community, 7–8, 17,
    146
Isabella, 108, 120–122, 126, 154, 158
    and Angelo, 121–122, 129–130,
        131, 139
    and Claudio, 139–141, 158, 190,
        194
    and Christianity, 130–131, 191
    and condition of her soul, 130–32,
        168, 170, 189, 190, 195
    and Duke Vincentio, 149–150, 192
    and Friar-Duke, 148–150, 183
    and jurisprudence, 121–122, 131
    and love, 144–145
    and Nietzsche, 118
    and patriarchy, 162, 192
    and Trial of Vienna, 160–162, 166–171

James, William, 197
Jessica, 36, 50, 58, 60–62, 63, 82, 87–88, 91, 93, 97
Jesus, 87
judicial decision making, 64–70
    and critical pragmatism, 64, 67–69
    and Dworkin, 64, 66–67
    and easy cases, 65–66, 67, 68
    and formalism, 68
    and hard cases, 65–66, 67, 68
    and Hart, 64, 65–66
    and indeterminacy, 65

judicial decision making, *cont'd*
    and justification, 66–67, 68–69
    and principles of legal interpretation, 69–70
    and right answers, 67, 68
    and the rule of law, 45–48
    and Trial of Venice, 59–64
Juliet:
    and Claudio, 106–108, 111, 132, 136, 157–158, 171
    and marriage contracts, 171–180
    and refashioning Viennese law, 152–153, 184–188
    and Trial of Vienna, 160–162, 166–171
justice:
    and Alien Statute, 59–61
    formal, 42–48
    substantive, 45–48

Kant, Immanuel, 105
Keepdown, Kate, 168, 193
Kierkegaard, Søren, 83–84, 88, 89, 129
    and aesthetic stage, 83, 88, 89
    and ethical stage, 83–84, 88, 89
Knight, G. Wilson, 168

last man, 116–117, 119
Law:
    Canon, 171, 172, 178
    English Common, 171, 172, 178
    Roman Catholic, 171, 172, 175, 178, 179
    Roman, 109, 110
    Viennese (imaginary), 178
laws, 119–20
legal cases:
    and rule of law, 42–48
    easy, 65–66, 67, 68
    hard, 65–66, 67, 68
legal moralism, 150–152
legal positivism, 67
    and Hart, 64, 65–66
legislative purposes, appeal to, 70
legitimation, 46–48
liberal-capitalism
    and rule of law, 42–44
libertarianism, and sexual morality, 133–134

life:
    biographical, 196, 198–199
    biological, 196–198
Lodowick, Friar, 160–162, 168, 175, 178, 180, 183–184
    See also under Duke Vincentio as Friar-Duke
Lone Ranger, 85
Lorenzo, 36, 50, 58, 60–63, 82, 87, 91, 93, 97
love, agapic:
    and Mariana, 162–166, 192, 193
    paradox of, 162–164
love, erotic, 28–32, 95–96, 194–195
    and Antonio and Bassanio, 50–51, 81–82, 86–87
    and Bassanio and Portia, 26–28, 29, 31, 32, 71–73, 75, 79, 83–89, 95–99
    and *Phaedrus*, 80
    and the condition of souls, 81–85
    and Socrates, 76, 77–80, 84, 89–90, 94
    and *The Symposium*, 74–80
    ladder of, 77–78, 79–80, 84
Lucio, 106, 108–109, 120, 122–23, 131, 149, 161–162, 168, 170–171, 183–184, 193, 199
Lucretius, 141
    and death, 144–148
lust, 126–128
    and Angelo, 126–128

Machiavelli, Niccolò, and delegation of authority, 102–106
Magna Carta, 158
Mariana:
    and agapic love, 162–166, 192, 193
    and Angelo, 123, 158, 162–166, 182
    and condition of her soul, 180, 182, 190
    and Duke Vincentio, 161–162, 167, 168, 169
    and Friar-Duke, 149–150, 154, 177, 180, 194
    and Isabella, 149–150
    and marriage contracts, 123, 171–180
    and patriarchy, 162, 192

Mariana, *cont'd*
    and Trial of Vienna, 161–162, 167, 168, 169
Marxism, and rule of law, 44–45, 46, 47
Mather, Cotton, 124
Measure for Measure, 101–128, 129–158, 159–99
    philosophical lessons of, 188–199
Medina, John, 127
Merchant of Venice, 5–33, 35–70, 71–100
    philosophical lessons of, 91–100
mercy, concept of, 52, 53–55
    and Angelo, 106–108, 111–112, 137, 139, 158, 160–162
    and Antonio, 60–62
    and Balthasar–Portia, 48, 59–64
    and Christians, 56, 62, 63
    and Duke of Venice, 60–61, 62
    and Duke Vincentio, 166–171
    and Isabella, 139–141, 194
    and law, 53–65, 64
    and Shylock, 40, 41, 48–49, 50–51, 53, 60–61
    and trial of Venice, 48, 53, 58, 60, 61–62
    and trial of Vienna, 166–171, 191
Miami Dolphins, 12
morality:
    adjusted conventional, 132, 133, 134
    conventional, 132
    objective, 132

Nerissa, 24–25, 36, 48, 71–72, 89, 91, 97
    and Gratiano, 58, 71–72, 82, 91, 96
Nietzsche, Friedrich, 114–120, 189, 193, 197, 198
    and *amor fati*, 119, 185, 197, 198
    and death of God, 114–115
    and last man, 116–117, 119
    and *Measure for Measure*, 117–118
    and nihilism, 114–120, 185
    and overman, 118–119
    and power, 117, 118–119
nihilism, 104, 114–120, 168, 170–171, 184, 185, 192, 193
    active, 115–116
    deconstructive, 115
    nonchalant, 170
    passive, 115, 116
    pathetic, 115, 116

Overdone, Mistress, 106, 113, 170, 171
overman, 118–119

patriarchy:
    and Isabella, 162, 192
    and Mariana, 162, 192
    and women, 192
Pausanias, 74–75
pessimism, 137–139
    and Claudio, 137, 140, 141
    and Friar–Duke, 137, 141
    and Schopenhauer, 138–139
Peter, Friar, 160, 161
Phaedrus, 80
Phaedrus, and *The Symposium*, 74
philosophical lessons:
    of *Measure for Measure*, 188–199
    of *Merchant of Venice*, 91–100
Plato, 20, 74–80, 84, 94, 119–120, 124, 138
Pompey, 106, 113, 114, 123, 149, 154, 155, 170, 171, 184, 193
Portia, 99–100
    and Antonio, 6, 72, 73, 86–87, 97
    and Bassanio, 26–28, 29, 31–22, 71–73, 75, 79, 83–85, 88–89, 95–97
    and condition of her soul, 85, 89–90
    and feminism, 99–100
    and human condition, 94–95
    and love, 29, 31, 71–73, 75, 79, 82–84, 88–89, 95–99
    and mercy, 48, 53, 58, 72
    as Balthasar, 48–52, 56–59, 59–64, 71
    See also under Balthasar-Portia
pride, contrasted with arrogance, 124–126
The Prince, 102–106
Prince of Arragon, 25–26
Prince of Morocco, 25, 89
Prodicus, 74
Provost, 107, 121, 122, 154, 158, 167

punishment, capital:
    and Eighth Amendment, 155–157
    and premarital sex, 155, 157–158, 187

Rawls, John, 15
religion, and jurisprudence, 180–182
Rogers, Roy, 85
Romagna, 102–103, 104
Roosevelt, Franklin Delano, 140
rule of law, 42–48
    and Alien Statute, 59–61
    and doctrine of desuetude, 109–111
    and equality, 42
    and formalism, 42–48
    and ideology, 43–48
    and liberal–capitalism, 42–44
    and legitimation, 46–48
    and Marxism, 44–45, 46, 47
    and Shylock, 42–43, 44, 45, 46, 47
    and substantive justice, 45–48
rule of lenity, 70

Sartre, Jean–Paul, 17
Schopenhauer, Arthur, 138–139
Scrooge, Ebenezer, 20
sex, premarital, 132–137, 150
    and capital punishment, 155, 157–158, 187
    and danger, 193–195
    and legal prohibition, 150–154
sexual morality in five tiers, 134–136
Shylock, 17–22
    and Alien Statute, 59–61
    and Antonio, 8–10, 18, 21, 23, 33, 38–40, 85-7, 91, 95
    and authenticity, 18–19, 20, 23
    and avarice, 20–1, 50
    and Balthasar-Portia, 48–52, 56–9, 59–64
    and Christians, 8–10, 17–8, 19, 21, 56, 62, 63, 93
    and condition of his soul, 81, 82
    and contracts, 8–10, 33, 35–36, 38–40, 40–42, 56–57
    and conversion to Christianity, 81, 88, 95
    and existentialism, 18–19, 20, 87
    and human condition, 87
    and Jewishness, 81–82

    and jurisprudence, 36, 42–47, 51–52, 57, 64–70, 103, 131, 167, 188, 194
    and legal trust, 60–63
    and mercy, 40, 41, 48–49, 50–51, 53, 60–61
    and principle of desert, 15
    and wrath, 21–22
Socrates, 28, 124, 129, 132, 165–166, 188, 194
    and erotic love, 76, 77–80, 84, 89–90, 94
Smisek, Amanda, 108–109, 153
spirit of law, appeal to, 70
Sponsalia per verba de futuro, 171–180
    and Angelo and Mariana, 171–180
    and Claudio and Juliet, 171–180
Sponsalia per verba de praesenti, 171–180
    and Angelo and Mariana, 171–180
    and Claudio and Juliet, 171–180
Standish, Myles, 124
stoicism, 127–128
Symposium, The, 74–80

Thomas, Friar, 101, 102
Trial of Venice, 40–64
    Stage One, 40–42
    Stage Two, 48–52
    Stage Three, 56–59
    Stage Four, 59–64
Trial of Vienna, 160–162, 166–171
    Stage One, 160–161
    Stage Two, 161
    Stage Three, 161–162
    Stage Four, 166–171
trust, legal, 60–63
Tubal, 91

US v. Weems, 156

Venice, 17, 21, 36, 59, 85, 95, 97, 100, 104
    and Belmont, 5–6
Vienna:
    and jurisprudence, 184–188
    and law, 84–88, 107–108, 111–112, 136–137, 152–153
    and sexual license, 102, 193–195
    and trial, 160–162, 166–171

Vienna, *cont'd*
    social conditions of, 102–105, 113–114, 152–153, 157–158, 182–184, 193, 199

Volstead Act, 185

wrath:
    and Shylock, 21–22
    contrasted with anger, 21–22

VIBS

The **Value Inquiry Book Series** is co-sponsored by:

Adler School of Professional Psychology
American Indian Philosophy Association
American Maritain Association
American Society for Value Inquiry
Association for Process Philosophy of Education
Canadian Society for Philosophical Practice
Center for Bioethics, University of Turku
Center for Professional and Applied Ethics, University of North Carolina at Charlotte
Central European Pragmatist Forum
Centre for Applied Ethics, Hong Kong Baptist University
Centre for Cultural Research, Aarhus University
Centre for Professional Ethics, University of Central Lancashire
Centre for the Study of Philosophy and Religion, University College of Cape Breton
Centro de Estudos em Filosofia Americana, Brazil
College of Education and Allied Professions, Bowling Green State University
College of Liberal Arts, Rochester Institute of Technology
Concerned Philosophers for Peace
Conference of Philosophical Societies
Department of Moral and Social Philosophy, University of Helsinki
Gannon University
Gilson Society
Haitian Studies Association
Ikeda University
Institute of Philosophy of the High Council of Scientific Research, Spain
International Academy of Philosophy of the Principality of Liechtenstein
International Association of Bioethics
International Center for the Arts, Humanities, and Value Inquiry
International Society for Universal Dialogue
Natural Law Society
Philosophical Society of Finland
Philosophy Born of Struggle Association
Philosophy Seminar, University of Mainz
Pragmatism Archive at The Oklahoma State University
R.S. Hartman Institute for Formal and Applied Axiology
Research Institute, Lakeridge Health Corporation
Russian Philosophical Society
Society for Existential Analysis
Society for Iberian and Latin-American Thought
Society for the Philosophic Study of Genocide and the Holocaust
Unit for Research in Cognitive Neuroscience, Autonomous University of Barcelona
Whitehead Research Project
Yves R. Simon Institute

Titles Published

Volumes 1 - 220 see www.rodopi.nl

221. John G. McGraw, *Intimacy and Isolation (Intimacy and Aloneness: A Multi-Volume Study in Philosophical Psychology, Volume One)*, A volume in **Philosophy and Psychology**

222. Janice L. Schultz-Aldrich, Introduction and Edition, *"Truth" is a Divine Name, Hitherto Unpublished Papers of Edward A. Synan, 1918-1997*. A volume in **Gilson Studies**

223. Larry A. Hickman, Matthew Caleb Flamm, Krzysztof Piotr Skowroński and Jennifer A. Rea, Editors, *The Continuing Relevance of John Dewey: Reflections on Aesthetics, Morality, Science, and Society*. A volume in **Central European Value Studies**

224. Hugh P. McDonald, *Creative Actualization: A Meliorist Theory of Values*. A volume in **Studies in Pragmatism and Values**

225. Rob Gildert and Dennis Rothermel, Editors, *Remembrance and Reconciliation*. A volume in **Philosophy of Peace**

226. Leonidas Donskis, Editor, *Niccolò Machiavelli: History, Power, and Virtue*. A volume in **Philosophy, Literature, and Politics**

227. Sanya Osha, *Postethnophilosophy*. A volume in **Social Philosophy**

228. Rosa M. Calcaterra, Editor, *New Perspectives on Pragmatism and Analytic Philosophy*. A volume in **Studies in Pragmatism and Values**

229. Danielle Poe, Editor, *Communities of Peace: Confronting Injustice and Creating Justice*. A volume in **Philosophy of Peace**

230. Thorsten Botz-Bornstein, Editor, *The Philosophy of Viagra: Bioethical Responses to the Viagrification of the Modern World*. A volume in **Philosophy of Sex and Love**

231. Carolyn Swanson, *Reburial of Nonexistents: Reconsidering the Meinong-Russell Debate*. A volume in **Central European Value Studies**

232. Adrianne Leigh McEvoy, Editor, *Sex, Love, and Friendship: Studies of the Society for the Philosophy of Sex and Love: 1993–2003*. A volume in **Histories and Addresses of Philosophical Societies**

233. Amihud Gilead, *The Privacy of the Psychical.* A volume in **Philosophy and Psychology**

234. Paul Kriese and Randall E. Osborne, Editors, *Social Justice, Poverty and Race: Normative and Empirical Points of View.* A volume in **Studies in Jurisprudence**

235. Hakam H. Al-Shawi, *Reconstructing Subjects: A Philosophical Critique of Psychotherapy.* A volume in **Philosophy and Psychology**

236. Maurice Hauriou, *Tradition in Social Science.* Translation from French with an Introduction by Christopher Berry Gray. A volume in **Studies in Jurisprudence**

237. Camila Loew, *The Memory of Pain: Women's Testimonies of the Holocaust..* A volume in **Holocaust and Genocide Studies**

238. Stefano Franchi and Francesco Bianchini, Editors, *The Search for a Theory of Cognition: Early Mechanisms and New Ideas.* A volume in **Cognitive Science**

239. Michael H. Mitias, *Friendship: A Central Moral Value.* A volume in **Ethical Theory and Practice**

240. John Ryder and Radim Šíp, Editors, *Identity and Social Transformation, Central European Pragmatist Forum, Volume Five.* A volume in **Central European Value Studies**

241. William Sweet and Hendrik Hart**,** *Responses to the Enlightenment: An Exchange on Foundations, Faith, and Community.* A volume in **Philosophy and Religion**

242. Leonidas Donskis and J.D. Mininger, Editors, *Politics Otherwise: Shakespeare as Social and Political Critique.* A volume in **Philosophy, Literature, and Politics**

243. Hugh P. McDonald, *Speculative Evaluations: Essays on a Pluralistic Universe.* A volume in **Studies in Pragmatism and Values.**

244. Dorota Koczanowicz and Wojciech Małecki, Editors, *Shusterman's Pragmatism: Between Literature and Somaesthetics.* A volume in **Central European Value Studies**

245. Harry Lesser, Editor, *Justice for Older People,* A volume in **Values in Bioethics**

246. John G. McGraw, *Personality Disorders and States of Aloneness (Intimacy and Aloneness: A Multi-Volume Study in Philosophical Psychology, Volume Two),* A volume in **Philosophy and Psychology**

247. André Mineau, *SS Thinking and the Holocaust.* A volume in **Holocaust and Genocide Studies**

248. Yuval Lurie, *Wittgenstein on the Human Spirit.* A volume in **Philosophy, Literature, and Politics**

249. Andrew Fitz-Gibbon, *Love as a Guide to Morals.* A volume in **Ethical Theory and Practice**

250. Ronny Miron, *Karl Jaspers: From Selfhood to Being.* A volume in **Studies in Existentialism**

251. Necip Fikri Alican, *Rethinking Plato: A Cartesian Quest for the Real Plato.* A volume in **Philosophy, Literature, and Politics**

252. Leonidas Donskis, Editor, *Yet Another Europe after 1984: Rethinking Milan Kundera and the Idea of Central Europe.* A volume in **Philosophy, Literature, and Politics**

253. Michael Candelaria, *The Revolt of Unreason: Miguel de Unamuno and Antonio Caso on the Crisis of Modernity.* A volume in **Philosophy in Spain**

254. Paul Richard Blum, *Giordano Bruno: An Introduction.* A volume in **Values in Italian Philosophy**

255. Raja Halwani, Carol V. A. Quinn, and Andy Wible, Editors, *Queer Philosophy: Presentations of the Society for Lesbian and Gay Philosophy, 1998-2008.* A volume in **Histories and Addresses of Philosophical Societies**

256. Raymond Angelo Belliotti, *Shakespeare and Philosophy: Lust, Love, and Law.* A volume in **Philosophy, Literature, and Politics**

t-compliance